Self-Making Man

This book describes one day in the communicative life of the owner of an auto repair shop in Texas: how he walks, looks, points, shows, and explains engines; makes sense by gesture; speaks, manages, makes his life-world, and in the process reproduces social structures and himself as an individual. *Self-Making Man* is the first comprehensive study of a communicating person; it reveals socially shared and personal practices, as well as improvisational actions by which a person inhabits and makes sense of the world with others. After decades of discussion on embodiment, this study is the first to investigate one body in its full range of communicative activities. Grounded in phenomenology and committed to the methodological rigor of context analysis and conversation analysis, *Self-Making Man* departs radically from contemporary research practice: it shows that, to take embodiment in human interaction seriously, we must conceive of it as individuation and organic, self-sustaining life: as autopoiesis.

Jürgen Streeck, a professor of communication studies and anthropology at the University of Texas at Austin, is known for his groundbreaking work on gesture, embodied interaction, and the bodily foundations of meaning. Among his publications are *Gesturecraft: The Manufacture of Meaning* (2009), *Embodied Interaction: Language and Body in the Material World* (edited with C. Goodwin and C. D. LeBaron 2011), and *Intercorporeality: Emerging Socialities in Interaction* (edited with C. Meyer and J. S. Jordan 2017). His articles have appeared in *Gesture, Journal of Pragmatics, Research on Language and Social Interaction, Annual Review of Anthropology*, and *Journal of Linguistic Anthropology*. He has been a fellow at the Center for Interdisciplinary Research (ZiF) at Bielefeld University, Freiburg Institute for Advanced Studies (FRIAS), and Carl von Ossietzky-University Oldenburg.

LEARNING IN DOING: SOCIAL, COGNITIVE, AND COMPUTATIONAL PERSPECTIVES

SERIES EDITOR EMERITUS
John Seely Brown, *Xerox Palo Alto Research Center*

GENERAL EDITORS
Roy Pea, *Professor of Education and the Learning Sciences and Director, Stanford Center for Innovations in Learning, Stanford University*
Christian Heath, *The Management Centre, King's College, London*
Lucy A. Suchman, *Centre for Science Studies and Department of Sociology, Lancaster University, UK*

BOOKS IN THE SERIES

(*continued after index*)

Self-Making Man

A Day of Action, Life, and Language

JÜRGEN STREECK
The University of Texas at Austin

CAMBRIDGE
UNIVERSITY PRESS

CAMBRIDGE
UNIVERSITY PRESS

One Liberty Plaza, 20th Floor, New York, NY 10006, USA

Cambridge University Press is part of the University of Cambridge.

It furthers the University's mission by disseminating knowledge in the pursuit of education, learning, and research at the highest international levels of excellence.

www.cambridge.org
Information on this title: www.cambridge.org/9781107022942
DOI: 10.1017/9781139149341

First published 2017

Printed in the United States of America by Sheridan Books, Inc.

A catalogue record for this publication is available from the British Library.

ISBN 978-1-107-02294-2 Hardback

For Ali, Ansar, Nada, and Mona Chmeis

If individuals are to reproduce society, they must reproduce themselves as individuals. No society can exist without individual reproduction, and no individual can exist without self-reproduction.

Agnes Heller, Everyday Life

Men make their own history, but they do not make it as they please; they do not make it under self-selected circumstances, but under circumstances existing already, given and transmitted from the past.

Karl Marx, The Eighteenth Brumaire of Louis Bonaparte

Contents

Videos and transcripts of the main episodes can be found at
www.jurgenstreeck.net/self-making man/

Acknowledgments

I owe infinite gratitude to Hussein Chmeis, the hero of this book, for allowing me to follow him with my video camera for eleven consecutive hours of his life—and to then devote an estimated 7,000 to 8,000 hours of my own precious life to scrutinizing them, slicing his life up into bits and pieces, and watching his every move. I also am grateful to him for traveling in digital form with me to so many workshops, conferences, and symposia as my subject and wingman, always there to carry the presentation. And for being my friend.

I thank the technicians who worked at Hi-Tech Automotive when the recording was made, and the customers and delivery people who showed up on that day in March 1995, for being willing to become research material, to have their pictures taken and published, and for their interaction skills, and, in some cases, hilarity. I hope you will find yourselves characterized with respect.

That I was able to devote so much time to studying one day in a single man's life was made possible in great part by the luxury and freedom of nearly three years spent as an unbridled fellow, two of them at institutes for advanced study, at the Center for Interdisciplinary Research (ZiF) at Bielefeld University and at Freiburg Institute for Advanced Study (FRIAS), and one as Gervinus-Fellow of the Minister for Science and Education of Lower Saxony at Carl von Ossietzky-Universität Oldenburg. At ZiF, I learned the little I know about neuroscience and was introduced, but not converted, to neo-Cartesian and engineering perspectives on embodied communication. And I fell into an unexpected and unexpectedly productive cooperation with J. Scott Jordan, an experimental psychologist. In Freiburg, I benefited from the brilliant friendship and team spirit of Peter Auer, Lorenza Mondada, and Anja Stukenbrock and their superb and precise understanding of moment-by-moment interaction and language use. Thomas Alkemeyer created the opportunity for me to spend a year in Oldenburg's large and frantic community of self-making researchers, and to learn from the intimate knowledge of bodies and their movements that its members, athletes all, possess. I thank Roderick Hart, dean of the Moody College of Communication, and Barry Brummett, chair of the Department of Communication Studies, for their sustained support. The Moody (!) College is a great workplace, and this is also due to the late Kamran Hooshmand, Rod Edwards, Larry Horvath, Brian Parrett, and Mark Rogers, whose technical support was equally important and dependable.

Many people have seen stages of this work and discussed it with me during its two decades of gestation. It has been inspired by Charles Goodwin and Adam Kendon, as can be seen on almost every page. In recent years, I have learned much from discussing and doing work with Mats Andrén, Elena Cuffari, Arnulf Deppermann, Marjorie Goodwin, Christian Meyer, and Federico Rossano. The habitat for this study has been the large and lively community of local and visiting faculty and graduate interaction researchers at UT Austin who have participated in our weekly data sessions. Senem Güney needs special mention: she wrote a wonderfully precise and carefully crafted master's thesis about Mr. Chmeis, titled 'Shifting frames in everyday interaction: the multiple personas of a car mechanic' (Güney 1997), a study of the style shifts and role segregation during Hussein's moments of multitasking. Unfortunately, because I did not focus on these processes much, her work does not get the representation here that it would otherwise deserve. In 1996, Elliott Malkin, now an information architect at the *New York Times*, produced an interactive CD-ROM about the flow of information and the *chaîne operatoire* at Hi-Tech, the synthesis of a senior fellows class project. Niaz Aziz provided me with some of the Arabic transcriptions and translations. Katie Bradford, Matthew Ingram, and, especially, Knud Lambrecht read and edited draft chapters.

Others who have inspired, responded to, and made an impact on the work here in Texas include Juanita Handy Bosma, Melissa Dalton, Maria Egbert, Katie Feyh, Josef Fulka, Andrea Golato, Jiwon Han, Johan Hjulstad, Tomoko Ikeda, Matthew Ingram, Alexandra Janetzko, Julia Katila, Elizabeth Keating, Jeong-Yeon Kim, Curtis LeBaron, Kristine Markman, Siri Mehus, Kate Mesh, Inger Mey, Sae Oshima, Katherine Stewart, Chiho Sunakawa, Carmen Taleghani-Nikazm, Julio de Tavares, Eryn Withworth, and Eiko Yasui: a self-sustaining research community with changing membership.

My children, Autri and Johannes, and grandchildren, Marley and Sunmi, give me more love and things to worry about than I could ask for.

Austin, Texas, November 2015, Thanksgiving Day

About this book and the man it is about

Meeting Mr. Chmeis

When the old Cadillac broke down that I had bought when I first arrived in America, my neighbor recommended the shop on the main avenue nearby. 'They're Iraqis', she said, 'but they're good people'. This was during the time when America geared up for Operation Desert Storm. When the war began, Hussein Chmeis, the owner of Hi-Tech Automotive, cut off his moustache and changed the nametag on his coat from his first to his family name.[1] Being from Lebanon rather than, as my neighbor said, Iraq, did not make a difference.

Satisfied with Mr. Chmeis' work, I became a regular customer, but I slowly also began to see in Hi-Tech Automotive a research site. It was a place to pursue two interests. First, it was (and continues to be) a site of complex and successful intercultural communication. Most research on intercultural communication seeks to explain what makes it difficult and to offer prescriptions for making it better, but I was more interested in how it routinely succeeds, which evidently it did at this shop. At Hi-Tech, the means of communication were multiple, but unevenly distributed. Only a few men spoke English—the lingua franca of the shop—as a native language; with the exception of Kenneth, Hussein's office helper, they spoke nonstandard varieties, and I often found them difficult to understand. Second, I had begun in my research on gesture to observe that what form a gesture takes and what 'job' it does often depend on the material setting, the things at hand, and that sometimes simply handling a thing in

---

[1] Hussein later told me that on the day the U.S. bombing campaign began, he had his day in court for a civil jury trial about an unpaid bill and his refusal to release the customer's car without payment. His lawyer was unwilling to stop the opponent's attorney from praising the heroic effort against the ruthless dictator. Hussein lost the case.

an unusual or even the usual fashion can be a communicative act. Gestures are often 'environmentally coupled' (Goodwin 2007; LeBaron & Streeck 2000; Streeck 1996, 2009: Ch.4). This observation gradually opened up a new view on the communicating body as 'always already' immersed in the material world, as its *inhabitant*, not a viewer (Streeck, Goodwin, & LeBaron 2011). An auto shop is a setting for *hands-on* practical and communicative action. It is cognitively complex, full of artifacts and technologies, a place of socially shared cognition (Hutchins 1995; Resnick, Levine, & Teasley 1991), practical work, talk, banter, and silent physical interaction. Interaction is centered around objects that are initially 'opaque', like a human patient with abdominal pain: what is the case needs to be found out, not just by looking or asking others, but by exploratory activities of the hands. While this did not initially concern me, the fact that the owner of an auto shop is also an institutional actor became relevant once I turned to his talk: Hussein's words—and sometimes his gestures—can create obligations for others and himself, beyond those that come with any conversation: he is the principal of an organization. Videotaping interactions at Hi-Tech, I concluded, would enable me to focus on a range of fundamental issues of human communication within a single corpus of data, and so I began to explain my work and my interest to Hussein and seeded the idea of videotaping him.

A workday

After a few tentative recordings,[2] I finally told Hussein that I would like to film him for an entire day, and he agreed. For one Friday in March 1995, I shadowed Hussein with my Hi8 video camera.[3] I spent the next days logging what I had filmed, activity by activity (for example, 'unpacks brake pads', 'orders injector', 'inspection', 'greets customer'), which yielded around 1,000 entries (see Appendix 1). There are, of course, many alternative ways to slice up the activities of a day in a human life; I simply made a new entry when I felt something new had begun. My interest was in part in changes in activity, in the very diversity and rapid shifting of communicative tasks with which one person has to cope in the course of one day. The number, 1,000, may give a sense of the frequency of such changes in Hussein's life.

---

[2] By Elliott Makin and myself.
[3] Follow the links on the author's website, jurgenstreeck.net, to view select video recordings of interactions at Hi-Tech Automotive.

This is how Hussein himself describes his workdays:

> I feel sometime I'm crazy:
> all day like this,
> all day like this (gestures).
> How I answer the phone,
> sometime I am handling two three line quick altogether
> and in meantime I'm checking invoices
> and I'm going sometime this way
> the technician here
> they expect me outside
> suddenly they see me in front of them
> then I done here
> then I change my way
> then I go this way
> to see something else going over there
> and then the technician they get confused
> they don't know how to catch me
> they don't know how to run away from me.
> This the only way I make money
> because I invest everybody time.
> I make my best.

A day is a natural unit for humans; we live and structure our lives by days, and workday by workday. A day seemed to be an adequate 'unit of analysis' for the study. From Hussein's perspective, a day was a long time to be videotaped, and I knew from having been at the shop enough that a day would yield enough data to analyze *forever*. (Had I known that 'forever' would turn out to mean twenty years, I would probably have filmed him for just an hour.)

A composite individual

Many ethnographies and ethnographic films have portrayed cultures through the prism of a single member. A study that has informed the present one is Harper's (1987) classic *Working Knowledge*, a study of a car mechanic in Upstate New York. Harper focused closely and intensely on the sensory knowledge of this man, how he can feel when metal has reached the right temperature under the torch so he can begin to bend it, how he knows what causes corrosion in a car part: his 'professional touch' (cf. Goodwin 1994). Hussein is very different from Willie, who would disparagingly call him a 'part changer', someone who does not mend, but replaces broken parts. Hussein is not much of a mechanic at all anymore; he is a manager, and my focus is on his communication.

A classic study in social and 'ecological' psychology is Barker and Wright's (1951) *One Boy's Day. A Specimen Record of Behavior*, which followed the same heuristic and produced

> a record of what a seven-year-old boy did and of what his home and school and neighborhood and town did to him from the time he awoke one morning until he went to sleep that night. It ... describes the actions of Raymond and the physical and social conditions of his life that could be seen and heard by skilled observers. ... *One Boy's Day* is a specimen of the behavior and the cultural and psychological habitat of a child. It is a field study in ecological psychology. ... It is an interpretive record too because it reports what these observers inferred as to the meanings to the boy of his behavior and of the persons, things, and events that he saw and heard and felt throughout the day. (Barker & Wright 1951: 1)[4]

This book picks up, as it were, where Barker and Wright left off; concerning Raymond, it would ask: How does he do the things he does? What are his *methods* for doing them? These questions characterize my *micro-ethnographic* perspective on Hussein's day at work.

Studying an individual over the course of a day—if it is a day filled with people, activity, and unpredictable circumstances—raises many interesting questions for researchers of social interaction, some of which I will take up in the following chapters. The disciplines that convene in the empirical, 'naturalistic' (observational) analysis of everyday interaction are usually and rightfully interested in 'social facts' (Durkheim 1982), in the words, grammar, rules, practices, and beliefs that members of a community share—in what is 'generic' about their interaction. The individual is regarded as a bearer of culture and social order, but not as a unit of analysis in its own right. It is assumed that the individual more or less consists of an accumulation of sociocultural 'stuff' (concepts, words, knowledge, beliefs, etc.) and sociocultural methodologies ('ethno-methods'; Garfinkel 1967) that are 'enacted' or 'used' in moments of social life. But observations of a person during an entire day irritate that picture, because so much of what he does appears improvised, handmade, invented for the moment and then forgotten: a solution for the single case at hand. Culture is a storehouse of routine solutions for *kinds* of problems or tasks (Hutchins 1995). The very culturality of the person is thus called into

---

[4] Another relevant study of an individual is Calbris' (2003) investigation of the gestures with which French Prime Minister Lionel Jospin expressed his political thinking. Various points of overlap occur between Calbris' account of gesture and the analysis in Chapter 5.

question when we observe how a person 'ad-hocs' (Garfinkel 1967) his way through the day. In Hussein's case anyway, his persona is sponsored by at least two 'cultures', and his actions and utterances are built from resources of multiple cultural and historical origin. Hussein is a *composite*, and so is every speaking human, because the system of human face-to-face conversation itself is a composite of systems of heterogeneous origins and with different evolutionary trajectories (Levinson & Holler 2013). But we rarely know where, say, a grammatical construction or a familiar gesture comes from (Arabic or proto-Semitic? The Eastern Mediterranean, Pan-Arabia, the whole world?). All we can observe, and can study rigorously, is what individuals make of cultural resources and personal habits and how they make meaning and create social moments from them together with others.

Focusing on an individual also, trivially, brings into focus the issue of *individuation*, which Agnes Heller explain this way:

> If individuals are to reproduce society, they must reproduce themselves as individuals. We may define 'everyday life' as the aggregate of those individual reproduction factors which, *pari passu*, make everyday life possible. ... Every human being has his own everyday life. ... The content and structure [are] not the same for all individuals. ... Reproduction of the person is always of the concrete person: the concrete person occupying a given place in a given society. ... Very few activities are invariant, and even these are invariant only as abstractions in the lives of all persons. We must all sleep (if not in identical circumstances, and not in the same way) and we must all eat (though not the same things and again not in the same way). (Heller 1984: 3)

In recent years, investigations of *habitus* by the late Pierre Bourdieu (Bourdieu 1990, 2000), of the inscription of culture and social class in the tacit dispositions of the body, and Foucault's late lectures on the 'techniques of the self' (Foucault 2005, 2010, 2011), have motivated a number of sociologists, who regard practices as the 'site of the social' (Schatzki 1995, 2002; Schmidt 2012), to study 'subjectivation' or 'subject formation' in 'communities of practice' (Lave 1991). Bourdieu defined habitus as

> a certain way of [the body of] orienting itself towards [the world] ..., of bringing to bear on it an attention which, like that of a jumper preparing to jump, is an active, constructive bodily tension towards the imminent forth-coming. (Bourdieu 1990: 144)

This raises the question of how this 'attention' is acquired or socialized, how individuals are molded and mold themselves into adequately skilled 'bodies of praxis'. This cannot be investigated with research methods that operate on the time-scale of moments, but requires long-itudinal study and other methods in the ethnographer's kit. And yet, individuation, the making of a viable self, also takes place in every fleeting moment.

Self-making/autopoiesis

It would not be productive to try to separate out which of Hussein's patterns and practices are cultural and which ones are idiosyncratic, as well as which cultures the cultural parts come from. Hussein is surrounded by global cultural material, and has previously been surrounded by it in Lebanon and Saudi Arabia, and he continuously fashions a viable communicative self out of them. As a communicator, he is the ongoing product of his own self-making. Different parts of his repertoire link him to different cultures, but do not always make him a 'member'. He is a member of his family, of an Arab American association, and perhaps a member and practitioner of international 'automotive culture' (whose lingua franca is English). But his cultural identity is a hybrid, and he himself does not apply ethnic or quasi-ethnic ('Shiite') labels to himself, but defines himself by his openness to relating to anyone. From member of a culture (or two cultures) and user and reproducer of sociocultural forms, Hussein thus transforms for us, without losing those identities altogether, into an ongoing product of individuation.

Modern biologists looking for a formal definition of life, as well as their philosopher allies, emphasize that individuation is a feature of all organic life. Thompson writes:

> Living beings affirm their own identities by differentiating themselves from their surroundings and thus demand to be seen from an autonomy perspective. Autopoiesis is basic autonomy in its minimal cellular form. ... A cell ... is a self-sustaining unity ... that dynamically produces and maintains its own identity in the face of what is other. (Thompson 2007: 149)

'The term "self" [is] unavoidable in any description of the most elementary instance of life' (Jonas 1966: 149).

The concept of *autopoiesis*—of self-making—thus took on relevance in this study of a person at various levels or scales: at the 'micro' scale of utterance, action, and action sequence, for example, when a spontaneous gesture makes itself and mediates the self-organization of the communicating ensemble; but also on the biographical scale, for Hussein's 'repertoire of practices' or *habitus* is a product of his own making. It is a by-product or *sediment* (Merleau-Ponty 1964) of his situated actions. Sedimentation itself—the slow incorporation of a practice—is not something that we can observe during the course of a single day, although there are moments when a practice or habit is being corrected and modified or replaced by another. But we can see sediments—or layers of sediments—in Hussein's linguistic repertoire (in Chapter 6). Hussein's English is not in full accord with standard grammar. His utterances often lack markers of tense and number and subject-verb agreement, and his word order is irregular at times. Yet he masters the all-important aspect of information design (or 'information structure'; Lambrecht 1994) with much subtlety and precision. Idiosyncratic constructions are sediments of his concrete, personal adaptation, and he does not share these with anyone. There is no community, no 'code' to which these constructions belong, in the way native speakers of English share a lexicon and grammar. Hussein's repertoire has emerged from unguided learning and autopoietic structuring and adaptation.

Hi-Tech Automotive: a self-made man's life-world

Hussein Chmeis is a prototypical American self-made man: immigrant, founder and owner of a successful small business (which has since grown to three locations), head of a large family, owner of a spacious home in a gated community, a respected man in the multiethnic, secular, Arabic-speaking community of his city. A self-made man is both a perfect and a problematic model of self-making: his self-making, while taking place under imposing and complex constraints, is in many ways less constrained than that, for example, of his employees. While everybody in the shop operates under economic and time constraints affecting the viability of the business, Hussein's actions are never constrained by what someone tells him to do. In this respect, self-made men are atypical self-makers, or self-makers as one finds them only in a socioeconomic class whose members own 'means of production'. (Car repair is not literally productive labor, but a repair shop owner belongs to the same socioeconomic class as a small factory owner.)

Mr. Chmeis' family hails from the Bekaa Valley in Lebanon, but he grew up in the town of Choueifat, near Beirut, as the eldest son of an illiterate baker, and gained his first business experience as a child helping his father run his business, especially the financial part. Hussein also told me that he never was a good student and in his youth had no interest in cars. When he graduated high school (at the bottom of his class), he did not even know that cars run on gas rather than water. Yet Hussein enrolled in a nearby technical college run by the German development agency GTZ, and graduated after three years, having discovered his skills as a mechanic. He then moved to Saudi Arabia, where he worked in the oil industry for four years before opening his first shop in Riyadh with a few associates, which over time would grow to become one of the biggest auto shops in the capital, employing forty-five men. In his thirties, Hussein tired of the restrictive life in Saudi Arabia and moved his family to Texas. After working out of his home for a year, he started his new business in 1987. Hi-Tech Automotive is located at a main thoroughfare near downtown Austin, with two locations, facing one another, in the vicinity of what were at the time two working- and lower-middle-class neighborhoods. Hi-Tech's customer base has always been ethnically diverse; only about 40 percent of the customers on the day when the recording was made were white. Today, Hi-Tech Automotive sits in the middle of Austin's main tourist drag, and the neighborhoods all around have been gentrified.

These were the employees at Hi-Tech Automotive at the time of recording, in approximate order of seniority (see Table 1): Hussein's closest confidant was Ashraf, who worked during most of this day in the shop 'across the street'. Ashraf apprenticed with Hussein in his shop in Riyadh and later followed him to Texas. The shop across the street was run by Hassan, whom Hussein occasionally consulted in technical matters, and whom he counseled in business affairs. Art and Victorio were Hussein's most trusted technicians, followed by Arturo, whose specialty was transmissions. Cedric worked on tasks of lesser technical complexity, including fixing tires and brakes. All men did much of their work independently, as did Uncle Ahm, the welder or 'body man' across the street, who, as Hussein said, could 'weld wood to wood'. There were two apprentices (junior technicians), Alex and Mike, and Omar, a distant relative from Lund, Sweden, who was doing a three-month 'internship' with Hussein. Kenneth worked in the office, advertising and selling cars, helping with billing and checks, and keeping tabs on customers with outstanding loans. A special role was played by Dr. M. (Hakim), a physician without a license to practice medicine in the United States, who served as the shop's runner, getting parts from suppliers, taking cars to the car wash, or giving customers rides home. Chito, the only one who does not appear in this book, was an independent contractor who refurbished transmissions. Hussein's sons Ali and Ansar made a brief appearance when Hussein sent them to the butcher across the street to buy ribs for a barbeque.

Since the 1980s, Austin has been a rapidly growing and economically thriving city, its growth rate now resembling that of cities in Asia. Several of Hussein's employees have left and started their own businesses. Today, twenty years later, Ashraf still works with Hussein, and Hussein has occasional contact with Art and Victorio. Hassan has long had his own shop, and Hussein's sons, along with their sisters, Nada and Mona, work in the three shops the family now owns, two children after graduating from a nearby Catholic university. Altogether, Hussein employs about thirty people today.

Because we are close in age, arrived in the United States at about the same time, and his shop is in the neighborhood, in the direction that my desk faces, I inevitably compared our lives at times, struck by the differences between them: here I was at home all day, seated; there Hussein was on his feet from morning to night. Here the blocked writer cursing and cursed by the loneliness of academic work, there a man giving work to dozens of people and never not talking to someone. But Hussein looked back at me and saw a teacher, and teachers he holds in high regard, often deploring their meager pay in America. The joy it gave him to be the object of my research had much to do with his own desire to be a teacher—of his customers, employees, and children. It was a role he was happy to perform. The videotapes would document his ubiquitous teaching.[5]

Methodology[6]

This book has the double ambition of illuminating both an individual person and his idiosyncrasies *and* the generic, socially and culturally shared practices this person enacts. The methodology is 'micro-ethnographic' (Streeck 1983, Streeck & Mehus 2004): the domain of social reality it is

[5] Throughout this book, and in contrast to my other publications, I consistently use masculine pronouns to refer both to Hussein and the men working with him, and to generic roles such as 'actor' or 'speaker'. I do so because choosing feminine pronouns to demonstrate gender neutrality would seem strange in this context, to Hussein, given his cultural background, but also in light of the fact that almost all of the instances cited to support general claims include only male participants.

[6] See also the note on methodology at the end of this book.

Table 1 The Men of Hi-Tech Automotive

Ashraf	Victorio
Art	Uncle Ahm
Hakim	Cedric
Arturo	Kenneth

Table 1 (cont.)

Alex	Mike
Omar	Chito
Hassan	Ali and Ansar

designed to capture are the communicative practices (or methods) and forms whose enactment by the members of a 'practice community' bring about intelligible actions and interactions, and, for moments at a time allows them to inhabit, make, and understand a piece of the world together (Streeck 2013a). The methodology will explain itself in the following chapters, and readers interested in its history, beginning in the 1930s with Bateson and Mead's photographic and cinematic analysis of the embodied culture of Bali (Bateson & Mead 1942), can turn to other publications for more detailed accounts (Kendon 1990: Ch.2; Streeck 2009a: Ch.2; Streeck, Goodwin, & LeBaron 2011). Still, a few remarks are in order.

Critical to research on communication among humans who are in each other's immediate presence is to recognize that every communicative act emerges as the result of interaction, in a particular 'place' or 'slot' within a sequence of social acts, and is designed to deal with the tasks of acting and securing understanding as they present themselves at this particular moment. Meaning does not inhere in forms (of speech and body motion), but is a *relationship* between form and context (Scheflen 1974). 'Context', in turn, in the first place means the interaction between the parties just prior to and at the moment: where they look, how they are positioned in relation to one another, but also 'where in the sequence' they are. For example, a certain gesture would not be seeable as a gesture of rejection if it were not for, say, its 'post-suggestion position', its being made following a suggestion (or other rejectable communicative act). We cannot understand how communicative understanding is achieved and action is accomplished unless we pay close attention to interaction's *sequentiality* (Schegloff 2007) and, more generally, *temporality* (Deppermann & Günthner 2015). Interaction builds itself within layered sequential matrices: an action-unit is produced within a turn-at-talk and is part of a sequence of actions within an interaction episode or encounter, which may or may not in turn be devoted to a particular project of collaborative action. This circumstance is at every point relevant to our investigation of Mr. Chmeis' repertoire of communicative practices, because it is within such contexts that these practices are enacted and for which they are designed. The term *multimodal communication* has become commonplace to describe these phenomena; the term alludes to the fact that human communication is a *composite* (Enfield 2011; Levinson & Holler 2013): each moment of understanding is the result of a local montage of heterogeneous resources, from prosodic contours to the grip with which one holds an object in one's hand, to the word someone uses, with the particular grammatical history and history of human migrations that may be embedded in it.

Overview

This book, then, is an investigation of the ways in which one man copes with the communicative tasks of an average workday: of his habits of walking and standing, of looking and pointing, his methods of showing others how things work and what should be done, for gesturing and speaking and organizing, or 'getting things done', mainly by others. It explores how its subject does these things methodically *and* spontaneously, as an improvising 'manager of the unexpected' (Weick & Sutcliffe 2011). To find a path into this unwieldy corpus of materials, I focused on 'uses' of the different modalities one by one: gait and posture, gaze, gesture, and so on. But of course, these modalities are not deployed one at a time, but always in combination, as whole-body products. Therefore, the case analyses in this book occasionally 'fold back' upon themselves, as new phenomena and layers of meaning are 'laminated' onto previously analyzed scenes (Goodwin 2011). We will accordingly enter some scenes repeatedly. There are also 'stories', episodes that feature a single car or customer, but unfold in multiple installments: in Chapter 7, we follow along with a car, a red Mercury Capri[7], as it goes through its 'patiency' in the shop. The Capri, the first patient to arrive in the morning, is also the last one to be discharged. It gets to spend an entire hour in Hussein's immediate care, because he has to remedy the effects of his own malpractice, but its *operating chain* in the shop (de France 1983) also involves a handful of technicians. The episode provides an opportunity to observe how Hussein 'soft-assembles' (Thelen 1994) his component skills during different types of organizational action, and how he 'executes', how he enacts his managerial roles. Our focus throughout is on communication, on how Hussein *makes sense* with others.

The sequence of chapters of this book follows a simple heuristic: it relies on the different parts of the body that are visibly involved in social interaction as a structuring principle. Beginning with the feet, in Chapter 1 I describe how Mr. Chmeis walks, both alone and with others, and how he positions himself and stands when he communicates with others or observes what is going on. Chapter 2 focuses on how Hussein uses his eyes, what kinds of vision-based activities he engages in, and how he communicates by gaze when facing others in focused interaction. Three chapters are devoted to the diverse and complex communicative work of the hands: in Chapter 3, I investigate how Hussein directs the attention and actions of others by pointing, perhaps his most important and most characteristic communicative action. Chapter 4 explores how Hussein reveals and illuminates features of objects at hand by touching, tracing,

[7] More than one car circulating through the shop on this day was named after a Mediterranean island. There was also a Corsica.

and manipulating them—what he calls 'showing'. A separate chapter (Chapter 5) is devoted to Hussein's spontaneous gesticulation during conversations. Even though it is the longest in the book, it captures only a fraction of Hussein's habitual gestures. Yet it is an attempt to break new ground in the study of the elusive phenomena of gesticulation, and it is in this chapter that the theory of autopoiesis—the self-making of living beings – and of motion as the most basic form of sense-making is explicitly applied. The chapter explains gestures as *living* phenomena—not as replicas of premade forms (see Cuffari & Streeck to appear). Chapter 6 takes stock of some of Hussein's linguistic routines, preformatted bits of verbal action that he has developed as he has been learning English on the job and by which he manages his shop, coordinates activities, and enacts institutional roles, and it also portrays him as a poet, as a speaker who occasionally is tuned to the music of his own language and relies on this tuning to build utterance after utterance. Chapter 7, finally, brings the parts together in an analysis of Hussein's *organizing*; communicative actions are analyzed within the context of the work of the *organization* 'Hi-Tech Automotive': the chapter shows how Hussein manages knowledge by acquiring and spreading 'situation awareness' (Norman 1993), how he participates in cooperative physical labor, which organizationally relevant *transactions* (Taylor 2011) he participates in, and how he 'performs' in his role as visible 'front' of the organization (Goffman 1959). Finally, Chapter 8 integrates findings from the previous chapters into a picture of Hussein as a 'generic' communicating person, representing everyone.

1 Moving

Beginning with Mr. Chmeis' first interactions in the morning, this chapter describes how he walks and stands, alone and with others, and how small modulations of his bearing and gait give off information about his purpose and destination and whether others can approach him. We see how Mr. Chmeis, through his posture and spatial positioning, discriminates between kinds of interaction partners and foreshadows the type of interaction in which he is willing to engage. These observations are set against the background of historical debates about the 'physiognomy' and morality of walking. A section of this chapter shows in close detail how Hussein and a customer negotiate conflicting definitions of a sales interaction and their social relationship by their feet: their 'dance' exhibits with great clarity the precise coordination of body motion in interaction that humans, like other animals, are capable of, but also how this ability is put to distinctly human social-organizational uses. Movement coordination, in turn, requires the ability to anticipate one another's movements; it is discussed in light of contemporary sociological research on dance and the neuroscience of movement perception.

1.1 The day begins

Mr. Chmeis' workday is a walk-day. Already during the first few minutes we notice that walking, for him, includes more than the technicality of getting from one place to another: its purpose is made apparent or it is accompanied by other activity or it is, in careful coordination, shared with others. Like others, Hussein uses his manner of walking 'to provide the person [he] is approaching with information about ... the focused interaction he intends and ... the theme it will be about' (Schmitt 2012: 8). We cannot, therefore, understand how Hussein inhabits his world without some appreciation of his locomotion, because he spends by far the better part of the day on his feet, walking, standing, squatting, and proceeding from one place of work to another. Because he moves about so frequently, Hussein's mind is also in motion most of the time, perceiving and scrutinizing a changing world from changing vantage points, always updating his mental image of the shop as he gathers information along his path. We all perceive the world, not from a fixed vantage point, but along a 'path of observation' (Gibson 1986: 197), a 'continuous itinerary of movement' (Ingold 2004: 331), but this is particularly visible in Hussein.

But before Hussein even begins to start the first of his numerous excursions, standing outside the front office, he already directs the movements of others. He does this by means of pointing gestures, and pointing will be a main device by which he coordinates movement, action, and coordination throughout the day. Thus, before we follow Hussein on his first walks around the shop, we will observe him standing and pointing.

After putting on his work coat, Hussein steps out of the front office and notices Hakim. They briefly talk to each other at a distance. Omar arrives with the shop's dog on a leash. He reports that the boxer had freed himself. Raising his arm to a pointing gesture, Hussein tells him to tie the dog up around the corner of the garage. Without lowering his arm, he then points out where Hakim should move the cars parked in front of the shop (Fig.1.1.1[1]). Then he steps forward and moves his pointing arm back and forth, insinuating a line on the ground, indicating how one car, a Celica, should be moved from its present to a future location (line 4, Fig.1.1.2). He then points to the taxicab parked to his left (Fig.1.1.3), and makes another pendulum movement that suggests another line on the ground, this time indicating the area where the cab should be parked (Fig.1.1.4). While Hakim takes off toward the Celica, Hussein performs a second, smaller version of the pointing gesture. With a final pointing gesture he indicates again where that car should go (Fig.1.1.5), in order to make room for the cars that are for sale (line 8). As he does with all other Lebanese employees and customers, Hussein speaks Arabic with Hakim and Omar.

---

[1] Figure numbers refer to the chapter, the example in the chapter, and the image in the image sequence associated with the example. Thus, 'Fig.1.12.3' refers to the third image associated with example 1.12. Not all examples are accompanied by images, and there may therefore be a gap in the numbering of the figures. Dots ('•') in transcripts identify the exact moments that figures show.

Figs. 1.1.1–5 The day begins with pointing gestures

(1.1)

1 Omar   Dayya' l-hableh.
           He lost the rope.
2   Bi-sharafeh fatah l-beb w-ma kemsho!
           I swear he opened the door and was not holding it!
3 H   Eh, biddak tshila halla' hay w-thitta some•where hek 'a janab.
           Yes, you need to remove this now and secure it somewhere on the
           side.
4 Hm   Wallah biddak thotta hon?
           Or do you want to put it here?

5	H	W hay deh l-Celica jehzeh, bi-twa'if awwal sayyara h•on, ha-Celica.
		And this Celica is ready, you park it first right here, the Celica.
6		W haydeh l-Capr•i jehzeh, bi-twa'if waraha hon.
		And this Capri is ready so you'll park it behind it over there.
7	(H)	Wih deh, tn•en.
		One and two.
8	H	W hay bitsheela 'a jan•ab w-minbalish nwa'if sayyarat lal-be'.
		And this one will be put aside and we'll begin to put up cars for sale.

Hakim for his part points to another car, a Honda, and Hussein, walking over, raises his left arm to form a large and sustained gesture. He points to the car, not with an index finger but a flat hand, the palm turned up (Fig.1.1.6). Besides identifying the referent of his talk, the shape and orientation of the hand also show a communicative action, namely that Hussein is asking a question (Kendon 2004, ch. 13): What is the matter with that thing? Hakim answers (his answer is inaudible for us) and points to the Honda as well, and the two men meet in an L-formation by the car, each orienting himself halfway to the other and halfway to the car (Fig.1.1.7).

9	H	W hay l-Honda, shu beha? Mniha sallahne•ha.
		This Honda, what's wrong with it? we fixed it.
10	( )	( )
11	H	Wen el-mifteh?
		Where is the key?
12	Hk	Eh ma ba'rif, • rajja'u.
		Ah, I don't know, they've returned it.
13	H	Eh.
		Yes.

Figs. 1.1.6–7 'This Honda, what's wrong with it?'

Pointing gestures coordinate the men's motions: they specify objects of shared concern and indicate paths toward them.

Hussein now walks away, coffee in hand. He tries to open a car door, finds it locked, and casually walks back to the shop. On the way there he calls on Art, who is in charge of the tow truck:

(1.2)
1   H   Art?
2   Let's park (- - -) the truck inside right now?
3   Temporary.
4   I'll see what we wanna do later.

Note how he mitigates his directive by including himself as a partner in the action: '*Let's* park the truck.'

A few minutes later, after a few transitory interactions, Hussein goes inside the shop, gets inside a car, and starts it. He gets out, closes the door, walks around the front, and turns his gaze to a pile of tires on the floor. He points to them with his left hand. He makes this gesture when he begins to talk before it is even clear to whom he is talking and who should therefore see his gesture. Cedric turns around (Fig.1.3.1, in the background) and walks over. Somehow he knows that he is the intended recipient of Hussein's directive. As Cedric turns his gaze to the tires, Hussein again points to them (Fig.1.3.2). For a moment, Hussein and Cedric look at the tires on the floor together.

(1.3)
1   H   Let's t•ake all the used t•ires across the street
2   those

Although the workday is only a few minutes old, Hussein has already initiated several encounters with pointing gestures. Each time the gesture

Figs. 1.3.1–2 Pointing to a group of tires

Figs. 1.4.1–2 Meeting the first customer of the day

is made at the beginning of the interaction or even before any word is spoken. Hussein's gaze during these moments is focused on objects of concern, rarely and only briefly on the other participant. This changes when the first customer arrives. Hussein's bearing changes, as does his gait (Fig.1.4.1). We see him, coffee still in hand, walking toward the customer who is waiting for him outside, and his posture is now erect, his shoulders are broadened, and he is taking long strides, but unhurriedly.

(1.4)
1   H   Go•od morning, Sir
2   C   (   )
3   H   Fine, how are you.

The customer walks to his car. Just before Hussein catches up with him, he turns around and leads Hussein to his car, where they enter an 'L-formation' (Scheflen 1972): positioned at a 90° angle at the car's front end, they look at the engine (Fig.1.4.2). It is the same formation Hussein had previously established with Hakim and Cedric, but the process in which it is formed is different. Hussein and his customer, before they focus their attention on the object at hand, for a moment maintain a face-to-face orientation. In contrast, when he interacts with employees, making pointing gestures, Hussein proposes a focus of joint attention 'out there', often even before he starts talking to them. There is rarely an initial 'phatic' communication phase (Malinowski 1922). A summons, a pointing gesture, and a visible movement by the addressee suffice to initiate an encounter. The change in Hussein's bearing when the first customer arrives is reminiscent of the changes in the comportment of wait staff transiting from the kitchen to the restaurant that Erving Goffman (1959) described: it marks a change from *backstage* to *frontstage* behavior. For the benefit of the customer, by modulating bearing, gait, and voice, Hussein assembles a *front* (see Chapter 7).

1.2 Practices

These initial observations suggest that Hussein applies routine methods for approaching employees and initiating interaction with them, and a different set of methods for approaching customers and initiating inter-action with them. These methods comprise both bodily actions and ways of speaking. We call these methods *practices* (Streeck 2013a). Practices are *methods for doing things*, for performing social actions. A practice, for exam-ple, is the way in which Hussein coordinates a pointing gesture, gaze, and some verbal device when he initiates an 'object-focused' encounter with a technician. A different practice (or coordinated set of practices) is the combination of bearing, gait, gaze, and voice projection as he recognizes and greets a customer. Another practice is the upward rotation of the flat hand while aiming it at an object, which displays a questioning stance toward an object. Practices, finally, are the uttering of a first name, spoken with loudness and question intonation, to summon someone, as well as the mitigating '*let's* directive', which attributes an action that is being requested of another person to an 'us', rather than a 'you'.

We can note a number of features of practices.

1. Practices are embodied. They are enacted through movements of the body (including those required for speech).
2. Embodied practices include practices for the performance of instru-mental, including solitary, actions and practices for social, commu-nicative acts. As methods of bodily action, the two modes are not necessarily distinct: the same motor-schema can be involved in performing an instrumental act (opening a soft drink can) and in giving a gestural version of it, a demonstration. Moreover, instru-mental acts can be transparent, 'speak for themselves', be commu-nicative in the way they are practical. It is implausible to consider the two realms, the practical and the communicative, as separate spheres (Leroi-Gourhan 1993). Yet, because our concern in this book is Hussein's methods of making sense with others, his practical actions (e.g., repairing cars) will concern us only insofar as they are reflected, in, or organized by, communicative action.
3. Practices may be modal or multimodal, comprising the acts of only one or a combination of body parts, often involving structured

relations between movements distributed across body parts and modalities (e.g., eyes/gaze, hands/gesture, voice/speech).

4. Practices are skilled, methodical. They are practiced ways of doing things, requiring bodily training, usually of the tacit, 'implicit' kind.

5. Practices are iterable; they can be applied to new circumstances. Usually, we will count an act as an enactment of a practice only if it is performed more than once.

6. Practices are adaptive; they mesh with situated particulars and common ground to produce local meanings and locally operative acts. (Moving the index finger like a pendulum to project a tract or path and to thereby evoke in the knowing listener an image of a track is an example of a locally adaptive imagery-making practice.)

7. The term 'practice' is scalable (Hirschauer 2013); we can apply it to the turning up and opening of a hand in a gesture of questioning, but also to the larger method of projecting a questioning stance toward an object of concern, which may not only consist of a gesture, but also include the movement of gaze and speech.

8. Practices are nested: displaying a questioning stance may be part of Hussein's coordinated practices for 'checking up' on the work of apprentices.

9. Practices are socially implicative: their enactment has consequences for both the agent and others. A pointing gesture can be an order to do something; the formula 'I will see later' commits the speaker to take some action in the future.

While the various versions of praxeology that are currently practiced define practices at different levels or 'scales', attributing to them different 'sizes', our investigation, micro-ethnographic as it is, will primarily focus on those that are usually enacted in seconds or fractions of seconds. However, at various points throughout this book, but especially in Chapter 7, 'lower-level' practices are implicated in 'higher-level' activities such as maintaining 'positive' customer relations. And the way in which Hussein incessantly directs the actions of his employees by pointing gestures (exemplified by the title picture) can serve as a metonymy for his specific agency and position in his world.

1.3   The physiognomy and sociology of walking

Close observation of Hussein's manner of moving, of his gait and bearing and of the way he moves his arms when he walks, clues us in to some of the many ways in which body motion can be meaningful beyond the immediate, instrumental tasks that it addresses and solves. That walking is more than a means of transporting, that its manner can reveal social information about the person walking, was recognized and led to extensive moral and scientific debates at different times during the unfolding of social thinking in the West, of which the Roman republic and the eighteenth and nineteenth centuries may be among the most interesting periods. The citizens and writers in the Roman republic considered movements of the body indications of the *motus*, the motions of the soul. Paraphrasing Cicero, Corbeill, in his book on body movement in ancient Rome (Corbeill 2004), notes that 'the properly discerning eye can recognize deviance in a human being's movement in the same way that it can judge an art object ... [so that] the reading of morality becomes an aesthetic practice, and one that can be learned' (Corbeill 2004: 109). At a time when politicians from the rural provinces, or those who borrowed their style (so-called *populares*), began to compete with the indigenous Roman elite (*optimates*), the stride of members of one party was contrastingly judged by members of the other as rustic or effeminate, respectively. Moral assessments of someone's movement style were justified by the conceit of naturalization: human beings, Cicero argued, 'are disposed by nature to disapprove morally of ways of sitting and standing that displease the eyes and ears' (Cicero 1942: 114). A politician would promote his own habitus as both natural and truthful, as a style that reveals the motions of the soul directly and efficiently and contrasts with shameful attempts by a member of the opposing party to feign qualities that he did not really possess or to suppress ones that he has, by appropriating someone else's gait. Motor habits thus became entangled in discourses around authenticity and style, elitism and populism, country and city. At the same time, ideas about movement and related systems of signification such as fashion served strangers as codes to make sense of one other's unfamiliar background and identities.

It is no coincidence that another, much more recent period during which people's gait was subjected to moral and sociological scrutiny was also an era of social and geographical mobility: the eighteenth and nineteenth centuries, during a time when the European capitals, notably London and Paris, grew on a massive scale and thus created the need to interact with—and assess—strangers from unknown cultural backgrounds by the visible characteristics of their conduct, including those shown when they walk across cities (Sennett 1977). Regulating one's body motions

according to a perceived moral code became a concern of the rising bour-
geoisie, and the famous writer of bourgeois life, Honoré de Balzac, endea-
vored to write a *théorie de la démarche*, a theory of physio-psychical
ambulation: 'Gait is the physiognomy of the body. ... Everything in us
corresponds to an inner cause' (Balzac [1833] 1968: 225, transl. J. S.).

Balzac's theory turns on the multiple senses of the word *démarche*, which
signifies not only gait and ambulation, but also a 'procedure' or 'manner of
proceeding', including the proceeding of thought. (In German, the analogy
is expressed by the word *Gedankengang*, 'thought walk', 'train of thought'.)
That walking is thinking in motion is a notion that lately has again gained
currency, for example, among neuroscientists (Llinàs 2001), philosophers
(Sheets-Johnstone 2010, 2012), and anthropologists (Ingold & Vergunst
2008), and we will return to their reasons for promoting this idea later. This
is how Balzac envisions practicing his *théorie de la démarche* as an observational science:

> I went to sit down on a chair on Boulevard de Gand, in order to study the
> gait of all Parisians who, to their own misfortune, would pass by me during
> the day. And that day, I collected the most profoundly curious observa-
> tions I have ever made in my life. I returned home loaded like a botanist
> botanizing who has collected so many plants that he is forced to give them
> to the first cow that comes his way. Only, the theory of the *démarche*
> seemed impossible to me to publish without seventeen engraved plates
> and without ten or twelve volumes of text and notes, enough to scare the
> defunct Abbey Barthélémey or my erudite friend Parisot. Finding out
> what is the sin of vicious forms of walking? Finding the laws to whose
> observation the beautiful manners of walking were due? Finding the
> means by which one can make one's gait lie, just like the courtiers, the
> ambitious, vindictive people, comedians, courtesans, legitimate spouses,
> spies make their features, their eyes and their voice lie? Investigating
> whether the ancient ones walked well, which people walks the best
> among all peoples? Brrr! The questions proliferated like crickets!
> (Balzac [1883] 1968: 225; transl. J. S.)

Balzac's project was, as his diction indicates, a critical, if not a satirical, one.
He meant to show that it is impossible to give a scientific basis to moral
norms of social comportment, that claims as to the superiority or greater
'naturalness' of one's gait, to seek to support class-based moral and esthetic
judgments with scientific experimentation and methodical observation,
were pure ideology. The circularity of the attempt was obscured by the
démarches of the proponents' own minds, their bias toward their own
idiosyncratic mental and corporeal habits.

Balzac's satirical comments notwithstanding, attempts to scientifically demonstrate the superiority of one mode of locomotion over others—and to relate 'mechanical' and 'semiotic' aspects of walking to one another—continued throughout the nineteenth century (Mayer 2013). On one side were scientists who aimed to understand the mechanics of human locomotion and to demonstrate either the superiority of the flexible human gait over the repetitive motions of trains and automobiles (or vice versa), or to identify, not least in the interest of the military, the most efficient ways of walking. On the other side were the French physiognomists with their comparative and forensic perspectives, which had found a home in the Société des observateurs de l'homme, established in Paris in 1799, that also inaugurated the comparative study of gestures and sign languages (Lane 1976). Balzac recognized that these projects could not be reconciled, that no social class would find scientific support for its claim to have the most natural—and thus the most esthetically pleasing—gait. The controversy continued in the twentieth century, when various countercultural *reform* movements in the 1910s and 1920s continued the quest for natural movement, while anthropologists such as Marcel Mauss stuck to the forensic or physiognomic agenda, expressed by Mauss' infamous claim, 'I think I can ... recognize a girl who has been raised in a convent. In general she will walk with her fists closed' (Mauss 1973: 73).[2]

In these 'physiognomic' accounts, from the Romans to Marcel Mauss, walking is construed as something that single bodies do. It is the individual body walking by itself that signifies and reveals something about the person. But when seen in this way, walking is deprived of aspects that make it interesting as a domain of social organization and cognition. There are neither those who keep the walker company (there is no 'walking with'), nor are there others whose oncoming trajectories make walking in public an obstacle course. Walking in public means navigating one's course among other walkers. Ingold and Vergunst note that walking is a profoundly social activity: 'in their timings, rhythms, and inflections, the feet respond as much as does the voice to the presence and activity of others. Social relations ... are not enacted *in situ* but are paced along the ground' (2008: 1). How we walk *together*, with and among others, is

---

[2] For a contemporary example of the physiognomic (diagnostic) perspective on walking, see Horowitz (2013).

a genuinely sociological question,[3] and answering it case by case reveals less about the individual than about the common code, the *interaction order*, by which we conduct our everyday lives. Investigating pedestrian traffic, the design of *vehicular units* (solos and 'withs'), and the 'body glosses' and 'tie signs' by which these units project their trajectories, Erving Goffman (1971) saw in the motions of walking not so much displays by which the individual reveals something about his character, but signals by which recurrent social problems—problems of social coordination and organization—are being solved. Body-glosses are processes

> whereby an individual uses over-all body gesture to make otherwise unavailable facts about his situation gleanable. Thus, ... in walking, the individual conducts himself—or rather his vehicular shell—so that the direction, rate, and resoluteness of his proposed course will be readable. (Goffman 1971: 11)

In Goffman's terminology, how someone walks is as much a matter of *giving* as of *giving off* information (Goffman 1959), of deliberately making one's intentions public, as of inadvertently disclosing something about the kind of person one is, for example, a miner, priest, or bureaucrat, how one uses one's body in one's daily work. These identities transparently reveal themselves in someone's gait. The analysis of walking thus becomes an exercise in the sociological analysis of bodily communication, an investigation of one set of ways in which communication makes social order possible.

Communication researchers used to proceed as if their work only begins once we have arrived at a place and are in each other's immediate presence, but in reality the way we approach one another is already part of our communicative exchange, and so are our spatial maneuvers when we move about together and in each other's midst. In recent years, more and more researchers have taken up the study of interaction in motion (Haddington, Mondada, & Nevile 2013), including how walking together is interactively organized (Schmitt 2012); how speaking and shared walking are coordinated (Relieu 1999); how modes of walking display definitions of the situation (Hausendorf & Schmitt 2010); how larger groups navigate and maintain shared foci of attention (for example, during guided tours; Kesselheim 2010); how interaction spaces are structured under conditions of mobility (Mondada 2012); and how new mobile communication technologies and old

---

[3] It also, of course, raises the philosophical question how we should conceive of the *subject* of walking together: Is it two (or more) individuals or a collective 'we'? (Gilbert 1990). For a phenomenology of the sensory, cognitive, and enactive coordinations and the co-subjectivization involved in joint *running*, see Hockey and Allen-Collinson (2013).

systems of spatial reference are brought together when people traverse territories in groups (Haddington & Keisanen 2009; Laurier 2001).

1.4   Walking alone and approaching others

Turning now to Hussein's movements and positionings—how he walks and positions himself—we are interested and prepared to study how he makes others see the 'intentional arc' (Merleau-Ponty 1962)—the purpose, direction, and destination—of his movement; how he responds to the presence of others as he moves; and how he prepares his arrival in an engagement.[4] These observations of one man's gait cannot claim to be more than structured impressions: I have not counted Hussein's steps or measured their length or tempo. Neither have I investigated the motion dynamics of his gait. Such means of objectivation are unavailable in messy natural settings like an auto shop, beyond the affordances of a handheld video camera, and outside the skills and methods of a micro-ethnographer. What micro-ethnographic research and the limited space of a book allow are analyses of exemplary moments and interactions whose representativeness can only be established by future studies of other cases. In the following, we follow Hussein on an idealized path: we follow him as he walks around the shop, alone, until he arrives in a formation with others; we watch how he stands and moves with them in changing spatial-postural formations; and we observe him when he eventually leaves the engagement and for a moment stands apart, contemplating the goings-on.

One of Hussein's walking modes can be called 'unmarked gait', a stride that does not disclose anything about his motive or destination. He strolls at a moderate pace, his hands free, both arms swinging in slightly asymmetrical alternation, the left hand moving a little bit more to the back than the right one does, the right moving a bit more forward than the left. Hussein's shoulders are pulled back and forth a couple of inches by the motions of his arms, and his gaze meets the ground about five steps ahead of his feet, unless he holds the head high and faces forward or scans the field around his path (see Figs.1.5.1–2).

This somewhat stereotyped description applies to moments when Hussein does not visibly attend to his visibility for others. When he does, he modulates his gait in a number of ways that make social information

---

[4] As I usually *followed* Hussein with the camera, he is most often seen from behind when he walks; occasionally, when he returns to a place of engagement where the camera has been waiting for him, we see him walking toward us.

Figs. 1.5.1–3 Hussein's unmarked, transparently purposeful gait

available: he motivates his trajectory and shows whether he is available for interaction. On short walks, for example, when he fetches a tool (Fig.1.5.3), he may convey a sense of purpose by leaning forward, a bearing that makes his body weight accelerate his pace. In contrast, returning from a completed job, he may walk at slower pace, one arm swinging, and if he has an object in hand he may position it in a fashion that shows that it is no longer being used. Or he turns his head left and right, surveying the scene along his path. If someone approaches him during this kind of walk, he will find a receptive Hussein. Finally, there is only one occasion when the camera captures Hussein rushing, taking long strides, as he hurries to catch Hakim before he leaves on a commission, to add an item to his to-do-list. Hussein never runs.

Hussein also keeps his path clear from unwelcome intrusions by others. He does this by the way he modulates his stride and pace. Putting extra effort into his steps (without increasing his pace), he may show that he has a purpose that allows no interference. Walking faster than usual, he may reveal that he has no time for anything other than the present task. His gaze contributes to this display: focusing straight ahead,

Figs. 1.6.1–2 Walking toward a task

Hussein avoids having his eye caught by anyone, but also allows others to locate the destination, and thus the purpose, of his walk. In (1.6), Hussein avoids eye contact with others until he reaches his destination. When he completes his task there, he instantaneously makes eye contact with a customer who has followed him.

Hussein has helped carry a motor block to the trunk of a car and is now returning to the shop to get a tool from the toolbox. He walks at a moderate pace, glances to the left, passes Cedric who is coming his way without looking at him (Fig.1.6.1), glances to the ground and throws a rag to the floor (Fig.1.6.2), and then begins to swing his freed left hand back and forth. Reaching the toolbox, he opens a drawer and looks for the tool, while Housem, a Lebanese taxi driver whom he knows well, enters the picture, rolling a tire toward him. Kenneth, his office worker, approaches him from the back, and Mike, a young technician, enters the scene from the left (Fig.1.6.3). Hussein, however, casts his gaze down and maintains a bubble or 'zone' (Kendon 1990) around himself, ignoring a question that Mike is asking; walking away a few steps, he mutters, 'Hold on.' He turns around (Fig.1.6.4) and walks to the car where the tool is needed, and turns his gaze to it (Fig.1.6.5). Now he holds up the wrench and rotates it like a rattle (Fig.1.6.6), calls out, 'Here,' calls again, and then, as he presents the tool to Cedric, who takes it, says, 'Here, number (- - -) eighteen' (Fig.1.6.7): the job is demonstrably done.

As soon as Cedric's hand encloses the tool, Hussein turns to the left, where his gaze meets Housem's, who becomes his next interaction partner (Fig.1.6.8). Right away they fall into synchronous steps (Fig.1.6.10). We see clearly in this scene how the configuration of Hussein's body is implicated in social organization: initially his manner of walking is designed to keep his path free from co-interactants; then he focuses his gaze on his destination

Figs. 1.6.3–7 Avoiding eye contact and engagement displays

and uses a tool in his hand to broadcast the purpose of his walk; finally he transitions to walking *with* another.

It is not uncommon for Hussein to broadcast the purpose of his excursions by demonstratively holding a tool. One time he stands in front of the toolbox, takes a large screwdriver out, and then closes and locks the box. Holding the screwdriver in his hands, he feels its length, looks at it. Then he holds it up, walking with it until he reaches the car he is working on. Another time, as he walks toward a motor block and prepares himself for helping to carry it to the trunk of another car, he

Figs. 1.6.8–10 Moving into walking together

fondles the rag he will use to protect his hand, and moves it from one hand to the other (Fig.1.7). Yet another time, as he approaches a car whose paint needs a touch-up, he loudly shakes the spray can (Fig.1.8). How he holds an object as he walks is an important conveyor of social information: it broadcasts Hussein's present engagement with the world and makes it intelligible to anyone concerned; it indicates a purpose and his inaccessibility to those who are not partners with him in the activity to which the tool belongs.

The ground on which Hussein walks is full of obstacles, things lying about that obstruct his course and require cautious circumnavigation. Accordingly, he clears the ground for later passage and rearranges things on the ground. Or he has someone else do the job: the day includes many brief interactions, framed by joint attention on objects on the floor, that result in their removal. What needs to be done, who will do what, and how the need for action is conveyed are incessant, on-the-spot, managerial decisions that Hussein makes as he navigates his shop, and often enough he decides to do the job himself. This saves the time investment communicating a request for action to a worker would constitute.

Figs. 1.7, 1.8 Holding a tool to convey purpose

Figs. 1.9.1–2 Transforming obstacles into resources

For example, when he walks to the shop across the street for the first time to check on Uncle Ahm, the welder, and then moves on, Hussein finds two fenders and a front end of a car in his path and rearranges the fenders so that their arrangement is more orderly and displays what kinds of parts they are; he turns them from a hindrance into a resource for action (Figs. 1.9.1–2). But, of course, not all problems can be dealt with right away and by him, and some must be delegated to someone else. In the following scene, Hussein removes an obstacle from his path as he delegates another task to Kenneth. Walking out of the shop where he has fixed a tire, Hussein glances to the left and right as he strides ahead. When he approaches his destination, he shoots a half-glance to the left and then points his right thumb over his shoulder, as Kenneth, who has appeared out of nowhere, approaches him from the back: the pointing gesture picks

Figs. 1.10.1–3 Connecting task, agent, and beneficiary

out the referent of Hussein's subsequent observation and turns it into an object for Kenneth's care (Fig.1.10.1). Hussein bends down to pick up a hose (Fig.1.10.2), rises, turns toward the shop, and says (Fig.1.10.3):

(1.10)
1 H This old man, he need oil change.

The sentence does not specify the actor of the oil change. This means that Kenneth can choose that person; he is simply responsible for getting it done (cf. Chapter 7).

Many of Hussein's walks end with him approaching someone else, either because that person was his destination from the outset or because that person simply appears on the scene, evidently in need of his attention. Once he enters the orbit of others, Hussein prepares his approach, which often 'projects' what kind of participation with one another he proposes for the ensuing interaction (Schmitt 2012). The approach is a slot for opening gambits that can facilitate or constrain subsequent moves. We have already observed this process during the first few minutes of the day, noticing the differences in the way Hussein configured his body for interactions with employees and customers, respectively. Employees, we noted, were approached with a visible focus on some external or 'third' object and without visual regard for the other. This bearing and orientation proposes a state of *joint attention* on an object at hand (see also Chapter 2). The customer, in contrast, received Hussein's prolonged gaze, and Hussein approached him with upright and open bearing, 'offering himself up' for focused interaction. These differences between participation frameworks, established during the initial phase of an encounter, were described as the result of the enactment of methodical practices.

In the following scene, Hussein and Victor (Victorio), a technician held in high regard by him, are trying to diagnose the engine problems of an Audi. Hussein says, 'This here, turn lot, probably that the problem,' when he notices a familiar customer approaching. Hussein turns his upper body so that he faces his customer, and then begins to approach him, offering a greeting (line 5):

Figs. 1.11.1–3 Customers are greeted face-to-face

(1.11)
1   H   This here,
2   turn lot.
3   Probably that the problem.
         (- - -)
4   Part of the problem.
         (1.0)
5   H   **Hi St**eve!
6   C   How you doing, ma:n.
7   H   **Fin**e Sir, how are **you**.
8   C   Not too bad.
9   I was gonna ask you about uh some of these parts off this van.
         (- - - -)
10 H   Okay.
11   Like which one.

Hussein's bearing and the sequencing of interaction with a customer are the same as earlier in the morning when the first customer arrived: his posture is erect and he fully faces the customer and looks him in the eye. Topical talk is initiated only after the greeting sequence has run its course.

In (1.12), one of Hussein's routine methods for approaching technicians, walking with a pointing hand, is on display. Hussein initiates interactions with three different employees within the span of twelve seconds, each time making a pointing gesture during his initial turn. First he addresses Art, then Mike, then Alex. Art, who is standing in front of the shop with a coffee mug in one hand, is trying to fish a cigarette out of the box with the other. Hussein rapidly walks toward him and asks, 'Are you going across the street now?' as he raises his right hand whose index finger is extended, pointing in the direction of the shop across the street (Fig.1.12; subsequent pointing gestures are marked in the transcript, but too small and distant from the camera to be shown).

(1.12)
1   H   Are you going • across the street now?
2   A   I'm just giving him some tips on this one here.
3   H   Okay.

Hussein slows down for a fraction of a second as he listens to Art's response (line 2) and then walks to the front end of the Audi where Mike and Alex are at work. Again slowing down, he says,

4   H   I need uh- (- • - -) this car up
5   and I need the front tire off
6   I wanna inspect the • brake.

Figs. 1.12 Pointing 'across the street'

Before he utters <u>this</u>, Hussein looks and points with his left hand to a red Mercury convertible (line 4). Mike rises from the engine of the Audi he has been working on with Alex and complies immediately, departing as Hussein utters <u>off</u>. At this point, Hussein is already focusing on his next object of concern, the Audi's engine. He moves to the front of the car and addresses Alex, pointing to the engine (line 7). Alex is positioned next to him, and both now look at the engine. A focus of joint attention is established.

7   H   This the original one here
8   A   No, this the original one
9   I mean thuh- from the other one car.

Thus, on a very brief journey, Hussein specifies three successive places or objects of concern at the outset of each interaction. He points at them and thereby provides his coworkers with an orientation within a 'task-scape' (Ingold 2000). We will explore pointing in Chapter 3.

In (1.13) we first see Hussein leaving the shop and then focusing his gaze on a transmission in the driveway. Hussein positions himself in front of the transmission, looks at it, and points to it as he begins to inquire what 'year model this 3.8' is (Fig.1.13.1, line 1). That the question is addressed to Victor who is working on the Audi on the south side of the yard, some distance away, is indicated only at the end of the turn. Mid-turn, Hussein raises his hand and

Figs. 1.13.1–4 Discovering an engine, inquiring about it

scratches his head, apparently rededicating his hand to a different task after
the pointing gesture clearly has missed its communicative function: there was
no way Victor could have seen it (Fig.1.13.2). But Hussein points to the
transmission again as Victor raises his head and looks over, and he walks a few
steps toward him (Fig.1.13.3). Thus, Victor finds Hussein pointing to the
transmission when he initially looks at him. Victor comes closer and looks at
the transmission during the subsequent exchange, whereas Hussein adopts
an akimbo posture and keeps his gaze focused on Victor Fig.1.13.4).

(13)
1   H   What • year model this • three-point-eight, Victor.
        (1.8)
2   V   Three-point-eight?
3   H   What • year model this Buick•.
4   V   Eighty-two.
5   H   Eighty-two? Oldsmobile?
        (1.2)
6   H   Uh- I better maybe find (- - - -) shorter block and two head
                                        [
7   V   Yeah
8   That's right.

This time, Hussein does not approach the technician, but rather makes him come to *him*, and when Victor performs the inspection that is necessary to answer Hussein's question, Hussein focuses on him, not the transmission. Different 'intentional relations' are embodied in Hussein's posture, orientation, and gaze direction than during previous moments when he was approaching employees. With the term *intentional relations* (Barresi & Moore 1996; see Chapter 3), I refer to (recursive) relations between agents and objects in embodied and mental activities. In the context of the auto shop, when Hussein and one or more of his coworkers together attend to and try to fix an automotive problem, they maintain, as co-agents, *parallel* intentional relations to an object. When they interact face to face, they are one another's intentional objects. Here, however, Hussein's attention is focused on Victor's inspection of the transmission; in other words, Victor's intentional relation to the object is Hussein's intentional object. In this sense, the relation is a recursive or nested one. When Hussein greets a customer, the customer is his intentional object as much as he is the customer's; they maintain reciprocal relations, not parallel ones (as they subsequently do when together they attend to the customer's car).

Hussein can rely on other practices and resources when he wants to structure his interlocutor's attention. In the following scene, instead of pointing to an object, Hussein *exhibits* it and uses his other hand to *annotate* it with gestures, as he asks a question about it. This is possible here because the object is itself a *representation*: a worksheet. Hussein is on his way back to the office, a worksheet in hand, but then suddenly turns around, walks back outside, and calls on Victor.

(1.14)
1   H   Victor!
        (2.0)
2   H   Victor, GMS just starter, • right?
3   V   Sta•rter-
        (3.0)
4   V   Yeah, just starter.
5   H   That's it.

As he walks toward Victor, Hussein makes a series of large, lateral *negation* gestures with his right hand (Harrison 2010; Kendon 2004). He holds the worksheet so that it faces Victor (Fig.1.14.1), who looks at it when he begins to answer (Fig.1.14.2). Hussein then turns the sheet so that he can write on it, and Victor looks on, repeating the answer (line 4), as Hussein finishes filling out the form. The positioning of the worksheet, the negation

Figs. 1.14.1–2 Pointing with and to a worksheet

gestures, and the question (a question about the object referenced on the form, of course, not the worksheet itself) together form a 'multimodal package': the positioning of the sheet communicates that it is the object of concern and anchors referential terms (GMS, starter), whereas the large negation gestures convey that there is *nothing else* to be done,[5] no other work to be performed on this car.

1.5 Standing with others

Many of Hussein's interactions with employees are transitory and do not require that he come to a halt. But it is just as common (and has been the case in most of the scenes so far described) that he and his counterpart take on a stationary position, at least for a brief moment. Many researchers, notably Scheflen (1972, 1974) and Kendon (1990),[6] have investigated the orientational and postural configurations that people build and maintain with their bodies when they engage in focused interaction, devoting most attention to how people stand together when they talk. Today, in our artifact-rich civilization, many face-to-face conversations are conducted in seated positions, constrained by furniture that implies a normative postural framework. (In contrast, members of standing groups can more easily alter the location and postural-orientational configuration of their interaction.) Following Kendon (1990), we call the postural-orientational configurations of the bodies participating in focused interaction *F-formations*. Kendon notes that

---

[5] See Kendon (2004) about ways in which negation gestures can negate presuppositions and implications rather than the overt propositions of utterances.
[6] See also Mondada (2013).

an F-formation arises whenever two or more people sustain a spatial and orientational relationship in which the space between them is one to which they have equal, direct, and exclusive access.

He suggests that

by arranging themselves into a particular formation [participants] ... display each to the other that they are governed by the same set of general considerations, ... a commonality of interest. (Kendon, 1990: 247)[7]

Scheflen used the term 'reciprocal' as a noun, to refer to joint posture frames of moments of interaction, and noted that

when people carry out 'reciprocal activities' they 'frame' them in space and time by the way they place their bodies. ... The twosome partners adjust ... aspects of their physical relation in order to indicate the degree of their involvement and the degree of their 'openness' or 'closedness' to third parties. (Scheflen 1972: 29)

It has sometimes been suggested that the distance people keep when they engage in conversation is a function of the culture to which they belong, as well as of their relative status, gender, and degree of mutual liking. The interpersonal distance of most F-formations Hussein and his interaction partners adopt, however, is due to the shifting and constraining contingencies of the auto shop and the activities conducted there. For example, when they engage in some sort of sensory exploration of a car (touching the body to inspect the paint, listening to the sounds emanating from the engine, etc.), perceptual requirements override other factors in bringing about the shape of the F-formation and the distances the parties keep.

However, personal preferences also matter. In sum, recurrent shapes of stationary ensembles appear to be motivated by three factors: the nature of the activity; the physical structure of the setting and/or the object of shared concern; and the habits making up the evolved relationship between the

[7] The spatial structure of face-to-face interaction includes the positioning of participants relative to their current status as focal participants, ratified participants, or bystanders, i.e., the 'embodied participation framework' (Goodwin 2007a) of the interaction at the moment. Goodwin notes that

the participation framework constituted through the mutual alignment of the participants' bodies creates a dynamic frame that indexically grounds the talk and embodied action occurring within it. (2007a: 57)

F-formations can also be regarded as participants' 'embodied answers to their *what is going on?* queries' (McDermott, Roth, & Gospodinoff 1978): the current configuration shows what is going on, and changes in the configuration indicate that something new is beginning.

parties. This latter aspect is of particular interest (and we will turn to it later), because it points to the *particularization* of social relationships that takes place even in routinized, functional interactions.

A side-by-side formation is common for Hussein and any category of partner (customer, technician, delivery personnel) when they are observing an event or object without directly engaging with it. During idle moments, Hussein always positions himself in this fashion if he finds himself with a customer, but only with a distinct subset of employees. Side-by-side marks engagements with other Lebanese, or people generally with whom he maintains a *personal* relationship. We can call this arrangement, to highlight the status equality it implies, a *fraternal* 'with' (Goffman 1971); Scheflen simply calls it 'side-by-side' (1972). The frequency and ease with which Hussein takes this position alongside certain individuals indicates that he sustains a different kind of bond with them than he does with others, even though the nature of that difference may not be transparent to us. Hussein maintained the most extensive fraternal framing when he walked 'across the street' in the company of Ashraf, his long-time associate from the time young Ashraf apprenticed with him in Riyadh.

Positioning also indicates, if in a different way, that Hussein has a particular kind of relationship with Hakim, the physician who serves as his runner: they often appear to 'hang out' (even as Hussein continues to review files, fix brake pads, etc.).[8] The special nature of their relationship may be a consequence of Hakim's social status as physician; the term by which he is addressed by everyone (which means 'Doctor') contributes to this distinction. But it may also be Hussein's charity that drives his relationship with Hakim, as he is saving him from desolation. When Hussein interacts with him, he frequently adopts a face-to-face formation— rather than joint attention—even if only for a short time. There is, in other words, a routine 'conversation slot' in their dealings with one another, which is not the case with most other employees, with whom Hussein interacts in 'functional' ways throughout this day. During the initial phases of his interactions with customers, Hussein invariably chooses a framework of vis-à-vis orientation, at a distance of three to ten feet. Later, when there are sustained periods of discourse, he may stand closer to customers, typically in an L-formation around the engine of their car.

Table 2 shows standard formations repeatedly adopted during this day at Hi-Tech Automotive.

---

[8] Hakim has long departed from the shop, but Hussein told me recently that, being again in need of a job and a place to stay, he may return after many years.

Table 2 Recurrent formations at Hi-Tech Automotive

joint attention with technician

joint attention with technician

face to face with customer

face to face with customer

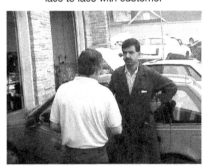

face to face with Hakim

face to face with technician

'L-formation'

'compromise formation'

While the preferred distance adopted by Hussein and a specific conversational partner is not a function of their cultural background, relative status, or gender, and while we therefore cannot predict from the 'official' identities of the parties the shape their conversational arrangement will take, some of Hussein's employees appear to have got accustomed to, and to actively maintain, a 'standard' habitual distance when they interact with Hussein, for example, when they 'reset' their positioning at this distance after contingencies of the joint activity have necessitated closer (or larger) distance.

A pair of episodes involving Arturo and Cedric illustrates this point. Each of these technicians comes to Hussein toward the end of the day and asks for an advance, but while Arturo maintains a distance of five or six feet, Cedric stands in closer proximity. We see Cedric waiting for Hussein, standing on the corner of the hydraulic bridge across the street. Hussein, who is approaching, asks him where he has been, as someone had come looking for him. As they deal with this topic, the two men stand side by side, Hussein on one side of the bridge, Cedric, with hands in his pockets, on the other (Fig.1.15.1). As they approach the end of the bridge, Cedric asks Hussein, 'Can I get ten dollars?' He steps off the bridge, stops, and turns around with light, dance-like steps. Hussein remains on the bridge, a bit above Cedric, who, belatedly noticing that Hussein has stopped, walks back toward him. As Hussein looks into his wallet and counts the bills, Cedric stands about two feet away from him (Fig.1.15.2). Hussein hands him some money, says 'eight dollar', and Cedric takes it, accepting the lower sum, thanks Hussein, and departs.

Figs. 1.15.1–2 Differential positioning: Cedric asks for an advance

(1.15)
1	Hussein	Where you were.
2		Somebody came asking for you
3	Cedric	Yeah I know.
		[
4		I say my son he said not there.
5	Cedric	Yeah well I- I:
6		I was getting around • on the floor
7		( )
8	Hussein	Uh huh.
9	Cedric	Yeah.
10		Can I get ten dollars?
11	Hussein	Ten dollar?
12	Cedric	Yeah.
13	Hussein	Sure.
		(2.5)
14	Cedric	Yeah anyway it's time- I'm gonna go
		(4.5) •
15	Hussein	Eight dollar.
16	Cedric	Okay. That'll do.
17		Alright. Thank you.
		[
18	Hussein	Uh huh. Bye bye.

When Arturo comes to Hussein with the same kind of request just a moment later, he maneuvers quite differently. He maintains a distance of about four feet, even when Hussein hands him the money (Fig.1.16.1). As Arturo approaches, Hussein, when he first establishes what Arturo wants (line 2), steps off the bridge, walks toward him, and stops about four feet away from Arturo, however, and moves a few inches back. The men

Figs. 1.16.1–2 Differential positioning: Arturo asks for an advance

banter at this time (lines 4, 9, 11, 12). When the transaction is complete, Arturo retreats another two steps and then remains in that place (Fig.1.16.2).

(1.16)
1	Hussein	Yes.
2		You need money?
3		Twenty I ha:ve.
4	Arturo	Ohh my gho:d.
5	Hussein	Go ask Cedric.
6		I gave eight
7		he need ten, I gave him eight.
8		Look.
		(1.0)
9	Arturo	Ohh my G(h)o:d.
10		O•kay, well
11		I gotta like it
12	Hussein	Yeah, don't worry, you get paid anyw(h)ay.
		[
13	Arturo	H(h)ah hah • hah hah hah
14		Okay

Arturo again moves in on Hussein. He launches another, more complex interaction: he asks for a larger advance the next day. For this request, he positions himself at roughly the same distance of four feet as before. He fondles his right ear in a gestural display of discomfort and lowers the volume of his voice, two acts that mitigate whatever imposition his request may constitute for Hussein (Scheflen 1972). Hussein, for his part, moves closer to him, lowering his head to hear him better (Fig.1.16.3). When Hussein shows that he understands him (line 24), Arturo again steps back (Fig.1.16.4).

Figs. 1.16.3–4 Arturo asks for another advance

15		Ah! Then, another one question.
16		Do you think uhh uhhhh
17		maybe you
18		I don't know if you wanna you wanna
19		give me a hundred dollars • for this job
20		uh for the uh-
21		whenever you pa- you pay me?
22		Then- you take it out of my check, okay,
23		a hundred dollars.
		(0.5)
24	Hussein	You want it tomorrow you mean?
25	Arturo	Yeah=
26	Hussein	=S•ure

The distance at which Arturo comfortably converses with Hussein appears to be four to five feet. Whether this is due to a cultural rule governing interaction with a person of higher status in his Mexican homeland or an ecological adaptation—Arturo's height is less than five feet—we cannot know. In this interaction we can also observe how different postures that Hussein adopts can bear on the development of the interaction he is in, how posture partakes in the self-regulation of interactional and interpersonal distance and cooperation. A posture he routinely takes on when customers or employees ask him a question that cannot be answered in a single sentence and perhaps require requests for clarification is the (*half-*)*akimbo*. This is a posture in which a hand or two are propped on the hips. Akimbo seems to signal that Hussein is prepared for a longer exchange and is responsive to the interlocutor's needs. In this episode, the akimbo posture alternates with 'arms folded in front'. The sequential evidence suggests that the latter posture indicates, by way of contrast, that he is done with a task, or temporarily 'off duty'.

At the beginning of the episode, Hussein is standing with his arms crossed, not doing much of anything, except half-heartedly answering questions the researcher poses to him. Arturo arrives. After he has made his request for an advance, Hussein changes his posture to retrieve money from his wallet. Having paid Arturo, he again folds his arms. When Arturo makes his second request, Hussein at first keeps his arms folded and looks on him with concentration. But, perhaps realizing that dealing with the new request will demand fuller involvement (Arturo's request-turn at lines 16–21 is full of self-repair and difficult to follow), Hussein changes his posture: he puts his left hand on a lever of the hydraulic bridge and the right in akimbo and bends down to hear Arturo out. Then he grants Arturo's request and

Fig. 1.16.5 Hussein in leisurely posture

treats the sequence as complete. However, Arturo is not done (lines 34–35). He keeps his gaze on Hussein, and another chunk of dialogue follows (up to line 52). Repeatedly here (at lines 39, 49, and 52), Hussein indicates by withdrawing his gaze from Arturo that the business at hand is done (see Chapter 2). However, Arturo, keeping his gaze on Hussein, indicates that there is more to come (Fig.1.16.5).

30	Hussein	Make you happy for the weekend.
31		If I say no
32	Arturo	h(h)eh
33	Hussein	you'll get mad
34		No. N(h)ok•ay
		[
35	Arturo	It's not that I- I-
36		I wanna pay the rent
37	Hussein	Sure
38	Arturo	and uh
39	Hussein	you got it
40	Arturo	See I wanna pay the rent
41		I don't wanna- wanna use the money
		[
42	Hussein	Sure
43	Arturo	( )
		[
44	Hussein	You got it.
45		Tomorrow I give you the money, no problem.
		[
46	Arturo	Okay I will just-
47		tomorrow I sure will be back

Hussein, as if to demand work in return for the advance, points out that
the next day, a nearby car will have to be 'kicked out' (line 48–49), and he
removes his left hand from the hydraulic bridge to gesture with it. His right
hand remains on his hip. At line 52, he puts his left hand on his other hip
and turns away from Arturo, thereby again treating the course of action as
completed. Now Arturo asks to get a day off (line 54). In response to this
question, Hussein changes his posture: he folds his arms (Fig.1.16.6). He
gives a noncommittal answer ('depend'), and then breaks out laughing.
Arturo joins in the laughter, turns, and walks away (Fig.1.16.7). It appears
that Hussein's folded-arms posture, along with his refusal to make any
commitment, indicates to Arturo that the moment at which he can make
serious requests of Hussein has passed.

(1.12–4)

48	Hussein	Ah yeah, sure, we need tomorrow maybe ten o'clock,
49		this car kick out
50		(nods)
51		and then next job will be the Cadillac
52		pull the engine
53	Arturo	(nods)
54		You think that ( ) give me- uh- uh- day (.) off
55	Hussein	.hhh Depend hhh •
		(- -)
56	Arturo	mh m(h)hh h(h)hhh huh
		[
57	Hussein	You need to work on that
		(- - -)
58	Hussein	.hhuh h(h)uh h(h)uh hhhh
59	Arturo	Okay
60	Hussein	Okay bye •

Figs. 1.16.6–7 Banter and departure

This interaction suggests that different significances are embodied in Hussein's two contrasting postures: akimbo is for task-related talk; it projects Hussein's commitment to a course of action that his interlocutor has initiated. In contrast, in this as in many other cases, Hussein stands with arms folded when he is either not engaged in interaction at all or when the interaction is not about solving a task. He changes into this when he transitions from task-related to leisurely talk.

Kendon (1990) defines the 'F-formation system' as an organization by which interaction participants maintain their encounter as a bounded social event and manage changes in their joint activity. But the system can also be invoked or enacted as a way of differentiating between different social relationships and types of recurrent engagements. Phenomena such as the spatial orientation and relative distance among participants are very much governed by perceptual requirements and spatial constraints of the activity and the setting. Yet the less constraining these constraints are, the more variables like distance and orientation become available as markers of relationship, even of 'nested' relationship representations. Moreover, in part because of the durability of some spatial arrangements (such as the F-formation), which can endure for hours, spatial organization in interaction not only concerns events on the time-scale of the single encounter. Rather, spatial organization is apt to serve as a representational 'interface' to express and transform 'abstract' social concepts such as status, status passage, hierarchy, in ritual orders of spacing.

1.6   Dance

Stable formations are, as Kendon (1990) has observed, the ongoing products of spatial maneuvers by the parties, who do interactional work to maintain (or alter) the formation. We can elucidate this interactional work by immersing ourselves in a few moments in which Hussein 'dances' with a female customer across the 'floor' of the auto shop (the driveway). The situation is unique because it takes place in a relatively large and unobstructed space, during times when the pair moves from one place to another—when they navigate as a *with* (Goffman 1971). This situation bears a formal resemblance to a dance floor, and the tasks of navigating together in unpredictable yet coordinated ways bears formal resemblance to that of tango dancers. Dance as an art form consists of genres and practices for decomposing and recomposing available patterns of human motion. Dance analyzes and represents forms of human relatedness and interaction by stripping away everything but the movement of co-present bodies in space. At the same time, it is a celebration of human abilities to interact (to court, deceive, seduce, escape, and so on).

An increasing number of interaction researchers are studying the social organization of body motion in dance and of body motion and language during dance instruction (Keevalik 2015; Müller & Bohle 2007). Sociologists interested in the behavioral foundations of social order (Alkemeyer, Brümmer, Kodalle, & Pille 2009) find in dance both a case in point and a metonymy. The adjustment of movements in a dancing couple, the viability of the dynamical system, is a function of individual mastery and shared membership in a community at once. The scripted *pas-de-deux* of classical ballet expressed esthetic values of the European elites—the ideal of weightless bodies—and presented formalized, ideological versions of gendered interaction and affect. Improvisational *tango Argentino* dancers seek to reach, through sequences of steps that are both practiced and improvised, the exalted moment when two bodies, one male, the other female, move as one—as a 'four-legged animal' (Elsner 2000). To get there, they must solve, step after step, an iteration of interaction problems, dilemmas of *contingency* and *intersubjectivity* (Haller 2009): because the order of steps is not fixed, each new step of each dancer must emerge as the product of the negotiated ability to anticipate the other's next step. For the couple to dance as a unit, each member must be able to glean what the other will do next. However, the immediate form of communication necessary for this coordination cannot take place in the feet themselves, which do not touch and cannot be seen. It rather takes place in the torsos, arms, and hands of the dancers, who are always in embrace. It is the sensitivity of that communication that holds the four-legged animal together, and because this is so, tango is also a paradigmatic case of the integration of modalities that make up embodied communication: the motions of the feet are connected to the ways hands touch.

Tango and other forms of dance exhibit the living body that Merleau-Ponty (1962) has written about, a body that, prior to any conscious recognition, responds to the moment's changing cues, but also, through its obstinate responses, moves the situation forward in unexpected directions, in constant intercorporeal interaction with other bodies/selves.

1.7   Negotiations on foot

The dance-like qualities of shared locomotion in everyday life are on display in a negotiation between Hussein and a female customer who is considering buying a white Jeep from him. As they discuss the car and the possible terms of sale, they move about the driveway, as if from station to station (Giddens 1984), inspecting and discussing the car and repeatedly stopping for a moment of face-to-face talk. We will examine how they maneuver together, how they 'negotiate space'—in other words, how they position themselves and move in relation to one another at different times and 'find their footing' with each other.

A joint beginning

The episode emerges through nineteen stages, each framed by a distinct 'reciprocal' (Scheflen 1972) or formation. It begins when Richie, the customer, an African American businesswoman who has been coming to Hussein's shop for years, arrives in an open white convertible, as Hussein is parking a customer's car. After a greeting and an interruption by a phone call, Hussein joins Richie in the driveway and they proceed together and inspect the Jeep. Moments of joint inspection alternate with face-to-face conversation, until Hussein begins his return to the shop and Richie follows him, a journey that is twice suspended by face-to-face 'reciprocals' and that ends in one as well. The episode ends when Hussein receives another phone call and Richie takes her leave, presumably to return on a later occasion. Nine moments during this episode show how the definition of the situation—the 'working consensus as to whose claims ... will be temporarily honored' (Goffman 1959: 9)—is negotiated and calibrated in dance-like fashion through the particular ways in which Hussein and Richie move together.

This calibration of the working consensus begins at the very beginning of the episode; it is achieved by the way Hussein maneuvers a customer's car (a Mercury Capri convertible, hero of Chapter 7). What is striking about the moment is that Hussein and Richie arrive in the driveway of the shop at the same time in near-identical cars, Richie in a white open convertible, Hussein in a red open convertible, coming to a halt at precisely the same moment. Close observation, however, shows that, as much as this is a moment of serendipity, it is one of serendipity being recognized and used: *how* they arrive in the situation together is the result of precision management on Hussein's part.[9] Driving the car out of the garage and onto the driveway in front of the office, Hussein is visibly looking in the rearview mirror where he can see Richie arriving in her convertible. At this point, she is still about thirty feet away from him. When Hussein reaches his destination, instead of turning off the car and getting out, he puts it in reverse and very slowly backs up while turning around so that he faces Richie in her car. At this moment, Richie turns

---

[9] This precision management (of speed and direction) cannot be seen in still photographs; but it is clearly visible in the videotape.

Figs. 1.17.1–2 Joining in arrival

her head toward him, and we can assume that they have eye-to-eye contact. Such eye contact would constitute a *distance salutation*, a minimal display of mutual recognition (see Kendon 1990: 172). When their cars are precisely aligned, they stop them at exactly the same time.

Hussein opens the door as soon as he comes to a stop, but he delays getting out by about a second, giving Richie time to open her door. As a result, when they do get out of their cars, they do so in synchrony (Fig.1.17.1). Once outside the car, Hussein turns around and looks toward Richie. When their eyes meet, he utters a greeting. Then, after closing the car door, he laughingly performs an action gesture, steering a wheel, and says, 'equal' (Fig.1.17.2). In other words, he expresses the situation that has just come to pass: they drive similar cars and are therefore, in one respect, equals. In the opening of this situation, then, Hussein, by using and modifying resources the situation offers him, picks out a contingent common identity and thereby lays an egalitarian, affiliative foundation for their subsequent interaction.

(1.17)
1   H   Hi Richie.
2   Equal.
3   (   )
4   How are you today.

Discrepant stances

Richie inquires whether Hussein still has the Jeep to sell. A brief dialogue ensues until Hussein's phone rings and he goes into his office for a moment. When he comes back out and finds Richie waiting for him, a trajectory unfolds through their spatial maneuvers that is quite different from the initial one. Now Hussein proceeds in a fashion that emphasizes differences in their approach to the task at hand. With his movements and positioning, Hussein anticipates Richie's spatial maneuvers, but he uses this anticipation, not to align with her, but to preempt the success of her moves. As he emerges from his office, Richie steps into his anticipated path and orients her body toward him (Fig.1.18.1), so that he would end up facing her were he to continue along the present path. But Hussein takes a small turn to the left (Figs.1.18.2–4) so that he does not arrive facing her, but by her side, and he maintains forward orientation, roughly facing toward the Jeep. By not taking up the vis-à-vis position Richie's positioning proposes, but rather proposing orienting to the Jeep, Hussein not only declines to join the formation she offers, but also declines to agree with the definition of the situation embodied in it (broadly, 'this is between you and me, about our relationship'). However, his own approach, implying that they jointly attend to the car ('this is about the car you want to buy, not about us'), is equally in need of ratification. She would need to move into a position aligned with Hussein's to 'ratify' a shared framework of participation. This is Richie's choice now: either insist on her approach by maintaining her orientation toward him and blocking his view of the car, or align with his. She chooses the latter and turns around (Figs.1.18.5–6). The two end up side by side, looking across the parking lot to the Jeep. Hussein's take on the activity, finding an answer to the implicit question 'what is it that we are doing together?', prevails.

This is their dialogue during this maneuver:

```
(1.18)
1   R   How much you're asking for it now.
2   H   Give me deal.
            ( - - - - )
3       You have money?
            ( - - - - )
4       Let's make deal.
5       You have money?
                    [
6   R               I-
        I have cash.
7   H   Good,
8       that what I need.
```

Hussein now proposes that Richie take the Jeep for a drive, and she responds that she has an appointment at 10 o'clock and will come back later to drive it. She makes a parting gesture, but then begins heading toward the Jeep, rather than her own car, while Hussein first seems to begin walking toward the shop, responding with a parting gesture of his own. But then he

Figs. 1.18.1–5 Refusing one F-formation, adopting another

abruptly changes directions, asks her if she has any questions, and follows her to the Jeep.

(1.19)
17 H You want to ask- q**ue**stion?
18   Hmm?
19 R Has the motor been rebuilt?
10 H Hmm?
11 R Has the motor been rebuilt?
12 H No no.

The interaction around the car that develops replicates this dance-like negotiation about discrepant takes on the joint activity (what Goffman calls 'lines'; Goffman 1959). Hussein walks around the car, points to various parts, and explains what work will still be done on it. Richie positions herself about five feet away from the Jeep, ready to engage in face-to-face conversation. Then she takes a step forward, moving in on Hussein, who initially also takes a step toward her as if to reciprocate her move, but in effect forces Richie to step back and make room for him, between herself and the car. Now a little dance unfolds. Hussein, who first seems to reciprocate her stances, instead takes a few steps past Richie until he gets to the car's open door and reaches inside, preparing to start it (Fig.1.20.1). Richie remains in lockstep with him, stepping backward and turning as he reaches into the car. She positions herself so that Hussein once again finds himself face to face with her when, having started the car, he turns around. But he maintains his distance from her, using the open car door as a barrier (Fig.1.20.2).

Richie asks Hussein for the price of the car, but Hussein turns away from her. He puts his right hand on the roof (Fig.1.20.5) and his left on his

Figs. 1.20.1–4 Answering a dispreferred question

hip in an akimbo posture, and only then turns his head toward her (Fig.1.20.4). Then he answers her question.

(1.20–1)

1 R What you bought-
2   what you bought-
3   what do I pay for this car, cash•.
          (- - • - -)
4 H Sixty-five•.
          (- -)
5 R Hm?
6 H Sixty-fi:ve.
          (-)
7 H It's very •clean truck.=

What can we make of Hussein's positioning? Is it possible to assign meaning to his posture? According to the principles of context analysis, the significance of body motions and positionings consists in the contributions they make to assembling the contextual frame of the interaction. Their significance lies in how they frame the *next* moment (McDermott & Roth 1978). Considered in this fashion, two features of Hussein's posture stand out. One is its demonstrative stability: Hussein gives support to his body by propping up one arm on the car, one hand on his hip; he thereby shows his readiness to engage in *sustained* interaction. Moreover, Hussein adopts this posture as he performs a distinct speech act: he names a price. By positioning himself in this fashion during this speech act, he frames it as the beginning of a possibly sustained state of engagement—perhaps expecting the price to be treated as his starting price. At the same time, Hussein's posture is one half of an asymmetrical configuration; he refrains from the alternative possibility of mirroring Richie's posture, opting instead to maintain close physical contact with the car. Again, the parties to the negotiation adopt positions and postures that embody discrepant definitions of the situation.

Now Richie changes ('steps up') her approach. Instead of embarking on a negotiation, she makes a counter-move. She takes a step forward, puts her right hand on Hussein's shoulder, states that she is not going to buy the car, and asks him how much *he* paid for it (Fig.1.20.5). Then she moves further to the left, positioning herself even closer to Hussein, proposing a full-face engagement. But Hussein, who maintains his akimbo posture, turns to the

Figs. 1.20.5–6 Changing the definition of the situation

right and looks away (Fig.1.20.6). (We will discuss his gaze withdrawal again in the next chapter.)

(1.20–2)

```
8    R    =Okay, ( - • - ) I don't wanna buy the car.
9         What'd you pay for the car.
          ( - • - )
10   H    Which car.
11   R    This car.
12   H    What I pay?
13   R    Yeah.
14   H    I bought it from the auction. ( - )
15        With- damage in the body and I have to fix it.
16   R    Right. Before you- before you fixed it,
17        how much did you pay for it.
          ( - - )
18   H    Thi- ( - ) it's not gonna help you this-
19   R    I know,
20        but I wanna know.
```

Two bodily acts frame Richie's verbal move: the 'tie sign' (Goffman 1971) of putting her hand on his shoulder and the close proximity she keeps. Neither correspond, in our culture, to the functional role relationship between buyer and seller. Here, too, the relative timing of the positioning and speech is important: by adopting the posture before she speaks, Richie prospectively *frames* her spoken utterance. Her positioning more forcefully than her talk, seeks to put the relationship on a special footing. Whether her move is intended as playful, as a counterfactual flight into fiction (of course she wants to buy the car!), is not clear at the outset. There

Figs. 1.20.7–8 Disalignment

is no evidence that Hussein takes it this way: he shows an entirely serious, perhaps bothered, expression and does not join her in redefining their activity as an event in and contribution to a special, personal relationship between them. Initially, Hussein maintains his akimbo posture, looking away. Then he effectively removes Richie's hand from his shoulder by making a gesture toward the interior of the car (Fig.1.20.7), before he returns his hand to its position on his hip and again looks away from Richie (Fig.1.20.8). Clearly, the two do not have a working consensus about the definition of the situation.

Synchronized movement

Hussein ends the dispute over whether he should reveal the price he paid for the Jeep by teasing Richie. He defines their bond as a 'joking relationship' (Radcliffe-Brown 1965). Radcliffe-Brown used the term to describe relationships in which structural ambivalence is managed by humor (his example were son/mother-in-law relationships). Through joking, contradictory meanings and sentiments can be simultaneously expressed, as in the following sequence, which marks the transition into a playful frame. Hussein laughs and smiles at Richie while telling her that 'she is so mean'. His joke laminates the insult 'you're so mean' onto her self-assertion, 'that's how I am'. Hussein glances at her, laughs, closes the car door, and then begins to walk to the front end of the car (Fig.1.20.9). Richie protests (line 26), yet follows him at a close distance (Fig.1.20.10).

(1.20–3)

21   H   Why you wanna know.
22   R   Because-
23   that's how I am.

Figs. 1.20.9–10 Play and movement synchrony

```
24  H   Why- because
25      you're- ( - ) so mean!
26  R   No I'm not!
          [
27  H       K(h)huh-
28      hah hah hah hah hah hah
29      huh huh huh huh huh huh.
```

Richie closely tracks Hussein's steps and matches his pace, and initially also holds her right hand in a fashion similar to his. Arriving at the front end of the car, Hussein opens the hood and looks inside. Richie positions herself next to him, all the while imploring him to tell her how much he paid for the car.

(1.20–4)
```
30  R   An honest person will tell you what you ask them.
31  H   No.
32  R   You're an honest person,
33      just tell me what you paid for it.
34      What'd you pay for it.
35      Three grand?
36      ( - - - - - - )
37  H   Whatever I may tell you will not help you in this case.
38      It's may- not make the deal.
```

The two are in a side-by-side formation (Fig.1.20.11). Then Richie grabs Hussein's right upper arm with both hands, and leans into him, asking him 'why don't you tell me?', and then she requests that he 'look her in the eye' (Fig.1.20.12).

Figs. 1.20.10–13 'You're a man; look me in the eye'

(1.20–5)

39	H	Whatever I may tell you will not help you in this case.
40		It's may- not make the deal.
		[
41	R	It's not.
42		So why don't you just tell me.
43		Look me in the eye!
44		You're a man,
45		look me in the eye!
46	H	I won't tell you.
		[
47	R	How much you pay for it.

Hussein turns to her and smiles, in effect complying with her request to look her in the eye. Then he turns his eyes to the engine, and Richie follows his motion, continually leaning in on him and holding on to his arm. Hussein does not look at her, but laughs. When she says, 'look at you', he looks at her, still laughing, and closes the hood. Again they are in a close 'F-formation' (Kendon 1990; Fig.1.20.13).

(1.20–6)

```
48  H   I won't tell you.
49  R   Why.
50  H   Wh(h)y?
51      It's m(h)y b(h)usiness!
                    [
52  R                   I've never seen you like this.
53  H   (Do you know I-          )
                    [
54  R                   Look at you!
55      Look at you!
```

Hussein begins to walk back to the driver's door, continually touching the body of the car. Richie follows him closely, turned toward him and never letting him get away from her, even as he once more opens the car door. She stays close to him and, as he reaches into the car to turn the ignition key, she tries to force him into another close F-formation. But Hussein now shifts his tone markedly, no longer laughing, and tells her that she has no business knowing the price he paid (lines 58–63).

(1.20–7)

```
56  H   Why should I tell you-
57  R   (      ) I've never seen you like this!
58  H   This-a question
59      I should not tell you how much I pay for
60      everything ha:ve here.
61      You should not know my pri:ce. ( - )
62      It's my price, it's not yours.
63      It's not for publish this price.
64      If you wanna buy it,
65      if the deal good for you, fi:ne,
66      if it's not give me offer,
67      I may tell you take it.
```

And indeed, Richie, joining Hussein's reframing of the exchange as a serious one, makes him a counteroffer. He rejects it out of hand.

(1.20–8)

```
68  R   I give you forty-five cash for it.
69  H   No.
        ( - - - - - - - )
70  R   What would you take?
71  H   Just ( - ) sixty-five.
```

Richie now begins to complain about the state the car is in and claims that the interior needs a lot of work, and the two look inside from the back. After an extended examination, Hussein closes the hatch and they begin their walk back to the shop. This walk, in particular, shares form features with dance. It is spontaneously choreographed in a fashion that allows them to anticipate each other's next steps (and go along with or derail them).

When Hussein has closed the rear door, he takes two steps back and Richie takes two steps forward (Figs 1.20.13–16). At the same time they make quarter turns, Hussein to the left, Richie to the right, so that their

Figs. 1.20.15–19 Dancing: moving into synchronized gait

Figs. 1.20.10–21 Dancing: moving into F-formation

facing formation becomes a side-by-side arrangement. They walk in syn-chrony, their feet reaching the ground within less than fifty milliseconds of one another (Fig.1.20.17). Hussein then slows down by shortening one step and delaying the next (Fig.1.20.18). Richie, who is presently looking down and thus witnessing this spatial maneuver, changes the orientation of her feet as she is setting them down: she organizes her steps so that she gradually makes a turn until she faces Hussein (Figs.1.20.19–21). The two come to a stop exactly at the same time: a symmetrical face-to-face arrange-ment emerges. It emerges not through action and response, that is, sequen-tially, but through the careful orchestration of each party's step with respect to the simultaneous steps of the other. They are now negotiating strategy, how to settle on a price and come to an agreement. They maintain this arrangement for about twelve seconds.

(1.21)
1   R   What year is it?
2   H   Eighty-eight.
3   R   It's a eighty-eight.
4   H   Yeah.
           (- - - - -)
5   And reconditioned.
6   H   It's not: uh- what they call Blue Title.
7   Reconditioned.
8   We bought it from the auction,
9   fixed, and for sale.
10   Reconditioned.
11   To me it's sold fine,
12   if not I sell in Russia though,
13   I sell it in Russia

Figs. 1.21.1–2 Teasing and tie sign

A stable, enduring face-to-face arrangement has emerged. Gesturing at the car, Hussein looks at Richie and nods vividly. Then he tells her that he will sell the car to Russia if he does not sell it to her. Richie replies, 'I don't wanna hear about Russia,' and Hussein, beginning to walk on, gives her a pat on the upper arm and teases her that 'Russia is [her] competitor now' (Figs.1.21.1–2).

They walk across the lot. For a moment, they walk in synchrony again, but then Hussein skips a beat and lets Richie step ahead of him and then turns toward the shop. He seems set on escaping her. But Richie matches the changes and holds Hussein to their engagement: she maintains synchrony with him, their feet reaching and leaving the ground simultaneously for at least seven steps (their feet are initially not visible on the tape), even though Richie is walking backward and Hussein forward. As their walking slows down, they turn toward one another (Figs.1.21.1–2). They come to a halt at the same time, and Richie takes one additional step to adjust the position of her feet so that she is again fully facing Hussein (Figs.1.21.3–9). Again they find themselves in a face-to-face arrangement.

As they stand face to face, Hussein appeals to Richie: 'You have to be very fair.' In response, she wants to know what he means by very fair. She removes her glasses and demands 'look me in the eye' as she steps up to him, once again 'getting in his face' (Figs.1.21.11–12).

Then she steps back to give him a better view and begins to perform: she mimes how Hussein would ache and moan from his bad conscience if he gave her a bad deal. She displays the physical pain he would suffer if he cheated her. She moans and grabs parts of her body like someone in pain: the stomach, thigh, and feet. What she is conveying is: this is what I don't want you to have to go through. Preventing such nocturnal pain is what she

Figs. 1.21.3–5 Joint walking and securing a face-to-face

Figs. 1.21.6–9 Serious negotiation: face-to-face

Fig. 1.21.10 'You have to [be] very fair'

Fig. 1.21.11 'Look me in the eye'

Figs. 1.21.12–13 Richie performing Hussein's nocturnal pangs of guilty pain

is trying to do for him (Figs.1.21.12–13). But Hussein just looks away from her, stoically pretends that this is not happening. Richie returns into a face-to-face, and Hussein resumes the sequence from there (line 6), disregarding the performance.

Fig. 1.21.14 Final face-to-face

Fig. 1.21.15 Parting gestures

Once again, then, Richie tries here to put their negotiation on a non-business footing, and once again she fails. It is Hussein's way or no way, and so they talk serious business from now on (Richie inquires about the actual properties of the car).

(1.21)
1   R   What do you feel is very fair.
2   Look me in the eye.
3   Tell me, tell me what you:- so that you: can sleep.
4   I don't want you to go Oh my God! Ohhh ohhhhoh!
        (- - -)
5   What is very fair to you.
            [
6   H   I'll give you firm-a price, and you can take it or leave it.
7   Don't give me o:ffer.
8   If I wanna give you my wo:rd, you don't give me offer.
9   Either take it or leave it.

They maintain this formation with only minor adjustments for the remaining minute and a half of their encounter (Fig.1.21.14), again framing by it a specific phase of their negotiation (a 'meta-communicative' exchange about ways to come to an agreement). The episode ends when Hussein gets a call on his wireless phone, and they exchange parting gestures (Fig.1.21.15).

1.8   Intercorporeality in motion

Earlier, it was suggested that Hussein's and Richie's motions during this episode occasionally take on structural features that they share with dance, specifically dance that involves dyads in movement sequences that are both improvisational and quasi-predictable, for example, Argentine tango in which couples improvise the order of steps and yet move like 'four-legged animals' or 'vehicular units/withs' (Goffman 1971). Hussein's and Richie's motions show a coordination that is similar to dance particularly during two kinds of moments: when they walk together and synchronize their steps so that their feet touch the ground at the same time. This is not possible without mutual anticipation of steps (their timing and tempo), which is facilitated by shared rhythm, which is in turn brought about by the synchronizing of steps (Richie and Hussein must make their own music). The other, similar, achievement is their simultaneous arrival in an F-formation, finding themselves in front of each other's faces and coming to a halt 'on the same beat', typically through coordinated footwork.

Haller (2009) has distinguished three levels of organization in Argentine tango: 1. the distribution of the roles of leader and led; 2. the couple maintaining itself in an embrace; and 3. the couple's navigation across the dance floor, among other navigating couples. Each level presents a separate task that must be solved moment by moment, step by step, through cooperation. These requirements and their methodical solution make tango a spectacle of 'carnal intersubjectivity' (Merleau-Ponty 1964; cf. Meyer, Streeck, & Jordan 2017), exaggerating tasks of movement coordination and joint navigation that also exist in everyday interaction. In the dyad at the auto shop, Hussein leads the movement, but he often leads from behind, slowing down or even coming to a halt as he walks behind Richie and somehow getting her to slow down or stop with him. Richie and Hussein, of course, do not embrace, but they maintain and hold each other in 'F-formations' (Kendon 1990), temporarily stable postural formations that embody a shared understanding of what they are doing at the moment (Goffman 1963; McDermott & Roth 1978). The floor is void of other dancers, but the two navigate in relation to co-present cars. Haller (2009) has argued that dancers acquire a particular *practical sense* (Bourdieu 1990) and that their subjectivity is to an extent that of 'inter-subjects', constituted through the interactions that they sustain and distinguished by a heightened ability to anticipate the acts and dispositions of others. 'In these movement processes, ... moving intersubjectivities show up in moving as a "with" [Goffman 1971, J. S.], as intersubjectivities that only develop through movements performed together' (Haller 2009: 102).

This fine-tuned ability to 'dance' with others is not something Hussein indiscriminately displays with everyone; he reserves it for situations or relationships that require extra care and perhaps afford a certain amount of closeness or *tactility*. Here, it is deployed in the service of maintaining a playful yet antagonistic relationship with a customer of many years. 'She always hug me and kiss me,' Hussein said, not without emphasizing the completely 'unsexed' nature of her affection. With Richie, antagonism is mitigated by signals of affection and framed as irony, teasing, and play (Bateson 1972). It appears that the context she provides brings out abilities to resonate and to transgress boundaries and to reveal aspects of his personality that remain dormant and may be less in demand in many of Hussein's more routine interactions.

Our bodily ability to resonate with others, to move and be moved by them, has recently received much attention by neuroscientists, notably those who believe that all cognitive phenomena are grounded in the human organism's 'carnal' interactions with other organisms and the world. Resonance of the type described here, exemplified by joint locomotion, explodes traditional psychological accounts of human action and perception in terms of stimulus and response: synchronized motion cannot be explained in terms of stimulus and response, because responses always only happen after some lag time (between 250 and 400 milliseconds). Synchronous motion requires some form of anticipation, as well as simultaneity of perception and action. Neuroscientists have proposed various models for mechanisms that enable the human organism to resonate and move with others. One mechanism proposed are 'forward-models' (Wolpert & Miall 1996). It is suggested that, whenever a human organism perceives the beginning of a familiar movement, it activates within itself the schema of the movement or action under way and can complete the act of another by activating a known schema within itself.

Using information about the movement properties of muscles and limbs, the forward model simulates the unfolding course of the movement, in parallel with the actual movement occurring in the external world. Any discrepancy between the forward model's simulated movement and the desired movement results in corrective commands being issued. (Wilson & Knoblich 2005: 466)

In other words, the act of another person does not need to be completed before a parallel or aligned action can be launched. Team sports provide a rich field to see forward modeling in action (Meyer & von Wedelstaedt in press). Cognitive scientists have suggested that forward modeling is a form of *covert imitation* (Wilson 2006): 'covert imitation' means that humans (among various other animals), in perceiving the motions of other humans, covertly activate the neural processes involved in producing the action. Covert imitation functions as a *perceptual emulator*, 'using implicit knowledge of one's own body mechanics as a mental model to track another person's actions in real time' (Wilson & Knoblich 2005: 463).

The various brain areas involved in translating perceived human movement into corresponding motor programs collectively act as an emulator, internally simulating ongoing perceived movement. This emulator bypasses the delay of sensory transmission to provide immediate information about the ongoing course of the observed action, as well as its probably immediate future. (Wilson & Knoblich 2006: 468)

Overt performance of emulated actions is inhibited in older children and adults by the central nervous system, but it is visible in infants who imitate facial expressions and other muscular actions of their caregivers. Kinsbourne (2009) argues that imitation *is* the form interpersonal perception takes in infants; imitation is the fashion in which infants perceive. A generalized version of the theory of covert imitation is the theory of *common coding* (Prinz 1997; Prinz, Foersterling, & Hauf 2005), which posits that the production and perception of action share the same neural resources: when we perceive an action, the same neural networks are activated as when we produce the respective action. The best-known and widely popularized version of this theory is the theory of *mirror-neurons* (Rizzolatti & Craighero 2004), which attributes common coding to a specialized subset of neurons, dedicated, as it were, to the production of intersubjectivity. Rather than offering a model of the human body and brain as fundamentally geared toward intercorporeality (Meyer, Streeck, & Jordan in press), the theory of mirror-neurons short-circuits the issue of 'carnal intersubjectivity' (Merleau-Ponty 1962) by positing a kind of apparatus that mechanically solves the problem of gaining access to other minds. Moreover, it is not even clear that humans have mirror neurons and, if they do, that they serve the same purposes as in the monkey brain. Moreover, there is little evidence that mirror neurons would enable either a monkey or a human to *understand* any action; understanding action involves conceptual knowledge and other areas of the brain (Hickok 2009). What mirror neurons (or comparable resonance mechanisms) are capable of is activating sensory-motor *knowledge* associated with an observed action (Mahon & Caramazza 2008) in those who already possess that knowledge. But resonance alone is indifferent to the conceptual features of human action (e.g., whether there was a blink or a wink).

This means that neural resonance mechanisms cannot *cause* individuals to act in certain ways; they *enable* modes of interpersonal relating, but require other cognitive abilities to count as social intelligence. As we have seen, Hussein's resonance abilities, whatever their neural shape, allow him to relate differentially to different others. For example, interacting with Yvonne, another long-time customer, an African American woman of approximately the same age as Richie, he repeatedly lets her take the lead in assembling an F-formation and mirrors her idiosyncratic posture. When she leans back against her car and props her arm on the door, he adopts a matching stance (Figs.1.22.1–2).

In contrast, when he interacts with Richie, Hussein takes the lead, and she must rely on her resonance abilities to stay connected with him. We also saw Hussein anticipate Richie's movement, but then preempt its desired upshot, a face-to-face formation with him, and instead leading Richie into a side-by-side. Resonance does not necessarily lead to alignment, let alone matching postures; it can serve the negotiation of discrepant 'lines' and approaches to the situation at hand.

Figs. 1.22.1–2 Customer drawing Hussein into a face-to-face

1.9   Walking with others

Just as he distinguishes types of others and engagements with them by the position he adopts as he stands with them, Hussein also chooses among ways of walking with others. Of course, how people navigate as they move from place to place is constrained by the space around them, but some preferences can nevertheless be observed. For example, Hussein rarely follows anyone. He is either being followed—that is, he leads—or he deliberately walks *with* someone, a type of movement that requires micro-management.[10] Kenneth usually trails him (Fig.1.23.1), as do his other junior technicians (Fig.1.23.2). These choices appear to parallel those Hussein makes in adopting a standing position relative to others: while he occasionally walks side by side with an employee, for example, if the employee comes to ask for his advice and has something to report as they walk to the job site (e.g., with Cedric, (Fig.1.24)), he normally reserves the mode *walking with* for customers and core members of his team.

We have already taken stock of some of the practices by which a state of walking together is achieved and we can now readily summarize them:

(1)   a state of synchronous walking is achieved by the parties' anticipa-
      tions of each other's next steps and the timing of their own next
      steps in relation to them, so that the parties' feet reach the ground at
      the same time;

(2)   the pattern is repeated until a shared rhythm is achieved (usually
      after the second step);

Fig. 1.23.1 Leading Victorio

---

[10]   Schmitt has analyzed *walking with someone* and *following someone* as distinct 'situated
       practices'; Schmitt (2012).

Fig. 1.23.2 Leading Art

Fig. 1.24 Talking and walking with Hakim

(3) subsequent steps are synchronized on the basis of rhythmic entrainment;

(4) when synchrony is disrupted, the pattern can be reestablished in the same fashion.

In (1.25) Hussein is seen walking with Hakim. The walk originates in the junkyard next door, where Hussein is inspecting the underside of a car. Hakim arrives with two boxes of spare parts so Hussein can verify that they are the right ones. Hussein rises, inspects one box, and tells Hakim to take the parts to Uncle Ahm, the welder. He closes the box and hands it back to Hakim. Hakim has his head turned toward the street and Hussein follows his gaze, and then they begin to walk in synchrony (Fig.1.25.1), picking up pace when they reach the sidewalk: whenever both men appear in the video frame, we see that their steps are synchronized, even though they move under different conditions, as Hakim carries two stacked boxes in his arms and repeatedly needs to adjust them. Eventually Hakim slows

Figs. 1.25.1–2 Coordinating a joint walk with Hakim

down and Hussein, who is still talking, keeps moving until he notices that Hakim has stayed behind. He turns around, Hakim slows down and stops, and they maintain a distant conversational positioning for a few turns (Fig.1.25.2). What is striking is how formally Hussein ends their interaction: while Hakim simply walks away, Hussein first looks toward his destination, the office, then to Hakim, and he announces what he will do next as he slowly walks on. He completes his talk with the address term 'Hakim' and looks back at him one more time before he turns toward his path and slowly walks away.

(1.25)
1 H   Hawdeh mnateehon la uncle '?', yazeem.
         We'll put these for Uncle Ahm, great.
2 H   Sho, bedak el lambah?
         What, you want the light bulb?
3 Hm   Aya lambah?
         Which light bulb?
4 H   Hay le ya taytneh yeha, ma yandeh.
         The one that you gave to me, I don't have.
5 H   Aza byiftahou bokrah min rouh en jeeba boukrah.
         If they open tomorrow, we will go get it tomorrow.
6 H   Heyeh jayeh bokrah tekhoud el seyarah, oh el tenen el soubouh.
         She's coming tomorrow to take the car, or on Monday morning.
7 Hm   Eh.
         Yes.

The most elaborate instances of walking together involve Ashraf as Hussein's counterpart. Hussein has known Ashraf for many years; he has trained him. In the following, Hussein is 'across the street' and Ashraf arrives with some report or question. Hussein walks toward him, but

Figs. 1.26.1–2 Walking and standing with Ashraf

instead of stopping, he slowly passes him without looking, and Ashraf joins him, and from the get-go they move their feet in parallel and in synchrony, even though their path is quite narrow (Fig.1.26.1). They only fall out of synchrony when they turn and then come to a stop and inspect some replacement parts strewn about. At some point they position themselves side by side and display their working consensus by matching postures (Fig.1.26.2). Then they move on.

(1.26)

1 H halla?, hæ:di lazbuna. ha:j.
　　　　Now, this is for a customer. This one.
　　　　shu: baʕd ʕindak tnen pruf.
　　　　You got two more repairs
　　　　bukrah ʕassari:ʕ bxallisʕon.
　　　　Get them ready quickly for tomorrow.
　　　　(1.0)
　　　　ħatʕetllak dʒank ja:rd ?tuʕʕa tnen. biddi txallisʕha pruf.
　　　　I have dropped the two pieces in the junkyard. I want you to finish them.
　　　　(0.2)
　　　　hæ:di I.malʸ ru:be min wara.
　　　　This one has been hit behind.
　　　　biddi ?asʕllihha li?annu lʕatʕi:lo ?utʕʕa bxamsi:n dola:r kulllum ka:mili:n.
　　　　I want to repair it because I intend to sell them to him altogether for fifty dollars.
　　　　bidhin ?asʕ?
2 A Do they need cut?
3 H hajaʕtʕu:ni lquwartar fener w l?zæz.
　　　　They will give me the quarter fender and the glasses (windows).
　　　　hajaʕtʕu:ni l?aʕda lwarranie: wa te:la:ijt kullum ʕala baʕlʸ.
　　　　They will me the back seats, bumper and taillight altogether.

Figs. 1.27.1–3 Walking with an old man

The kind of interactional work Hussein must often perform to achieve
a state of 'with-ness' with a customer can also be gleaned from an interaction with an old man who has come to have his old Plymouth checked. For
nearly twenty steps, the walking of the two men is aligned so that they
always set a foot on the ground at almost exactly the same time. Twice,
Hussein slows the downward movement of his foot, at one time adding
a slight upward kick to it, so that the old man can take two steps while he
takes one; still the feet land in synchrony. During the middle third of the
walk, Hussein's right hand holds his left arm behind his back, and he
maintains a slightly stooped posture, amplifying the measured character
of his gait and showing that he is *with* the old man (Figs.1.27.1–3).

1.10   Walking and knowing

Anthropologist Tim Ingold has argued that 'walking is a highly intelligent activity'; the feet's movements,

> continually and fluently responsive to an ongoing perceptual monitoring of
> the ground ahead, are never quite the same from one step to the next.

> Rhythmic rather than metronomic, what they beat out is not a metric of constant intervals but a pattern of lived time and space. It is in the very 'tuning' of movement in response to the ever-changing conditions of a task that the skill of walking ... ultimately resides. (Ingold 2004: 332)

Social life, Ingold continues, is walked along 'paths of observation' (Gibson 1979) and embedded 'in the actual ground of lived experience, where the earth we tread interfaces with the air we breathe':

> It is along this ground, and not in some ethereal realm of discursively constructed significance, over and above the material world, that lives are paced out in their mutual relations. ... The body itself is grounded in movement. Walking is not just what a body *does*; it is what a body *is*. ... Walking ... [is] thinking in movement. (Ingold & Vergunst 2008: 2)

That body motion is a form of thought and that thought has evolved from body movement and motor control is a point that philosopher Sheets-Johnstone (2012) has emphasized. After all, only organisms that control their own movements have brains (Llinàs 2001). Arguably, however, the movements of the hands tell us more about, and are more characteristic of, human cognition than those of the legs; we will explore the cognitive nature of body motion when we investigate Hussein's hand gestures. Moreover, like most members of industrial civilizations, Hussein wears shoes and rarely explores the world through the sensory capacities of his feet.[11] But undoubtedly, walking around his shop, alone or in the company of a technician, is an important source of information for him; it is a main way for him to gain *situation awareness* (Donald 1991; see Chapter 7).

1.11 Standing apart

After ending an exchange or a joint activity, Hussein sometimes just stands in place for a moment, *scanning* the scene, as if looking for the next task awaiting him (Fig.1.28).

Scanning can lead to the discovery of a problem, and this discovery may in turn call for a decision about what to do next. In (1.29), Hussein had been leaning over the engine of an Audi, inspecting Victor's work. He concludes his visit with an instruction (line 1) and a juncture marker (okay) as he rises. Then he stands for a moment, puts one arm akimbo, as if undecided what to do next.

---

[11] An exception is his pressing of foot pedals when he test-drives a car.

Fig. 1.28.1–2 Hussein scanning the scene

Figs. 1.29.1–3 Scanning, discovery, inquiry

He turns around, scans the front of the shop, and announces his plan to take a rest (i.e., a restroom break; Fig.1.29.1). But then he fairly jerks back as his gaze finds a Maxima inside the shop. Immediately his right arm and index finger form a pointing gesture (Fig.1.29.2). Holding the gesture, he turns to Victor, who has risen from the engine (Fig.1.29.3, line 4) and asks 'Is this ready?'.

(1.29)
1   H   ... reset everything on the fifth.
2   Okay.
        (2.5)
3   H   I'm gonna go take some rest now=
4   =>Is this< ready?
5   Maxima?
        (- - -)
6   V   Yes.
7   H   Ready?
8   V   (nods)

Victor turns to the Maxima as he answers (line 6). Hussein repeats his question, reconfiguring his hand to a bunched shape as if grasping for an answer, while looking at Victor, who nods. But at this point, although still pointing, Hussein is already on his way to that car, as if guided by his own pointing gesture.

When he stands by himself or apart from those around him, Hussein takes on a number of standard postures. Most of these are adaptations to—and thus indicative of—the activity in which he is engaged. But there are also a number of *signature* postures, postures that are context-adaptive, yet distinctly personal. Among these are the positions he prefers to take on when he conducts what promises to become an extended phone conversation. Fig.1.30.1 shows Hussein with his right elbow forming a bridge between the roof and the open door of a car; he gestures with his left. As he talks, he intermittently monitors the goings-on in front of the shop (Fig.1.30.2). (Hussein had walked to this place when he received the phone call, after leaving Hassan and their joint work site when he received the call.) In Fig.1.30.3, we see Hussein sitting on the trunk of a car, having received a call from Lebanon. In this position, he needs his left hand to support himself. At one point, he attempts to gesture. One hand goes on an excursion but then quickly returns to and takes hold of the knee, stabilizing what has become a precarious posture. When Hussein is alone at the counter in the front office, he rarely props up his arm, not even during phone conversations. Instead, he always has some paperwork in front of him, unless he takes a call, for which he then uses the counter as support for a sustained posture.

In Fig 1.31, we see Hussein standing akimbo as he observes what is going on in the shop, at a juncture between activities. Sometimes he folds his arms during such moments (Fig.1.32). There is a contrast between the two postures: akimbo marks a stance of expectation; folded arms do not. They rather signify nonparticipation, because the hands are prevented

Figs. 1.30.1–3 Resting postures during phone conversations

Fig. 1.31 Akimbo postures

from gesturing. Akimbo is a position Hussein repeatedly takes on when he inspects the work done on a car from a distance, alone or with others.

Other postures appear almost as icons of Hussein's status, for example, how he directs others with pointing gestures (see Chapter 3). His bearing is erect and his voice raised (since he talks at a distance and needs rapid compliance), as in (1.33), when he directs Victor's attention to coolant leaking from a car.

Fig. 1.32 Arms folded, a leisure posture

Fig. 1.33 Authority in pointing

(1.33)
1   H   Look look look look.
        (1.0)
2   H   Antifreeze leaking.
3   Why?

1.12 Conclusion

In this chapter, I have introduced the term *practice* and the multiscale way I use it in this book: to refer to a habitualized method for performing actions, in this case, mainly communicative actions. The term is applicable at multiple scales because it is possible and entirely coherent, for example, to call Hussein's entire 'multimodal' habit of approaching customers a 'practice', but also the way he carries himself during such approaches, or how he directs his gaze. Practices (the know-how they contain and require) reside in individual human bodies, who acquire the majority of them from 'the society' and 'the culture' by participating in their public commerce, but adapt them and blend them with 'self-made' practices, routinized solutions to recurrent tasks and circumstances in the life-world, and perhaps infused with personal style (signature). Always, someone's repertoire of practices—or *habitus* (Bourdieu 1990)—is indicative of an individually embodied, lived life. Embodied communication practices, although deeply rooted in millennia of cultural evolution and shaped to a large degree by social norms, are in each case an individual's equipment for living, and this equipment is the interim outcome of the living body's self-organization and organization of its *Umwelt*, and thus its participation in the society's (and local community's) reproduction. 'Persons ... reproduce society ... by reproducing themselves as persons' (Heller 1984: 4). While this must seem trivial to those researchers of the human body who have investigated it for its trainability—and are forever confronted with the idiosyncratic obstinacies of single bodies—it is not trivial when considered from the perspective of conversation analysis and most other sociological accounts of human action. Sociology, as well as social and cultural anthropology, are by disciplinary fiat interested in the behaviors, meanings, and norms that are *shared* by groups of people. But cultural action *is* individuation, and individuation is the product of enactments of the very practices that also sustain society and culture (and whatever lower-level social organization they partake in). Cultural development is possible because embodied persons adaptively and creatively sustain and reproduce themselves. We must therefore turn to the *individual* body if we want to understand the reproduction—or re-instantiation and 're-inscription'—of embodied culture. Thus, in the study of embodied communication practices, biological, phenomenological, sociological, linguistic, and anthropological perspectives merge.

We have seen how Hussein modulates his gait and bearing in ways that broadcast purpose, destination, and whether he is open to being approached by others. His own methods of approaching others are also enactive distinctions between classes of them (technicians and customers), as well as between types of engagement he is seeking or entering. Furthermore, whether Hussein has his arms folded or akimbo can signal to someone familiar with him whether he treats the interaction at hand as serious and in demand of close attention, or as an open-ended moment of inconsequential leisure. Most iconic of Hussein's role in the organization and his mode of participation in its activities is what I have called the 'point walk', which is captured in the cover photograph: Hussein walking with a pointing gesture, directing the attention and future action of a technician who is walking with him.

The crucial and most interesting moments from the viewpoint of communication theory were Hussein's 'dances' with Richie around the white Jeep. For here we saw two individual bodies walk as a 'four-legged animal' (Elsner 2000), in perfectly synchronized steps, finding their path even though the leader is walking backward—a fleeting, but in its details impressive display of *intercorporeality*. This form of social being is not attributable to the agency of individuals, but only *exists* 'at the level of the dyad' (or ensemble or *we*). It is a purely social *dynamical system* (see Streeck & Jordan 2009). And yet it is not a system that is closed to individual agency: we saw how Hussein transformed the 'F-formation system' by not playing the part Richie's actions afforded him, which conditioned re-adaptations on Richie's part. Richie, in turn, anticipated Hussein's path and adjusted her course so that she could draw him into a face-to-face formation and derailed his return to the shop. These are processes that cannot be explained as individual action and individual reaction, because each step is itself a joint product of ongoing interaction, and this requires the participating bodies' ability to mutually anticipate each other's moves. This biological capacity is itself thoroughly social in nature, a part of the human body's socially geared neuro-anatomy.

2 Looking

This chapter describes how Mr. Chmeis uses his eyes during the course of his workday. It identifies his main vision-based activities and the practices of gaze allocation he enacts in face-to-face communication: when he looks at, and when away from, his interlocutor, and how he uses his eyes to refer to objects in the surrounding area. Particular attention is paid to mutual gaze: when and why Mr. Chmeis seeks it. It appears that mutual gaze is less a means for displaying attention, as previously assumed, than a form of mutual recognition, a minimal social contract by which a communicative act is certified as part of the conversation's 'official record'. Conversely, looking away while answering a question or receiving advice is a way of disengaging, of marking the talk and action of the moment as dispreferred. Overall, two prevailing frameworks of visual attention can be distinguished at the auto shop: *face-to-face* and *joint attention* on an object, a 'third'. When focused on an object, Hussein and his interaction partners display mutual recognition by a transitory compromise orientation, slightly turning to one another while maintaining their visual focus on the object at hand. In face-to-face communication, gaze (where speaker and listeners look when) appears to be the socially most regimented of the communication modalities, giving the parties little freedom to turn their eyes without consequence.

2.1 A moment's glances

The German word for moment is 'eye-glance', *Augenblick*, but a moment can contain many glances. During this moment, Hussein and Uncle Ahm, the welder, are bending over the front end of a Corsica that is in the final stages of remodeling. Ahm presently explores the backside of the radiator grill, which, according to Hussein, needs adjustment. Hussein watches him (Fig. 2.1.1) and then lets his gaze wander over the engine and front right fender (Fig.2.1.2). Repeatedly, his gaze falls on an area to his right (Fig.2.1.3).

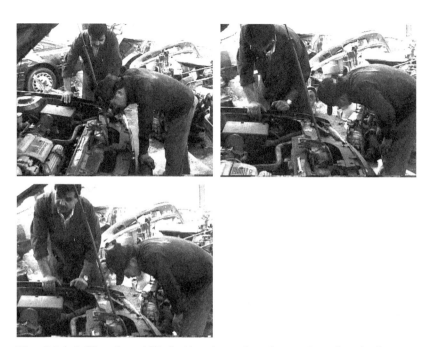

Figs. 2.1.1–3 Hussein and Uncle Ahm determine what work needs to be done.

Then Hussein looks back to Uncle Ahm (Fig.2.1.4). He turns his gaze to the right and reaches with his hand toward the area he had just focused on before (Fig.2.1.5). Then, keeping his hand in place, he looks at Uncle Ahm and speaks to him. Ahm at first does not react (Fig.2.1.6, line 1).

(2.1–1)
1   H   If you find the other pie:ce

Now Hussein requests Uncle Ahm's gaze explicitly (line 2); he keeps his own eyes on him until Ahm looks up, and as soon as he does, Hussein returns his gaze to the object his right hand is touching ('this'). Ahm rises and looks toward Hussein (Fig.2.1.7, line 2). Hussein still holds the object in his right hand, but now looks and points with his left hand to the other side of the car. Ahm's gaze follows the pointing gesture (Fig.2.1.8). Hussein explains that Ahm will need 'one piece like this' (line 4, Fig.2.1.9): apparently, there are two identical parts, one for each side of the car, and one of them is missing. Hussein's goal is to direct Ahm's attention to the part (on Hussein's right) that is present so that he knows what part is missing on the other side ('over there').

Figs. 2.1.4–6 Uncle Ahm explores the front end with his hand.

Figs. 2.1.7–9 'Over there you need one piece like this.'

Figs. 2.1.10–12 'Missing.'

(2.1–2)
2 • look.
  (- - - -)
3 This also.
  (- - -)
4 Over there you need one piece like this.

Uncle Ahm offers no response. Hussein silently makes another pointing gesture, this time with his left hand (Fig.2.1.10), but receives no answer. Then he turns to Ahm and points across the car, this time with his right hand, and says, 'missing' (Fig.2.1.11). Then he reaches for the part on his side of the car and says, 'one like this' (Fig.2.1.12). Ahm impassively follows Hussein's motions with his eyes.

(2.1–3)
5 Missing.
  (- -)
6 One like this.

Hussein rises and looks to his left, away from the Corsica, perhaps searching for the missing part. He makes a HOLD gesture (see Chapter 5), his

Fig. 2.1.13 'One like this.'

Fig. 2.1.14 'Finish' gesture: 'We find it for you.'

palms facing one another, but the significance is not entirely clear: perhaps the positioning of the hands is supposed to figure the 'fitting' of the missing part in its place (Fig.2.1.13). Finally, Hussein turns his gaze to the engine and makes a wiping motion with his right hand over it, a gesture that, as we will see in the next chapter, is a habit by which Hussein often accompanies directives like 'finish everything'; it refers to a job's completion (Fig.2.1.14).

(2.1–4)
7   Maybe in (-) (   )
8   we find it for you.

Thus, in a period of less than twenty seconds, we see Hussein employing his eyes for a range of purposes: he *observes* or *supervises* the welder's actions; he *scans* the field, *searching* for objects that need further attention. In connection with pointing gestures, with his gaze he *directs* the welder's *attention* to objects and areas of concern; and he also *monitors* Uncle Ahm's responses to his pointing gestures. These are some of Hussein's ways of looking, all displayed within a few seconds of a single activity.

2.2 Gaze

The study of vision in human interaction since the 1960s has developed along two paths that we can associate with two verbs, *looking* and *seeing*. On one hand, researchers have investigated how gaze—specifically gaze direction—operates in the regulation of face-to-face interaction, particularly conversational interaction. On the other hand, investigators have inquired what it takes in various contexts of activity and professional practice, for example, among scientists, to actually *see* relevant phenomena at all. Looking is an activity; seeing is an achievement (cf. Ryle 1949). One line of research consequently addresses the question where and when people look in interaction; the other the question what people—for example, the members of a professional community—can *see* when they *look at* a 'domain of scrutiny' (Goodwin 1994), and how they manage to see it and see it together. Both dimensions are in play in the brief interaction shown between Hussein and the welder: Hussein scrutinizes a car to figure out (see) what work needs to be done and simultaneously monitors (looks at) the actions of his employee. Throughout, he engages in *professional vision* (Goodwin 1994). Hussein also seeks to direct the welder's gaze with his own. But, as we will see, a simple dichotomy between looking and seeing does not give us an adequate picture of the uses of the eyes in social life and interaction, and certainly not at Hi-Tech.

Sociologist Georg Simmel wrote at the beginning of the twentieth century:

> One cannot take with the eye without at the same time giving. The eye unveils to the other the soul that seeks to unveil the other. [It is] in immediate eye-to-eye contact ... that the most complete mutuality in the whole realm of human relations is produced. ... Among the individual sense organs, the eye is applied to a fully unique sociological accomplishment: to the bonds and patterns of interaction of individuals who are looking at each other. Perhaps this is the most immediate and purest interactive relationship. ... And so strong and sensitive is this bond that it is borne only by the shortest, the straight line between the eyes, and that the least diversion from this, the slightest glance to the side, fully destroys the singularity of this bond. (Simmel 2009: 571)

In ordinary interaction, this 'bond' of mutual gaze is usually brief, and how it is achieved and sustained and how it (or its absence) impacts the conduct of interaction has been a key question in research on gaze.

That work began with a seminal study by Adam Kendon (1967, republished in 1990) in which he showed that the amount of speaker and listener gaze is unequal: speakers usually direct shorter glances at listeners than listeners at speakers. While listeners express sustained attention to speakers by looking at them and only occasionally look away, speakers look more briefly at listeners, and these glances, according to Kendon, serve a monitoring function. The speaker 'appears to "place" his ... gazes at those points in his discourse where he ... [appears] to be looking for a response from his interlocutor, by which his subsequent behavior may be guided' (Kendon 1990: 82). Kendon concludes that speakers and listeners use gaze direction to 'regulate each other's behavior' (71).

This appears to be the mechanism involved:

> In withdrawing gaze, [the speaker] is able to concentrate on the organiza-
> tion of the utterance and at the same time, by looking away, he signals his
> intention to continue to hold the floor, and thereby forestall any attempt at
> action from his interlocutor. In looking up, which ... he does briefly at
> phrase endings and for a longer time at the ends of his utterances, he can at
> once check on how his interlocutor is responding to what he is saying, and
> signal to him that he is looking for some response from him. And for his
> interlocutor, these intermittent glances serve as signals to him, as to when
> [the speaker] wants a response from him. (Kendon 1967: 71)

Bavelas, Coates, and Johnson have suggested that speaker gaze not only serves to monitor the listener's behavior, but also to actively solicit responses (such as acknowledgment tokens) from him:

> The speaker typically seeks a response from the listener by looking at him
> or her, which begins a brief period of mutual gaze. When the listener
> responds within this gaze window [i.e., the period of mutual gaze, J. S.],
> the speaker quickly looks away, terminating the window and continuing to
> hold the turn. (Bavelas, Coates, & Johnson 2002: 570)

Goodwin (1980, 1981) developed Kendon's analysis of gaze further. He showed that gaze between speakers and hearers is *sequenced* in specific, normative, and describable ways: the listener should look at the speaker before the speaker looks at the listener; a speaker who initiates a turn at talk expects to find the intended listener looking at him; if the listener is not looking at the speaker at this point, the speaker will perform corrective acts to solicit his visual attention. These corrective acts can be 'self-repair initiators' such as restarts:

> When [a] speaker's eyes reach a recipient who is not gazing at him, he treats the talk in progress as impaired by producing a restart, an action that simultaneously has the effect of acting as a request for the gaze of [the] recipient. (Goodwin 1981: 73)

A speaker who finds himself gazing at a non-gazing listener can, alternatively, interrupt his turn, look away until the listener's gaze arrives, and then return his gaze to the listener and continue speaking. Speakers choose between these devices according to whether a listener has already begun to turn his gaze to them: if he has, they pause; if not, they restart their utterances from the beginning. Participants also use gaze withdrawal to temporarily disengage from a conversation or to enter a period of diminished participation or a side engagement such as eating, drinking, and lighting a cigarette, which neither require nor accommodate the co-participation of another. Where side activities require or warrant the other's participation, for example, when the parties are attending to an object of interest that has entered the scene, one can often see one party strive to redirect the attention of the other.

When speakers make gestures that depict objects or events and that need to be seen by the listener, speakers shift their gaze to their own gestures, triggering a parallel gaze shift by the listener (Gullberg 2003; Gullberg & Holmqvist 1999; Streeck 1993). Shared focus on the speaker's gestures can be considered a case of *joint attention*, to be distinguished from *mutual attention*. During mutual attention, each party looks to the face and eyes of the other. Developmental researchers have observed that human infants, who can indicate their focus of attention early on, are initially most interested in the faces of interaction partners. However, around six months of age, they begin to join adult interaction partners in turning their attention to objects in the world (Moore & Dunham 1995). 'Joint attention' refers to the sustained focus, shared with another participant, on an external object, and the simultaneous mutual monitoring and awareness of one another's attention. Joint attention is realized when 'both participants are monitoring the other's attention to the outside entity ... [and therefore] know that they are attending to something in common' (Tomasello 1995: 106). Around nine months, children begin to actively seek to direct caregivers' attention (Butterworth 1995: 30), and around the end of the first year of life, they move toward longer bouts of joint attention. It is within this 'participation framework' (Goodwin 1981) of joint attention that much of the early acquisition of words takes place: acquiring a new word often requires that child and caregiver attend to—and know that they attend to—an object in common. Joint attention evidently is a constant concern during cooperative manual work, but equally important are organized, joint shifts between joint and mutual attention.

2.3   Looking and seeing

Despite the paramount relevance of gaze direction for the regulation of face-to-face conversation, evidently regulative functions are only one of many different things interaction participants do with their eyes. As the opening scene shows, in a complex work setting such as a car repair shop, gaze is critically involved in a variety of types of cognitive, communicative, and practical activities, and often multiple demands concurrently are placed on the parties' visual attention. Much of the early research on gaze has been conducted in conversational contexts, often only involving two parties, where demands on the other's gaze as a visual display of attention may be uncommonly strict, whereas they may be relinquished when the participants simultaneously conduct complex practical activities that demand their visual attention. Rossano (2012) has already shown that the need for speakers to obtain their listeners' gaze, or for speakers to gaze at listeners, is not the same for every kind of conversation or activity or action sequence. For example, it is common for speakers who are asking a question to keep their gaze focused on the addressee, who in turn may not need to look at the questioner—a pattern that reverses what Kendon (1967) had documented in 'longer utterances' (e.g., storytelling).

The term 'gaze' itself is problematic. It obscures the variations that occur in the ways humans look at the world (and each other) and that are captured by the rich vocabulary for ocular actions in our everyday languages. The term 'gaze' typically refers to gaze *direction*, and, when applied to interaction, specifies *where* a person's visual attention is focused. But it does not designate the *activity* performed with the eyes. Coulter and Parsons point out that, instead of referring to a speaker's (or listener's) visual orientation as 'gazing at the listener' (or speaker),

> alternative possible (conventionally available) characterizations of . . . visual orientations . . . [by] speakers and recipients of . . . talk [exist]; these . . . include staring at, looking at, sizing up, or scrutinizing. To say of someone that he is/was 'gazing at' a speaker (as distinct from, inter alia, 'looking at' him) while speaking can be to imply distractedness or disinterest. We may also use the concept of 'gaze' when describing one who is failing to display

any discernible attentiveness to another during the course of a conversation. (Coulter & Parsons 1990: 267)[1]

Visual actions occur in the context of more embracing activities. The focus of analysis must therefore, as Goodwin writes, be on

> the systematic practices used by participants in interaction to achieve courses of collaborative action with each other ... [and] demonstrate how the participants themselves not only actively orient to particular kinds of visual events ..., but use them as constitutive features of the activities they are engaged in. (Goodwin 2000: 160)

For example, Hussein's gaze shift from a timing belt to a gauge will be recognized by his coworker as a constitutive and indispensable feature of the activity diagnosis.[2] Interaction at the auto shop is also notable for the frequent shifts between joint and mutual attention. As in the settings Goodwin (1981, 1994, 2000) studied, parties 'continuously shift between actions that invoke and ... require gaze toward specific events in the surround and ... [actions] that make relevant gaze toward no more than each other's bodies' (Goodwin 2000: 164).

In traditional accounts of visual perception, no distinction has been made between looking, seeing, and other types of visual events denoted by natural language verbs; visual perception was simply explained as

---

[1] Coulter and Parsons present a whole battery of vernacular vision verbs and recommend them for the scientific description of visual activities:

> There are many diverse verbs of visual orientation ..., some of which can combine with diverse complementizers, marking diverse perceptual modalities in the domain of vision: attending, beholding, browsing, catching sight of, checking out, discerning, discriminating, distinguishing, espying, examining, experiencing, eyeing, gazing (at, through, upon, around, in[to], up at), glancing (at, over, through, upon, around, into), glimpsing, having in sight, holding in view, inspecting, leering (at), looking (at, for, over, into, through, up, under, around), making out, noticing (that), observing (that, through), ogling, peeking, peeping, perceiving, perusing, picking up, poring over, recognizing (as, that, how), scanning, scrutinizing, searching (for, among, around for, under, through), seeing (as, that, through, into), seeking (for), setting one's eyes on, sighting, skimming, spotting, spying (on), squinting, staring (at), studying, surveying, taking in, taking notice of, viewing, watching (for, over), witnessing, and others.... For the application to self or other(s) of any of these verbs to work, diverse sorts of circumstances must obtain which are not interchangeable throughout the set. (Coulter & Parsons 1990: 261–262)

[2] In the repair shop, these 'courses of collaborative action' may be contextually remote from (reside at a 'higher level of social integration' than) the concrete visual actions in which Hussein engages. For example, he may diagnose the repair needs of a car and look up replacement part numbers on his own to enable one of his technicians to then repair the car on his own. The overall activity in this case is still collaborative.

a process in which light hits the retina and the information from the retina is then transmitted to the brain and interpreted by it as a picture of a stable world of objects. Seeing, in this account, is an invisible, interior, private process. However, this account, as so many given by psychologists who offer physiological explanations for overt behaviors, runs afoul of everyday language, as Ryle (1949) has pointed out (see also Sharrock & Coulter 1998): 'seeing' is not a process at all, but an accomplishment.

> 'See' ... and 'find' are not process words, experience words, or activity words. They do not stand for perplexingly undetectable actions or reactions, any more than 'win' stands for a perplexingly undetectable bit of running, or 'unlock' for an unreported bit of key-turning. (Ryle 1949: 145–146)

When I say 'I *see* it,' I claim *success* in trying to visually locate (make out) or identify (recognize) an object or a state of affairs ('I see that it has stopped raining').

Traditional accounts of seeing also cannot explain how we can see the *absence* of something (such as rain; Nishizaka 2000)—an important ability for Hussein, for whom seeing 'what is missing' is an essential ability. Being able to see things (or the missing of things)—to achieve relevant, agreed-upon seeings—in the context of collaborative activities requires far more than the ability to use one's eyes. 'The ability to see something is always tied to a particular position encompassing a range of phenomena including ... a larger organization, a local task, and access to relevant material and cognitive tools' (Goodwin & Goodwin 1996: 61). In the context of the auto shop, such resources for shared perception include diagnostic practices, instruments, perceptual categories, and various forms of automotive knowledge. What can be seen at any moment is not an individual affair, but a matter of shared perception and a shared normative order: 'seeing belongs within the public and normative order of activity, rather than taking place under an individual's skin' (Nishizaka 2000: 106).

2.4 Vision-based activities

These are the main vision-based activities other than face-to-face conversation that Hussein performs during the course of the day.

In Fig.2.2.1, Hussein is concentrating on the wheel of a car whose brakes he has exchanged. The practical activity in which he is engaged requires *hand-eye coordination*; his vision is absorbed by the practical activity's demands, but the activity itself is primarily a manual one. In Fig.2.2.2, we see him *reading* a printout from a computer; he is acquiring written

Fig. 2.2.1 Hand-eye coordination while repairing a car

Fig. 2.2.2 Reading a computer printout

Fig. 2.2.3 Retrieving printed information

information, a primarily visual activity that is supported by the actions of his hands (see also Chapter 7).

In Fig.2.2.3, Hussein is retrieving information from a voluminous list of car parts and then (Fig.2.2.4) places a call to a supplier while keeping his gaze anchored on the shelf where this list belongs.

Fig. 2.2.4 Anchoring gaze while on the phone

Fig. 2.2.5 Checking a timing belt

Fig. 2.2.6 Reading information from an instrument

Anchoring gaze—fixating an object—is a common practice for him when he is on the phone.

In Fig.2.2.5, Hussein checks the behavior of a timing belt; in Fig.2.2.6, he is reading off information from an instrument Victorio presents to him;

Fig. 2.2.7 Tactile exploration of paint

Fig. 2.2.8 Discovering a problem spot

the activities alternate with each other within the larger activity of diagnosing the cause of engine failure.

Fig.2.2.7 shows a tactile exploration of a newly painted car. Gaze is coordinated with the motions of the hand; the hand is the primary acquirer of information. Fig.2.2.8 captures the moment when a problem is discovered.

Figs.2.2.9 and 2.2.10 are taken from the same event; in 2.2.9, Hussein inspects the edge of a hood—he is gathering information—in 2.2.10, just a split second later, he looks at the hood while closing it. Now he looks at it merely in the service of a manual action; his looking is not *primarily* a cognitive act.

When Hussein has completed a task, his eyes sometimes wander. Having completed the inspection of a newly painted car, Hussein turns away and scans the area nearby (Fig.2.2.11). Not finding anything that needs his attention, he lets his gaze wander toward the road (Fig.2.2.12).

Fig. 2.2.9 Inspecting a newly painted hood

Fig. 2.2.10 Hand-eye coordination for closing the hood

Fig. 2.2.11 Scanning

We saw in Chapter 1 that Hussein often uses moments of transition between activities, for example, when he walks away from a work site, to scan the part of the shop that he is traversing, prepared for objects or events that need his attention. Scanning is also captured in Fig.2.2.13,

Fig. 2.2.12 Wandering gaze

Fig. 2.2.13 Scanning

Fig. 2.2.14 Discovering a problem

while 2.2.14 shows a moment of discovery: Hussein notices engine parts lying about (which he then asks an employee to remove).

Yet another visual activity is supervision. In Figs.2.2.15 and 2.2.16, one sees Hussein supervise the work of technicians as he waits for them to complete their jobs.

Fig. 2.2.15 Supervising an employee

Fig. 2.2.16 Supervising an employee

In the activities shown in the images in this section, the eyes are enlisted in the acquisition of information. The remaining images (Figs.2.2.17–19) show Hussein *giving* information by the direction of his gaze. Such uses of gaze are typically combined with pointing gestures of the hand (these will be addressed in the following chapter).

Despite the centrality and frequency of purposeful looking, it would be inappropriate to assume that 'professional vision' (Goodwin 1994) is a strictly visual competence: Hussein's other senses, especially olfaction, hearing, and touch, are equally important components of his professional skills, they have been subjected to as much specialized training as his eyes, and they are often simultaneously involved in cognitive acts that are guided by vision. However, our focus is on communication, and we can take Hussein's cognitive-perceptual skills into account only insofar as they inform communication. The focus in the remainder of this chapter is therefore not on what Hussein can see, but on what he communicates to others, and how he manages the actions of others, through the ways in

Figs. 2.2.17–19 Directing the visual attention of others (pointing with hands and eyes)

which he uses his eyes. Central to that are practices for whose description, pace Coulter and Parsons, the terms 'gaze' and 'gaze direction' are sufficiently distinctive. We examine Hussein's methods of looking, specifically where he looks when, in contexts of face-to-face conversation, for example, at the counter, then during states of joint attention on cars. However, because joint visual attention is very often brought about by acts of pointing, we will investigate joint attention more thoroughly in the next chapter.

2.5 Gaze and social action[3]

Researchers of face-to-face interaction have explained the patterning of gaze in terms of the display and negotiation of speaker- and listenership during turns at talk. Specifically, Kendon (1967) and Goodwin (1981) have described mutual gaze as a form of mutual monitoring by which speakers make sure that their talk is being attended, and listeners monitor speakers

[3] A version of this section of this chapter has previously appeared in Streeck (2014).

for cues as to when the turn is being relinquished to them. Linguistic and paralinguistic features of the emerging utterance—its syntactic structure, the intonation contour—provide the parties with a matrix for identifying moments when mutual monitoring becomes relevant. Recently, however, Rossano (2012) has modified this account of gaze sequencing as a matter of regulating attention and turn-taking and given evidence that gaze sequencing is contingent on the specific *courses of action* participants pursue; it is sequenced by reference to types and sequences of *action*, rather than turns at talk. For example, while it is true that during extended turns occupied with actions such as storytelling, listeners spend much time focusing their gaze on the speaker, and speakers, in turn, frequently and for extended periods withdraw their gaze from the listener (Kendon 1967); the opposite is often the case during question-answer sequences: speakers who ask a question typically look at the addressee, at least until an answer is begun, while recipients of questions are not always expected to look at the speaker while listening to them. In sum,

> [S]ome activities require more sustained gaze by the recipient toward the speaker . . . or by the speaker toward the recipient . . . than others, suggesting that this relative freedom actually depends on the gaze expectations associated with the ongoing course of action. (Rossano 2012: 37)

Rossano furthermore observed that when an action sequence (e.g., an adjacency pair such as question-answer) is completed, its participants withdraw gaze from one another. In contrast, when one or both parties maintain gaze on the other, the sequence is thereby treated as in need of further expansion. Sequence completion conditions mutual gaze withdrawal.

> Sustained gaze by even one of the participants in the transition relevance place [after a sequence-completing act, J. S.] displays an orientation toward more talk or general uptake by the other participant. On the other hand, gaze withdrawal at possible sequence completion displays an orientation toward the possibility of ending the sequence. (Rossano 2012: 229)

2.6   Moments of mutual gaze

The questions I pursue in the following are: When does Hussein look at, and when does he look away from, his interlocutors, at what *kinds of moments*? What is implied by his shifts of gaze for the further course of action? Where do his interlocutors look at different points during sequences of action? I use the following transcription notation to mark Hussein's and his interlocutors' gaze:

H/X	H turns gaze to X
H\X	H turns gaze away from X
(H/X)	round brackets indicate an ongoing state
H….X	slower gaze shift by H to X; position of 'X' marks point of gaze arrival
H:X	H is oriented toward X, but gaze direction is uncertain
[H/X H\X]	Square brackets and boldface mark the beginning and end points of mutual gaze
<X/H X\H>	initial and final gaze shifts of a sequence
H = X	joint arrival in state of mutual gaze
h ≠ X	joint break-up of mutual gaze

In (2.4), Hussein is in the process of finishing up business with the owner of a red Mercury whose brake pads have been replaced (see also Chapter 7). The customer wants to know if the rotors of the brakes need to be ground down any time soon. As he utters the question, he turns his gaze to Hussein (line 1), who briefly looks at him. (It is common for the person asking a question to look at the addressee more than the addressee looks at the questioner; Rossano 2012.) Not understanding the question, Hussein requests a repeat (<u>hmm</u>?, line 2). He briefly looks at the customer during this request for clarification, but he looks away during the answer. When he begins to answer the customer's original question (in line 1), Hussein turns his gaze to him, and the two sustain mutual gaze (Fig.2.4.1) until Hussein concludes the answer ('still in good shape', line 7). When the customer acknowledges it ('oh', line 8), they look away from one another (Fig.2.4.2).

Fig. 2.4.1–2 Mutual gaze during sequence initiation, gaze withdrawal during sequence completion

(2.4)
```
              <C/H    [H/C        H\C]
1   C    You gotta grind it down in a couple of months, huh?
         ( - - - - )
         [H/C
2   H    Hmm?
                        H\C]
3   C    uh- grind down the rotors in a couple of months?
         [H/C
4   H    No! Check if you have any probly- find any problem by squealing
5        then we may need to taken 'em and grind 'em
6        now I left them as is
                        H\C]
7        still thick and in good shape I think
         C\H>
8   C    Oh.
9   H    We may not need it
```

This moment of interaction instantiates what we can consider to be a basic (unexpanded) gaze sequence (cf. Schegloff 2007). It has this form: the initiator of the sequence looks at the addressee at some point during the initiating act and often secures brief eye contact in this fashion. The initiator and interlocutor turn their gaze away from one another when they complete the sequence and course of action.

The pattern is also enacted in (2.5). Here, Hussein is standing by a blue Subaru whose owner has just brought it to the shop. 'And it die, you said?' Hussein says, turning his gaze to the owner, who is already looking at him. When the owner confirms, Hussein responds with a preliminary diagnosis, and, that project completed, the two turn away from each other.

(2.5)
```
         (C/H) <[H/C
1   H    And it die, you said?
         ( - - - - - )
2   H    It die?
3   C    Yeah
4   H    That because the idle low I believe.
         H≠C]>
```

In (2.6) (which occurred right after [2.4]), Hussein volunteers a bit of advice to the Mercury owner, who takes it. The owner at first is not looking at Hussein, but Hussein solicits his gaze with a bit of self-repair ('but uh (- - - -)'; cf. Goodwin 1980), and the customer turns to him. In other words, the two establish mutual gaze at sequence beginning. Hussein briefly looks toward the customer again when he utters the 'focused' constituent of his utterance (see Chapter 6), the main advice or invitation, 'stop by one day'. They have brief eye contact and then they both look away as the sequence concludes.

(2.6)
```
                        C/H
1   H   But uh ( - - ) about the oil leak
                    [H=C    H≠C]
2       if you have a chance to stop by one day?
3   C   Yeah, I wanna- I- yeah
            [H/C C\H]
4       Okay
            C\H>
5       yeah
```

In all of these extracts, the sequence initiator looks at the interlocutor during the sequence-initiating act; if the listener is already looking at him—as is the case here—he thereby achieves mutual gaze. Hussein and his customers turn their gaze away from one another when they bring the ongoing action sequence to completion.[4]

The small 'gaze window' (Bavelas, Coates, & Johnson 2002) that opens up when the parties look at one another can provide a view of visually communicated meaning when the speaker gestures as he talks. (2.7) occurs during Hussein's interaction with the owner of the blue Subaru. Seated in the driver's seat after having started the car, he explains what he is doing: waiting for the choke to disengage so that he can assess the car's operation under normal operating conditions. He looks toward the customer, who stands by the car. Unable to complete his utterance because he lacks a word to describe the action of the choke he is waiting for ('disengage' or 'go off'), Hussein freezes the gesture of his hand. In response, the customer repeats and completes the gesture, moving the hand down, indicating the lowering of the speed (RPM) at which the engine is running. While this does not describe the action of the choke, it describes its consequence. Understanding is thus achieved by gesture, and Hussein completes the sentence by replacing the description of the state of the choke (disengaged) by a description of the engine ('warm'). At the same

---

[4] To be aware of each other's gaze withdrawal, depending on the current focus of their gaze, it can be necessary that one or both parties must first turn their gaze to the other so that *mutual* withdrawal of gaze can then be mutually perceived. There are sequences in the corpus in which Hussein and his interlocutor briefly turn gaze to one another just before sequence completion and then withdraw gaze during it.

time he returns his attention to the car, and the customer turns his away
from him.

(2.7)

```
       (C/H)                      <[H/C
1   H  Now idle high, I wanna wait the choke-
       H raises, spreads hand
       _____|_____
       |      _____|
2      |          | C raises open hand, stroke down
       ( - - - - - - - - - - - - - )
       H\C]                    C\H>
3      warm, and then I'll see it.
```

Here, too, mutual gaze is established during the beginning, and broken
during the closing, of the sequence.

Even when sequence initiation and sequence completion are many
turns apart, during expanded sequences (Schegloff 2007), this sequencing
of gaze can be observed. The next example is taken from an interaction
between Hussein and a tool delivery man, and it is a request-compliance
sequence. Hussein's request to provide him with additional documentation
about the purchase of tools from his company that have since been stolen,
documentation he needs for the insurance,[5] requires a great deal of explaining on Hussein's part, and the delivery man's compliance statement ('okay,
I'm gonna get that for you', line 71) occurs only after forty-five turns.

At the beginning, Hussein and the delivery man (D) are in the front
office of the shop, Hussein behind and the delivery man in front of the
counter. The latter has made a small delivery and then asked about new
orders, and Hussein has asked him how much money he owes. He reaches
for the wallet in his pocket and discovers that he does not have enough cash

---

[5] The request is never fully stated:

```
51   H   Anything you able to provide
52       that it helps me
53       because until no:w
                 [
54   D            (Right)
55   H   they can't pay me nothing
                 [
56   D            Ri:ght
57   H   And I'm out of about of about ( - - - - ) between
58       tools about maybe between seven eight thousand dollars
```

Figs. 2.8.1–2 Mutual gaze at sequence beginning and during the sequence

on him. At the same time he formulates a request preface and turns to D, who has been looking at him (Fig.2.8.1).

```
(2.8)
          (D/H)          <[H/D  H\D              H/D
1    H    .hhhhh You remember when we had the- ( - - - - ) OTC from you
2    D    Yeah
          [
          [  H\D]
3    H    or scanner from you
                         [
4    D                      Yeah
5    H    OTC
6    D    OTC
          (1.0)
7    H    Now the insurance company
8         we have a problem with the insurance
          (D/H)  [H/D   H\D]
9         about the invoices.
10   D    Alright.
```

When Hussein looks away from D (at line 3), he first looks in his wallet. Without looking back at D, he then turns to the right and begins to walk out from behind the counter, toward his adjacent office. He looks back one more time to D (Fig.2.8.2), who is at this point looking toward him (line 9), and then turns his gaze back on his path. Continuing his explanation, Hussein walks into his office, sits down in his chair, opens a desk drawer, reaches for an envelope with dollar bills, takes them out, gives the delivery man twenty dollars, and begins to sort the remaining bills. Occasionally,

Figs. 2.8.3–4 Mutual gaze and gaze withdrawal before and during sequence
completion

mutual gaze is established between the two (Fig.2.8.3). The delivery man
finally promises to get Hussein the documents he is asking for (line 46), just
after withdrawing gaze from Hussein, who has already turned away from
him. Turning his body away from Hussein, the delivery man begins to leave
(Fig.2.8.4).

```
              (D/H)                              [H/D
42    H    I can't cover everything unless they pay me
43    D    Right.
           ( - - - - - - - - -)
           H\D]                             D\H>
44    H    I(h)I don't know how long its takes (most)
                                            [
45    D                                     Heh heh
46         Okay, I'm gonna get that for you
47    H    Thank you Sir
                  [
48    D              (So you can get) your tools.
49    H    I appreciate that, thank you
50    D    See you la:ter
76    H    Mh hhm.
```

A deviant gaze pattern

Not always does the sequence initiator secure mutual gaze. During the intake
of the red Mercury, when Hussein and the owner are positioned in front of
and behind the counter, the customer asks Hussein several questions without

looking at him. This interaction appears to be a counter-example to the basic pattern I proposed. But let us follow the interaction step by step. The customer is in the process of filling out paperwork for his car. As he does this, he revisits a topic that had previously been discussed; he requests that Hussein also check the source of an oil leak (line 1). His gaze remains focused on the worksheet, and Hussein does not respond. The customer now formulates his own hypothesis about the leak, again without looking at Hussein, who does not look at him either. Then the customer cannot remember the name of an engine part (line 4); instead of providing the term for him or otherwise helping with the talk, which would be a common trajectory for word-finding problems, Hussein disregards the customer's talk and reasoning altogether and simply promises to give him a call, thus canceling the action project the customer has initiated. Hussein's announcement is accompanied by a glance at the customer, but he does not meet his eyes. No eye contact at all occurs during this sequence.

```
(2.9)
1   C   Yes, see where it's coming from
            (1.8)
2   C   I don't think it's really coming from
3           maybe anywhere from the head-gasket.
4           It's running down and getting on that uh-
            (- - -)
                H/C      H\C
5   H   I'm gonna give you call
```

Now Hussein gets busy doing other things. Eventually, the customer, still filling out the form, begins to wonder aloud whether it might be possible to have only one brake repaired, and Hussein moves closer to him, but he does not look toward him nor does he look up when the customer keeps repairing his talk (lines 6–10), as could have been expected (in light of Goodwin's findings about how self-repair solicits gaze; Goodwin 1980), and instead continues the paperwork. Hussein only once briefly looks up at the customer (line 13). But he fully turns his gaze to him when he asks for clarification ('on the brake?', line 14, i.e., 'you mean spend a hundred on the brake?'). What is happening here is that Hussein disregards the customer's sequence-initiating speech acts as long as the customer does not look at him, but when he himself initiates a sequence to clarify his understanding of the customer's talk, he does turn his gaze to the customer (line 14). And now the customer reciprocates. They maintain mutual gaze for the rest of this course of action until they agree that brakes should always be padded

on both sides. During the formulation of this agreement, they withdraw
gaze from one another in quick succession (lines 21–22).

```
6        C        I just wonder if
7                 maybe if it has something to do:
8                 just on that one si:de
9                 to uh-
                  (1.8)
10                uhm
                  (3.0)
11                'course if it still costs fifty dollars
12                might as well spend a hundred dollars
                        H/C      H\C
13                but- you know (that)
                  (1.8)
                  <H/C    [C/H
14       H        On the: break?
15       H        Yeah
.
.
.
                              C\H]
21                yeah, you should do it on both sides.
                               [        H\C>
22       H                 it should go both together.
```

Thus, twice during this interaction, when the customer does *not* turn gaze
to Hussein as he initiates a sequence, he does not receive a response from
Hussein. However, when Hussein initiates an action sequence of his own
and turns his gaze to the customer, the customer reciprocates the gaze shift,
mutual gaze is established, and the sequence runs its course. This seeming
counter-example in effect confirms the pattern of gazing during these
courses of action that I described earlier. Initiating an action sequence
under conditions where gaze to the addressee is possible, but withholding
it, may allow the recipient to treat the sequence as not having been initiated
at all.

2.7   The significance of mutual gaze

Kendon has interpreted brief mutual gaze as a display of mutual attention,
and extended mutual gaze as an indicator and vehicle either of a more
intimate or a competitive relationship between the parties:

> By looking at q, ... [p] signals to him that he is giving him his attention, and thus if, in looking at q, p sees that q is looking at him, he sees that he is being 'received'. The mutual gaze, momentarily held, at least, would thus appear to be an integral part of the set of signals that people are on the look-out for in interaction as indicators that each is still taking account of the other. But the mutual gaze, especially in certain situations, appears to signify more than this. For where it is extended in time, or where one or other participant tries to extend it, he indicates that his attention has shifted away from the common focus which both share in the encounter, and that his attention is specifically directed to the other person. And extended mutual gazes appear to be indicative of an intensifying of the direct relations between the participants. (Kendon 1990: 48)

Once an extended sequence is under way—initiated by one party and ratified by the other—when and how often mutual gaze occurs varies. Kendon attributes these variations in frequency and duration to the type of relationship and the distinct working consensus between the parties.

Hussein shows considerable variation in how often and for how long he looks at listeners during conversations, but this variation is greater within than between encounters, and greater also than variations in relation to categories of others, such as customer and employee, with which he interacts.[6] Of course it is contingent also on whether Hussein is multitasking. This is evident in another interaction with the owner of the red Mercury. Here, the customer launches two inquiries about the price of having the brakes repaired. During the first inquiry (lines 1–9), Hussein looks at the customer for the duration of five words (lines 8–9), but during the second inquiry (lines 10–22), he keeps his gaze focused on the customer for seven and a half lines (lines 14–21).[7] Whereas Hussein attends to the paperwork in front of him during the first inquiry (lines 1–9), he disregards this activity entirely and concentrates on dealing with the customer during the second (lines 14–21). In other words, he treats and formats two successive installments of the same speech act differently.

---

[6] Here I disregard the initiation of encounters. As I have pointed out in Chapter 1, at the beginning of an encounter with a customer, Hussein always looks at her or him, whereas his gaze is often focused on an object when he initiates interaction with a technician, the object then becoming the topic of talk.

[7] During the entire interaction in this extract, the customer faces away from the camera, toward Hussein. While we cannot be sure, it is likely that he has his gaze focused on him.

(2.10)

1   C   I don't know if uh-
        (- - - -)
2   Hey how about-
3   did you- you talked about (- - -) new-
        (- - -)
4   C   pads and stuff. About a hundred dollars (   )?
                                              [
5   I think so.
6   H   If- uh pa:d and rotor need to be turned
                    (C:H)
7   it's just to be about hundred dollars
                                          H/C
8   if it's just pa:d without turning rotor
            H\C
9   it will be less.
                    H/C   **H\C**
10 C   Bu::t- (- - - - - - - -) °ye know° there's not a way: ye know
                            H/C
11   if there's anything che<u>a</u>per maybe
12   Well ye know (   )
                    [**H\C**
13 H   Yeah, if the ro<u>t</u>or good
                H/C
14   the:n (.) just (- -) about maybe sixty-nine ninety-fi:ve.
15   If the rotor bad
16   then we need to knock the rotor
17   and grind it.
18   If the rotor were ou:t
19   then more hundred
                H\C   H. . ..C
20   more than hundred because
                            H\C
21   you have to change them both.

What accounts for the differences in Hussein's gaze behavior in these two sequences? Perhaps this: his response to the customer's first question is 'affiliative': repairing the brakes will cost as much as the customer suggests, if not less. This is, as it were, an unproblematic course of events. In response to the second question, however, while Hussein also gives an affirmative answer, it comes with a caveat: the repair will cost as much as the customer proposes—or *more*. This is a more delicate response, and it is important that the customer hears it properly if Hussein wants to prevent later misunderstandings. In other words, it may be intuitively important to Hussein that this part of his answer (lines 15–20) 'registers' with the customer, that it becomes part of the 'record' of the interaction. Given that Hussein's visual attention is initially occupied by another task, the fact that he fully turns it to the customer now elevates his talk and asserts its salience. It warrants suspending another activity and devoting visual attention to monitoring whether and how his utterance is being received.

The episode[8] suggests that, if Hussein and his interlocutors enact normative cultural patterns and are in this way representative of the culture, what is generally at stake when conversation participants seek mutual gaze is not the securing of one another's attention, but a perceived need to get an action recognized, acknowledged, ratified, and *registered*: Hussein makes sure that his interlocutor 'gets' the social act he is committing (which may be a *transactional* act; see Chapter 7), and that the listener understands the impact of what he is saying. The listener, by looking at the speaker without displaying disbelief, lack of understanding, disagreement, or other stances that would warrant suspending the progression of the course of action, *ratifies* the speaker's speech act. Whatever business is transacted in the sequence is thus mutually recognized as an 'achieved' social fact. Mutual gaze in conversation partakes in the logic of 'mutually perceived perception' (Hausendorf 2003): what is attended in this fashion is accorded the rank of a 'deed' that is given mutual and explicit recognition by the parties. This could explain why speakers often seek recipient gaze during sequence initiations: because it is important that the parties recognize—and each recognizes that the other recognizes—that a new course of action is under way and what kind of action it is. Mutual gaze, then, might serve as a minimal 'contractual' format by which interactants explicitly ('meta-communicatively') ratify specific acts as ratified social facts (Streeck 2014).

The organization of mutual gaze appears to be similar to that of the use of continuers such as 'uh hmm' (Schegloff 1981): a continuer signals that its producer foregoes the opportunity to request repair or register disagreement, and so on, at the end of the speaker's turn and thereby gives the speaker the go-ahead for further talk. Similarly, when a gazing listener who receives the gaze of the speaker does not produce a facial or vocal display of disagreement or non-understanding, he thereby treats the speaker's act as mutually understood and done. Brief mutual glances in

---

[8] For further examples, see Streeck (2014).

conversation are a practice for mutually affirming that intelligible (recognizable), contextually appropriate, and accountable social acts are being performed.

2.8 Joint attention

The attentional framework known as 'joint attention', in which the parties, rather than attending to one another, jointly focus their attention on an external object, constitutes a distinct mode of relating in which the methods for allocating and sequencing gaze that govern face-to-face conversation cannot work: when Hussein and his partners attend to an object of shared concern (e.g., a timing belt), they do not seek each other's gaze in the ways we have seen them do in face-to-face conversation. They rarely turn fully to one another. But how, then, do they ratify each other's acts, if such ratification is indeed necessary?

In example (2.11), Hussein talks to Ms. Nancy while he checks the electrical system of her car with a handheld instrument. When the camera first captures them, Hussein and Ms. Nancy are looking at the instrument in Hussein's hand ('i' in the transcript, Fig.2.11.1). Hussein points to it as he

Figs. 2.11.1–4 Movement of joint attention

reads out the text on the display (lines 3 and 4). Ms. Nancy, looking at the instrument, nods profusely. Then Hussein dramatizes what the instrument reveals, namely that 'we receive fourteen volt' from the car's charging system: he makes a large 'pulling' motion.

(2.11)
```
1   H    Charging system is perfect.
         (1.3)
                 (H/i N/i)
2   N    Uh huh.
              [
3   H          Here you see it where it says on the oka:y?
    N    ((              nods            ))
4   H    Inside on the green it says okay okay?
                         N/engine
5        Fourteen volt then
         ( - - - - - -)
         "pulling" gesture
         _____|_____
         |   N/hand    |
6        we receive
                 N:i
7        from alternator
8        fourteen volt output.
    H    ((       nods      ))
                 H/m                 H/engine
9        Then the alternator doing the job right.
```

This sequence shows a pattern that is common at this auto shop: rather than fully suspending the state of joint attention to an object in favor of face-to-face orientation, Hussein adopts a 'compromise' orientation by which he maintains focus on the object while at the same time letting his interlocutor sense that he is seeking her engagement. A small change in Hussein's head orientation and a reciprocal interim reorientation by the co-participant appear to function similarly to mutual gaze in a face-to-face conversation, namely as a ratifying practice by which an action and its cognitive focus are marked as 'ratified' and shared. (This orientation is marked 'm' in the transcript, referring to gaze broadly aimed at center space without focus on any object.) This attentional framework is a compromise between the need for the recognition and acknowledgment of one another's co-participation and the requirement for object-focused joint attention.

Obviously, being in a state of joint attention does not preclude anyone from looking at the other; it is only a preferred attention structure (Chance & Larsen 1976). A moment later, directing Ms. Nancy's attention to the instrument in his hand by demonstratives and small pointing gestures, Hussein twice looks at her and thus sees her response, not as a way of soliciting her gaze to him, but of securing that she is reading the words on the display. We will examine sequences of this kind in the next chapter.

2.9 Referring by gaze

Often during the day, Hussein can be seen directing brief glances to some place or object, or in a certain direction, but there is no gaze shift by the listener. Here, we are dealing with a different, yet equally familiar (and potentially universal) practice for directing the listener's 'virtual' or 'cognitive' attention. These glances can be described as 'reminders'; they support the listener's tracking of the referents previously introduced in the talk. For example, before Hussein and the delivery man (see 2.8) begin their conversation, the latter is waiting in a corner of the front office while Hussein is finishing up business with a pair of customers. Once they leave, he moves to the counter and looks at the delivery man, who simultaneously looks at him. The delivery man puts a small object in front of Hussein and rests his arms on the counter. Hussein looks at the object, and the delivery man says, his eyes raised to Hussein:

Figs. 2.12.1–2 Indexical gaze

(2.12)

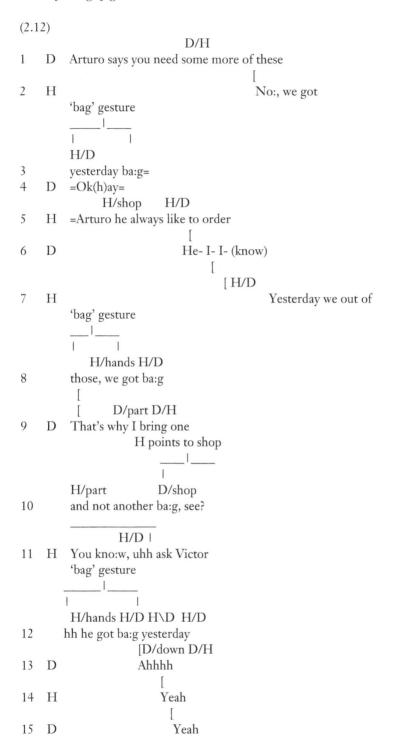

```
                              D/H
1   D    Arturo says you need some more of these
                                      [
2   H                                 No:, we got
         'bag' gesture
         _____|_____
         |          |
         H/D
3        yesterday ba:g=
4   D    =Ok(h)ay=
              H/shop      H/D
5   H    =Arturo he always like to order
                              [
6   D                         He- I- I- (know)
                                  [
                                  [ H/D
7   H                                      Yesterday we out of
         'bag' gesture
         ___|____
         |       |
            H/hands H/D
8        those, we got ba:g
           [
           [       D/part  D/H
9   D    That's why I bring one
                      H points to shop
                      ___|____
                         |
         H/part        D/shop
10       and not another ba:g, see?
         _____
                 H/D |
11  H    You kno:w, uhh ask Victor
         'bag' gesture
         _____|_____
         |         |
            H/hands H/D  H\D  H/D
12       hh he got ba:g yesterday
                      [D/down D/H
13  D                 Ahhhh
                          [
14  H                     Yeah
                            [
15  D                       Yeah
```

In this extract, the delivery man tries to solicit an order for some unidentified replacement parts from Hussein: 'Arturo says you need some more of these.' Hussein disagrees: they got a bagful from another supplier yesterday. Hussein's answer contains a depictive gesture. His hands appear to hold a bag much bigger than the one the delivery man has put before him: without saying it, Hussein makes it obvious that they will not need any more of these parts for a while. 'He always likes to order,' he says about Arturo (line 5). And then he elaborates that they ran out of 'these' yesterday and already got a bag, the bag again depicted by a gesture. The delivery man replies that, for this reason, he brought only one bag and no more.[9] Finally Hussein refers the man to Victorio ('go ask Victor'), who has placed that order.

During this interchange both men, in addition to glancing at one another, repeatedly turn their gaze to 'proxies' of the things and people they are talking about. They use eye gaze in referential fashion. When Hussein first talks about Arturo (in line 5), he briefly turns his head and glances toward the shop floor, which is to the left of him, the place where Arturo would be working at this time. When he makes bag-depicting gestures (lines 8 and 13), he glances at his gesturing hands. The delivery man glances at the object in front of him as he points out that he brought only one part (line 9), and not a whole bag. By these eye glances, the speaker does not manage turn-taking or gather information, but rather provides it. His glances support his speech and gesture in the task of enabling the listener to identify and keep track of referents.

2.10   Turning away

Occasionally, when Hussein is the addressee, not the speaker, of a speech act, he turns his gaze and head away from the speaker. In the sales negotiation with Richie (see Chapter 1), Richie asks Hussein how much money he is asking for the white Jeep, before she has inspected the car, just after Hussein has started the engine for her benefit. She needs three attempts to get the question under way.[10] During this time, Hussein has his face turned toward her, although we cannot be certain that he is looking at her. When she finally succeeds in articulating her question (line 3), he first looks at her and then, as she utters 'pay for this', his eyes wander off to her left; when she utters 'car', he turns his head to the right of her. As she utters 'cash', he looks down, and then, during the

---

[9] The utterance is ironic because the single part the delivery man shows to Hussein is just a sample, not the actual object meant to be sold.

[10] It is possible that she was going to ask 'what you bought this car for?', as she later does (line 11).

Figs. 2.13.1–3 Hussein disengages from the speech act under way

following pause, he steps back and makes a further quarter turn with his entire frame away from her, so that he ends up answering 'sixty-five' as he is fully facing away (Figs.2.3.1–2.3.4). He has his back turned to her when he answers.

(2.13–1)
```
          (R/H) H:R
1   R     What you bought-
2         what you bought-
          [H/R    H\R]
3         what do I pay for this car, cash.
          ((H turns away))
          ( - - - - - )
4      H          Sixty-five
```

While Hussein turns to Richie when he understands that she is producing a question, he turns away from her once he can recognize what he is being asked, and then turns away further as he answers. He dis-aligns from her, from his own action, and from the sequence under way. He treats her question as dispreferred.

There is a pause of about two seconds during which Hussein takes a step back, halfway turns to Richie, and then looks her in the face. Only now does Richie say 'hm?', asking for a repeat (line 5), and Hussein's answer is given while his gaze is on her.

(2.13–2)

```
                        [H/R
        ( - - - - - - - - - - - - - - - - - - - - )
5   R   Hm?
6   H   Sixty-fi:ve.
```

Richie remains silent and still. We cannot see whether she is looking at him. After five and a half seconds, Hussein says, 'It's very clean truck.' In response, disregarding this statement, Richie turns to Hussein, puts her arm on his shoulder, and says, 'Okay, I don't wanna buy this car. How much did you pay for this car?' Hussein once more turns away from her when he answers and looks down the avenue (see Figs.2.13.4–7).

Figs. 2.13.4- 7 Hussein avoiding to answer a question

(2.13–3)

s8	R	=Okay, (- -) •I don't wanna buy this car.
9		What'd you pay for this •car?
		(- -)
10	H	Which car.
11	R	This •car.
12	H	What I pay?
13	R	Yeah.
14	H	I bought it from the auction. (-)
15		With- damage in the body and I have to fix it.
16	R	Right. Before you- •before you fixed it,
17		how much did you pay for it.
		(- -)
18	H	Thi- (-) it's not gonna help you this-
19	R	I know,
20		but I wanna know.

In this sequence, Hussein's withdrawal of gaze shows his reluctance to answer and ratify the course of action Richie has embarked on; he tags the course she takes as dispreferred. If mutual gaze is a practice for ratification, as I have proposed, then refusing or breaking mutual gaze can be understood as a practice for rejecting to ratify.

In (2.14), Hussein repeatedly refuses to agree with an assertion Art keeps making and to align with Art's perspective on the issue at hand.[11] But here he does not turn away from Art's gaze, but from the gesture Art persistently makes and treats as essential to understanding what he is trying to say. Hussein is inspecting the air conditioner of a car with a flashlight. He calls on Art and asks him to listen to the sound of the compressor 'when it's kicked' (i.e., engaged). Hussein believes that 'the clutch [is] kind of loose', and Art initially agrees with him, specifying that the clutch is 'warped'. For a couple of minutes the two men are bent over the car, inspecting the engine with a flashlight, poking around with a screwdriver, and seeking to confirm that, indeed, the clutch is warped. But then, as they rise from the engine, Art concludes that, rather, 'the *drive* is warped': 'The clutch is alright. We just need the drive.' The drive and the clutch proper together make up the clutch. The question is which of the two parts is warped.

In line 1, Art revises his hypothesis that the clutch is warped and attributes the problem to the drive. At the same time, he makes a hand

---

[11] This scene is more extensively analyzed in Streeck (2008b).

Fig. 2.14.1 is w•arped

Fig. 2.14.2 loo•ks like

gesture that depicts the way in which the drive is warped. Hussein, who first
is turned away, turns around and looks toward Art.

(2.14–1)
```
                           1              2
1  A   The- ( - - ) dri::ve is warped, 't looks like
       ( - - - )
2  H   Hmm
       [
3  A    The drive-
4  A    The drive-plate that pulls in
                                    [
5  H                                Uh huh
6  A   is warped.
```

Fig. 2.14.3 (- • - -)

Fig. 2.14.4 Hmm•

As Hussein turns around to Art, his gaze passes Art's hand as it moves up to his face. He minimally 'takes in' the gesture without really looking at it. He sees it, but does not acknowledge it. Although he sees the gesture and presumably hears what Art says. Hussein initiates repair: he requests a repeat ('hmm', line 2). Art's diagnosis, in other words, is kept from going on record at this time.

By now Art has begun to repeat his statement (line 3); the two utterances overlap, and Art proceeds to recycle his turn from the beginning, producing a more elaborate version (lines 4, 6): 'The drive-plate that pulls in is warped.' He accompanies this utterance with a two-part gesture: the first, a repeat of the 'drive' gesture, sets up the referent, the drive-plate; the second, the hands crossing one another, depicts the engagement of clutch and drive ('pull in'). But while Art has Hussein's gaze for the first part of the gesture (line 5), he loses it for the second, which provides the new information; Hussein looks the other way (line 6). Hussein begins to turn his gaze away from the gesture at the very same time that Art is turning his gaze to it. Hussein overtly disattends what Art shows to be in need of attention. Then, as Hussein is oriented toward him without, however, looking at him (instead he looks at the engine), Art completes the gesture-phrase, repeating the rotation previously introduced as a depiction of 'warp'.

(2.14–2)
```
                        5              6
4   A    The dri:ve-plate that pulls it
                                       [
5   H                                  Uh huh
               7
6   A    is warped
```

Art keeps his hand in its exposed position for a second, until Hussein begins to respond (see Fig.2.14.8). Before he speaks, Hussein raises his left hand with a rapid, attention-grabbing motion, and, evidently in response to this motion, Art drops his hand. The floor is thus cleared for Hussein's talk (which begins in line 7).

Fig. 2.14.5 the dr•i:ve-plate

Fig. 2.14.6 that p•ulls it

Fig. 2.14.7 is w•arped

Fig. 2.14.8 it's b•een hit

Fig. 2.14.9 he•::re

(2.14–3)

```
                8       9
7   H   It's been hit he:re.
8   A   Yeah (        )
                [
9   H           I don't think the drive
```

Fig. 2.14.10 I don't think the dr•ive

Hussein's statement, 'it's been hit here,' motivates his subsequent disagreement ('I don't think the drive'). As he utters 'it's', Hussein raises his eyes, and they reach Art's eyes on 'been'. For a brief moment the two men have eye contact: Hussein's explanation, in other words, gets on record. Now Hussein blinks and, when he opens his eyes again, looks to the engine. Art's eyes follow. Hussein moves a step closer, and Art moves his coffee cup from the left to the right hand and quickly extends his left arm, pointing to the engine with a flat, supine hand, a presentation gesture (Fig.2.14.10, at line 9; see Chapter 5). What Art says cannot be heard because Hussein interrupts him: 'I don't think the drive.' The disagreement continues, but now the car is in focus.

(2.14–4)
8   A   Yeah (   )
                    [
                    [10
9   H   I don't think the drive
                 11
10 H   I don't think-
                  [
11 A   It probably got hit
                            [12
12 H   The clutch by itself I think it's hit.

Interrupted, Art abandons his pointing gesture and brings his hand to his head, scratching it (Fig.2.14.11, at line 10). He repurposes the gesture, which has lost its point, as a 'self-adaptor' (Ekman & Friesen, 1969). When Hussein says, 'the clutch by itself it's hit', he repeats his 'hitting' gesture, and Art looks up at him (Fig.2.14.12, at line 12). Now the two are back in a state of mutual orientation, but no shared agreement is in sight.

Fig. 2.14.11 I don't th•ink

Fig. 2.14.12 The cl•utch by itself

Art returns his gaze to the engine, and Hussein follows this gaze shift with his eyes. But Art is in fact now looking at his own hand, which is initiating yet another version of the 'drive' gesture. For the second time Art succeeds in performing the gesture under Hussein's eyes: he enacts it just as Hussein glances in the direction of his hand. Art's gesture 'models' the motion of the drive: his arm represents the rod, and it pushes forward, just like the drive-plate would move toward the clutch (Fig.2.14.13, at line 13).

(2.14–5)

12 H   The clutch by itself I think it's hit.
                13
13 A   The- the clutch
                [14   15
14 H   Because the- first of all the clutch it's hit

Fig. 2.14.13 the- th•e clutch

Fig. 2.14.14 fi•rst of all

Fig. 2.14.15 the cl•utch

But again Hussein looks away from the gesture, raising his gaze to Art's face as he reiterates that the clutch has been hit (line 14). He also repeats the hit gesture. With its rapid onset, it attracts Art's gaze. Hussein performs the stroke as Art is looking at him. Hussein thus gets his gesture on record. Thus, just like Art when he positioned his hand so that his gesture would be seen, Hussein times his talk so that salient parts are spoken when he has the hearer's undivided attention. This is the kind of labor conversationalists routinely perform for the sake of getting their talk acknowledged.

By now Art has abandoned his gesture. But he has held his hand at the ready to make another one (line 15). He makes yet another attempt to get the drive gesture seen and acknowledged. Now, for the first time since the beginning of this extended sequence, he succeeds in keeping Hussein's gaze for the duration of the gesture. This is because he has placed his hand in Hussein's line of regard, near the engine.

Fig. 2.14.16 the cl•utch is alright

Fig. 2.14.17 you just need the dri•:ve

(2.14–6)
                          16
15 A I say the clutch is alright
                          17
16   we just need a dri:ve.
       (- - -)
17 H Yeah.

Now Hussein acknowledges everything: he voices token agreement ('yeah', at line 17). He moves to end the interaction by taking a big step back, as Art reiterates his diagnosis one last time, pointing to the engine one more time and leaning over it: 'We just need drive.' Hussein calls the matter closed (line 20).

Fig. 2.14.18 I say the cl•utch

Fig. 2.14.19 we just need the dr•ive

(2.14–7)

18

18   A   I say the clutch (before here) (- -) is probably okay?

19

19   We just need the drive.

(2.0)

20   H   I will see. If we don't have anything else then

That Hussein averts his eyes from Art's gesture does not, of course, mean that he has any particular aversion to the gesture, that he does not want to see it, that it is the gesture itself that he disattends. Rather, turning away from the gesture is an artful method of disaligning and 'turning away' from Art's diagnosis, of registering disagreement without making it overly overt. The practice is the same as his turning away from Richie's question: 'How much do I pay for this car, cash?' In that case, though, Hussein's disalignment targets the speech act itself—the question being asked at a premature moment—whereas here he disaligns from the substance of Art's diagnosis. In either case, the organs of vision, the supreme gatherers of environmental information and central to the human and many other life-forms, are narrowly tasked in the conduct of distinctly human activities: agreeing and disagreeing with a perspective on a situation. In conversational interaction, the activity of the eyes is severely constrained; what we call 'focused interaction' is an achievement that comes at the expense of utter restrictions on the freedom of the eyes. In this regard, Rossano's (2012) discovery that conversation participants withdraw their gaze from one another when they finish a project of action also means, at least for a moment, that the eyes regain their freedom and can attend to one or more of their other occupations: scan, stare, or contemplate.

2.11   Conclusion

In order to account for the ways Hussein uses his eyes during this workday, I introduced a number of conceptual distinctions, namely between *looking* and *seeing*—'looking' is a process verb, 'seeing' an achievement verb (Ryle 1949; Sharrock & Coulter 1998); and between *gazing*, a form of looking, and vision-based activities that call upon Hussein's professional vision (Goodwin 1994). Hussein glances, scans the environment, searches (looks for), scrutinizes (probes), inspects, monitors, and supervises, and his eyes take control of his hands when he works on a car or unpacks a spare part, none of which would adequately be described as a case of gazing (Coulter &

Parsons 1990). But 'gaze' is indeed an adequate descriptor for most of the looking behavior Hussein and his interlocutors display during face-to-face conversations, when all that matters is whether one party looks at the other and the other looks back and thus *sees* that he or she is being looked at.[12] Conversational gaze in two-party interactions is little more than a two-state system, comprising the states 'look at other' and 'look away from other', as well as the movement of gaze between the two (that is, can one party see that the other party's gaze is moving toward her, or are the eyes still?; Goodwin 1981).

Previously, gaze and mutual gaze in conversational interaction have been explained as ways of displaying and monitoring attention, and it has been assumed that attention and its display are required for demonstrating listenership and for the ordered transfer of speaking turns (Goodwin 1981; Kendon 1967). However, Rossano (2012) has correctly pointed out that such visual display of attention is not really required, as vocal 'back-channel' signals are usually sufficient for this task and abundantly used. And by far not all talk is accompanied by mutual gaze. Rather, as the data (both Rossano's and mine) show, whether mutual gaze is required is contingent on the type of action under way, and gaze is thus implicated less in turn-taking than in the collaborative production of particular types of *action sequence*, whose successful completion is marked by the coordinated mutual withdrawal of gaze.

We have observed what I have called a 'basic gaze sequence' in face-to-face interactions: Hussein and his interlocutor establish mutual gaze during the initiation of the action sequence and withdraw gaze from one another during its completion. We have found this sequencing of gaze during brief as well as extended speech act sequences, and we have noticed that a speaker who initiates a sequence without seeking and establishing mutual gaze may not get a response to the initiation. Mutual gaze thus turned out to be not a matter of showing attention and regulating turn-taking, but of *social recognition*: it is a minimal form of social contract by which an action under way is certified as mutually recognized and ratified, becoming part of the 'official record' of the interaction. During longer turns, for example, when he informed a customer about prices or counseled Hassan about the best way to deal with a delinquent customer, Hussein

---

[12] Here I refer to 'mundane', 'uneventful' conversations, disregarding what can happen when there is prolonged mutual gaze, as is characteristic of both flirtatious and threatening behavior.

sought mutual gaze for 'transactive' speech acts (Taylor 2011), that is, those that have institutional consequences.

This analysis has then also enabled me to account for other patterns or practices in the data: Hussein's gaze withdrawals when he answered questions (by Richie about prices) and disagreed with a diagnosis (by Art about the cause of a rattling noise). And why speakers, including Hussein, may seek recipient gaze to depictive gestures, gestures that must be seen for the utterance to be understood. When the parties' gaze is primarily focused on an object—an engine, a carburetor, a battery tester—a state commonly labeled *joint attention*, we can see that the role of mutual gaze is taken over by minor posture and head reorientations; the parties turn to each other enough to allow each other to notice this turning, while keeping their eyes focused on the object at hand. Indeed, when I have discussed gaze and gaze direction, I have almost always tacitly included, if not relied on, changes in the orientation of the head. Arguably, this is also how participants take note of each other's visual and cognitive orientation.[13]

Eye-to-eye communication shows the simplest organization among the bodily modalities, much simpler than, for example, facial action or gesture, but also far more restrictively regulated. While speaker and listener have some, perhaps unequally distributed, opportunities to let their gaze wander, focus somewhere else, or glance around, at certain determinate points during utterance sequences, they must turn their gaze to each other, lest the conversation derails, because the course of action under way is no longer treated as 'licensed'. Gaze leaves little room for individuation, and nonstandard gaze behavior is often taken as a warrant for attributions of deviance (autism, shame, dishonesty, and so on). Yet, we also know that the regulation of conversational gaze is not a human universal. Gaze aversion and avoidance, for example, are *topoi* in anthropological research, and gaze (or restrictions on gaze) is often related to social stratification. Hussein's gaze behavior appears entirely familiar to us. Whether this is the result of cultural adaptation to the U.S. or we witness the practices of his urban, multicultural, and modern homeland, I do not know.

---

[13] The relationship between gaze, visual focus, and head orientation would need a more precise investigation; for example, a distinct feature of human eyes is the white around the retina, which makes gaze direction a more conspicuous phenomenon. Humans thus have a more precise view of one another's gaze than other primates, who lack this feature and therefore seem to rely on head orientation to gauge one another's visual and cognitive focus. See Call and Tomasello (2005).

3   Pointing

This chapter investigates how Mr. Chmeis directs the attention of others. Pointing is one of his most frequent and iconic communicative acts. It is shown how pointing gestures emerge within and adapt to complex and shifting material settings and communication ecologies, as well as the variety of communicative functions that pointing gestures serve beyond directing attention, such as aiding linguistic reference to objects and their features (*deixis*), including ones whose names are not shared knowledge, as well as framing the addressee's perspective on the object, the aspect under which the object is to be seen. Finally, pointing gestures can direct not only the attention, but also the actions of others, in which case they become embodiments of the speaker's authority. This is captured in the cover photograph of this book.

3.1   A pointed answer

We saw at the beginning of Chapter 1 that one of Hussein's preferred 'vehicles of being in the world' (Merleau-Ponty 1962) are pointing gestures; from the get-go, he directs others around the shop by pointing things out to them. Pointing is a main vehicle of his agency, and we can understand a great deal about his status in the shop—that is, his power and say over the actions of others—by studying his entitlements to point, or rather to achieve certain effects through pointing. Pointing is not only a means of social control, but a knowledge-sharing device, and it is in that capacity that pointing is usually studied: as a 'technology' or 'resource' that, coupled with the 'deictic system' of the language involved, serves to impart knowledge or 'situation awareness' (Norman 1993). It is this usage of the communicative praxis 'pointing' that we will now turn to, before we reexamine pointing as a set of methods for social control and

Figs. 3.1.1–2 Uncle Ahm answers a question by pointing

transfer of physical agency. We will find that pointing is a rich and variable praxis, accomplishing far more than focusing visual attention or supporting verbal reference. But it can also be a demanding practice, requiring extra interactional work to succeed.

The moment captured in (3.1) is Hussein's first arrival 'across the street', where he greets Uncle Ahm, the Chinese welder, and checks whether he has everything he needs to get the job done. In response, he gets an indecisive <u>uhhhh</u> and a pointing gesture: Uncle Ahm points to the gaping hole in the car's front end, the socket where the headlight goes. In response to that pointing gesture, Hussein also makes a pointing gesture, a two-component one, and then repeats it right away. Thus, the silent moment in the transcript (lines 5–7) in fact shows a *pointed* question-answer sequence, and a slightly troubled one at that. The problem is inherent in the perceptual ecology of pointing gestures, as we will see.

Figs.3.1.1–2 show Ahm's gestured response to Hussein's question. He moves his index finger from right to left, near the top of the putative headlight.

(3.1)
1 Hussein Hi, Uncle Ahm.
2 Ahm   Hello.
3 Hussein How are you.
4 Hussein We got all the part you need?
5 Ahm   Mmm?
            (- - - - - - - - - - - - - - - -)
6 Ahm   Uhhhhh hhh
            (- - - - • - - - - - - - - - - - - -)
7 Ahm   (   )
            (- - - - - - • - - - - - - - - - - -)

Figs. 3.1.3–4 'This 'cross the street.'

Hussein's pointed response is shown in Figs.3.1.3 and 4. In 3.1.3, we can see Hussein gearing up for his first pointing gesture (the hand is moving toward Ahm), while Ahm is still deeply into pointing himself. Hussein moves his right hand a few inches toward Ahm, and then he retracts and raises his arm and moves it to his left, the index finger extended (Fig.3.1.4). In effect, he points 'across the street', to the junkyard next to the main shop. When the gesture reaches its full extension, Hussein looks to Ahm. He can see that his gesture has attracted gaze, but by the time Ahm has looked up, the first half of the two-gesture unit is over, and Ahm is nonresponsive. He utters a hesitation marker, 'uhh' (line 9).

(3.1–2)
8   Hussein   This 'cross the street.
9   Ahm   Uhh.

Without missing a beat, Hussein repeats the gesture. Now he distributes it between the two hands. With the left index finger he points to the socket; with the right he points across the street, thus linking one object or location to another. This time Ahm nods, affirming that he has seen and understood. Hussein thus is free to elaborate his answer ('I have another car to cut' [up].), but he does so as he is already walking away. He points back over his shoulder, to the junkyard that is now, as he is moving on, receding into his interactional past: 'everything over there.'

10   Hussein   This (–) 'cross the street.
11   Ahm   (nods)

Fig. 3.1.5 'This

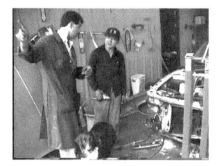

Fig. 3.1.6 ''cross the street.'

Fig. 3.1.7 'another car to cut.'

12   Hussein   I have another car to cut.
13   Hussein   Everything over there.

In this interaction, the success of the pointing gesture is only secured by an act of repair, that is, a redoing of the gesture. The gesture needs visual attention, but it is also the means to attract it (Heath 1986). Thus, Hussein's

Fig. 3.1.8 'Everything over there.'

two-part pointing gesture attracts Ahm's attention, but that attention then arrives too late. The gesture needs to be redone, and such redoing is, as various studies of pointing show, quite routine for pointing gestures. Pointing is repair-prone, perhaps more than it is trouble-prone: some of the repair may be preemptive.

In (3.1), then, pointing operates in the service of knowledge distribution: pointing gestures carry much of the 'information load' in this exchange about needs, things, and locations—what one might call 'resource management'. Notice that Ahm and Hussein do not ever point to an object. Rather, they point to its absence, the place where the object 'would go'. Ahm knows that Hussein will infer the absence of the headlight and make information about it available if he can. In other words, just as it is possible to see that something is missing, it is possible to make someone see that something is missing by pointing at an empty place, so that that missing object becomes available for further topical talk (Kita 2003a; Nishizaka 2000).

3.2   Pointing and reference

Pointing gestures ostensibly refer to objects and locations. They serve functions of reference. Frequently, pointing serves to disambiguate an otherwise vague or ambiguous (pronominal or nominal) term. Pointing is part of the *deictic system* that speakers have at their disposal. Linguists have tended to disregard pointing in their treatment of the deictic systems of spoken languages, even though Karl Bühler, in his well-known and influential *Sprachtheorie*, had insisted, on account of the word 'this' ('dies' in German), that 'the pointing gesture that is observed in the actual perceptual situation is indispensable' (1934: 103). In other words, 'dies'/'this' are words specifically designed to support pointing gestures. Moreover, Bühler also recognized the multimodality *avant la lettre* of pointing:

> The entire body and the head and eyes can be involved, and an actor knows how to work out dynamic moving gestures with these resources when he wants, he can make *turns* that have the character and make the impression of having a goal. . . . In mute human contact, controlled fixation of the eyes on something in the field of vision is also a familiar, usual means of indicating a goal. (Bühler 1934: 112)[1]

What these diverse forms of pointing appear to have in common is that they are 'communicative body movement[s] that project a vector by a body part. This vector indicates a certain direction, location, or object' (Kita 2003b: 3). We understand pointing gestures

> by projecting a straight line from the furthest part of the body part that has been extended outward, into the space that extends beyond the speaker . . . This object or location may be something that is currently visible to all participants, or it may be an object or location that exists somewhere in the real world, but cannot be seen, as when one points in the direction of objects that lie beyond the walls of one's house. (Kendon 2004: 200)

Thus, 'tracing a path from the gesture to a thing', as Fillmore defined the task of the beholder, is rarely a trivial affair. Stukenbrock (2009, 2015), in particular, has explained the routine organization of pointing as having a built-in 'fail-safe' or 'repair' mechanism. It is needed because the gestural act itself can be ambiguous: where the vector ends may be difficult to ascertain. This is a perceptual problem. Or, the target may be inherently ambiguous. To paraphrase Quine's (1960) classic example: it may not be certain whether I am pointing at a running rabbit or just a rabbit or to the rabbit's running, skill, speed, or feet. Context, of course, will always matter. As Goodwin reminds us, pointing is constituted as a meaningful act 'through the mutual contextualization of a range of semiotic resources including . . . a body visibly performing an act of pointing; talk that both elaborates and is elaborated by the act of pointing; . . . and the larger activity within which the act of pointing is embedded' (2003: 219). It is the activity in particular that gives semiotic objects in the environment of the gesture their particular occasioned significance (222).Thus, the pointing gesture recipient's problem, 'to trace a path from the gesture to the thing' (Fillmore 1982: 46), can require the mobilization of different kinds of knowledge and is not exclusively a perceptual or geometric problem.

---

[1] 'Goal' here means what we call *target*: the object indicated by the pointing gesture.

Stukenbrock distinguishes the *perceptual* 'vector-goal problem' (where does this gesture 'go'?) from the *cognitive-semantic* 'problem of establishing reference' (what in the area where it 'goes' does it pick out?; Stukenbrock 2009: 293). Working out the reference of the gesture requires local knowledge, or even layers of knowledge, including normative ontologies of what is there to be seen in the first place. Whatever epistemic asymmetries and symmetries may be required, Stukenbrock has shown that the attendant problems of intersubjectivity are solved through sequential interaction. One characteristic of interaction during pointing are repeats. For example, Stukenbrock shows that people, before they point by hand, typically glance in the direction of the subsequent pointing gesture. She calls the space defined by the initial glance 'Verweisraum' (roughly, 'reference space'), i.e., the space to which indexical elements, including gestures, refer. She observes that the speaker characteristically establishes the reference space by briefly *facing out* of her 'transactional segment' (i.e., the space she occupies; Kendon 1990: 212). While maintaining the lower body oriented to the other, the speaker briefly turns head and gaze (sometimes also the shoulders and torso) in the direction of the target, and then turns back. The actual pointing gesture can then, in the next step, be performed while the gaze remains on the recipient monitoring what he or she is doing. Stukenbrock calls this deployment of the body *Ressourcenspagat* ('resource split'). Pointing—the kind intended to redirect the addressee's visual attention—is thus an activity rather than an act, intersubjectivity achieved through sequential interaction. We can see the elements of this, in the following moment, in which Hussein instructs a customer to see something, to perceive a symptom, smoke.

Hussein is standing by the left fender of a Ford Fiesta. The owner, Ms. Nancy, is at the front end, while Kathy, her daughter, is in the driver's seat. Hussein is performing various tests to find out why her car would not start when she called. He has just instructed Kathy to start the car (Fig.3.2.1). He waits for a few seconds, nodding, then looks to Kathy and says 'push gas more' as he makes a one-armed down-pushing gesture. He nods and says, 'uh huh'. Then he turns his head and looks toward the car's rear (Fig.3.2.2). He raises his arm, makes a large pointing gesture, and says (Fig.3.2.3): 'You see the smoke in the back. Watch the smoke.' As he utters 'smoke', Hussein briefly turns his gaze to Ms. Nancy, at the same time as she is turning her gaze toward him (Fig. 3.2.4). This is a moment Stukenbrock has described with the term 'resource split': while the pointing gesture directs the other's

Figs. 3.2.1–5 'You see the smoke in the back? Watch the smoke.'

attention, the speaker's gaze is not aligned with the pointing, but rather monitors the other's response to it.

(3.2)

```
          ( - - - - - - - - - • - - • - - - • )
1  Hussein  You see the sm•o:ke in the ba:ck.
2           Watch the sm•oke
            ( - - )
3           More gas!
            ( - - - - - - - - - - - - - - - - - - - )
4           Okay.
```

Figs. 3.2.6–7 Ms. Nancy joins Hussein's line of vision

Still pointing, he looks back to the car's rear (Fig.3.2.6). 'More gas', he demands, making another push gesture, while Nancy moves over to him, joining his line of regard. Silently, Hussein points again and then turns to Nancy and finds her nodding (Fig.3.2.7). He ends the gesture with a flourish and says, 'okay'.

Pointing in this episode is successful due to the interactional work expended by both parties. As Stukenbrock has predicted, Hussein points with his hand only after having selected a sector of space by his gaze and orientation in space. He also monitors what Ms. Nancy does with her head and face. Ms. Nancy, in turn, goes out of her way to align her visual perspective with his pointing gesture, making sure she gets to see what the gesture shows or points up. And she produces displays of understanding that assure Hussein that the pointing has worked and she can see the smoke.

A common, if somewhat surprising and spurious, way to show that one has understood a pointing gesture is to respond with a pointing gesture of one's own. This is the case in (3.3) and (3.4). First, Hussein is the addressee, then the initiator of a pointing act. Both interactions take place by the toolbox in the shop. In (3.3), Hussein calls on Arturo, who arrives a few seconds later. Hussein asks him if he has any work to do, and Arturo says 'yeah, the truck', as he turns his head and upper body to the right and makes a large pointing gesture (Fig.3.3.2). Hussein looks up, his eyes following the path of the gesture. Arturo drops the arm and looks up to Hussein, but Hussein does not look at him; he still looks in the direction of the target, clearly unable to see it. Hussein's body enacts non-understanding: he steps forward, slightly lowers the head, and transparently searches for the target. When he locates it, he utters a token of recognition ('ah', line 5) and then points to it (Fig.3.3.4).

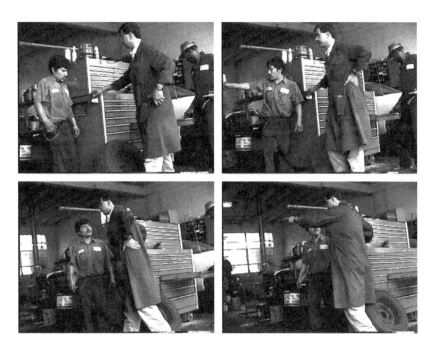

Figs. 3.3.1–4 Arturo points out what car he is working on; Hussein confirms

(3.3)
1   Hussein   Arturo?
2   Arturo!
          (8.0)
3   Do you have anything •to do right now?
4   Arturo   Yeah the• (truck).
5   Hussein   Ah you- • did wanna paint this, • okay.

Hussein's return pointing gesture and his acceptance token, 'okay', conclude the inquiry sequence.

   The interaction sequence is similar to (3.2): through a shift in gaze
direction and an orientation of head and torso, Arturo selects a field of
reference, and then he selects the target from within this field by
a pointing gesture. Hussein, the recipient, like Ms. Nancy in (3.2),
moves toward Arturo, aligning his perspective with Arturo's line of
regard. And then he affirms his understanding (i.e., his ability to
identify the referent) with a return pointing gesture. In Fig.3.4.1, we
see Hussein summoning Cedric. Having noticed that Cedric is looking
at him from a distance, he makes an 'index up' gesture ('I need your

Figs. 3.4.1–4 Hussein summons Cedric, directs and adjusts his gaze; Cedric confirms

attention.'). As Cedric approaches him, Hussein points with the left hand to the 'front right-side tire' of a car, which is some distance away (Fig.3.4.2). Cedric turns and moves backward as he approaches Hussein so that he already looks in the same direction when he arrives next to him. With Cedric next to him, Hussein raises his other hand and points to the tires again, precisely aligning his gaze with the vector of his arm, as if he were shooting a gun (Fig.3.4.3). Cedric responds with a pointing gesture of his own. In response Hussein tilts his head and flips his fingers (palm-vertically) a few times to the side, indicating 'further to the left' (Fig.3.4.4). Thus, Cedric's responsive pointing gesture, on whose precise orientation hinges whether he will identify the proper tires, is fine-tuned by Hussein. Hussein's palm-side gesture is a method for fine-tuning Cedric's gaze. He says, 'this side'.[2]

---

[2] 'This side', combined with the palm-vertical point, replaces Hussein's previous formulation, 'right-side tire'. It appears that the combination pointing gesture+indexical 'this side' is deemed more reliable than the less indexical phrase 'right-side tire'.

(3.4)
1   Hussein   (summons Cedric with an 'index up' gesture)
             (5.5)
2   Hussein   The • front right side tire
3   the fro:nt •
4   Cedric   (   )
                 [
4   Hussein   • this side
5   Cedric   Ok•ay

Then, Hussein refers to 'that tire' inside the shop as he makes another
large, right-handed pointing gesture. Like in his interaction with Uncle Ahm,
he relates one object/location to another through a two-component gesture.
Inexplicably, Cedric co-performs this second pointing gesture. Now Hussein
looks at the brake pad in his hand and looks up, over to his right, toward the
back of the shop, and begins to raise his right hand, as he says, 'you need'
(line 6). At precisely the same time, Cedric's right hand also begins to rise.
The two men end up making simultaneous parallel pointing gestures. While
Cedric's arm does not rise to the same level as Hussein's, its movement is
perfectly synchronized with Hussein's. The men also lower their arms at the

Figs. 3.4.5–6 Joint pointing

same time. The synchronous pointing to some known-in-common object is a powerful demonstration of the 'synching of the minds' of the two men.

6   Hussein   you need to switch with th•at tire
7   Cedric   Okay.

Note that this sequence, repair action and repetition aside, is, like Hussein's exchange with Uncle Ahm, a two-part pointing sequence, relating 'this' to 'that', 'this side' to 'that tire'. Two successive pointing gestures select (individuate) two distinct objects, while the verb phrase 'need to switch' explicates the nature of the relationship. The bilateral structure of the body is frequently used to display relations between objects, as we will see later.

In the three sequences we have considered so far, pointing gestures lead to a change in gaze direction by the addressee. Having both parties look at the target together—and thus displaying *joint attention*—appears to be the goal of the interaction. But, as Hanks (2005) has pointed out, the deictic field is also embedded in a social field, and, other things being equal, the type of response required or expected in response to a pointing gesture may depend on the position the recipient occupies in the social field. Hanks writes:

> [T]he phenomenal context is embedded in a broader social one, which over time determines aspects of relevance and provides an *already established* space of positions and position takings. This vastly simplifies the task of resolving reference by providing a ready-made universe of objects, boundaries, and relations to others which any deictic utterance can articulate. Without this universe, much deictic practice would be radically indeterminate. (Hanks 2005: 210–211)

Art, Hussein's partner in (3.5), is regarded as the most senior mechanic by Hussein, and this may be a factor in his response to Hussein's pointing. But Art is also in charge of operating the tow truck. After his exchange with Cedric, Hussein is still standing by the toolbox. Now he is in an F-formation with Art, who is facing him from a few feet away. Hussein is giving Art instructions which cars to load (and remove from the premises), and he misnames a car, calling a Mitsubishi a Chrysler. He tries to solve the problem by making a large pointing gesture and pointing out that the car can be seen ('the one over here', line 5), but Art does not turn around to look where Hussein is pointing. He seems unengaged, and yet he does display that he knows which car Hussein is talking about. Hussein holds his pointing gesture beyond his turn, demonstrably waiting for a reaction from

Figs. 3.5.1–2 Art claims knowledge by pointing at the target without looking

Art (Fig.3.5.1). He adds a small stroke when he adds the description, 'the one over here'. This is when Art reacts: he raises his left hand and points, with his thumb over his shoulder, to the back (Fig.3.5.2). Pointing gestures with the thumb are often made when the target is known. By making one and not turning around, Art presents himself as a knowing listener. He offers a 'try-marked' understanding, 'The little Mitsubishi?' Hussein confirms, and Art agrees to do as told.

(3.5)
1	Hussein	… and bring through the-
2		load the- (1.0) uh-
3		the • Chrysler over there
4		the- the Mitsubishi
		(1.0)
5		the one over here
6	Art	The little • Mitsubishi
		(0.4)
7	Hussein	Yeah
8	Art	Okay.

This episode illustrates Hanks' observations about the embeddedness of the deictic field within a social field. Pointing behavior is not self-contained and not exclusively occupied with cognitive and attentional demands of the activity and interaction. By assuming the authority to point—that is, to make demands on others' attention—a speaker makes epistemic and pragmatic claims: when Hussein points (i.e., directs) Art to the Mitsubishi, he claims (or presupposes) that Art does not already know what car behind him needs to be loaded and that Art needs to look to see which car he means. Art, by keeping his gaze on Hussein and not turning around, rejects that claim. He does not need visual instruction. The thumb gesture suggests that 'the Mitsubishi' is known information.[3] Art positions himself in the social field in a way that markedly contrasts with how he would have positioned himself had he turned around. A small battle over epistemic authority is fought here, and Art prevails: he needs no education. And yet, his thumb-pointing gesture shows that he is 'in the know' so that no time needs to be wasted on further negotiations about the right designation.

3.3   Spotlighting

In all of these episodes, pointing is done in the service of referring: it is done to help the listener 'disambiguate' which object the speaker is talking about. That this disambiguation was done by pointing—that pointing served as referential practice *du jour*—was a matter of contingency: given the perceptual ecology of the situation, the 'arc' of pointing gestures appears to be a robust and reliable reference device, usually guiding the path 'from the eyes to the thing'. But if we include other configurations of artifacts and humans in our investigation, we will quickly find moments when other measures for raising an object to prominence are chosen for selecting it as the target of a referential act, in short: for focusing the spotlight of attention on it, are chosen. They appear to be better adapted to the situation. Thus, while so far we have discussed cases where the target is some distance away from the gesturer, it is also possible, of course, that the speaker holds the object that is at the center of attention in his hands, so that a different perceptual ecology governs, even if the communicative tasks and the ways they are solved show parallels as well. In (3.6), Hussein is taking a reading of the charging system of Ms. Nancy's car and explicates the information displayed on the battery tester. Holding the battery tester in his hand, he beckons Ms. Nancy to come. The beckoning morphs into a pointing gesture, directed toward the instrument. Ms. Nancy moves in, looks at the display, nods, and utters an acknowledgment ('uh huh') as she takes her position next to Hussein. Both keep their eyes focused on the display, and Hussein's index-finger pointing is replaced by a tapping with the middle finger. This is the equivalent of a large pointing gesture, but 'resized' to fit the constraints of a small 'surface' or 'reference domain'.

---

[3]   The area behind one's back is treated as the field where past experiences remain and can be found: things one has dealt with, places one has visited, actions in which one has participated before. See Nuñez' various studies of gesture and contrastive cultural conceptions of time (Cooperrider & Nuñez 2009; Nuñez & Sweetser 2006).

Figs. 3.6.1–2 Directing attention to an object in hand

(3.6)

```
         ( - - - - - - - - - - - - - - - • - - - )
1   Hussein  • Charging system is perfect.
         ( - - - - - - - - - - )
2   Nancy    Uh huh
2   Hussein   Here you see where it says on the okay
3            inside on the green it say okay okay
4            fourteen volt
```

We notice that, in contrast to previous extracts in which speakers monitored listeners' facial responses to their pointing gesture, no such monitoring takes place here: Hussein does not look at Ms. Nancy. (However, there will be, as I have described in the previous chapter, a halfway 'compromise' orientation between them in the next moment.)

Spotlighting takes place when an object—the target or figure—is 'elevated' or highlighted or otherwise made the center of attention. Spotlighting means raising the figure from the ground. Pointing is one method of spotlighting. *Placing* is another one, showing partly similar, partly different features and implications. Placing, or *placing-for*, means 'placing an object for [the co-interactants'] … attention' (Clark 2003: 256). Placing has a distinct temporal organization: objects placed for communicative purposes remain in place, 'accessible to everyone in a conversation for an extended period of time' (262), in contrast to the targets of pointing gestures, which decay with the gestures.

Placing means to 'position-for'—to expose to others—an object within a static environment. Hi-Tech Automotive is largely a mobile environment. People are in motion and arrangements of things undergo constant change. Whereas in placing, the work of making the object salient is off-loaded to the environment, in cases of positioning-for in motion, 'maintaining' is the hands' ongoing concern: the object must be actively kept in play. In (3.7), Hussein, who is inside the garage, has just asked Ashraf to move a truck. He enters the picture holding out an ignition key with his right hand while pointing it toward a truck (Fig.3.7.1), which is off camera. Using the key as a pointer, he points it to a truck (Fig.3.7.2). But at the same time, he also holds out the key for Ashraf so he can get it and use it in the moving of the truck (Fig.3.7.3). The gesture is simultaneously an act of offering and keeping ready for,

Figs. 3.7.1–6 Hussein points with a car key, addressing successive co-participants

and what it has in common with placing is that the object is 'maintained' (literally, held in hand) in a place where it can be retrieved. Hussein keeps holding out the key, as Ashraf is still some distance away. Just before Ashraf arrives, Hussein changes tracks. He rushes outside and calls on Kenneth, all the while holding out the key toward the truck. Kenneth arrives and takes the key from Hussein.

(3.7)
1   Hussein   Kenneth!
                  (1.3)
2   Drive that truck,
3   turn around the block
4   and come here next to the Audi please.

A single 'multimodal' act, which combines the exhibition of an object with a pointing gesture, is carried over from one interaction to the next. The activity pivots around the elevated key—the object in the spotlight— which is never mentioned or talked about, but whose positioning in space is motivated by its dual roles as index and tool. The key is kept in the spotlight because it ideally synthesizes appellative (directive) and indicative meanings. The dynamic, 'multimodal' pattern of sign, tool, and physical action can easily be passed from one co-participant to another. Of course it is the need for a handover of the key that gives it this significance, not its positioning alone. Its positioning says: 'come get me.'

   To the extent to which the 'point' of an action is to bring an object to the attention of another, any method that raises the figure from its ground will do. There is no need for conventionalization. Indicating actions (Clark 2003), conventionalized pointing gestures notwithstanding, do not tend to have very stable forms, because they live in richly textured environments to which they fluently adapt. (3.8) shows, quite literally, *elevation* as a method of spotlighting. Hussein and Alex are trying to diagnose why the engine of an Audi will not start—a problem that will occupy a succession of people throughout this day (and which is in fact not solved until the day after). At this moment Hussein is trying to 'make sure that [there is] enough spark', and he explicates his actions. He simply raises one of the cables that connect to the spark-plugs and then lowers it again. Altogether, this action takes three seconds. But in between the raising and lowering of the cable, he raises it further, so that its metallic end (which screws onto the plug) becomes visible, and he first holds it in the left hand, tapping with the index finger of his right, and then puts it in his right hand and taps it with the fingers of his left. The first tapping comes with 'make sure',

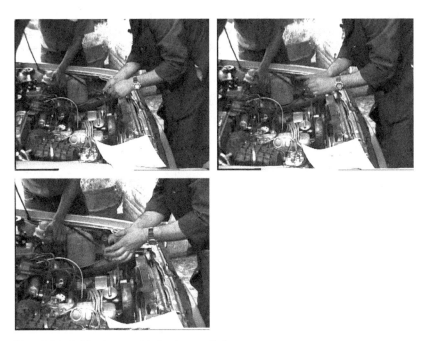

Figs. 3.8.1–3 Putting a cable in the spotlight

the second with 'enough spark'. The entire action is but an ornamentation, a three-second elaboration of a day-long activity. Yet it focuses attention, spotlights the talked-about object, highlights what the actor is doing, and perhaps also conveys something about the object.

(3.8)
1   Hussein   Okay now.
              (0.3)
2   I wanna make sure we got enough spark now.

The spotlighting action adapts opportunistically to the context that the object is found in: to be exposed and visible, the cable will need elevation, freedom from the cavity it is in. The shape of the spotlighting action—the quick, double tapping—abstractly figures something about the object, namely, that there might be a 'spark', a tremor.

   If we were to arrange varieties of spotlighting gestures by the degree to which the embodied form stands on its own or is derived from the context, large pointing gestures such as Hussein's 'see the smoke' gesture (3.2) mark one end of the continuum. They reign supreme in their moments and relegate other bodily activity to inferior ranks. On the other end we find cases where the spotlighting of an object results from a minor modification of an ongoing practical activity involving it. What is needed or suffices to meet the need for deictic reference, or spotlighting, varies from situation to situation, and degrees of explicitness may also vary for stylistic reasons and according to the relevances and time constraints of the situation.

J. J. Gibson (1962) has coined the term 'active touch' to describe the active gathering of tactile experience, for example, by actions of the hands. Active touch aims to bring out the features of things, their texture, consistency, and affordances for action. When active touch is conducted in public, under the eyes of another, once it is successful and yields findings, it also spotlights these findings and makes them available for further referential action. In (3.9), Hussein is interacting with a customer who has come to his shop to ask for free spare parts, which need to be lifted from a car in the junkyard by the shop. We meet Hussein and the customer as they are positioned by the car; Hussein has removed a door hinge and begins to explore it. He discovers that it is in proper order and proceeds to demonstrate this to the customer. This scene shows what we can call 'deictic manipulation': depending on its affordances and its 'degrees of freedom'

Figs. 3.9.1–3 Deictic manipulation

within its material context, the object is manipulated in ways that reveal relevant features. This scene requires a fine-grained description.

```
(3.9)
1    C   Yeah, that's it.
2        That right the:re
         (1.0)
3        (well) I thank you very much
4        h(h)eh heh heh
                      [
5    H              (    ) you need this too?
6    C   No:, I don't need tha:t.
                          [
7    H                    Hold on, look what.
         (0.3)
8        You see the bushing here
                          [
9    C                    Ooh, I might need that
10   H   You see the bushing's fa::st
                          [
11   C                    Yeah.
         (0.4)
12   C   That's what I need then
                  [
13   H            then you need too this
```

Hussein holds up the hinge and asks, 'you need this too', and the customer declines. But Hussein demonstrates that, while bushings often get warped, this one is in proper order. He should take it. Hussein holds the hinge in his right hand and 'pinches' the bushing with his thumb and the index finger of his left hand. As he says, 'if that's

Figs. 3.9.4–5 Pointing and handover of object

warped', he raises his hands, exposing the object, and taps the precision-gripped part several times with the tip of his index finger while he explains (lines 13–16) that the customer may need the bushing too (and thus the hinge, in which it is firmly embedded). The customer points his index finger and then grabs the bushing, bringing his other hand to the hinge, the pointing gesture transforming into a handover of the object. When Hussein releases it from his hands, he makes a handover gesture (see Chapter 5).

1	C	Yeah, that's it.
2		That right the:re
		(1.0)
3		(well) I thank you very much
4		h(h)eh heh heh
		[
5	H	( ) you need this too?
6	C	No:, I don't need tha:t.
		[
7	H	Hold on, look what.
		(0.3)
8		You see the bushing here
		[
9	C	Ooh, I might need that
10	H	You see the bushing's fa::st
		[
11	C	Yeah.
13	H	then you need too this

Here, too, the manual patterns chosen to select parts of the object are adapted both to the physical shape of the objects and to the instrumental acts in which the hands are currently engaged. Hands easily turn instrumental into communicative actions. Actions by which a figure is elevated from a ground are context- and object-adaptive. All they need to accomplish is to bring the target into the foreground of the perceptual field.

3.4 Construal

Often, indicative gestures are not only adaptive, but also evocative: they *construe* the target in a certain way, show it *as* something (see Goodman [1968] 1976 on 'representing-as'). 'Construal' in the context of pointing and other attention-focusing gestures means: the target is not only selected,

but also 'figured', that is, represented *as* something, in some way. Kendon
has similarly observed that '[O]ne can combine with the pointing action
components that seem to *characterize* the object pointed at. ... The form
of pointing is systematically related to the way the object being referred to
is presented in the speaker's discourse (Kendon 2004: 201, emph. J. S.).
He noted that in his video recordings from England and southern Italy,
pointing hands are shaped and held in a variety of distinct ways. Kendon
distinguished seven different hand shapes and orientations which
correspond to different aspects under which the target is presented. For
example, 'index finger extended supine' is used when some quality is
attributed to the target. A change from the neutral to the supine orientation of the hand while keeping the index finger extended can therefore
mark the transition from reference to predication or, in Kendon's terminology, from topic to comment: 'as the focus of the discourse shifts from
individuating an object ... to making some comments about the object, so
also the mode of index finger pointing changes' (208). Kendon and
Versante show that pointing can easily be elaborated by additional features of hand shape and movement 'so that the gesture not only indicates
but at the same time accomplishes something else, such as depicting
a characteristic of the object indicated' (2003: 112). Wilkins (2003) gives
another example of distinctions of 'aspects' under which the target is
spotlighted by different pointing gestures. The Arrernte in Australia
distinguish between *pointing at* an object X and *pointing Y-wards at X*.
In the former case, the object is individuated by the gesture; in the latter,
only the general direction in which it is found is identified (as in 'the tree
that stands in the direction of the camp'). This conceptual distinction
corresponds to a morphological one between a pointing gesture and
a 'horned sign' in which index and little finger are extended and middle
and ring finger bent, and the hand 'moved toward the target and then
rapidly retracted, and ... never held for any length of time at its apex'
(185). In Stukenbrock's German data, and in the data under investigation
here, this difference would be communicated by the choice between
'pointing by gaze' and 'pointing by hand', and the former would precede
the latter.

Hussein 'sheds different spotlight' on targets, construes them in different ways, by selecting from among hand shapes and spotlighting actions.
In (3.11), he is walking across the shop and notices a stack of tires. He
proceeds to tell Cedric what to do with them: 'Let's take all the used tire
across the street.' As Hussein begins this utterance and Cedric is still in the
back of the store, he directs his left index finger to the tires, without much

changing the position of his hand (it is in 'walking position'). The movement shape of his gesture is not a point, but a line. Drawing a line, Hussein selects a set of objects grouped along this line as the target of the pointing gesture. The gesture projects a line onto a set of adjacent objects and thus makes the recipient see them as one, as 'connected by a stroke of the hand' (Figs.3.10.1–2). The gesture spotlights tires, but does not individuate any single tire. Hussein draws another line in the direction of the tires, as he says 'those' (Fig. 3.10.3). Cedric, when he answers (line 4), makes an 'inclusive' movement with his open hand over the tires as well (Fig.3.10.4). He repeats this gesture when he says 'these' (Fig.3.10.5, line 5). Clearly, both Hussein's and Cedric's gestures are designed to refer to the whole set of tires. The communicative function of this gesture is not different from individuating pointing gestures: they identify an object. But in this case, the object is simultaneously construed as a set.

(3.10)
1 H Let's take all the used tire across the street,
2   those
3 C Okay.
4   Okay they belong in the (hallway)
        (- - -)
5 H These (   )
        (1.5)
6 C belong (in the hall) anyway

In (3.11), we encounter index finger pointing and open hand pointing, and it appears that these alternate hand shapes are conveniently utilized to spotlight locations/objects in contrast to regions. Hussein inspects the engine of the Mercury Capri. Addressing the researcher, he says: 'you wanna see this early, lots of oil'. His open hand, held face down and moved over a section of an engine, projects the shape of an area or domain (Figs.3.11.1–2). In other words, we are invited to see the shadows or traces of the moving hands in the terrain, the engine. The gesture adds spatial information not given in the talk: it demarcates the area covered by oil. A moment later, Hussein repeats the gesture, when he points out that Dr. Marwan 'steam(ed) this area'. Then he grabs a cable and fondles it between index and thumb, an exploratory action probing the state the cable is in. Combined with the statement 'I like to have maybe new wires later', it conveys that the wires are frail. The customer interrupts him with a pointing gesture and the statement that Hussein 'replaced all this once', and Hussein points out that the

Figs. 3.10.1–7 Pointing to a group of objects

water drawn by the cables is the result of the damage the oil has done to them, which is itself the result of a leak in the valve cover gasket. He supports this account with a pointing gesture whose stroke falls on 'oil' (line 15): here the finger identifies the precise location of the leak and lets the listener see the oil. Thus, the complementary tasks of showing areas and points within areas are met by simple but embracing changes in the shape and action of the hand. Adaptive as they are, hand gestures keep the recipient's gaze and cognitive attention properly focused across changing activities and settings.

Figs. 3.11.1–5 Spotlighting a cable

(3.11)

1	Hussein	We did the break a:nd
2		a:nd he m- mention about the leak
3		and you wanna see this ea•rly
4		lot of oil?
5	Customer	Yeah
		[
6	Hussein	I send with Dr. Marwan
7		I tell him here, go to the car wash
8		and • steam this area.
9		And I like to have maybe new • wires later
10		in the future.
11		It look • like the:se
		[
12	Customer	Awww, but you replaced all this once
13		they must get water somewhere
		[
14	Hussein	Maybe we should this
15		Yeah. From the • oil.
16		The oil is damage all the rubber, all the seal,
17		that's what I believe.

Then Hussein moves on to his diagnosis: the car has been sputtering after it was in the shop because it has a crack in the distributor cap and water got in when Dr. Marwan steam-cleaned the engine (see Chapter 7). When he says, 'Dr. Marwan', Hussein begins a gesture whose stroke coincides with 'washed this'. The gesture is a rotation and back-and-forth motion of the index finger, which delineates the area previously shown to have been covered by oil. The gesture blends *deixis*—it points to and delineates an area—with an enactment of the movement performed when the area is steam-cleaned: delineating the area by gesture and cleaning it with a steamer are structurally similar actions. Thus, the viewer not only gains an understanding of the area that has been cleaned, but also of the cleaning action. A small modification of the pointing posture adds a predication to the reference: the target is presented as undergoer of a certain type of action.

Hussein turns his hand up and points the area out to the interlocutor (the researcher) with a palm-supine gesture, which, according to Kendon, presents a target as an exemplar, as a bearer of certain traits. He reaches into the engine and taps the distributor with his middle finger, the stroke falling on the accented syllable of 'distributor'. He retracts the hand, rises, turns to the researcher and makes a large cutting motion with his flat right hand, and says: 'cracked'.

Figs. 3.12.1–3 Hussein explains what happened

(3.12)
18   Hussein   What I thi:nk
19   when Dr. Marwan he w•ashed this area probably
                    (- - - - - -)
20   the distr•ibutor cap could be cra•:cked
21   but can't be seen

Thus, pointing something out easily turns into showing it in a certain way, or showing it—construing it—*as* something. The fluidity of gesture and its adaptability to 'contextures' (Goodwin 2011a) makes it indispensable from communication in settings that, while always at hand, are often opaque, their features not fully understood by the participants. This by definition is the case in auto shops, where what is wrong with a car remains, to an extent, an open question until the repair is complete and the car running.

There is no dividing line between gestures that draw attention to a target and gestures that characterize a target. The orientation of the hand, its stance and 'prehensile posture' (Napier 1980), while perhaps falling short of depicting the target (for which there would also be no need), nevertheless reveal something about the fashion in which the speaker orients to the target or what kind of an object it is to him at the moment. The phenomena in question are perhaps most comparable to classifiers in sign languages of the deaf, which characterize broad classes of objects and have pronoun-like functions. The kinds of semantic profiles generated by the gestures under consideration are classifier-like: 'bunch', 'set', 'handful', 'one', and so on. An organic elaboration of the referential act of pointing are acts by which the object or target is related to another target or location. Such gestures draw on the bilateralism of the body, on the experiential schema that we can establish relationships between objects by 'channeling the energy flowing between them', that is, by holding one in each hand. This schema can be abstracted into the domain of pointing.

3.5   Intentional relations

A pointing gesture is easily followed by another, and rather than marking two separate targets or locations, when pointing gestures are made in close succession, they typically display some relation between target and location for example, where an object should go, or between one object and another. In (3.1), we saw Hussein, as he was responding to a 'questioning' pointing gesture by Uncle Ahm, make two two-part pointing gestures, linking 'this' (or, rather, the 'place for this', a socket for a headlight) to a place 'across the street', the junkyard where a headlight is kept. Hussein moved his right hand first toward the socket and then to the back, across the street. Then he pointed the left index finger to the socket and his right index finger to the back, across the street. Often, when two hands cooperate in pointing gestures, they play complementary roles, one referring to an object, the other to a place or destination. The hands project intentional relations between multiple agents, objects, and places. They not only direct someone's attention to an object, but also anticipate that object's relations to other objects within a future course of action. We can call these relations that are established in a course of action— between agent and object, or object and instrument, 'this and that', agent and co-agent, and so on, following Barresi and Moore (1996), *intentional relations*.

In (3.13), the camera follows Hussein as he walks from the front office to a white car in front of the garage that has the hood open. He calls on Victorio, who is inside the garage: 'Done?' When Victorio answers, 'yeah', Hussein points his right hand toward the engine and aims his left, palm forward, at Victorio, in a 'stop' gesture, and says: 'your mixture, you adjust

Figs. 3.13.1–4 'Get that. We can get the reading on this.'

mixture?'. One hand focuses the car, the other presents Victorio with a sign that signifies 'stop, done'. Here, a referential gesture is combined with a predicative one, and together they figure an abstract sense of 'this is done'. The right retains its pointing posture throughout the following dialogue (until line 7), and the left hand remains in a gesture-ready position. Finally, Hussein points his left hand to the shop and says, 'get that' (Fig.3.13.3). What 'that' refers to is never stated, presumably the strobo-scope that is subsequently used to read the car's R.P.M.

(3.13)
1 Hussein   Do:ne?
                (2.0)
2 Victorio   Yeah
3 Hussein   Your mixture, you adjust mixture?
4 Victorio   (   )
5 Hussein   And the mixture, we just did mixture ever-
6   Get that,
7   we can get the reading on this (.) here.
                (0.6)
8   Will you hook it on and we'll get the R.P.M. also.

The only linguistic markings of a relationship between the two objects are the demonstratives 'that' and 'this', which imply a distinction between degrees of proximity to the speaker. The speaker's body, however, embodies their relationship more explicitly and indicates their connection in a future course of action: the object Victorio is directed to fetch will be used in the location Hussein's other hand singles out. The intentional structure of the activity is thereby made visible.

In (3.14), incidentally, Hussein's pointing gesture also relates to 'mixture'. Hussein interacts with a customer who has returned with his truck

Figs. 3.14.1–5 'I'm gonna put this on the machine.'

because he is unhappy with the way it has been tuned. Hussein points to the car when he says 'mixture', and to the shop when he refers to the machine where he will check it.

(3.14)
1   H   I don't wanna do it by listening
2   I'm anna put th•is on the machine
3   R   Good deal
            [
4   H   and do it right
5   H   I should just get eight hundred R P M:
6   set • the timing right
       (- - -)
7   H   by • specification I will get the • book
8   of this (year's)
          [
9   R   Yeah.
10   Just so (- -) that I get enough gas
       [
11   H   and • get the mixture right

Here, as well, the intentional structure of future activity is laid out by the gestures: the truck will be moved inside the shop, to the machine. This is the prospective structure of the situation. Until then, nothing can be said about the mixture. In other words, the pointing serves a purpose within an argument.

In (3.15), Hussein holds up a form as he explains to me, 'those going to salvage auction'. Holding up the form may be a way of exhibiting what is written on them: inscriptions that identify 'those' cars. This action, both

Figs. 3.15.1–2 Pointing with a document, pointing with a finger

curious and entirely commonplace, selects the cars as both real and symbolic entities: the real cars are pointed *at*, their symbolic representations on
the sheets are exhibited and pointed *with*. The listener gets a glimpse of an
activity system in which car bodies must routinely be matched to 'sign
bodies', that is, to paper documents (called 'titles') that are unique, irre-
placeable physical bodies.

(3.15)
1   H   Those going to sa•lvage auction now the•se car.

The bureaucratic existence of the cars is certified by and contained in the
titles Hussein has in his hand. When the cars cease their existence at the
salvage auction, so will their titles. They become meaningless pieces of paper.

Pointing gestures, then, can position the subject in relation to a field of
concern; turning to the side and raising an arm, holding it and then aiming
the other arm somewhere else can display the spatiotemporal embeddedness of the person in a field of action. Pointing gestures, their sequence and
bilateral simultaneity, can incorporate and express the anticipated unfolding of a situation, the ways in which objects will enter into relations with
one another. Similarly, pointing gestures can designate and map out relations between interactants. We are all familiar with being goaded and
guided into a room, a cluster of people, and an interaction by inviting,
guiding, and pointing hands. In (3.16), Hussein goads a visitor into interacting with the researcher. The pictures tell the story of this forging of an
engagement. Hussein's pointing gestures define a path for an engagement
between others.

(3.16)
1   H   Ask him ask him!
2   Uh-huh, go ahead, ask him.

3.6   Self-emplacement

Like everyone else, Hussein, when he points in some direction (say,
'across the street') and perhaps formulates where he is pointing, implicitly
also defines where *he* is now. We 'read' pointing gestures by following
them *away* from the body. But by pointing into the world, human bodies
also *emplace* themselves: they take a position in relation to, or rather in, the
world. In Bühler's terms, an act of pointing re-anchors the 'origo' (Bühler
1934). But there are close and distant horizons against which Hussein,
through his talk and gestures, emplaces himself. We can gain a sense of

Figs. 3.16.1–5 Forging relations among co-present parties

these horizons in the following three extracts. In (3.17), the researcher had been asking Hussein about some of his employees, and talk has been about Mike, a young apprentice mechanic presently at work inside the shop. Then I ask him about Ashraf, and Hussein explains that, like Mike now in Austin, Ashraf once apprenticed with him in his shop in Saudi Arabia. Hussein points east when he refers to the shop and when he refers to Saudi Arabia. Both gestures roughly point in the correct direction. While neither gesture is made to direct the listener's visual attention to these places—their actual location is of no significance to the talk—

Fig. 3.17.1 'in Saudi Arabia'

Fig. 3.1.17.2 'business across the street'

Fig. 3.17.3 'When he start the business'

inevitably they position the speaker—the 'sign-post' (Bühler 1985) in relation to them. Making such gestures routinely can become a kind of 'dead reckoning' device, aiding the person in keeping track of their location in space.

Fig. 3.17.4 'like Mike now'

Fig. 3.16.5 'he get teach in my business in Saudi Arabia'

(3.17)
1   J   Is he a nephew of yours?
2   H   No, he's from my country;
3   he used to work in my business in Saudi Ar•abia
4   and now he run b•usiness, with Hass, across the street.
5   J   Oh, so he's worked for you for a long time
6   H   Yeah, long time he used to work in my business
         (0.4)
7   When he st•art the business
8   J   Uh huh=
9   H   =he ha-
10   like M•ike now
11   he don't know nothing
12   we teach him
13   He: get t•each in my business in Saudi Arabia.
14   He start=
14 J   =Oh really

When Hussein goes on to explain that Ashraf now runs the business 'across the street' with Hassan (Hass), he briefly glances and points across the street. In this sequence, Hussein situates himself and the person he is talking about in the world at large and the world around him. 'Across the street' is a frequent anchor point for Hussein, in either of the shop's two locations on opposite sides of the avenue.

In (3.18), Hussein and Alex are working on an Audi that a succession of technicians has been unable to start. Hussein is in the process of removing the starter cable and the starter cap and believes he has discovered the cause of the problem: the people across the street have put in the wrong cable. He points his index finger across the street just before he says 'across the street'. This combination of verbal and gesture phrase is almost automatic for him.

(3.18)
1 Alex   Let me put this
2 Hussein   Hold on
             (2.0)
3 Hussein   Sure those we lose power like this, you know tha:t?
4 Alex   Uh-huh.
5 Hussein   That's why they'll- across the street they have problem.
             (1.3)
6 Alex   Like this
                  [
7 Hussein   You got this wire and the • cap from across the street?
8 Alex   Uh huh=
9 Hussein   =That's wrong.

(The gesture does not coincide with the phrase 'across the street', but rather with reference to the starter cap: it *prepares* reference to 'across the street'.)

Fig. 3.18 Pointing 'across the street'

Figs. 3.19.1–3 Pointing to a past encounter

Anchoring (or self-emplacement) by pointing gestures at Hi-Tech typically happens during activities that involve forward motion. Pointing often means pointing ahead, targeting a next or future site or object of concern, indicating the path of the activity through the shop. Pointing to the back can refer to the site of action one is moving away from, and thus to the past. In (3.21), Hussein has inspected a Corsica with his nephew Omar. They now move on and Hussein keeps pointing to the car. Then, moving on, he calls on Uncle Ahm, changes hands, and continues to point backward with his thumb.

(3.19)
1   H   (- - • - -)
2   Uncle Ah:m!
          (2.0)
3   You got the part • for the Corsica.
          (1.0)
4   Corsica part.
5   Yester•day, junkyard, they bring Corsica part.

In this fashion, Hussein, we might say, stays 'moored' to the place as he moves about. As a pointer, his arm, to cite a dictum by Wittgenstein (1953), points both ways: as it points to a target, it also positions and anchors its owner in relation to the target.

3.7   Gestures of authority

In (3.20), Hussein touches Mike by the shoulder, then points to a customer ('him'), then to the shop, and subsequently to a red Honda. Here, Hussein's two-handed act incorporates an intentional relation between the acting body of Mike and the place of Mike's action, and this intentional relation is itself recursively embedded in Hussein's relations with Mike and the beneficiary of Mike's future actions, his customer. In other words, by directing Mike in this way, Hussein takes

Fig. 3.20.1 'You can't go nowhere'

Fig. 3.20.2 'just give him ride'

Fig. 3.20.3 'and come to me'

Fig. 3.20.4 'because I'm not settled yet'

Fig. 3.20.5 'Take the red Honda'

action in the context of his own relationship with his customer, and Mike becomes an instrument in it. An 'instrumental' stance toward Mike's body, though held in respectful restraint, is embodied in Hussein's gestures. Finally, with the other hand, he summonses Art.

Fig. 3.20.6 'the red Honda over there'

Fig. 3.20.7 'Come in, Art'

(3.20)
1   H   You can't • go nowhere
2   just • give him ride and come • to me
3   because I'm not se•ttled yet.
4   Take • the red Honda.
         (- -)
5   The red • Honda over there to give him ride.
6   Come in • Art.

Not always do pointing gestures, then, only serve to direct and structure the addressee's attention. Occasionally we can see Hussein hold a pointing gesture beyond the point in time when the listener has clearly identified the target, or when there is no need to direct his attention at all. In (3.21), Kenneth is approaching from the office and alerts Hussein to the activities of a customer: 'What's the customer gonna do with that?'. He self-interrupts and completes the utterance with a pointing gesture. We can only see Hussein's torso, and we see him turning around. He answers, somewhat angrily, 'check what he's doing; go find out.' He is briefly off camera, but when we see him again he has adopted a signpost posture, aiming his left arm and hand in the direction of the suspicious customer. He holds his arm still while he tells Kenneth that there still are things to be done with the car (before it can be sold.) As is common for him (see Chapter 7), he motivates the directive, but his continued pointing gesture also embodies his authority in the situation, his ability as principal of the auto shop to tell his employees what to do. The arm remains extended, displaying the continued 'conditional relevance' of complying with his command. Then (line 6), Hussein steps forward, extends his index finger again, and asks Kenneth 'Is this the owner?' Then he lowers his hand.

(3.22)
1	Kenneth	What's the customer gonna do with that?- •
2	Hussein	Check what he's doing
3		go find out.
		(0.6)

Figs. 3.21.1–4 A gesture of authority

4   what he's doing in the car
5   We • need to make- to mechani-• clean again that car•.
6   Is that the owner
7   Kenneth   Uh huh, she wants to buy it.
8   Hussein   We can't sell it.

Hussein's pointing gesture is evidently not made to alert Kenneth to an event—after all, it was Kenneth who alerted him to it—but it is rather a component of a directive sequence, directing Kenneth to take action: 'Go find out.' Pointing gestures are too narrowly conceived as acts geared only toward directing attention; often, they are made when the speaker, rather, directs someone to *do* something. They are directive, not only directional. Of course, directing attention itself means directing someone to do something, namely to shift gaze (or listen for a sound), but this is distinct from pointing acts that, having focused the addressee's attention, then become implicated in the interactional machinery for transferring agency to someone else. We will return to this in Chapter 7. However, it is relatively rare for Hussein to take on this iconic posture of authority. Far more commonly, from the first moments, he rather embodies his authority in the shop by pointing gestures that are made in motion and that direct others toward an activity in which he will then also participate, a situation captured in the cover photograph.

3.8   Conclusion

In the previous chapter, we observed Hussein looking; in this chapter, we have investigated how he directs the gaze of others. Pointing must be one of the most ancient communication practices of the human species, given how essential it is to the coordination of attention, movement, and action in so many forms of physical cooperation. It is fundamental to knowing and making an *Umwelt* together, to sharing perceptual experience and information. Tomasello (2006) claims that among the great apes, only humans point to share information, others only to make requests. Pointing in the human fashion, he argues, requires an understanding of the information needs of others, empathy, even 'Theory of Mind'.[4] Pointing is the most

---

[4] 'Theory of Mind' is a neo-Cartesian explanation of understanding other minds. 'Theory of Mind' is conceived as an innate 'theory' according to which other minds have the same desires and motives as one's own; Baron-Cohen (1995); Dunbar (1998). Evidently, this account is incompatible with an interactional, pragmatist account of mind, and of understanding other minds, as it was envisioned by G. H. Mead (1934), which guides the present work.

extensively researched and best-understood gesture practice (Kita 2003a). How pointing practices reflect cultural systems of spatial cognition and wayfinding (Levinson 2003), what body parts are used for pointing and under what conditions in various cultures (Enfield 2009), as well as the sequential order of pointing actions (Stukenbrock 2015), have been described with great precision.

We have found the elementary structure of pointing sequences realized in Hussein's interaction with Ms. Nancy, when he showed her the smoke coming out of her car, and with Cedric, in which the two men pointed to 'these tires' and 'those tires'. Pointing was prepared by a turn of the head and eyes to the target, and the pointing gesture itself coupled with a shift of gaze to the addressee, whose gaze direction indicates whether she sees the target. When this did not seem to be the case, Hussein added gestures to fine-tune the addressee's line of regard. Pointing gestures were occasionally confirmed by return pointing gestures, aiming at the same target. We have also found many minor pointing gestures, which Quintilianus ([1922] 100) labeled 'gesture pronouns'; they refer anaphorically to objects, characters, or places that have already been introduced into the discourse or are taken to be common knowledge. We saw an example in Hussein's interaction with the delivery man, when he slightly turned his head and made a thumb-pointing gesture in the direction of the shop floor, as he referred to Arturo. 'Small' pointing gestures do not require a shift in the addressee's visual attention, only recognition of the direction of the point.

That humans have two arms enables them to relate objects to other objects, locations, or actors, and when the head is added, trilateral relations can be displayed. 'Full' pointing gestures elevate an object-figure from a ground. But they are only one among many practices by which such elevation can be achieved. When the target is at hand, other methods are used, each fitted to the material context and the type of object under scrutiny: a cable is raised a little bit and held, a spark plug is tapped, a radiator knocked on. Each of these acts serves the same purpose as a pointing gesture: a target is brought to the addressee's attention. But instead of constituting schematized, culturally standardized practices as are involved in 'pointing proper', here we rather find improvisational, adaptive solutions to the spotlighting task at hand. In fact, 'spotlighting' recommends itself as a more embracing term to refer to all of those practices of which pointing by hand is a subset.

When the hand is used for pointing, modifications of its shape can lend the gesture the additional capacity of making the target appear in a particular light, of framing the *aspect* under which the target is to be seen: as discrete individuals or a set, as a part or a whole, and so on. Pointing gestures that have these features thus participate in the human *construal* of the world within sight (or within earshot). They show, if in a minor way, what *kinds* of phenomena there are to be seen or otherwise attended.

Finally, I have named a few of Hussein's 'full' pointing gestures 'gestures of authority', to allude to the fact that they do more than directing and framing attention, namely directing the *actions* of others, or directing others to act. They are embodied directives and, when accompanied by speech, typically couple with directives. That a pointing gesture carries this force can be gleaned from the response it elicits: whether the addressee just shifts gaze or 'gets going' to take action; as well as from its timing. When is the pointing hand withdrawn—when the addressee shifts gaze or when he initiates practical action? When Kenneth did not 'get going' in response to Hussein's prolonged pointing gesture, Hussein said, 'Go find out!' Performing such directive gestures is an *entitlement*, which comes with the rank Hussein occupies within the shop, the *institution* Hi-Tech Automotive. Like looking, pointing is deeply implicated in the social order, in the reproduction of a stratified organization.

Finally, we have seen how pointing can be extended to become an order, an embodiment of the demand that something be done by the other. It is thus an embodiment of what one can consider a particular form of social (interpersonal) agency that consists in the entitlement to transfer physical agency to another person: making P do X. The authority the gesture embodies at Hi-Tech and elsewhere is the authority of someone entitled to choose actions for others and expect that they will be taken. Adopting a pointing *posture* is thus an icon of this form of authority, embodying 'go do X'. It is (a component) of what, following Taylor (2013), I call *transactions*, acts that have institutional force. I will return to Hussein's embodied agency in Chapter 7.

Pointing at Hi-Tech Automotive is often an element of more complex, manipulative explanations of engines and car parts. Hussein calls these explanations 'showing'. How he shows it is the subject of the next chapter.

4   Showing

Pointing is always a part of those interactions that Mr. Chmeis calls *showing*: the hands-on illumination of a defective auto part or of the way an auto part functions in context. Showings emerge frequently from diagnostic manipulations when these are observed by another person. They are of paramount importance in the dissemination of automotive knowledge at Hi-Tech. Mr. Chmeis has a battery of practiced methods of showing at his disposal, gestures as well as explicative manipulations, ways of handling objects so as to highlight their physical properties, affordances, and proper and improper uses. A sample of such practices is described in this chapter. Their close analysis reveals that key to the way hands communicate in the 'manipulatory zone' (Schutz 1982: 306) is *sensory transformation* or 'transmodality': tactile, haptic, and enactive experiences are visualized, gesturalized, and thus enfolded in shared symbols. This chapter also describes another mode of showing that is rare on this day at the auto shop, depiction, the gestural representation of scenes and objects beyond the here and now. There is evidence that this is not a favorite mode of communication in this workplace; the preference is for indexical, hands-on communication.

4.1   Showing chokes

When we use the verb 'point' with a human subject, we commonly refer to a pointing gesture. Of course, the verb can also take other, inanimate subjects ('The arrow points north.'). At times, when we refer to a pointing event, we use the verb 'show' ('He showed me the way north.'). By referring and pointing to the smoke coming out of Ms. Nancy's car, Hussein 'shows her the smoke'. The verb 'show' has a far greater range of applications in English than 'point'; it can take any number of categorical subjects and objects and, in contrast to 'point', that- and how-complements ('This utterance shows that Hussein articulates Hi-Tech Automotive in nonstandard fashion.'). Hussein himself uses the verb 'show', when he speaks of himself, in a distinct and coherent fashion: it means explaining something to a customer or technician *in the immediate presence of a car* (or car-related object). It means 'illumination'. And he regards pointing as a sub-activity of showing. He says to Ms. Nancy, 'I don't have anything to point it; I wanna show you something.' And showing requires watching. Hussein continues, 'Watch this.' This chapter is about that kind of activity.

At the beginning of the last chapter, we observed Hussein run a test to find out why Ms. Nancy had trouble starting her car: he asked her daughter to turn the ignition and then to 'push gas more', and the result was smoke, an indication that the car was using too much gas and the choke might be the underlying problem. He now proceeds to inspect the carburetor with the choke under Ms. Nancy's observant gaze. We see his index finger moving toward the carburetor, almost touching it, and then held in place while Hussein looks up to Ms. Nancy, monitoring her gaze. He finds it focused on the carburetor. He tells her to 'see' and 'watch'. He curls his index finger and points his middle finger to the choke. He lightly taps it, then gives up and retracts his hand: 'I don't have anything to point it; I wanna show you something.'

(4.1.–1)
```
10    Somebody • clogged the choke by accident.
11    You see • what's happened here,
12    watch this.
      (2.0)
13    I don't have anything to point it.
14    I wanna show you something.
      (11.0)
```

Figs. 4.1.1–2 Hussein directs Ms. Nancy's attention to the choke

Hussein goes to get a screwdriver to be used as a pointing tool. He points it at the choke and suggests that somebody 'opened this to do some work', as he makes a 'palm up' presentational gesture with the other hand (see Chapter 5). Then he removes the air filter.

(4.1.–2)
15 Probably, for some reason,
16 you asked for help
17 or you open this to do some work
18 to think you can fix the car.
   (1.0)
19 And somebody did mistake,
20 I wanna show you where the mistake.
   (1.5)

Hussein nearly pokes his index finger into the opening where the choke is located, tapping it: 'this here' (Fig.4.1.4). Then he adds a verbal-gestural predicate: he raises his hand and opens it, palm down, the fingers spread widely, the hand in rotation (Fig.4.1.5). This gesture shows what he calls 'flipping', that is, rotating an object by 90 or 180 degrees.

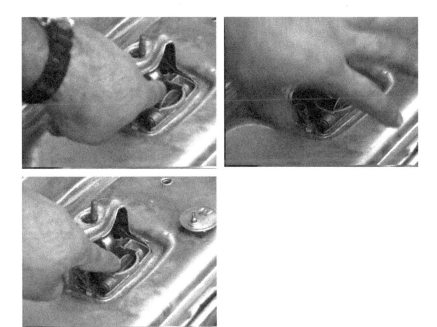

Figs. 4.1.3–5 Hussein points to the choke and shows how the bracket was 'flipped'

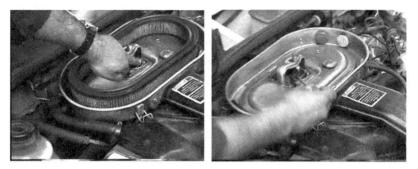

Figs. 4.1.6–7 Pointing without and with tool

As will now be revealed, 'this here', the target of Hussein's pointing, is the *inner carburetor bracket* (ICB), underneath which sits the choke, which must be able to change position according to the engine's temperature, but whose movement can be obstructed by a misplaced or unsecured bracket. Hussein tries to show the possible misplacement of the ICB by two index-finger pointing gestures, the first to the frontside of the choke, coupled with 'this' (line 22, Fig.4.1.6). Hussein tries but gives up to point to the other side as well: his hand aims for the location but is retracted. Instead, his right hand appears, holding the screwdriver, which he inserts underneath the outer carburetor bracket so that its tip turns the choke and reaches the opposite side (Fig.4.1.7). (The choke is a round, quarter-sized thin metal plate; Hussein's finger touches it in Fig.4.1.5 above.)

(4.1.–3)
21   This • he:re (- -) they • flip it
22   and it came here in between • this and- (.)• thi::s
      (- - - - - - - - - - - - - - - • - - - - - - -)
23   and they clo:se it.

Hussein now lifts the lower half of the air filter container so that the ICB becomes accessible and comes into view. For nine seconds, Hussein's hand is obscured by his arm. When it comes back into view (as he says 'by accident', line 28), we see it holding the ICB, as Hussein says 'I just pick up like this' (Fig.4.1.8). Hussein retracts his hand, picks the ICB up again and turns it 90 degrees so that Ms. Nancy can appreciate how, as a result of such mis-positioning, the ICB could have closed the choke (line 21, Fig.4.1.9–10). He takes the ICB in his hand, holding it with his three outer fingers, and uses the thumb to, again, show how the ICB would close the choke

Fig. 4.1.8 'I just pick up like this.'

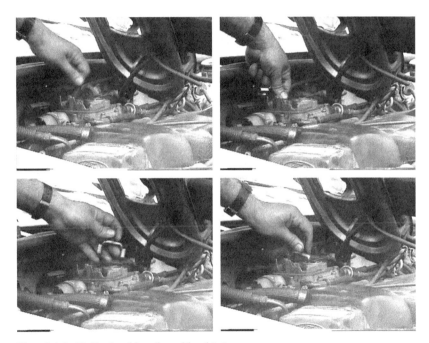

Figs. 4.1.9–12 'It should go here like this.'

(Figs.4.1.11–12). Two methods for showing states and actions, manipulating the object and performing a gesture, are enacted in alternation (see also LeBaron & Streeck, 2000). Hussein repeats the gestural and the manipulative display, the latter several times. Then he reinserts the ICB in its right position, as he announces that he will 'do something to make it stick here'.

(4.1.–4)
24		This (- -) I just pick up this like •this
		(- - - -)
25		It should go here like this.
		(1.0)
26		You see?
		(1.0)
27	Ms. Nancy	Kathy di:d?
28	Hussein	By • accident.
29		That's why it make no power,
30		it's • closed on the cho•ke he•re.
31		It's close the choke like this, you see?
		(- - -)
32	Ms. Nancy	Oh, but before ( )
		[
33	Hussein	By accident somebody did this.
		(- - - -)
34		Like this.
		(- - - -)
35		Like this.
36		You push ga:s it won't accelerate good.
37		But I wanna do something to make it stick here now.

We see pointing give way to manipulative action as Hussein strives
to bring relevant features of the carburetor (specifically: the choke-ICB
'subsystem') into Ms. Nancy's view: its affordances (how it can be
positioned and mis-positioned), that is, what can but should not be
done with the ICB, as well as the operation of this car part in the
context of other, interlocking parts. The differences between these
two modes of action, pointing and showing (in the specific sense in
which I use the term here), are gradual: pointing leads to tapping, which
becomes holding the choke in place. A more precise term to refer to
these semi-gestural activities than 'showing' would perhaps be the
phenomenologists' 'disclosing' (Dreyfus 1991), because these are
actions and practices geared toward testing and revealing the *dispositions*
of objects, unveiling hidden parts, and gathering such local data
together in a haptic and visual understanding of the object at hand.
Heidegger, to whom this term is attributable, rightly insists that disclosing is not the result of communication, nor does it require consciousness. Every act discloses something about its object or instrument
and context. 'Disclosure' is a feature of human action. (The same point
has been made by ethnomethodologists; Garfinkel 1967.) I use the term

'disclosing' in the narrower sense of 'showing', to refer to actions whose very point it is to make public—transparent to a less informed spectator—features of the object at hand that disclose themselves to Hussein during his routine investigative activities. If Hussein were to investigate Ms. Nancy's carburetor alone, his hands would disclose its features to his eyes only. But they would not devote any extra effort to highlighting them, as they do for the benefit of Ms. Nancy. It is this 'extra' that I investigate in this chapter. Showing (by hand) also includes the gestural depiction of worlds not presently seen. This otherwise common practice was rare on this day at Hi-Tech Automotive, but we will nevertheless look at a few depictions by gesture at the end of this chapter.

4.2   The antenna hand[1]

We can distinguish between two kinds of showing by hand. On one hand we find manipulative practices that disclose hitherto undisclosed features of objects and settings, making them apparent or transparent, that is disclosing them. On the other are gesture methods by which reality is, in a sense, 'augmented': the gestures show what *can* be done or elucidate what transparently needs to be done, or what was done, and thereby augment the visible world at hand by visual sketches of future or past action. Gesture practices of the first kind are *exploratory practices* by which humans gather sensory knowledge (Gibson 1962; Klatzky & Lederman 1990; Streeck 2009a: ch.4) or are abstracted from them. Those of the second kind are abstracted versions of other types of action that the object at hand, in its present or a possible state, affords.

Some of the most common forms of exploratory action are those of the 'antenna hand' (Napier 1980), a hand configured for the gathering of tactile sensations as it travels along a path. In (4.2), Hussein's fingertip probes dirt—or what lies underneath it (Fig.4.2). While Ms. Nancy is watching him, he makes tactile information vicariously available to her: revealing what is underneath the surface, the finger alludes to a possible cause of the dirt (oil?). The exploratory act, not in any way different from what it would be were Hussein inspecting the car by himself, is intelligible and needs no elaboration.

[1] Napier (1980).

Fig. 4.2 Hussein senses dirt

Fig. 4.3 Hussein explains the battery tester

(4.2)
1   H   This kind of dirt
        (- - -)
2   I wanna clean little bit.

Better suited than an antenna index finger for gathering *thermal* information is a flat hand. How that hand is held and moved can convey to
spectators the warmth or heat it feels. When Hussein is testing the charging
system of Ms. Nancy's car and holds the tester in his left hand, his flat right
hand, held frozen until then, moves to the tester and touches it ever so
slightly: a method for cautiously exploring—and thus displaying—heat.

(4.3)
1   H   Now I wanna see
        (- - - - - -)
2   if the battery good, okay?
        (1.5)

3   I'm loading the battery
4   we'll look-
5   we heat this
6   it's mean we drain the battery down

Still cradling it in his hand, Hussein then rotates the charger so that Ms. Nancy can see the display. A moment later, he puts his flat hand near one side of the charger, without touching it, responding and alluding to increasing heat. As he rotates it once more, he holds his hand in continuously cautious exploratory position, which has now become an indexical sign for heat. It configures a local experience for the parties and, as a gesture, is reusable (Hutchins & Johnson 2009). Hussein's hand's handling of the battery tester could give rise to a range of displayed senses associated with heat. In sum, gesture can make heat visible.

(4.4)
1   H   And this burn red
2   and this still okay.

Such *sensory transformation*—the recoding of a tactile sensation in visual form—is common whenever gestures disclose significances of the world at hand (and, as we will see in the following chapter, in other modes of gesturing as well). In (4.5), Hussein taps a car part, not to spotlight it, but to produce a sound, which is indicative of a significant feature of this part. Hussein reaches into a slot between the front panel and the radiator of a car (Fig.4.5.1), then taps it from the inside (Fig.4.5.2). In this fashion, he directs Uncle Ahm's gaze to this car part.

Fig. 4.4 'And this burn red'

Figs. 4.5.1–2 'This here Uncle Ahm'

(4.5)
1   H   This here Uncle Ahm
         [reaches]
2   See?
         [taps]

The following is a somewhat different example. The men have moved to the side of the car, and Hussein directs Ahm's attention to the back door ('door', line 1) by knocking on it, as one would do a neighbor's, but rarely a car door. The cultural practice of knocking on doors to be granted entry, the routine coupling between action, sound, and object, is creatively applied here in a simple act of reference in talking to someone who barely speaks English.

(4.6)
1   H   Door?

This is a characteristically opportunistic, adaptive act, responsive to the material the moment offers up. It can serve as a language lesson in which Uncle Ahm learns the word 'door'. In the first place, it is a directive to Ahm to check out and take care of the door.

At another time, Uncle Ahm is standing in front of the hood of a car, which is leaning against the garage wall. He brings his hand to a dent as Hussein is approaching. Arriving, Hussein says. 'There is damage, yeah, because used.' Ahm draws a circle with his index finger, and Hussein brings his flat hand to the dent, moves his hand over it several times so that the tip of his index finger feels its texture, and says, 'need to fix this little bit'. By copying Ahm's indexing gesture, Hussein signifies the sharing of sensory experience. By touching the dent, however, he simultaneously gathers information about its properties: its depth, potentially whether there is a crack, and so forth. This makes the gesture an exploratory action. But because the rest of his hand is spread, 'summing up' the damaged area, the gesture also evokes schematically what is to be done to it. He says, 'Fix this little bit.'

In the meantime, Uncle Ahm has moved on to another, smaller dent in another part of the hood. He brings his hand to it and attracts Hussein's gaze. He draws a circle around this dent as well, as if marking the place where further action will be taken, 'annotating' the object at hand. Hussein confirms this schematic proposal ('yeah', line 4), brings his flat hand in the vicinity of the dent without touching it, and then closes his hand swiftly, projecting a sense of completion (see Chapter 5), as he instructs Ahm to 'put bond'. Ahm annotates yet another problematic area by drawing a snaking line with his index finger, and Hussein swipes his open right hand quickly over that area as well, as he repeats the instruction, applying it to this area as well (line 5).

(4.7)
```
1    Hussein    There is damage, yeah
2               because used.
3               We need to fix this little bit.
                (0.3)
                yeah put bond do ya
5               ( ) put bond do you
```

In this exchange, Hussein moves from performing an exploratory action—the four-finger touch of the dent Ahm has pointed out to him—to an indexical gesture that only hints at such a move but now enfolds the meaning gathered the first time around, projects sense gathered in one area onto another, draws an analogy between them.

Figs. 4.7.1–2 Uncle Ahm and Hussein explore a dent

Figs. 4.7.3–5 'We need to fix this little bit.'

Figs. 4.7.6–7 'Yeah, put bond, do you?'

4.3   Transmodal gestures and the 'logic of sensation'

Murphy has introduced the helpful term 'transmodality' to describe the 'sequential generation of linked semiotic chains' (2012: 1969) in professional communication work that has so far been characterized as 'multimodal'; his case in point is design practice, in which ideas are inscribed and transcribed in a succession of media. Murphy points out that

> [W]ithin these chains, the forms or meanings of given modes do not simply correspond with or support one another, but they also exert some degree of sway over the manifestation of subsequent action. ... Viewed from the perspective of transmodality, modes like speech, drawing, and gestures, ... sequentially perforate and interpenetrate each other, acquiring a certain co-morbid resemblance. When viewed longitudinally the meanings expressed in the different modes dynamically blend, shape, and reshape each other in different ways, and consequentially transform the 'shape' of an emergent interactional product. (Murphy 2012: 1969)

Hussein's practices for showing indicate that even single gestures can have transmodal qualities. Transmodality—transposing sensory experience from one modality to another—is characteristic of the way in which all hand gestures make sense.

To illuminate the transmodality of gesture in the service of showing, we can benefit from Deleuze's *Francis Bacon: Logic of Sensation* (2003), a study of the gestural and representational properties of the brush strokes and other painting actions of Francis Bacon. Deleuze distinguished different ways in which hand and eye interact in Bacon's painterly actions, how, in the words of Sinclair and de Freitas (to appear), 'the eye and the hand compete for control of meaning.' Deleuze called these the digital, tactile, haptic, and manual modes. 'The first term designates situations where the eye dominates the hand, while the next two terms track an increasingly more dominant hand in relation to the eye' (Sinclair & de Freitas to appear: 6). Deleuze argued that,

> [T]o describe the relationship between the eye and the hand, and the values through which this relation passes, it is obviously not enough to say that the eye judges and the hands execute. The relationship between the hand and the eye is infinitely richer, passing through dynamic tensions, logical reversals, and organic exchanges and substitutions. ... There are several aspects in the values of the hand that must be distinguished from each other: the digital, the tactile, the manual proper, and the haptic. (Deleuze 2003: 124)

The digital seems to mark the maximum subordination of the hand to the eye: vision is internalized, and the hand is reduced to the finger; that is, it intervenes only in order to choose the units that correspond to pure visual forms. The more the hand is subordinated in this way, the more sight develops an 'ideal' optical space, and tends to grasp its forms through an optical code. . ... A relaxed subordination of the hand to the eye, in turn, can give way to a veritable insubordination of the hand: the painting remains a visual reality, but what is imposed on sight is a space without form and a movement without rest, which the eye can barely follow, and which dismantles the optical. We will call this reversed relationship the manual. Finally, we will speak of the haptic whenever there is no longer a strict subordination in either direction, either a relaxed subordination or a virtual connection. (Deleuze 2003: 164–165)

Painting by and large is a one-handed activity; the non-dominant hand fulfills ancillary functions. This may have made Deleuze disregard a mode of action and sensation-production of human hands that is principally bi-manual. It is also the most distinctively human mode of using hands: *making*. By 'making', I mean the molding and putting together of artifacts, the ability to make something out of something, productive labor. Making things is a distinctive mode of human action, and it produces distinct kinds of sensations and experiences. Making, or 'the gesture of making' (Flusser 2014), is perhaps the most characteristic type of act of the human life-form. Hand gestures are more thing-like than other forms of communicative bodily action such as gaze shifts and smiles: not only are they made by hands, but they are also discrete, bounded, individuated, and countable, features they share with things. More importantly, the actions of some forms of gesturing, just like the actions of painting, bring into existence phenomena that are representations of other phenomena. The most thing-like gestures are hand postures designed to model things. The human ability to gesture, in other words, is predicated on the human ability to make things, to have created a world of artifacts.

Sense-making by gesture involves varieties of transformation, synthesis (or blending, condensation), and reconfiguration of sensations. Always and inevitably, gestures produce *enactive* sensations—*feelings of action*—in the maker; but they are objects of visual perception to the addressee. Moreover, exploratory gestures can make tactile sensations visible. And gestures, though visual, are capable of generating covert enactions in those who see them (see Chapter 5). McCullough writes that

[W]hereas the eyes stay fixed on the outer surface of things, hands have a way of getting inside, and so they contribute more to our belief in the reality of the world. . . . Hands also discover. They have a life of their own that leads them into explorations. For example, a sculptor's feel for a material will suggest actions to try, and places to cut. Learning through the hands shapes creativity itself. (McCullough 1996: 8)

All of these sensory features and capacities come into play when hands are used to show, to illuminate an object at hand.

4.4 Sharing perception

In the moments of showing we have looked at so far, one party—the one 'in the know'—stages an action or show in an explicative manner for a listener-spectator. As Hussein discovers features of the object at hand, he discloses them—makes them intelligible—to another person. In the next two interactions we visit, what is at issue is the actual *sharing* of sensory experience, or having parallel sensory experiences. The activity gets structured in ways that enable Hussein and his interlocutor to experience, and *make sense* of, tactile features of the object at hand. The first scene is still from Hussein's and Ahm's inspection of the Corsica in which they are figuring out what final touch-ups need to be done before the car can go on sale. At this point, Ahm is scanning the front end, and his gaze fixates on the corner of the radiator. It remains anchored as he steps around the fender to get closer to it. Now, Ahm and Hussein simultaneously reach for the grills, but they do so with different and differently timed actions. While Uncle Ahm takes the grill's rim between thumb and index finger, Hussein reaches under it from the back and feels the inside by moving his four fingers back and forth. He concludes:

Fig. 4.8.1 'Put cover here'

(4.8)

1   H   Put cover here maybe .hhh

Hussein thus gathers tactile sensations, feeling the condition of a relevant part of the grill, but he also repeats and thereby marks the exploratory act, suggesting a certain contextually implied feature. Exploratory act and gesture are one and the same.

Hussein and Ahm take a step back and Hussein bends over, his hands, fingers adducted, reaching forward (Fig.4.8.2). He says:

2   H   This here Uncle Ahm?

He reaches for the radiator behind the grill. Ahm looks intently, and Hussein asks (Fig.4.8.3):

3   H   See?

Fig. 4.8.2 'This here Uncle Ahm?'

Fig. 4.8.3 Uncle Ahm inspects the radiator by hand

Fig. 4.8.4 'Need to push little bit.'

Ahm looks closely, but now Hussein produces acoustic information: he taps the radiator repeatedly, evoking a clanking noise, which, presumably, provides Ahm with insight into the identity of the part that needs fixing, or into a contextual feature, such as the improper arrangement of parts. The interaction becomes manifestly multimodal: visual, tactile, and acoustic resources are configured so that Ahm can see and judge what he sees. Then Hussein retracts his hands and makes room for Ahm to inspect the area up close. After a few seconds, Hussein offers his own diagnosis: he says 'need', raises his right hand, the palm facing Ahm; with 'to', he pushes the palm forward, enacting the schema before naming it; then, retracting his arm, he says 'push little bit'.

4   Need to- (- -) push little bit
5   and put bo:lt.

In this sequence, language and tactile acts are used to elicit an acoustic phenomenon, which in turn is a symptom of the material quality of the unnamed object of concern. Hands and talk recommend targets to the audience's eyes for closer haptic inspection. When interacting with Uncle Ahm, Hussein does not request or require ratified mutual understanding. He trusts that Ahm's hands will find out everything he needs to know to do his job, as other episodes show. In contrast, when Hussein inspects a car with an apprentice, generating the same sensations through the same kinds of actions is more important, because this is also an education in feeling, and the sequences are structured to make parallel feeling possible.

In (4.9), Hussein goes on an inspection walk around a car with Mike. Before they go to the car, Mike formulates his circumstances:

(4.9–1)
1   H   Yes.
2   M   I'm tryin' to finish the (Ford) over there.
3   H   Which, with this?

They walk to the car, and Mike points to a spot on the body, and Hussein points to further spots.

(4.9–2)
4   M   This is ( ) here.
5   H   He:re, and this here.
6   M   Right.

Every time he says 'this' or 'here', Hussein points to a spot, but keeps walking, closely looking at and touching spots on the car. Mike repeatedly

Fig. 4.9.1 Inspection

Fig. 4.9.2 Inspection

Fig. 4.9.3 Inspection

touches and feels the spot that Hussein has touched before him, confirming Hussein's sensation, making it a consciously shared experience.

(4.9–3)

7	H	Come see this
		(1.0)
8	H	fender here.
		(1.4)
9	H	Need to be everything in order.
10		Make sure if you're going to buy the car
11		what you're going to see wrong,
12		correct that.
13		This here, yeah.
		(0.7)
14	H	Everything.
15	H	If there is tha- any paint
16		I saw paint yesterday
		(1.5)
17	H	and one tire,
18		maybe this.
		(3.2)
19	H	He:re
		(1.3)
20	H	We'll go all around these tire
21		maybe clean em little bit

The granularity of shared sensations is finer in the following interaction. Omar has come from Sweden on a three-month apprenticeship with Hussein. Here he shows Hussein a car that has been professionally repainted and only needs a few touch-ups. This requires closer tactile

Figs. 4.10.1–4 Hussein and Omar assess a paint job

inspection. Hussein leans over some areas, runs the tip of his index finger over them, and then demonstrates for Omar what to do. Omar carefully touches every spot that Hussein has touched before. 'Tactile common ground', needed for a shared understanding of a paint job to be done, is achieved through methodical sequential interaction.

(4.1)
1 Hussein: kello mniħ badnā jinaʃef bas halla^q
              all is good we just want it to dry now
              hone• niḍəf [mniħ
              here it's clean [good
2 Omar: [ʔe mā
                         [yes {cause}
              ʃilto bil-ʃu [ʔismo •mā bjinḍaf ʔaktar min hek
              I took it away [with what it's called it can't be cleaned more than this
3 Hussein: [mniħ (0.1) mniħ bas hedi ḍajaʕnejā
                           [good (0.1) good but this we lost it
              miʃ hejk
              isn't it

4 Omar: hajdi ḍāʕit
this was lost
5 Hussein: ba:siṭa
nevermind {not a problem}
6 Omar: niḥna min la^{q}ilnā ʃī sajjāra nafsi-l-euh: tanak
we will find a car same heu: scrap metal
nafsi-l-ʒilid [ʕandā
same leather [{it has}
7 Hussein: [• ʃwajet (0.2) ʃī glue ʕa-hajdi wu
[some (0.2) {like} glue on this one and
Ɣaṭṭīhā b-tilza^{q} ^{q}abəl mā t- jikamlūhā [• ḥadā
cover it you'll glue it before it/ they finished it [someone
8 Omar: [ʃū huwe
[what is it

Thus, in 'disclosing' interactions such as this one people perform active sensory scanning to identify intrinsic object features such as shape, texture, and substance, or the generic category to which an object belongs. To extract these features, we must move our fingers: 'the stimulus has to be a change in time' (Gibson, 1962: 479). It is the *moving* body that feels and communicates its feelings (Streeck 2009a: 52–53).

> By using one's body in the same way as others in the same environment one finds oneself informed by an understanding which . . . remains grounded in a field of practical activity. (Jackson 1989: 135)

4.5 Decomposing

Yet another method of 'explicating' objects is to indexically or figuratively decompose them, that is, to exhibit them as things made of separate parts. In (4.11), we see Hussein's hands adapt differentially to two different parts of a composite object, a headlight and the bracket or 'door' that frames it. The technical term is 'light-door', even though Hussein calls it 'door-light', a mistake that remains unnoticed until later, when he makes a call to order one (see Chapter 6). Hussein is seeking Uncle Ahm's advice. The 'door' is broken, and he wants to know whether the door frame 'is sold separately'. Hussein presents Ahm with the headlight and points several times with his left index finger to a corner and then takes it between thumb and forefinger: he foregrounds one part of the headlight by a precision grip. Then he taps

Figs. 4.11.1–2 'Uncle Ahm, they sell this separate you think?'

the glass with the hand. The pointing gestures and precision grip separate the headlight door (the figure) from the headlight (the ground), which is marked by a wide, flat hand, referring to the entire object to whose shape it is fitted. As we saw in Chapter 3, differences in hand shape during pointing gestures can display different aspects under which objects can be seen. In this case, the contrast between index pointing/precision grip and patting with the flat hand figures the semantic contrast between specificity and entirety.

(4.11–1)
1	Hussein	Uncle Ahm. (-)
2		<u>Uncle Ahm?</u>
3		They sell this separate you think
4	Hussein	The door-light?
		(- - - - - -)

Now Hussein says, 'this junkyard but broken', and repeats, 'they sell door-light separate, you think?', tapping his index finger several times along the length of the light-door and elevating it from the headlight, highlighting its shape. He points a few more times at different parts of the light-door and then fixates his fingertip on one of its corners while moving the headlight closer to Uncle Ahm, waiting for a response. Ahm's answer is incomprehensible to Hussein and the researcher.

(4.11–2)
5		This junkyard but broken.
6	Hussein	They sell door-light separate, you think?
		(3.0)
7	Uncle Ahm	( )

Figs. 4.11.3–4 Selecting the whole and a part

Figs. 4.11.5–6 Specificity: precision grip and pointing

Hussein tries one more time. This time he looks to his left and then makes a pointing gesture toward the Corsica, the car into whose front the headlight will go, and repeats 'door-light'. He taps at the light-door and then takes one corner between index finger and thumb again: 'this door-light broken'. Then he pats the glass one more time as he refers to the (entire) 'light' (line 11).

(4.11–3)
```
 8   Hussein   Door-light.
 9             This door-light broken.
10             They sell them at dealer's separate-
11             We got the light from junkyard.
               (1.0)
12             But we need the door-light.
```

Figs. 4.11.7–8 Selecting a part, figuring the whole

The fact that Hussein repeats the same illumination procedures several times may indicate that no others are at his disposal, that he has no practiced methods for dealing with this type of understanding problem, where the other person is incapable either of understanding him or of displaying his understanding in a manner that he, Hussein, can understand. The interaction remains unsuccessful: there is no intelligible response from Uncle Ahm and Hussein resorts to letting him simply try to fit the headlight into its socket, allowing him to discover with his own hands the nature of the problem. (Later, Hussein goes on and orders a new head light-door anyway.)

We see two distinct actions, each of which elevates or focuses one part of the object. The actions are haptically adapted, coupled with conspicuous affordances: a small 'rim' (the 'door') elicits a fingertip (precision) grip, a plane (the glass) couples with a flat hand. The gestures construe the objects as a compound of two distinct parts. They show it as a composite object. In the present case, this 'compositionality' is in some sense itself in question: 'They sell this separate, you think?'

4.6   Augmenting reality by 'action figures'

In the auto shop, discovering and disclosing what is the case often leads to an immediate decision and display of what is to be done, and while spoken commands certainly do most of that work, particulars of an instruction may be delivered by the hands, or the hands may perform a formulaic gesture that, superimposed on the area of concern, allows it to be seen as a stage for kinds of action. Perhaps the most frequent and generic action schema (or family of actions schemas) by which Hussein 'marks up' a field is a wiping or circular motion with the palm facing the target area. Because it routinely co-occurs with spoken directives in Hussein's communication, we could call it the 'make sure' or 'finish everything' gesture.

In (4.12), Hussein is talking to Art at a car both Art and Ahm are working on; moving his arm toward a fender, he says:

(4.12)
1 H   I want to just to make s•ure
2   the door back together
3   because he don't know how to put the wires

In Chapter 5, I will refer to this typified gesture as WIPE.

When Mike shows Hussein the work he has done on a trunk and asks his permission to take the car to the car wash, Hussein wants him to finish the other work first. His directive, 'finish before the interior', is coupled with the WIPE gesture.

Fig. 4.12 Hussein's 'make sure' gesture

Fig. 4.13 'Finish'

(4.13)
1   M   Can I go over there real quick and do that?
2   The interior is done already
                                      [
3   H   Fin•ish before the interior
4   everything uh need to- (- -)
5   be fixed without car wash
6   and at the end I'll let you go out to car wash
7   (- - - -) clean inside
8   and then come by here
9   to wax outside

We see a common figure: a palm-down motion made in reference to a work in progress can carry a sense of 'finish everything, make sure everything'.

But Hussein also makes gestures that profile a *specific* action to be taken, as can be seen in the following two scenes in which Hussein checks up on the work Mike is doing and will do on cars that will be sold. In (4.14), Hussein performs a first action gesture when he searches for the name of a particular type of paint: he rubs index finger and thumb, insinuating the paint's viscosity (Fig.4.14.1). Then he enacts spraying, moving a hand with spread fingers over a part of the trunk (Fig.4.14.2). In other words, the first action gesture is made to evoke an object--or better: a mass-- the second an action the addressee is to take.

Figs. 4.14.1–2 Figuring paint

(4.14)
1	H	If you have any closer paint
2		Or at least uh-
3	M	(Etch it?)
4	H	Uh- no:!
5		The uh- (- - - - - - - - - - - - - - - - -)
6		The-
6		undercoat
7		spray

A minute later the spraying gesture is made again.

(4.15)
1	H	and spray undercoat in this area

Thus, pointing and action figure are near-complete instructions for Mike: deal with this part, do that—a proto-sentence comprising gestural reference and predication.

In (4.16), Hussein scrutinizes the underside of another car near the front wheel. The car is raised above them on the lift. Mike approaches and Hussein says, 'this he:re', pointing to a spot, and looks to Mike, who approaches more rapidly now. Seeing that Mike is focusing on the spot, Hussein returns his gaze to it too, moves his hand a foot to the right, and then drags it twice along the edge back to its prior location, thus modeling in abstract fashion the 'fixing' of the problem, as he says 'need to be'. A moment later he clarifies, 'this here need to be tied all', and grasps the edge of the car at two points, modeling the 'tying'. Mike tries to insert a statement of his own, but is cut off by Hussein (at line 7), who continues with his instructions. He taps another spot with his index finger, then four more along the edge (line 7). He taps and then rubs his index finger in a spot by the wheel, taps once more in the middle of the car, each time identifying a point that needs Mike's present and future attention.

Fig. 4.15 Spray-painting

Figs. 4.16.1–2 Scrutinizing the underside of a car

Figs. 4.16.3 'This here need to be tied all.'

(4.16–1)
```
1   Hussein    • This he:re (- - - - - -) needs to be ( - - - - • - - - - -) all fixed
                                                      [
2   Mike                                              (All-)
3              Okay
4   Hussein    This here need to be • tied all.
5   Mike       I see a we' (     )
               (0.3)
6               But uh-
                [
7   Hussein    That need to be tied, look • here, all these
                                            [
8   Mike                                   Uh huh
```

Fig. 4.16.4 Split orientation: directing attention, monitoring response

9   Hussein   Even this here should have something
10   we need to figure what should have.

Gestures and talk combine to project a layer of significance onto the underside of the car; Hussein instructs Mike what to notice, how to see. Gestures such as these 'transform settings into "spaces of possibilities" and enable the shared understanding of the "involvement-whole"' (Dreyfus, 1991: 189) of the activity.

In (4.17), Hussein and Mike are inspecting the trunk of another car. Mike is explaining to Hussein what he has done and what he thinks he still needs to do. Here, Mike's gestures are of interest. At the beginning, Mike moves his left hand, fingers spread and palm facing down, in irregular patterns above the floor of the trunk; this action displays the large, unbounded area where the carpet was dirty (line 4). Then he turns the hand, which is still open, up, making a presenting gesture; a little upward stroke is added when he utters 'change' (the seats), a minimal display of removal, and then he configures his hand to a power grip, the posture with which one holds many tools and instruments, and moves it about the trunk, showing the action of vacuuming the carpet. Although vacuuming is never mentioned, it is shown and understood.

(4.17–1)
1   Mike   The interior was really clean and this rear light
2   all this is fine,=
3   Hussein   =Yeah.
              [
4   Mike   Maybe the carpet is so di•rty,
5   I don't wanna cha•nge the seats

6   because it ta•kes too long
7   'n I have to work full-time.
8   You know.
9   At the c•ar-wash it's real quick
10   and it p•icks up all the dirt and •
             [
11 Hussein Yeah.

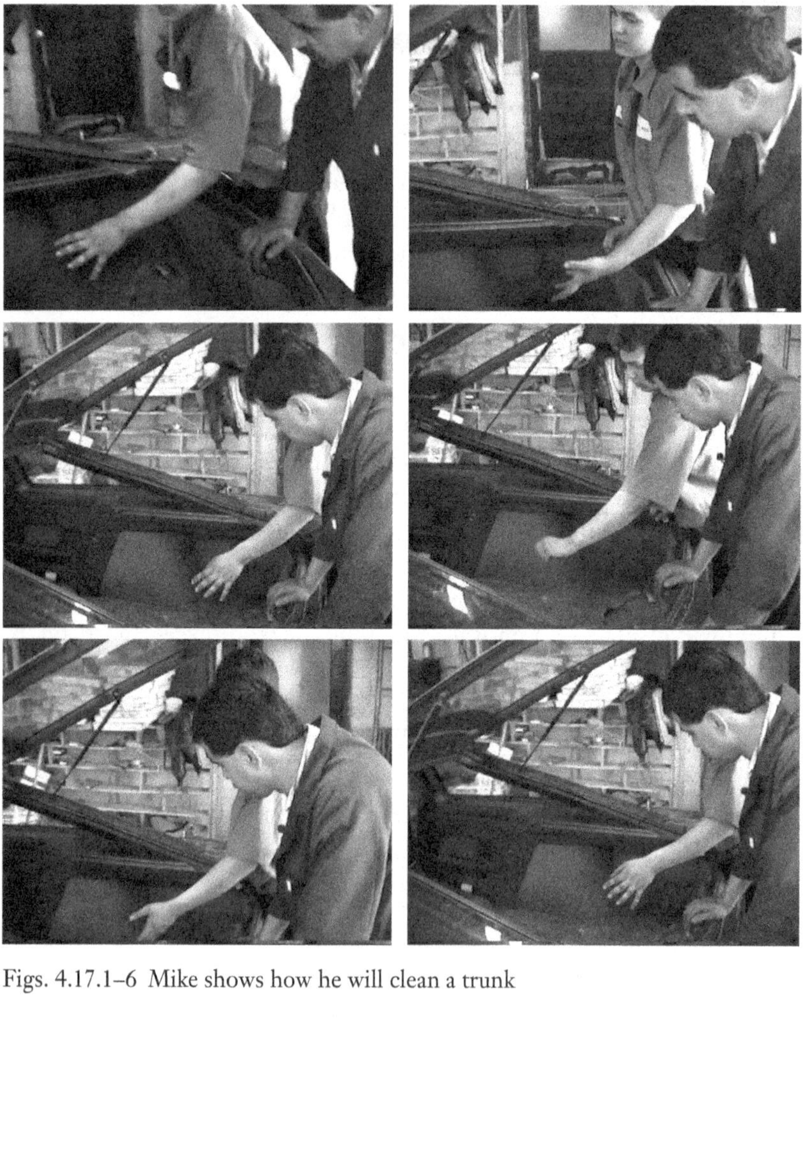

Figs. 4.17.1–6 Mike shows how he will clean a trunk

A moment later, Hussein discovers and then grasps a bolt on the left side of the back door and asks, 'what this bolt here for'? Immediately, Mike puts his open hands to both sides of the open hatchback door and then quickly, the index fingers now extended, to the tracks inside the trunk where these bolts go, and moves them back, forth, and back, along the tracks. In this fashion he insinuates the movement of the bolts in the tracks when the hatchback is opened and closed, and gives a visual account of their function.

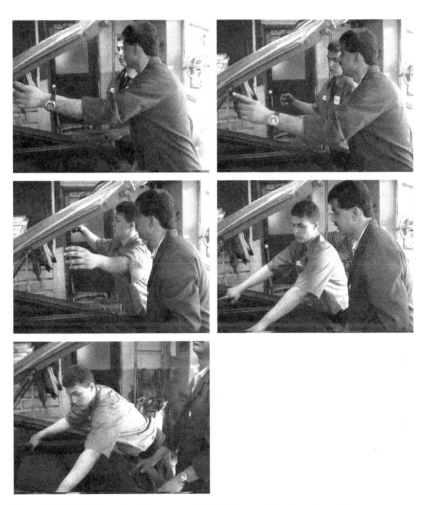

Figs. 4.17.7–11 Hussein discovers a bolt; Mike explains how it works.

Fig. 4.17.12 'just inspect everything'

(4.17–2)
1   Hussein   • What this bolt here for.
2   Need to go ins•ide?
3   Mike   Oh no, there's- an (- - - - • - - - - - - -)
4   Hussein   Something to hang from this?
5   Mike   For the co•ver right he•re.
6   Hussein   Okay. (- -) You just inspect everything.

Human hands are extremely well suited to illuminating the world at hand, which, after all, they know so well. They find solutions to the task of enhancing what is there with ease: elaborating actions to make them more conspicuous, extracting an object's features and giving them visible form, providing concrete versions of abstract instructions ('make sure'). Naturally, gestural and manipulative practices of the 'showing' type are indispensable from apprenticeship, the transmission of both embodied and factual knowledge.

4.7   Another kind of showing: depiction

Conversations that take place in the setting that they are also about have been studied for a much shorter time than those taking place at the dinner table or in other, 'leisurely' settings where the world talked about is not immediately present. In auto shops, and presumably many similar places, exemplars of relevant categories of objects are often available, and there is no need to represent them. The object in question—or, if not it, a replica—is almost always at hand. Depiction, as I have described it elsewhere (Streeck 2008a, 2009), is thus comparatively rare at Hi-Tech Automotive, or, at any rate, was on the day I filmed.[2] But spareribs

---

[2] Machinists often have elaborate repertoires for manually explicating the workings of an engine, even in the absence of the engine. It is entirely possible that Hussein utilizes similar methods in similar situations, but I have no videotaped evidence for this.

are not among the objects available for a *demonstratio ad oculos*; they
need to be retrieved from the butcher shop across the street. One of
the few moments of extended gestural depiction occurs when Hussein
instructs his sons to go and get ribs for a barbeque on the weekend.
Hussein is keen to show their approximate size and cut. He makes
a 'bounding' gesture (a HOLD, see Chapter 5), that shows the desired
size (width) of the meat. With the index finger Hussein then draws cut
lines into the virtual meat in front of him, and subsequently performs
a series of evenly spaced cuts.

Figs. 4.18.1–6 Hussein depicts the spareribs Ali is supposed to buy; Ali shows that
he understands

(4.18)

1	H	Ali, Mumken namel smoking yal weekend?
		Ali, perhaps there's going to be a barbecue this weekend?
2		Rooh yand el laham honeek ou shoof aza yandon ri•bs.
		Go to the butcher over there and see if they have ribs.
3		Bas sh•ahef ezgheereh.
		But small pieces.
4		Jhiblak shi yashreen pound aza yandon.
		Bring about twenty pound if they have it.
5	Ali	Ayya naw?
		What kind?
6	H	Mish kteer, ma e koon kteer kabeer, ey'yes ezgheer.
		N•ot a lot, n•ot too big, the sm•all size.
7	A	Mish lem atyeen ezgheer.
		Not the o•nes they've cut into small pie•ces.
8	H	Fe ematyeen ezgheer kil wahdeh hek, lahk.
		There are ones that are cut into small pieces, each one like this, no.
9	H	Ribs le halad kil shakfeh, mish hek.
		I want ribs where each piece is this much, not like this.

Ali shows his understanding by holding a 'rib' of proper size in front of him and cutting it with his flat hand (rather than the index finger, as Hussein did). Occasionally, Hussein mimes or reenacts events, as in a playful interaction with a delivery woman getting his signature: he reenacts his reaction and others' reaction when, as he was backing out a car into the driveway, he 'almost hit her'.

(4.19)

1	H	You know what?
2		You almost involve me in big accident.
3	D	Oooooooooooh (what's that).
4	H	You're lucky.
5		You're just-
6		I get inside this ca:r
7	D	Uhhh
8	H	and nobody behind me
9		and then I put reverse to get i:n
10	D	Oh my go:d
11	H	and you just p•ark
12		and I almost hit you
13		the old man he say Oo ooh
		(- - -)
14		and I quit
15		we're almost in a problem.

Figs. 4.19.1–3 Hussein reenacts a near-collision

It is likely that Hussein, on other days, depending on the explication tasks presented to him, depicts objects and events by gestures with greater frequency than on this day, when most depictions were brief and transitory. Another context in which Hussein produced elaborate depictions was a conversation with me about the stresses of his workdays. We will look at these in Chapter 6, in the context of other rhetorical practices Hussein deploys.

4.8 Preference for indexicality

One moment shows particularly clearly that Hussein, or people in his position, with their need to be exactly understood in a context rich in objects with highly specific category names, may prefer indexical to iconic or verbal communication. In this scene, Hussein is planning a job with Alex, and he needs to order a part, of which there is a left and a right version. From a distance, he asks Alex which side he needs, thumb-pointing to his back, in the direction of the car Alex is working on. Before Alex can answer, Hussein moves to 'point-walk' him to a car in the vicinity, which is then recruited as

Figs. 4.20.1–2 'Which side of the engine'

a model for the car they are talking about. Approaching the car, Hussein asks
Alex to show him, presumably by pointing gestures, which side of the car he
is talking about (line 17).

(4.20)
1   H   Which • side of the • engine
2   because they going to ask which si:de

3   To- show • me on which side
4   A   Well this is in the front
         (1.0)
5   H   Here the- here the motor.
6   The one go up-front?
7   A   Yeah, two in the front
8   H   In the front underneath, right?
9   A   Yeah.
10 H   That bracket you nee:d
11   This side • okay?
12 A   Yeah, this-
13 H   Is that • side okay?
14 A   Yeah that side-
15 H   But you still had that or you fix it already.
16 A   No I gotta fix it.
17 H   You want to fix it, okay then.
18 A   Okay the part is by the barrel.
19 H   Okay outside, okay thank you.

Thus, instead of undertaking the linguistically difficult task of referring to
the left and right side of an absent object, in decontextualized terms, Hussein
realizes the opportunity provided by a like car at hand, which he can then

Fig. 4.20.3 'Show me on which side.'

Fig. 4.20.4 'Is this side okay?'

Fig. 4.20.5 'Is that side okay?'

use as a model to anchor indexical expressions that refer to the car 'across the street'. This appears to be a general preference for Hussein.

4.9   Conclusion

While pointing serves to direct attention and action, showing explicates what is thus attended. Showing in Hussein's sense makes objects intelligible, discloses their dispositions and hidden features, reveals how they behave within their material and practical contexts, and prefigures actions to be taken on them. While pointing is about directing attention and action, showing is *pedagogy*. It is part of the ubiquitous learning that takes place at Hi-Tech Automotive. Showing, of course, is rarely silent; objects are 'languaged', 'encoded', and explained in terms of cause–effect relations, hypotheticals, diagnostic assessments and predictions. In keeping with my focus on the embodied foundations of human communication, I have paid much greater attention to the gestures and manipulations involved than to the talk accompanying them and identified a handful of showing methods in the video-corpus. The most interesting perhaps are practices involving an 'antenna hand', a hand out to gather sensory information and, while gathering it, make it available to others. The antenna hand is a collector and distributor of sensory experience and information, and different shapes that it takes during exploratory actions correspond to the type of sensation gathered (temperature, viscosity, surface texture, air pressure, etc.). Undoubtedly, Hussein's exploratory actions are *practiced* actions, as is their modulation to communicative ends. Other modes of showing include 'decomposition', suggesting ways in which an object might be divided up or taken apart, and what I have ironically called 'augmenting reality by action figures', the gestural annotation of objects by gestures that figure future actions to be done with them.

'Environmentally coupled gestures' (Goodwin 2007) and explicative manipulations always involve *sensory transformation*, reorganization or 'recoding' of sensory information, what Murphy (2012) calls *transmodality*. I have made use of Deleuze's (2003) typology of modes of hand–eye interaction to shed light on the ways in which hand gestures translate tactile, haptic, and enactive experiences into visible figures. This will occupy us again in the next chapter, in which I dwell on the kinesthetic dimension of hand gestures, the fact that they evoke feelings of action in their makers.

5   Making Sense

While pointing and manipulative gestures are practices that Mr. Chmeis purposefully and methodically enacts in his interactions with technicians and customers, his conceptual and rhetorical gestures during extended face-to-face conversations—his *gesticulation*—are of an entirely different kind: they are spontaneous, emerging unbeknownst to him, and attended by no one. And yet they are meaningful and intelligible and appear to articulate fluidly with the conceptual and social activity of the moment, giving form to significances emerging in the situation. In this crucial chapter, a dozen or so recurrent gestures of this type are isolated in the midst of Mr. Chmeis' gesticulation, seemingly practiced forms that may be cultural conventions or personal habits, adaptive manual solutions to recurrent communication tasks. Conventional gestures and personal habits combined constitute his self-made repertoire of manual conceptualization practices. These gestures are examined across the various contexts in which they are made, with close attention to their temporal unfolding.

Conceptual gestures, both those that construe content and those that are about the moment of interaction, are abstracted versions of practical actions. This is shown in one of Mr. Chmeis' phone conversations in which he instructs a customer how to 'push-start' her car, as well as during the account he later gives of the problem and how he fixed it. This chapter makes a number of fundamental and unorthodox claims about gesticulation (or conceptual and pragmatic gesturing). Seeking to answer the question, 'what do conceptual gestures tell the speaker (who is not aware of making them)?', I interpret the neuroscience of motor cognition as showing that gestures evoke enactive kinesthetic sensations—*feelings of (familiar) actions*—in the speaker that, by way of the meanings inherent in them, provide conceptual structure for the content or situation at hand. They are, as it were, the enculturated body's autonomic and unrecognized contributions to the processes of conceptualization and social action during speaking, and they structure this process as if it were concrete material (manual) activity.

5.1   'I make sense when I talk to the people.'

When Hussein is on a job, his gestures connect with the things at hand, putting them in the spotlight, characterizing or explicating them. In this chapter, we see Hussein's hands 'left to their own devices', but also free to play and, through their play, contribute to his conversation. We visit Hussein in his office, where he is seated behind his desk, talking to the researcher and, later in the day, a customer who, after an accident, is in dire financial straits. Here we find Hussein with without cars nearby and without manual labor to be done or ordered. Usually, due to the origin of most gesture research in research on language, language processing, and verbal interaction, conversational settings are treated as primary. But arguably, it is more characteristic of the human life form to have the hands engaged in, and getting a hold of, the material world. Hussein gestures as much or more than he is simultaneously engaged in manual action but his gestures are quite different from those we have studied in Chapter 4, where he gestured at the world or depicted it. What we see here is what, in everyday parlance, is called 'gesticulation'. Gestures embody features of Hussein's communicative acts or provide conceptual structure that somehow, but generally in elusive ways, contributes to the meanings of the moment. Previously, I have called these modes of gesturing 'pragmatic' and 'conceptual' gesture, respectively (Streeck 2009a). These modes of gesturing are not understood very well at all, and comparatively little research has been conducted into them.[1] This chapter is one of only few attempts to understand, in light of current 'motor science', how they 'work'. I will subject Hussein's gesticulating to particularly close scrutiny, hoping to learn more about how, in general, this mode of sense-making by hand works, and to reflect on how we achieve intuitive 'seeings' of gestures as meaningful acts. I use the ambiguous term 'making sense' purposefully, because in our present theoretical context, beyond its ordinary uses, it also alludes to the 'made' character of gestures, that they—and the sense they make—are products of human *hands*. And Hussein himself alludes to his embodied experience and communication when he declares that he 'makes sense when he speaks with his customers'. How his gestures contribute to sense-making in conversational contexts, rather than during 'hands-on' cooperation, is the subject of the present chapter. How does Hussein make sense with his hands, or perhaps: how do Hussein's hands make sense when they gesture, for it is not evident how we should conceive and refer to the 'subject' or 'agent' or 'maker' of these gestures. This chapter thus combines an analysis of a subset

---

[1]   But see Bavelas, Lawrie, and Wade (1992); Bressem and Müller (2014b); Kendon (2004: chs. 12 and 13).

of Hussein's conversational gesture practices with an attempt to give a broader explanation of sense-making by pragmatic and conceptual gestures, that is, by gesticulation. I begin to answer this question by analyzing a section from a long monologue in the morning (see Appendix 7) in which Hussein talks to me about his days at work (see also Chapter 6). I will inevitably try the reader's patience as I ask to consider every gesture Hussein makes during these forty seconds of conversation. I proceed gesture by gesture, treating each as new.

In the following short extract, we see how heterogeneous Hussein's conversational gestures are and how the *kinds* of meaning they convey can shift from moment to moment, but also that some gestures are made repeatedly, at different points, which gives us some clues as to how they may signify across contexts. Hussein says:

(5.1)

```
121   H   But I don't know what
122       I don't understa:nd
123       about your uhh- ( - - - - - - )
124       it makes sense to me
125       when you tell me about ( - - ) ta:lk,
          ( - - - - - - - )
126   J   Right
          [
127   H   people they talk not just by mouth or language
                                        [
128   J                                 Right right
129   H   because ( - - - ) I fee:l
130       when the customer came to me
131       and I'm behind the counter
132       I make sense when I talk with the people
                                     [
133   J                              Right right
134   H   not because my language
135       my language it is the la:st one I have
136   H   If I have good ( - - - - ) vocabulary
137       and I have good experience
          ( - - - )
138       to spea::k
139       as ( - - ) people they study in school
140       to better than my knowledge
141       if I ha:d tha:t
142       I would make more money
143       but ( - - -) with this ( - ) information
144       I make sense when I talk with my customers
```

Hussein's first sentence, roughly, states: 'It made sense to me when you told me about talk, that people use not only their mouths and language.' At the beginning of this turn, before he begins the sentence, 'It makes sense to me ... ', Hussein's hands gesture toward me. The gesture emerges in two parts. First he points his index fingers to the interlocutor (Fig.5.1.1) when he says, 'about your uhh- (- - - - - -)'. But as he hesitates, his hands open and turn up, forming a vessel or 'bowl' (Scheflen 1974), and move forward, the fingers curling inward several times, as they would when beckoning (Fig.5.2.3). Intuitively, we see the gesture soliciting a contribution by the other (me), given that Hussein cannot complete the phrase begun by 'your'. But it is also possible that the repeated curling of the fingers is a manual enactment of speaking; after all, he eventually settles on 'talk' as the final and focal element of his new sentence. When I, the addressee in situ, watch it on tape, I sense that Hussein's gesture was part of an act of reminding me of something, such that my formulating that memory would take care of his speaking problem. I see the gesture as an (unfulfilled) request to participate in his speaking.

Figs. 5.1.1–3 'I don't understand about your-'

121   H   But I don't know what
122   I don't understa:nd
123   .hhh •about y•ourrr uhh- (- - - • - - -)

Hussein abandons the sentence and speaks a different one: he asserts that what I had previously told him about talk made sense to him. Initially he completes the bowl-shaped gesture with another forward stroke, but then his hand changes shape.

124   its make s•ense to me

With his next gesture, Hussein gives a motor image of talk (line 125, 'when you tell me about talk'): he closes both of his hands twice so that the thumbs touch the fingertips, corresponding to the movement of the lips while speaking. A motion pattern is thus transferred by the gesture from one body part to another. Then Hussein's hands open up in a 'palm up', utterance-final gesture (see Section 5.8).

Fig. 5.1.4 'It makes sense to me'

Figs. 5.1.5–6 'Talk': moving fingers like lips

125   when you tell me about (- • -) t<u>a</u>•:lk,

Hussein performs yet another enactment of talking. This time, he casts talk not as speaking, but as interaction: he leans forward, and his two hands make one large forward motion in the sagittal axis ('people they'), and this has a direct sensory impact on the interlocutor. It puts me in the position of co-interactant: I am made not only to see, but to physically experience talk as physical engagement between people, not as movement of the lips. (Gesture is physical action in interpersonal space.) Then there is a third gesture related to talking. As Hussein says, 'talk not just by', his right hand, bunched, goes to his mouth, its shape figuring lips pursed for talking. Then the hand opens up and moves forward and rises, along with the other hand, to become part of a big shrug as he utters, 'by mouth'. The point Hussein is conveying here is that, even though he considers language the least of his communication resources, he is demonstrably able to achieve shared understanding with his customers.

Figs. 5.1.7–8 Talk as physical interaction

Figs. 5.1.9–10 'People talk not just by mouth or language'

126 J   Right
          [
127 H   pe•ople they t•alk not just by m•outh or l•anguage
                                                    [
128 J   Right right

Hussein's spontaneous gestures thus construe (conceptualize) 'talk' in three different ways within a very short time span, and each 'cept' (Streeck 2009a: ch.7) corresponds to an experiential dimension of talking in interaction.

In support of his claim that he makes sense when he talks to customers, Hussein now reminds me of the interaction with the Mercury owner I had filmed earlier in the day. He points to the counter next door where that interaction had taken place.

129 H   because (- - -) I fee:l
130   when the customer ca•me to me
131   and I'm beh•ind the counter

That interaction, Hussein is implying, was an example of him 'making sense when he speaks with people'. Hussein adds, 'not because my language': emphasizing 'not', his index fingers point up; 'my language' is coupled with a two-handed 'hold' gesture in which the open hands face each other. It appears that the gesture embodies a form of possession, holding something in one's hands: 'my language' (see [5.9]).

132   I make • sense when I talk with the people
                                      [
133 J   Right right
134 H   no•t because •my language

Figs. 5.1.11–12 'When I'm behind the counter'

Fig. 5.1.13 'I make sense'

Figs. 5.1.14–15 'not because my language'

Fig. 5.1.16 'the last one I have'

Then he adds that his 'language is the last one I have'. 'Last one' amalga-
mates the sense of 'least' (apparently the intended word) with that of 'last
item on a list', and this sense—or the sense of diminished importance—is
also conveyed by a swipe of the right hand over the palm of the left,
figuratively removing whatever was left in it.

135 my language it is the la•:st one I have

Note the way the acting body and an abstract concept ('last one') are matched: something that was left is being removed. A schematic action of the type 'clearing the table', 'wiping off/wiping clean' is enacted in the context of 'last one'. The form of the gesture is abstracted from concrete acts commonly associated with 'last one', and one can understand the projection of meaning by the action schema in multiple ways: completing an action by cleaning up after it, discarding a bit of speech—or a capacity to which it refers—as not needed, debris, trash.

What Hussein means to say next is not entirely clear.

136 H If I have good (- - - -) vocabulary
137   and I have good experience
        (- - -)
138   to spea::k
139   as (- -) people they study in school
140   to better than my knowledge
141   if I ha:d tha:t
142   I would make more money
143   but (- - -) with this (-) information
144   I make sense when I talk with my customers

Hussein's verbs and nouns are often unmarked for number, mood, or tense (see Chapter 6), and he does not use all available conjunctions of English. On rare occasions, these absences and an underdetermined context make an utterance ambiguous. It appears that he wants to say that he could make more money if he spoke English as well as the people who have studied it in advanced schools. Yet, given the experience he has, he makes enough sense with his customers. Or, alternatively, even though he has not studied the language, his vocabulary, combined with his experience, allow him to do just as well, communicatively if not economically, as those who have. Other readings may be possible. What we are interested in are the gestures he makes.

At the beginning of the conditional clause, 'if I have good', Hussein makes a precision-grip gesture (see [5.9]). Then, hesitating as he searches for the next word, he opens the hand to a grasping posture and then lowers and closes it, performing the grasp as he utters 'vocabulary'.

136 H If I have g•ood (- - - • -) vocab•ulary

The gesture is transparently coupled, not with 'vocabulary', but 'have vocabulary'. Hussein repeats the grasping gesture with the next, parallel phrase, 'I have good experience.'

Figs. 5.1.17–19 'If I have good (- - - -) vocabulary'

Figs. 5.1.20–22 'I have good experience'

137   and • I have g•ood expe•rience

Here, as at other moments, we face an interpretive dilemma: while the gesture presents a schematic, enactive image (an 'action figure'; cf. Condillac 1746) that is easily recognized (or, in the proper context, lends itself to being recognized) as a distinct action, we cannot determine what the gesture is about, that is, which of the cues or components of the current communicative moment (the referent, the speech act?) it is responsive to. Does the grip gesture in this segment signify possession, understanding, or word? Possession can always only be the possession of something; it is a predicate with two arguments, and thus the gesture, by its dynamic form, insinuates what kind of object it is targeting, but leaves us room to 'figure it out'. And the figuring out is usually, in the case of conceptual gestures, as tacit and implicit ('subconscious') as is their production by the body of the speaker. Hussein frequently makes grasping gestures, and we will examine more instances in (5.6) in a variety of discourse contexts.

When he refers to 'people they [=that] study in school', Hussein's hands move toward me, the interlocutor (Fig.5.1.23), paralleling their action at lines 123–124, associating me, a professor, with 'people who study in school'.

Figs. 5.1.23–25 'study in school to better than my knowledge'

Then he raises his right hand, palm down, in two steps, figuring stepwise upward motion, a visual concept corresponding to the educational careers or self-improvement or superiority of people who 'study in school to better than my knowledge'. Referring to *his* knowledge, Hussein makes an inward movement with one hand (5.1.25).

139   as (- • -) people they st•udy in school
140   to better than m•y knowledge

Then, when he anaphorically refers back to knowledge of language ('if I had *that*'), Hussein repeats the 'hold' gesture, and here its temporal coupling with 'have' suggests more strongly that the gesture corresponds to a state of physical possession. The accented syllable of the clause, that, comes with a small downward stroke of the hands, which are turned to face down.

141   if • I ha:d tha•:t
142   I would make more money

Hussein's hands now resume a bilateral holding posture, as they are moved in the direction in which the pointing gestures before were made, toward the counter where the interaction with the Mercury owner took place. He says, 'but with that information'. In other words, his possession of experience, expressed by the hold, explains how he was able to make sense in the place his hands are directed toward. At the end of the gesture, his left hand closes into a grip.

143   but (- - -) w•ith this (-) info•rmation
144   .hh•h I make s•ense when I talk with my customers

Figs. 5.1.26–27 'if I had that'

Figs. 5.1.28–29 'with this information'

Figs. 5.1.30–31 'I make sense'

5.2 Features of gesticulation

This turn, which lasts forty seconds, illustrates what everyday language calls 'gesticulation', which is quite different from the practices of pointing and explicating things we have investigated in the previous two chapters. Those gestures served clear functions within activities of 'shared cognition', whereas the gestures in this turn are not so obviously 'functional', although each one demonstrably furnishes some experienced structure and perceived meaning to the interaction. We have identified thirteen distinct gestures, in this order: pointing (to listener, self, and the counter); a 'bowl' or 'receptacle' gesture; three offering/presenting gestures (not all discussed); a shrug; three different enactments of talking; five grasping/ taking hold gestures; a 'wiping away' gesture ('the last one I have'); a precision grip; an index-finger up gesture; three two-handed 'holds'; and an enactment of 'step up'. We can take stock of some features of these gestures.

1. Each gesture is a single, indivisible act. But a gesture can be followed by an act that repeats it, or uses some of its structure, which then can be seen as an instantiation of the same gesture or an 'elaboration'.

2. Hussein makes some gestures several times, and these are potential 'habits', elements of a 'habitus' (Mauss 1973), patterns or practices that he routinely enacts. However, these enactments are not mechanical and predictable. But even the enactment of a routine is an improvisational act: multiple habits are at Hussein's disposable at every moment, and he follows no rules when choosing them. Gesticulation is spontaneous.

3. The *kind* of significance conveyed can shift from gesture to gesture. By 'kind of significance' I refer to the dimension of the communicative situation to which it relates and for which it provides a form. For example, Hussein proceeds from a gesture that relates to the semantic content of his talk (e.g., a grasping gesture coupled with 'have experience') to an open-handed 'presenting' or 'offering' gesture by which the content of his utterance is figuratively 'handed over' or 'presented' to the interlocutor, which, in linguistic terminology, is a pragmatic, not a semantic function (see [5.8]).

4. Every gesture is significant and conveys something in relation to something. In other words, hand gestures are never meaningless, even if it may be impossible to recover exactly how they contribute meaning to the communicative situation. This is so because humans perceive *any* living motion as meaningful, oriented to an object or a goal. Because gestures have the features of living, not mechanical, motion, interaction partners will always perceive them as inherently meaningful, even if this perception is as autonomic and unrecognized as the making of gesture is on the part of the speaker. Very rarely do we see a gesture that 'does not make sense', and this is usually possible because it is treated as such by its maker: abandoned, stopped in mid-course, corrected, and so forth.

5. At the present time, each attribution of meaning I have made here has been conjecture. In making these attributions, I have inevitably relied on intuitive judgments, made on the basis of tacit everyday knowledge, as well as on those studies of pragmatic and conceptual gestures that are available (notably Calbris 2011; Kendon 1995, 2004; Müller & Bressem 2014a). Thus, each attribution of meaning, even each identification of a given gesture as a 'token' or a 'type', are hypotheses, offered up to other researchers for confirmation or disconfirmation.

6. Each gesture (and this is an important feature) is a single act and can only provide a single meaningful gestalt. It couples a single enactive form with a single 'intentional object', in the same fashion in which we can only take hold of one object, or set of adjacent objects, at a time with a single grip, or gather a diversity of objects into a single grasp, subsuming them under one prehensile schema. In *Gesturecraft* (Streeck 2009a), I coined the term *ceiving* to refer to a gesture's subsuming of an intentional object under a manual *cept*—a prehensile posture and motor schema—to allude to the provenance of the term *conceiving/concept* from the Latin root <u>cap</u>, which signifies grasping or taking hold of. The metonymy 'understanding is grasping' is not uncommon in human languages (German *be-greifen*, *er-fassen*, English 'grasping (an idea)'). Neither is it uncommon for gestures to construe abstract content or depict objects by various grasping schemata. Incidentally, in its Greek root meaning, 'schema' also refers to a kind of grasp, the 'hold' of a wrestler. In *Gesturecraft*, I furthermore distinguished between 'conceptual' and 'pragmatic' modes of gesticulation, according to their different 'intentional arcs', one being about a theme of the discourse, the other about discursive action. However, there is no observable behavioral difference between these gestures, nor in the attendant behavior of the parties, as there is, for example, between pointing and depicting. Pragmatic and conceptual gestures typically remain unattended, doing their work in the background or at the periphery of the attentional field.

7. Although each gesture can, in principle, only pick out a single significance, it is also possible, though apparently less frequent, that a single gesture 'condenses' two (or perhaps more) significances into a single form, in ways not unlike what Freud (1913, 1960) detected in the symbolism of dreams and jokes: the symbol highlights an analogy between disparate experiences. We will notice some instances of condensation in the coming pages.

8. To reiterate: what 'kind' of meaning is conveyed from gesture to gesture is impossible to predict, and this is one aspect of what we perceive as the spontaneity of gesticulation. Yet, as addressees and observers, we do not appear to have any difficulty tracking these changes from gesture to gesture.

9. Our perception of gesture, finally, is informed by our own 'tacit knowing' of the world we inhabit. Polanyi said about the logic of tacit knowing that

The way we see an object is determined by our awareness of certain efforts inside our body, efforts which we cannot feel in themselves. We are aware of these things going on inside our body in terms of the position, size, shape, and motion of an object to which we are attending. In other words we are attending from these internal processes to the qualities of things outside. These qualities are what those internal processes mean to us. The transposition of bodily experiences into the perception of things outside may now appear, therefore, as an instance of the transposition of meaning away from us. (Polanyi 1966: 13–14)

Although it is clearly impossible to discern what a particular enactive form 'means' and 'does' without analyzing its specific interactional and linguistic context, this must not foil our attempt to explain the *gestalten* of these gestures, however underspecified, to investigate in which ways they may be meaningful, and thereby hopefully understand more broadly how meaning is 'manufactured' by gesticulation. In order to do that, we need to investigate recurrent forms across their contexts of occurrence.

5.3   Habits/types

I have identified approximately 440 'gesture-rich' conversational moments in the data corpus, that is, sequences of talk during which Hussein makes one or several gestures that are not either pointing gestures or gestures about objects at hand (which we have already covered). I have transcribed and annotated each of these moments and identified thirty-eight 'types', that is, gestures that are either made repeatedly during the day or that, in a few cases, appeared familiar to me from other conversational experiences or prior research. In the following, these presumptive 'types' or discernible 'habits' are labeled (glossed) by names in capital letters, following the convention of sign language research. Some of these types are instantiated by a single occurrence, others, especially gestures of the GRASP/TAKE HOLD and of the PRESENT/OFFER/ GIVE variety, by dozens. A single day is obviously not enough to record a man's entire repertoire of habitual gestures; common sense tells us that many additional ones would have been gathered on subsequent days. But while the number is difficult to gauge and inherently indefinite— new habits emerge, others, no longer needed, might fall away—it is certainly not infinite. My estimate is that it might be somewhere between 60 and 100 types. 'Types' are 'iterable' routines. Among these, many, and, in the case of pragmatic gestures probably most, are conventions, shared with other members of a borderless community. Others, I assume, are personal habits, routinized methods to cope with recurrent, field-specific communication tasks. Some are enactments of identifiable, object-related action patterns; others seem to be more broadly grounded in the body's position in the world, conveying senses like 'away' (Bressem & Müller 2014a), 'holding at bay', or the speaker's connection to the interlocutor. Emphatically, this typology is a heuristic; its adequacy can only be established by a great deal more research, focused on communities, not individual speakers.

Among transparent actions (gestures transparently abstracted from a real-world action), we find GRASP, HOLD, RECEIVE, TAKE BACK (retract), TWO-HAND HOLD, PUT TOGETHER, PRESENT, GIVE, as well as SLICE, SWEEP, WIPE, RUB, and FOLD. A rare schema in this corpus is THROW. A more abstract (and highly conventional) one is DISMISS, a gesture that appears to toss an object. Among recognizable action schemata we also find emblems, that is, conventional or lexicalized gestures (Efron 1972). These include HANDS WIPE EACH OTHER ('finish'), COUNT, and a highly specific one, WRITE. There are also gestures that conventionally express abstract concepts such as fairness or equality (a BALANCE movement).

Not readily associated with material-world actions are gestures that draw in more generic ways on the affordances of the body and its position in the world (Calbris 2011; see [5.12]). These include AWAY, HANDS APART, HANDS TOGETHER, HAND TO SIDE, ALTERNATION (left-right/up-down, etc.), as well as PALM-DOWN and PALM-SIDE, and their inflections by motion (e.g., PALM-SIDE to side). These cannot be linked to specific real-world actions, but they display an intentional orientation toward an object or the situation. Similarly, there are acts that lack distinctive dynamic features; they are straight, evenly paced motions. These gestures typically convey that an object moves in a direction and thus convey directionality in the most generic way. In this corpus, they include UP and DOWN (for example, 'business going down'). We also find motions that project generic motion patterns and trajectories, including CIRCLE, FORWARD ROTATION, TWO-HAND ROTATION. And there are body-indexicals such as INDEX-FINGER TO FOREHEAD, HAND-TO-HEAD, HAND-TO-CHEST, as well as conventional embodiments of subjective states, such as HEAD ON HANDS (thinking posture) and HOLDING HEAD. Besides personal 'conventions' (Hussein's habitualized responses to the particular significances in his life-world), occasionally we seem to witness a 'symbolic invention' (Donald 1991),

Hussein's locally improvised gesture response to the 'direction of the situation' (Merleau-Ponty 1962). This category may include the wiping gesture accompanying 'the last one' (see [5.1], line 135). Obviously, assigning a single gesture action to one of these types is necessarily a tentative, reversible judgment.

That the activity of gesturing and many forms that gestures take are grounded in manual activity in the material, tangible world—that the 'language' of gesture is a 'language of action' (Condillac 1746)—is critical to the theory of gesture I proposed in *Gesturecraft*, but other researchers have also made the same point. How can we imagine the process of 'abstracting' gestures from everyday action? Andrén (2010) has reported important observations of this process.

5.4   Abstracting gestures from practical actions

Andrén (2010) studied the developing hand gestures of young children (from eighteen to thirty months) and showed that these first emerge as 'frozen stages' of practical actions. One such action, and one of the most basic ones, is taking an object and giving it to another person. This action comprises the following stages:

1. reaching for the object
2. touching or grabbing the object
3. handling the object in interaction space ('center space')
4. moving the object toward a target
5. putting the object down
6. withdrawing from the object (Andrén 2010: ch.9).

At each of these stages, the movement can be frozen, and this 'frozen stage' can then be deployed as a communicative gesture, for example, by bringing the hand in a position where it can be seen. For example, by 'making a reaching gesture', rather than reaching for the object, a young child may *solicit* the object; that is, the gesture can become a *practice for making a request*. Similarly, moving the object toward a target 'in central space', in the direction of, but not all the way toward, the other, it may become a *gesture of offering*. Acts of transfer and transportation are among our hands' most ubiquitous occupations and the acts involved the most practiced ones. A 'vocabulary' of transfer and transportation movements, comprising minimal acts of seizing, holding, setting down, and so forth, is also pervasive in gesture, where these acts are typically 'bleached out', simplified beyond recognition.

Observing how gestures emerge from children's practical actions, Andrén has noted subtle, yet essential steps or degrees of separation and semiotization, that is, 'sign-like-ness', of gestural acts. One dimension is 'communicative explicitness', that is, the (visible) degree to which a bodily act is designed to communicate. Andrén distinguishes these degrees or 'levels of communicative explicitness':

1. communication as a side effect of co-presence
2. action framed by mutual attunement
3. visibly other-oriented action
4. reciprocated action (Andrén 2010: ch.2.2.2).

Simply by reaching for an object (1), the child communicates her desire for the object; child and adult can be jointly focused on the object and jointly observing the child's act (2); the child can gesture its desire by a 'reaching gesture' (3); and the child can perform a communicative gesture that necessitates or calls forth a response (4).

The other dimension, more relevant in our context, is 'level of semiotic complexity'. Andrén distinguishes three general levels:

1. This level comprises physical actions that only respond to the material contingencies of the situation at hand. 'There is no differentiation between the form of the action and its meaning or purpose, and the action is a direct adaptation to a current local situation in its uniqueness' (30). An example would be reaching for 'this particular glass' on 'this cupboard'. However, Andrén notes that 'already at this level actions may invoke the world at hand in various ways, such as making a certain object relevant by means of handling it somehow. Therefore, already at this level, a basic form of reference is possible' (30).
2. Typified actions are 'recognizable as [exemplars of] pre-established action types, i.e., as tokens of a type' (31). A gesture, for example, may highlight the typical aspects of an action it depicts: the turning, not the exact width of a steering wheel.
3. 'Semiotic signs' are actions modulated in one or both of two ways:

   The first kind of modulation is modulation of the act itself: its movement and configurations, with regard to its form as it would have been performed the way one would typically have performed it when performing it for practical purposes. An example is when an act such as writing with a pencil is performed, but where this is done without a pencil in the hand: i.e., as an empty-handed gesture.

> The second kind of modulation [occurs] when a modulation of
> typicality is a result of factors outside the performance of the bodily
> movements and configurations in themselves, such as various sorts
> of highlighting, modifications, concretizations or vaguefications,
> and re-contextualizations of an action [as in 'rehearsals' and
> 'replayings'; Goffman 1974; J. S.]. (Andrén 2010: 34)

Other researchers have made similar observations. For example,
Haviland (2013), Sandler (2012), and others have shown that the earliest
signs that have emerged in 'home-sign systems' of families with deaf members are abstracted from ordinary actions of the hand (see also Kendon 2009),
and researchers of sign languages such as 'Plains Sign Language' (Mallery
1978) have described degrees of metaphorization in the meanings of signs
grounded in manual actions. A particularly interesting analogy can be found
in the spontaneous production of gestures among bonobo infants,
humans' closest relatives. Hutchins and Johnson describe the abstraction
of gestures from the fluid haptic engagements of an infant being picked up
to be carried by its mother. As some part of the action is abstracted for
communicative purposes, it is transformed from a haptic/kinesthetic
schema into a visual one:

> Mothers and experienced infants come together for the carry activity in
> a very fluid way.... Mothers often sweep up infants and move off while
> looking at their destination.... The infant simultaneously moves its
> body and hands in ways that fit and take advantage of the mother's
> motions. Mother and infant just come at one another, interdigitating
> (grab, climb on, lift, etc.) mainly by feel. Bonobo mothers experience
> most carries as tactile and proprioceptive events rather than as visual
> events.... For example, a common part of the infant's role in establishing
> a ventral carry is to lean back and reach out and up. Infants assume this
> pose and hold it as a solicitation to the mother to pick up the infant and
> carry it.... The infant's gesture is made available to the mother as
> a visual experience, yet it seems to refer to an activity that consists
> primarily of tactile, motor, and proprioceptive experience. (Hutchins &
> Johnson 2009: 535)

Hutchins and Johnson note four dimensions along which communicative forms separate from practical acts: (1) the gesture is removed in time
from the actual course of the activity; (2) the gesture is performed outside
its indigenous spatial context; (3) it has a different motor dynamic than its
practical counterpart; and (4) it is decontextualized by the transposition of

the kinesthetic and tactile to the visual mode in which it is experienced by others (Hutchins & Johnson 2009: 539).

In human communication, once gestures have separated from actions and become independent (in Hutchins and Johnson's terminology: iconic) communicative forms, reusable independently of any particular practical context, there is no limit to their further semiotic development. As Andrén writes,

> once expression and content/referent have been 'detached' by some kind of differentiation, actions may be changed along a veritable array of further dimensions of variation into ever more complex and abstract forms of semiotic signs. Content may become metaphorical ... or metonymic so that a gesture invokes some content which in turn stands for something else. The techniques of realization involved in the articulation of various expressions ... may depart formation-based logic into much more indirect forms of realization, where the hand is no longer seen as a hand. ... As expressive actions begin to be detached from the concrete spatio-temporal domain of practical action in the world within reach, i.e., the core of the Lifeworld ..., there are increasing degrees of freedom in the many ways in which semiosis may be achieved. ... Semiotic complexity explodes into a multidimensional progression along many different dimensions. (40–41)

5.5   Relations between actions and gestures

Hussein's gestures during and after the following phone call he received from Ms. Nancy, before she came to the shop (see Chapter 4), as well as those he made to me after he repaired her car, illustrate some of the manifold relations between gesture actions and their physical-world counterparts[2]; the fact that Hussein makes these gestures as he is talking on the phone and the listener cannot see him, and that he also makes them when he talks about that phone conversation, suggests that concepts like 'push' and 'turn key' have an inalienable motor component for him.

Hussein is taking his lunch break. He has warmed a pita bread in a microwave and is eating it with vegetables and hummus, seated on a desk in the garage. The phone rings and he answers. On the other end is Ms. Nancy, distraught because she cannot get her car to start. After a few inquiries to find out whether the battery is dead or the starter might be the

---

[2] For a more detailed analysis of this episode, see Streeck (2002).

Figs. 5.2.1–2 'Turn the key on.'

source of the problem, and having established that the battery has not entirely expired, he gives her what he later calls a 'phone start'; he instructs her how to 'push-start' her car. That way she can drive it to the shop, rather than having to pay for a tow truck. Ms. Nancy does not seem to understand, and Hussein asks her if there is 'a man over there' he can talk to; absent such a man, he explains again. This time, he begins to gesture as he instructs her over the phone, and some of his gestures enact actions he is asking her to take, such as turning the key (Figs.5.2.1–2).

(5.2–1)
1 H If you have enough light
2   the car it should be cranked.
3   When you try to turn the key and it crank
4   do you hear any response
5   crank but won't start or not.
          (2.2)
6   Then you have light
7   if you put in second gear
8   push the clutch
9   and turn the key o•n
10   let somebody push the car
11   you should get the car to st•a:rt

In the following extract, Hussein makes five different gestures, two of them twice at different times: repeating his instruction to turn the key (line 23) and to see if there is light on the dash (line 24), he opposes the thumb to the curled fingers and then rotates the hand 90 degrees to the right, enacting the motor schema of turning an ignition key (line 23, Fig.5.2.3); as he refers to the light on the dash (line 24), his hand reaches forward, the thumb opposing the index finger in a grasping posture, and slowly moves sideways, as if he were tracing or feeling the light on the dashboard, or the dashboard itself (Fig.5.2.4). Along with the inference he hypothetically draws ('ignition okay', line 25), he moves his flat hand diagonally downward, in an abstract gesture that eludes interpretation (Fig.5.2.5).

Fig. 5.2.3 'turn your key'

Fig. 5.2.4 'light on the dash'

Fig. 5.2.5 'is okay'

(5.2–2)

17   Okay.
18   But you have light,
19   then you have little bit left in the battery.
20   Now to push-a start the ca:r,
21   you need to put- second gea:r,
22   turn the key to see light on the dash.
23   When you notice when you t•urn your key to start the car,
24   you see li•ght it's on the da:sh.
25   That it's mean your ignition is ok•ay.

A moment later, Hussein repeats the 'turn key' gesture, but this time while he says, 'you need to see light on the dash,' the two component acts Ms. Nancy needs to perform—turn the key to 'on', see whether there is light on the dashboard—are distributed between an enactment and a spoken directive, even though, of course, Ms. Nancy cannot see the gestured one. Then, when he says, 'somebody push' (line 28), Hussein's free hand pushes forward, and it is rapidly raised when he says 'take off clutch'. In real life, in contrast to 'pushing', this second action would not be done by hand, but by foot. The motor schema is thus transferred from one body part to another, not unlike the speaking movements of the lips were in (5.1).

(5.2–3)

26   You need to see light on the dash,
27   push the clutch, in second gear,
28   and while the car somebody p•ush,
29   just take off the clutch
30   and then, in that way it's called jump-a start.
31   It may start like this,
32   but make sure the key on, in on position.

Fig. 5.2.6 'Somebody push'

When he formulates a coda ('in that way it's called jump-a start'), Hussein repeats the uninterpretable gesture he made before, a slow downward movement, and, like before, the gesture is coupled with a summarizing statement, a 'statement of gist' (cf. 'that it's mean', 'in that way it's called'). The slow downward motion may figure the arriving at an endpoint.

Two of the gestures made on the phone, then, are schematic enactments of the actions Hussein instructs Ms. Nancy to perform: turn key, push. Another 'traces' the object talked about. Yet another is more vaguely related to a concrete, specific action: 'take off clutch'. It transposes the act of raising or retracting from the foot to the hand. Finally, there is an abstract gesture, a movement gestalt not transparently related to kinds of things and kinds of actions in the physical world: a downward motion of the flat hand. The forms of the gestures are simple: each is made by a single, unbroken movement and the hand's postures do not change while they are being made. Each is, in a word, a basic gestalt that cannot be decomposed into smaller components.

After he hangs up the phone, Hussein explains the problem to the researcher, who wants to know what happened. Now Hussein addresses a seeing co-participant, and he repeats some of the previously made

Figs. 5.3.1–3 'her car broken down'

gestures and adds another, an enactment of shifting gears ('put second gear', line 8).

(5.3)
1   J   What happened?
2   H   She's outside of New Brownsville, and her car broken down
3   (- - - - -) I'm a tryin' to help her to start the car,
4   cuz towin' too much money,
5   and she has nobody to know about this.
6   I said you have light, she said yes.
7   Turn the key o•n,
8   put second g•ear,
9   somebody p•ush,
10   take off,
11   maybe start.

Hours later, after Ms. Nancy has come and gone, Hussein again explains to the researcher what the problem was, how it may have been caused, and how he solved it. We saw him in the previous chapter taking the carburetor apart and disclosing the cause of its malfunctioning to Ms.

Figs. 5.3.4–6 'Turn key on, put second gear, somebody push'

Nancy. After that, he fixed the problem by reinserting the inner carburetor bracket in its proper location, thereby freeing the choke, and secured it in place, in the mode of the *bricoleur*, by inserting a wire. Now he repeats some of these actions: the schema of flipping the carburetor that he enacted repeatedly during the diagnosis is reenacted, an extended index finger is 'inserted' in place of the piece of wire, and the air-filter cover is opened and closed.

(5.4.–1)
1	Hussein	And accidentally she p•ulled that,
2		and it's missing the sa•fety lock.
3		And when she put it b•ack together
4		she don't know how it should g•o.
5	J	Right.
6	H	And she put it d•ifferent way,
7		she fl•ip it,
8		and she make the choke clo•se.

Figs. 5.4.1–2 'she pulled that and it's missing the safety lock'

Figs. 5.4.3–4 'When she put it back together, she don't know how it should go.'

Figs. 5.4.5–6 'And she put it different way; she flip it'

Fig. 5.4.7 'and she make the choke close'

The link of these gestures to real-world actions is immediate and close, as the gestures reenact recent actions, although in a manner adapted to the communicative situation. But the link can also be more remote, oblique, vague. A gesture can *construe*, rather than depict or reenact, bodily action and experience. Thus, when he diagnoses Ms. Nancy's car and directs her daughter to start it, he says to Ms. Nancy, 'You hear the engine cranking?' As he utters 'cranking', Hussein rotates his index fingers near his ears (Fig.5.4.8). The gesture blends the figures of rotation and listening. Like his spoken utterance, it instructs her to hear a certain sound as the result of an action (the rotation of the machine).

(5.4.–2)

| 11 | Hussein | When she came to start the car, the car flooded her. |
| 12 | | She cr•ankin'. (- -) She misdescribed to me. |

This gesture, rather than being abstracted from an action, emulates one, but frames it as an object of perception: a turning that is being heard.

Fig. 5.4.8 'Cranking'

The gesture is made again when Hussein explains to the researcher what the problem was. The fact that Ms. Nancy's car *was* cranking is important to him, because it means that the battery was working. Ms. Nancy had been in the shop a few weeks before for a new battery. She might have complained on the phone that the battery was not working. Here, Hussein repeats the 'cranking' gesture.

The link of the last of Hussein's gestures during this conversation to a material action appears to be more difficult to establish. But this is so not because the action of the hand is in any way more obscure, but because the gesture has no semantic link to content. The spoken utterance does not cue us in to the gesture's significance, as it did in the previous extracts. Holding one hand with the palm up, Hussein performs three successive 'handing over' motions toward the hearer, the first ending on 'smoke', the second on 'gas', and the third, made with both hands, on 'power'.

(5.4.–3)
9   All the car sm•oke,
10   wa•sting gas,
11   no po•wer.

Seeing these repeated movements as acts of 'handing over', even though nothing is in the hands, is not more difficult than seeing a hand 'pushing a car' or 'shifting gears'. The abstractness is not a feature of the gestures, but of the ways they relate to the context of communication: they embody an inherently abstract communicative act, that of 'presenting consequences', an act for which there is no concrete model other than this gesture itself (or a gesture of its kind). The situation is different when a gesture shows pushing: we know what pushing looks like. But what

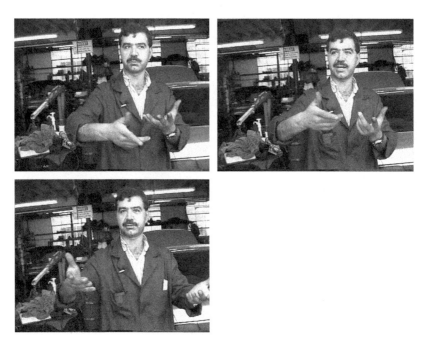

Figs. 5.4.9–11 'All the car smoke, wasting gas, no power.'

does 'presenting consequences' look like? Only a gesture—an embodied action—can give us a concrete, tangible understanding of such an abstract discursive activity. 'Give and take' appears to be a viable, widely enacted gestural model for conversational action.

Keeping this perspective, I now return to Hussein's conversational gestures, following Andrén's (2010: ch.9) heuristic for grouping and making sense of some of them, a heuristic that takes as its point of departure the stages of a basic act of object transfer: reaching, grabbing, handling, moving toward target, putting down, withdrawing. ('Handling', I should add, can be plain holding.) Pragmatic gestures, Hussein's and those of others, though transparently abstracted from one of these stages, usually present a fuzzier picture. For example, a hand that closes can close around an object, or it can close to become used as a fist, or the fingers may simply return to a rest position. These are, in their contexts, entirely different actions, but the motor schemata involved are similar or the same. Accordingly, abstracted from their contexts, as gestures, we may not be able to tell the difference between these motor acts. Similarly, reaching and grabbing are continuous, yet distinct when real objects are involved. In gesture, the distinction can collapse: there is only a continuous prehensile act that never meets an object.

5.6 Closing hands, grasping, taking hold

Closing a hand—curling the fingers, adducting the thumb, and making a fist (or nearly a fist)—is one of the basic actions we can perform with it. Phenomenally, in the context of gesture, closings of the hand can simply involve that the fingers come to rest as they relax and curl into the palm, for example, at the end of an open-handed gesture. But hand closings also occur as separate, 'free-standing' gestures in which the hand appears to take hold of, to seize, an object. The task, then, is, in Andrén's (2014) words, to find the 'lower limit' of gesture, the point at which a hand closing becomes significant. This point cannot be found in the form itself, only in its relation to a context (Bateson 1972). In the following, I offer a systematic analysis of a sample of Hussein's hand-closing gestures. Taking as the starting point their experiential gestalt, as well as variations of this gestalt, including how the making of these gestures *feels*, and the contexts in which they occur, I seek to lay bare a common enactive and kinesthetic core that allows us to explain why Hussein offers a grip schema when he says that he 'makes sense', but also when he considers something complete.

In Hussein's discourse on language and sense-making occurs a closing of a hand that I have not mentioned before because it simply is the conclusion of a gesture—not a stroke, just an inconspicuous return of the fingers from the prehensile posture formed for a stroke, into their curled rest position.

(5.5)
141   if • I ha:d tha•:t

Even though this clearly is not a gesture (if indistinguishable from one in the picture), even a mere closing of the hand can be meaningful, depending on the point in the conversation at which it happens.[3]

In (5.6), Hussein depicts a 'rocker panel', drawing it with an index finger, then 'pushing it into place'. Being done with the gesture, his left hand closes.

(5.6)
1   H   and the •rocker panel
2   where the door is sitting•

---

[3] Several of the following samples are taken from another longer office conversation, 'A Customer in Distress'.

Fig. 5.5.1–2 Hussein's left hand closes after gesturing

Figs. 5.6.1–2 Hussein's left hand closes after gesturing

The closing of the hand is again simply the 'return phase' (Kendon 1980) of a gesture. Upon completion of a gesture, the hand can return to a rest position or remain in 'cocked position' (Sacks & Schegloff 2002), from where a next gesture can be made, and states in between are also possible. Here (Fig.5.6.2), the fingers come home for a moment, while the hand remains somewhat raised.

Having 'returned home', the hands are ready for another gesture. To separate a new gesture, and perhaps a new clause, from the prior one, some form of return may indeed be needed. If the hand remains in 'cocked position' and is seen, a simple curling of the fingers can be enough for the listener to be alerted to a present or upcoming unit boundary of some unspecified kind.

In the following, Hussein is counseling a familiar customer who has wrecked a car for which he is still paying off a large debt and now does not know how to pay for its repair. He is also unsure about his insurance coverage. Hussein presents him with different hypothetical scenarios.

During his turn in (5.7), beginning at line 24, Hussein closes his hand several times, and there seem to be subtle variations in how these instances are perceived. The sequence begins with a large shrug, which, as will be argued later, displays an attitude of retraction or withdrawal, but which here seems to be related to the hypothetical nature of the talk: Hussein indicates that the scenario, 'I have no money; I cannot do anything' (line 25), is a hypothetical one, sketched for the sake of argument. The hands are then held up and perform several more gestures before returning home and then leaving again for a shrug. The shrug displays a neutral, indifferent stance toward the scenario, 'it cost six-thousand dollar' (line 28); the amount does not matter now (Streeck 2009a, 2009b). This shrug is completed with a quick and effortful closing of the hands.

(5.7)
```
20   V    See- see what I'm sayin is
          ( - - )
21        I'm not gonna lose my credit
22        because ( - ) I'm gonna pay that car
23   H    .hhh I'm not saying ( . ) this here.
24        Let's say different way.
25        You have no money to fix the ca:r
          ( - )
26        and because you don't have full-cover insurance
27        you have no money to fix it for-
28        it may cost si•x-thousand dollar.
```

Here, the closing has the features of a stroke: it is 'marked', effortful, made by fast-flexing muscles. It coincides with the syllable that carries the clausal accent, which marks the utterance's focal element. The gesture, by its production features, appears to contribute to this focusing. In other

Figs. 5.7.1–2 Marked hand closing during gesture completion

words, the closing of the hand is not only the end of a gesture-phrase, it is also a gesture. It is a movement-phrase that is 'elevated' from its surroundings and minimally elevates the moment, recommends what is being said to the listener's attention.

Clearly, these hand closings are not 'mere' closings, but timed and shaped for communicative effect. As I describe elsewhere (Cuffari & Streeck 2017), 'marked' hand closings frequently occur at the end of a unit of talk; they mark the unit's completion, blend it with a bodily sensation of closure.

In (5.8), the closing of the hand appears more as a grip. Whether there is an objective difference in the execution of marked closings and grips we cannot know without subtle motion-detection technology; there is always the possibility that the linguistic context impacts our perception, especially during the analysis of videotapes when we already know what is going to be said next. This grip coincides with 'time', at the end of the clause 'I invest everybody time' (line 5), to which is then appended 'hundred percent'. The gesture is not about time. Rather, it appears to convey a sense of, and enact a primordial form of, achievement, the achievement of grip. This sense articulates with (the achievement of) investing everybody's time 100 percent.

(5.8)
1   H   This the only way I make money
2   because I keep it- I invest everybody ti:me.
3   I make my best
4   Every technician here they working ha:rd
5   I inv•est everybody ti•me hundred percent

Closing gestures are made with varying degrees of effort, definition, or markedness, ranging from effortless relaxations of the fingers into

Figs. 5.8.1–2 Precision grip before hand closing

a curl to free-standing, 'stressed', grips. There is no cut-off point separating one class from another, no criterion comparable to the look at the hands during depictions, which indicates that some hand closings (and, thus, not others) are salient gestures. Perhaps the more 'marked' a hand closing is, the more likely it will 'register'. Clearly this is true from the listener's visual perspective: we hardly ever attend to a gesture's end, but are more likely to unknowingly notice a free-standing hand-closing act. The same is true for the maker of the gesture: a relaxation of the hand after a gesture has much less kinesthetic prominence than an effortful grip (if any at all).

In this respect, the following instance is of particular interest. In (5.9), Hussein is finishing up a series of instructions for Hakim, which have been accompanied by large gestures of the right hand (lines 1–3, Fig.5.9.1). Now Hussein turns away to return to the shop, and he performs a single, rapid closing of the *left* hand, which is not in anyone's line of regard. It appears as if Hussein unwittingly makes a gesture to himself.

(5.9)
1 H Bddi ʔaqib staːrter.
       I would bring the starter
   2   ħna nʃtɣul
          to make it work.
2   nkun mħamliːn lak hona.
          We would carry it
          miʃ jaːxu•o.
          in order not to be towed
          |

Certainly, Hussein does not become conscious of this gesture, as he, like the rest of us, remains unconscious of the overwhelming majority of all

Figs. 5.9.1–2 Hand closing as completion gesture

Fig. 5.10 'capacity'

gestures he ever makes. But it is possible that the gesture nevertheless registers as a kinesthetic, enactive sensation, a *feeling of action*. The act picks out a significance of the moment, that it is over. By making it, Hussein, 'objectivates' himself, produces a material form. This objectivation is accessible to him as it is to others, but not in the same way. I will return to this issue in Section 5.12.

Hands can close, but they can also close around something: grasp, seize, take hold of. The absence of objects from most gestures can make it difficult to distinguish grasping from closing gestures. This issue notwithstanding, the following gestures readily appear as schematic grasping acts. In (5.10), Hussein makes a grip gesture as he utters the word 'capacity' (whose root meaning, incidentally, is 'ability to take').

(5.10)
1   H   it's mean the battery
2   still has good cap•acity

This gestural conceptualization of capacity as grip is similar to what I have alleged for the gesture in (5.8). In Hussein's analysis of his own communicative abilities that we have examined, the grip gestures, in their linguistic contexts, convey a sense of 'cognitive possession' and 'communication capacity': 'have vocabulary', 'have experience', 'with this information', 'I make sense'.

(5.1)
136   H   If I have g•ood (- - - -) vocab•ulary
137   and I have g•ood expe•rience
143   but (- - -) w•ith this (-) information
144   .hhh I make s•ense when I talk with my customers

Figs. 5.11.1–2 'professional'

Fig. 5.12 Seizing sound

In (5.11), the gesture is coupled with the word 'professional', another word related to capacity, which appears to be the beginning of an uncompleted phrase (for example, 'professional skills', 'identity', or 'ethos'), or perhaps he meant 'profession'.

(5.11)
146 H   a::•nd
147 H   .hh this (.) part of my pro•fessional
148   the way I talk with my customer
149   the way I diagnosis their problem
150   the way I treat him

In ordinary English, we use manual action verbs such as 'seizing upon' and 'getting a grip' as metaphors to describe discursive and cognitive operations. In (5.12), Hussein 'seizes upon' a sound. He is test-driving a customer's car in her company and that of the researcher. At one point, he takes the left hand off the steering wheel and forms it into a grasping posture, as he says:

(5.12)
1   H   Did you hear this so•und?
2   Exhaust leak somewhere
3   C   Really?
4   it <u>shhhhhhhhh</u> when I accelerate gas

The grasping posture appears at the very moment of Hussein's noticing; it is an immediate and spontaneous response to the sound. In (5.13), the closing/grasping gesture marks the success of a word search (<u>copy</u>, line 7). At the beginning of the word search Hussein self-interrupts, turns his eyes up, thereby embodying his mental search, then pushes his hands forward and closes them with effort as he 'gets' the right word. Here, the gesture embodies the dynamic of Hussein's speaking, the searching for and finding—seizing upon—a word. The content (copying someone) is unrelated to cognition.

(5.13)
1   H   And mo- some of the technicians they ha:te me
         (- - - -)
2   and some of the technicians they l<u>o</u>ve me
3   more than their family
4   They build themselves
5   in my experience
6   and they do lo:t better
7   when they uh- (- • - -) •c<u>o</u>py me.

These last two examples in particular allow us to describe the mechanism or 'motor logic' (Berger & Schmidt 2009) of this type of gesture. Clearly, these gestures are not made 'in order to' express a concept.

Figs. 5.13.1–2 'when they uh- (- - -) copy me'

The temporality of the actions and cognitions involved precludes us from claiming that, in (5.13), Hussein is making a grasping gesture *in order to* express that he is completing a word search: the gesture is made at the very moment he completes it. In Wittgensteinian parlance (Wittgenstein 1953), the gesture is part of his 'word-search completion' or 'word-finding behavior', and so is his adopting a prehensile posture in advance. 'Getting ready to seize' (forming a prehensile posture) and seizing are a human body's spontaneous responses to this class of circumstance: getting ready to catch. The body can be seen to respond to a discursive and cognitive circumstance with meaningful acts. This is what makes these gestures legible and explains how 'pragmatic' gestures provide meaning and structure for the communicative situation, at the same time as they make sense of it: that they are familiar bodily responses to circumstances that are the mental analogues of physical circumstances. They can therefore be called 'metaphors' (Cienki & Müller 2009).

To sum up, hand-closing gestures form a phenomenal continuum from returns to rest position to forceful seizings, and they appear to convey senses ranging from completion to capacity and knowledge. There is no clear cut-off point where a closing/completion gesture becomes a grip gesture. I will refer to the respective prototypes—the enactive schemata, conceived as 'real life' action schemata—as COMPLETE and SEIZE/HAVE. It is interesting to observe that similar adjacencies of sense as between COMPLETE and SEIZE/HAVE are also found in grammatical expressions, mainly of aspect, in many spoken languages. We have already noted that 'cognitive seizing', that is, understanding, is often expressed by the metonymy 'grasping'. Similarly, possession of various kinds is expressed by the verb 'to have', and the primordial form of having, arguably, is having something in one's hand. Equivalents of the verb 'to have' are also used in many languages (including English, German, Spanish, and French) to express a 'completive' or 'perfective' aspect. If used as an auxiliary, the verb signifies that the action has run its course, that its goal has been achieved. Thus, it is not entirely surprising that the thematic contexts in which we have seen Hussein make hand-closing gestures also range from completion to cognitive possession or capacity.

While it is not possible to draw a line between closing and seizing gestures, another gesture variety can be readily distinguished, even though it also sometimes involves the closing of the hand. The difference is one of temporality. The examples we have examined in this section have all *ended* in a closed hand or fist. But when the hand is fully closed *in preparation* of a gesture, we face a different gesture (or gesture component): a fist. As a fist,

Fig. 5.14 'power'

Fig. 5.15 Impact gesture

it can then be wielded in the stroke. The gesturing hand embodies a weapon, controlled by the arm. This is a different gesture whose closing phase is irrelevant to the meaning it projects. But, ironically, both the fist and the grip can transparently signify 'power'. The fist is, apparently in many societies, an emblem of power.

When he diagnoses Ms. Nancy's car, Hussein makes fists and then pushes the hands forward, as he utters 'power'.

(5.14)
1 H   That's why sometime you start the car
2   the engine run
3   you get no p•ower

A different variety of the 'fist/power' gesture is a hitting of the palm of one hand with the fist of the other. In (5.15), Hussein makes this gesture as he describes a near-collision, when he tells a delivery woman that he 'almost hit her [car]'.

(5.15)
8   H   and nobody behind me
9   and then I put reverse to get i:n
10 D   Oh my go:d
11 H   and you just p•ark
12   and I almost hit you

At other times, the gesture figures a more abstract notion of 'transitivity', of a 'subject acting on an object', an 'agent' on an 'undergoer'. Thus, we can arrive at two similar conventional gestures that are indistinguishable in photographs and that can convey the same meaning, 'power', but along different lexicalization paths, originating in different ways of being of the hand: from the power grip (Napier 1980), the hand wielding an instrument such as a hammer, and from the (empty) fist, used as weapon.

5.7   Holding

In object-taking-and-transfer acts, the stage following 'seizing' or 'grabbing' is 'handling' in the space shared with the recipient. Handling includes as a default possibility holding. Holding can involve one hand or two; here we only look at examples of two-handed holds. In a two-handed HOLD, the open hands, flat or slightly curled facing one another, appearing to hold on object.[4] Calbris (2003b) calls this gesture 'cadre' ('square'), selecting the shape formed by the hand as defining feature. She gives several meanings for the gesture: *path*, where 'the vertical palms, face to face, constitute two lines bordering a space that is open before the self'; 'boundary', where 'the palms figuratively delimit a field of action or mental operation'; 'measurement and delimitation'; and 'definite object' as meanings of this gesture. She suggests that 'the gesture of definition serves the verbal designation of the abstract object. Gesture and speech show intimate solidarity' (ibid.). HOLDs are often 'ontic' gestures, positing the existence of an object, similar to an existential quantifier: 'there is'. The intentional object of the action, however—what is being 'held'—is often quite elusive.

We have seen an instance of a holding gesture in Hussein's discourse about language. He formed a HOLD gesture and then moved his hands in the direction where a prior interaction with a customer had taken place.

---

[4] Sowa (2006) describes this as a delimitative gesture by which the extent (width) of an item is shown.

Fig. 5.16 HOLD: 'with this information'

The gesture was made during the phrase 'but (- - - - - - - -) with this (- - - -)
information I make sense when I speak with my customers'. The stroke of
the gesture fell on 'with'.

(5.16)
143   but (- - -) w•ith this (-) information

The preposition 'with' expresses, among other concepts, 'being in possession of' and 'using an instrument' ('with your experience, you will come
out best', 'he did it with a knife'). Both senses seem to be enfolded in the
gesture: possessing something and doing something with it (moving it,
putting it somewhere). Framed by the talk of the moment, we see
Hussein's hands holding information. Hussein *has* information and brings
it to bear on conversations with his customers. This appears to be
a common form of coupling or 'semantic interaction' (Kendon 2004)
between gesture and speech: while the gesture figures an act, the direct
object of the sentence (or another focal referring expression) cues us in as
to what the gesture is about, the object of the action.

Several two-handed holds occur near each other when Hussein
counsels Victor. In one instance (5.17), the coupling of hands and
speech is quite 'literal'. Out of a one-handed gesture Hussein forms
a two-handed HOLD and moves the configured hands toward Victor
with the word 'back', as he says 'get the car back [to you]'. Of course,
this is not how a car is literally returned, but how a hand-sized object
can be returned to someone; yet the distance between the form of the
action and the sense that is locally conveyed by it is minimal. The
gesture enacts a concrete schematic *sample* of the type of act to which
the talk refers.

Fig. 5.17 HOLD, GIVE: 'get the car back'

Fig. 5.18 'put together'

(5.17)
12   .hhhh let me fix mechanical
13   to get the car ba•:ck
14   and then you drive your car

In the third instance, the hands are positioned at a greater distance from one another, and they are moved down, toward Victor. Here, the gesture is coupled with 'put together'. Like trying to find a proper fit, putting together is an action hands routinely do when they are holding something. In the course of practical action, the two schemata are 'adjacent', following each other or alternating with one another when we are handling a composite object, an artifact made from several parts.

(5.18)
25   and .hhh I will order the pa:rt
26   put the ' (- -) ca:r to•gether as mechanical
27   then you able to drive your car.

Fig. 5.19 HOLD, GIVE: 'give you your car back'

In (5.19), the hands are held in a HOLD posture as the forearms perform a downward stroke. The gesture, by its coupling with speech, selects 'necessary' as the focal element of the sentence, a word that also carries contrastive stress (which conveys: the necessary work, not all of the work).

(5.19)
36   Let the men work on our car for sale and customer car
37   and do nec•essary work to give you your car back.

The material this gesture is made of, the posture, has now been in play for a while, and it is not uncommon that new gestures reuse materials provided by prior gestures, a phenomenon McNeill (1992) has called 'inertia'. It is also common that redoing a gesture is an anaphoric device, linking back to what was being said when the gesture was made before. Or, the recurrence of the gesture might betray an underlying or sustained theme of the conversation, what McNeill (2005) calls a 'catchment'. Here, the gesture gathers several senses together in a broadly 'summarizing' enactment, what we might call a 'gisting gesture', a gesture that condenses the gist of what has just been said: HOLD delimits the work to be done, firmly affirms the existence of something, and then hands this something over to the other: the car, but also the offer and the turn, which thus returns to the interlocutor. The gesture can condense these senses because they 'fall under the same enactive gestalt': we easily 'see', and it makes sense to us, that hand-sized things, cars, and proposals can all be *handed over*.

Our last example of a two-handed hold comes from Hussein's diagnosis of Ms. Nancy's car. Hussein forms it as he utters 'able to', and he holds it as he searches for the word 'prove'. Note that the HOLD gesture often involves tension, a firm grip, as it does here. The gesture's relation to the

Fig. 5.20 HOLD: 'we're able to prove'

talk is ambiguous: the firm hold may signify 'able to'; it may be an enactment of the search for the right word, not unlike a frozen prehensile posture
one can see in such circumstances; or it can be the manual equivalent of the
type of cognition that 'prove what happen(ed)' adumbrates: a firm grip on
the situation.

(5.20)
    H   And then (- -) we're a•ble to: (- -) .hhh p- to- to- to pro:ve
2   what exactly happen with you
3 N   Okay

5.8 Releasing, presenting, offering, giving

The last stage of object transfer can either be withdrawal of the hands from
the object or handing the object over to another person. One type of
gesture abstracted from this stage are versions of 'release', of hands opening
up or moving apart. This is how Hussein ends the hold gesture in (5.19): he
says to Victor, 'less damage for both of us', and, as if releasing the consequence, letting go of something, relieving oneself of something ('less
damage'). Again a gesture makes sense by synthesizing different relevances
of the moment into a single form.

(5.17)
15   Less damage for both of us.

When he talks to the researcher in the morning about the stresses of his
workdays, Hussein reenacts the advice his wife's uncle, who is into 'spiritual
stuff', gave him, namely to occasionally take a five-minute break and
meditate, and leave everything. When he refers to 'giving himself five
minutes', Hussein encloses his head and vision between his hands. Then,

Fig. 5.17.2–3 'less damage for both of us'

Fig. 5.21 'leave everything'

at 'leaving everything', he opens them wide, in a large 'releasing' gesture (Fig.5.21).

(5.21)
1   even if you give yourself five minute
2   lea•ve everything

If associated with hands, verbs such as 'release', 'leave', and 'let go of' all describe similar actions.

The most frequent gestures, by several orders of magnitude, that Hussein makes during the day are abstracted from the presentation and handing-over stage of object transfer, and from the subsequent or reciprocal stage of holding the hand out in anticipation of receiving an object: the hand is open, the palm turned up. When the hand is brought into position and held, the action looks more like a presentation or offering; when the hand is moved to the interlocutor, like a giving or 'handing over'; and when the hand is quickly retracted, or its turning into palm-up position is combined with a raising of the eyebrows and shoulders, it is part of a shrug (Streeck 2009a, 2009b). This 'family' of gestures has received a great deal of attention. Kendon treats it as a sub-branch of the 'o-[open hand] family' and calls it 'open hand supine' (2004: ch.13). Referring to Müller's (2003) overview, he writes:

> [T]he gestures of this family are very widely used, and various versions of them have been described ... from Quintilian down to the present day.... The various meanings that have been attributed to Open Hand Supine gestures have in common the idea that it is a gesture of offering or giving, or a gesture of readiness to receive something. (Kendon 2004: 264)

Streeck (2007a) has shown how a palm-up gesture can change from a giving hand into a receptacle by the sheer passage of time: for example, 'offering an assessment', the open hand, held in place, can signify with increasing urgency that the speaker is waiting for a response. Usually the hand is retracted and/or closed when the response begins. The gesture, Kendon writes, 'serves to define whatever might be the content of the utterance of which the gesture is a part as something "being given" or something "being asked for"' (ibid.). McNeill (1992), drawing on Reddy (1979), has called these gestures 'conduit gestures'.

The frequency of presenting, giving, and expecting gestures is not Hussein's idiosyncrasy. To the contrary, it appears that gestures of this kind are universally the most ubiquitous in almost any conversation, the gesture any individual makes far more often than any other gesture during a conversation with someone else. I do not remember traveling anywhere where I would not see these gestures wherever people were in a 'state of talk'. This is one of the mysteries of human gesticulation: how can we explain the abundance and global distribution of gestures that embody a model of talking with one another as give-and-take?[5]

I have identified more than 200 instances of open-hand supine gestures in the first six hours of the recording; further collecting appeared redundant. Examples of three versions will suffice to illustrate contexts in which Hussein makes gestures with an open, supine hand; I call these 'handing over', 'presenting', and 'shrug'. The groups overlap. Presenting and handing over are different stages of transfer acts, but in gesture, the difference is

---

[5] Open-hand supine gestures can project different meanings when they are made before or at the beginning of a turn. When the speaker looks at the open hand at the same time, these gestures typically project an imminent 'telling'. The gestalt is that of someone looking at a domain, the 'universe of discourse' of the forthcoming report; Streeck and Hartge (1992).

often washed out, noticeable only in a minimal forward movement of
the hand.

Handing over

In (5.22), Hussein frames an offer by moving his open hand toward a
customer. When he initiates the offer (line 1), his right hand is presented,
palm up, to a listener. Then his hands come together and nearly touch in
a hold-like posture (line 2), as he talks about the time she will 'get the title
here' (perhaps narrowing down the timeframe or figuring the coming
together of 'here' and 'the title'). They move apart and then fold near the
end of the clause ('title'), and then they open again, toward the customer,
along with the invitation to come back and get a free oil change. On 'free'
the hands are folded again, but then the left hand moves forward and makes
a two-step 'giving' gesture, turning up and spreading (with 'oil') and then
moving further toward the customer (with 'change').

(5.22)
1   H   Maybe you come by: Tuesday
2   or Wednesday when you get the ti•tle here
3   come by all we give free o•il change

That we can see the gesture as an embodiment of an offer has much to do
with the highly conventional nature of the gesture. In Kendon's words, the
gesture 'serves to define whatever might be the content of the utterance of
which the gesture is a part, as something "being given"' (Kendon 2004: 264).

In (5.23), Hussein performs a series of increasingly large two-handed
hand-over gestures; the upgrades appear to be responsive to Hussein's speaking trouble and the listener's trouble understanding. Hussein does not

Fig. 5.22.1–2 'give free oil change'

Fig. 5.23 Hand-over gesture during word search

manage to distinguish 'spiritual' and 'spiritist'. He utters 'spirished', recognizes his mistake and looks away, without receiving any input from his interlocutor, and returns his gaze to him, who then says, 'Sorry?'. Hussein's fourth hand-over is even larger and coupled with a forward posture shift, as if he were bearing into his interlocutor to come up with an image of a man who believes in spirits, like those that can be seen on TV.

(5.23)
```
1    H    My wife uncle
2         he's about seventy years old
3         they came from- ( . ) New York
4         to visit us
5         and first time I met him
          ( - - - - - - )
6         This ma:n, he really spiruts-
7         spirished ma:n.
          ( - - - - - - - - - - - - )
8    J    Sorry?
9    H    He- he'll (leave) the sprit or:-
10        or he believe in spirit
11   J    Oh. ( )
            [
12   H      and he do s•ome thing
13        like people on TV.
```

The size of a hand-over gesture and the effort with which it is made appear to play a part in how its significance is perceived. In (5.24), Hussein has told the researcher that he sometimes has stomach pain; when the listener shows minimal concern in his response ('you do?'), he mitigates the statement: 'sometime sometimes'. His hand-over gesture here is but a brief, one-handed, and lax offering motion: his non-dominant hand briefly turns up from its current position. (The tension of a hand cannot be shown in a picture.)

(5.24)
1 J You d-?
2 H Yeah so•metime sometimes

In contrast, when he appends an 'aggravating' clause, 'that's for at least twenty-three years', to the assertion that he always eats while working, the left hand makes a large hand-over motion to the listener. Here, the gesture appears as one of the methods for aggravating the statement, along with the phrase 'at least'.

(5.25)
1 H I always eat while I'm working.
         (- - - - -)
2   And that's for at •least twenty-three yea:rs

The same physical action, described here as 'handing over', is sometimes seen as a gesture of soliciting. This is typically the case when it is coupled with a question. In (5.26), Victor assures Hussein he will pay him, and Hussein emphatically responds, 'I know that,' and then asks, rhetorically, 'How many years have you been dealing with me?', lowering his open hand into a palm-up posture.

(5.26)
1 V I- I'm gonna pay you.
1 H I know tha:t.
2   Ho•w many years you're being dealing with me?

We may refer to this contextual sense of the gesture by the term 'receptacle hand': a hand in expectation of an object.

Fig. 5.25 'At least twenty-three years'

Fig. 5.26 'How many years you're being dealing with me?'

Figs. 5.27.1–2 Presenting gestures

Presenting

Neither perceptually nor semantically is there much of a difference between hand-over gestures and presentings, by which I refer to gestures appearing in their contexts to be offering an object up for inspection. When the object that is being presented is at hand, the gesture resembles an act of pointing (cf. Kendon 2004), but, in apparent analogy to that situation, hands that face up may also present arguments, information, opinions, and other discursive objects. In (5.27), Hussein's hand leaves the steering wheel of a car he is driving to make an open-handed, palm-up gesture. He is test-driving Yvonne's car in the company of Yvonne, with the researcher in the backseat. Hussein 'presents' Yvonne to the interlocutor as an example. Talking about how he acquires new customers through referrals, he presents Yvonne to me by moving his open hand toward her. Then he returns the hand to the wheel.

(5.27)
1 H   like Yv•onne
2   she sent me customer
3   she has (a year) or two
4   a friend.
5   Yo•u sent many friend

But then, when he elaborates and addresses Yvonne (line 5), Hussein takes both hands off the wheel and makes two wide, two-handed presenting gestures. The gestures take part in affirming Hussein's point. This is a version of what I have I called 'spotlighting' in Chapter 3, which is a referential act: the object is presented as an exemplar of a kind (Kendon 2004).

A strong sense of 'presentation' is conveyed when the gesture—the configuring and moving of the hand into a palm-up posture—occurs when Hussein comes to a conclusion or draws an inference, for example, during the diagnosis of a car. Here, the gesture accompanies 'that's why': both hands turn up, and one of them points toward the engine. 'That's why' could even serve as a category name for one usage of the gesture.

(5.28)
1 H   Probably you have choke problem
2   th•at's why
3   the car has no power sometimes

Similarly, on the phone, where the gesture combines with the phrase 'in that way', which marks the gist of his message: 'in that way it's called jump start'.

(5.29)
1 H   and then in th•at way it's called jump start

Fig. 5.28 'That's why'

Fig. 5.29 Presenting the gist of an instruction

Shrugs

Even though they are made in the same conversational environment, near the transition place between turns at talk, or along with the completion of a unit, and while they are sometimes indistinguishable by form from other varieties of presentation, we often recognize a very different kind of action in open-handed supine gestures: we see them as *shrugs*. Turning the hand(s) up and opening it is a standard component of full-fledged shrugs, combining with the raising of eyebrows and shoulders. But, given the right environment, a single hand can do the shrugging. Elsewhere (Streeck 2009b), I have described a series of manual shrugs Hussein performs during an interaction with a customer as he is reluctantly complying with the customer's request. The shrug expresses a noncommittal stance.

Shrugs have been called 'pragmatic operators' (Kendon 2004): they display a stance toward an intentional object, an attitude of detachment, of withdrawal from full commitment to a course of action (Streeck 2009a, 2009b). As is the case with offering and presenting gestures, the scope of the operator 'shrug' varies and can be difficult to determine. In (5.30), Hussein frames a hypothetical statement by a shrug, and the shrug, like 'let's say', appears to work as a 'subjunctive marker': it lowers the relevance of the proposition, displays the irrelevance of the number, or the hypothetical nature of what is being said.

(5.30)
1   H   Let's say cost - • - six thousand like-

Similarly, when he talks to the researcher after getting off the phone with Ms. Nancy, Hussein makes a one-handed shrug (he turns an open hand up) before he begins to speak, following with another and then a bigger, two-handed shrug.

Fig. 5.30 'Let's say it costs six thousand'

Figs. 5.31.1–2 Two-part shrug

(5.31)

       (- - - - - - • - - - - -)
1 H   She's outside of New Brownsville,
2   and her car broken down
       (- - - • - -)
3   I'm a tryin' to help her to start the car,
4   cuz towin' too much money

At the end of the report, there is another two-handed shrug, which corresponds to the modal adverb, 'maybe'.

(5.32)
1 H   take off
2   may•be start

These shrugs frame the noncommittal stance Hussein takes in his reporting of the call: these are the circumstances, I am trying to help her, but I cannot guarantee what will happen.

In Chapters 3 and 4, we have seen how small, 'opportunistic' changes in the shape of a motion, coupled with what is at stake in the situation, can

Fig. 5.32 'maybe start'

convey subtle changes in meaning that recipients seem able to track. The changes in the position and shape of the hand in the realm of 'pragmatic' gesticulation are equally subtle, but their significances are more elusive. Looking closely, we may see the thumb separating from a hand and forming a V-shape as a transformation of a 'presenting' into a shrug and find that change to resonate with a change in the speaker's stance. Often, it is *change* in form, not the form itself, that cues us in on a significance, especially when a gestural form is already in play and the significance it enacts continues to matter. Adding a bit of form by reconfiguring the hand or altering the motion in a minor way can maintain one significance while adding another.

5.9 Other gesture types

We now turn to a handful of typified pragmatic gestures that Hussein repeatedly makes during the day and that are not related to acts of object transfer. Given the limited space we have, we can only investigate a small number in any depth. Hopefully the sample will suffice to illuminate the logic of sense-making by conceptual and pragmatic gestures. (It is important to keep in mind that other modes of gesturing are characterized, at least in part, by an altogether different logic of operation.) The types have been chosen and arranged to illustrate that Hussein's gestures vary in their degree of transparency: the meanings of some gestures appear obvious, perhaps because they are conventionalized, while others are opaque. Accounting for the way their forms make sense eludes us.

Precision grip

The so-called ring or precision grip gesture, in which the tip of the index finger and the thumb touch and may exert pressure on one another, has been described, and its function discussed, since antiquity (Lempert 2011; Quintilianus [1922] 100). Kendon writes that the gesture is 'derived from the "precision grip", the use of the thumb and index finger to pick up something small and hold onto it' (2004: 238–247), and that 'the semantic theme that [precision grip gestures] share is related to ideas of exactness, making something precise, or making prominent some specific fact or idea' (240). This also describes the contexts in which Hussein makes precision grip gestures. In (5.3.1), the gesture is coupled with 'exactly'.

(5.33)
1   H   I'm happy because my business going good.
2   And •I know ex•actly

Equally in (5.34):

(5.34)
1   H   Let me verify something
2   to make sure •exactly what is wrong

Fig. 5.33 'I know exactly'

Fig. 5.34 'exactly what is wrong'

Fig. 5.35 'correctly'

Fig. 5.36 'This the only way I make money.'

In (5.35), the precision grip foreshadows 'correctly'.

(5.35)
1   H   The part you take
2   put back •correctly

In (5.36), it is coupled with 'the only way', which implies specificity.

(5.36)
1   H   They don't know how to run away from me.
2   Th•is the only way I make money

The gesture can, of course, also project the semantic feature 'precision' when no corresponding word is said. In (5.37), Hussein is talking about checking a car's mileage as he makes the precision grip, as if picking out the exact number.

(5.37)
1   H   when the car came in
2   what the •mileage was

Fig. 5.37 'what the mileage was'

Fig. 5.38 'one hundred percent'

In (5.38), the precision grip is coupled with 'every technician' and then sustained over two lines, the posture held through a succession of strokes. Thus, while the precision grip initially seems to signify 'every *single* technician', the gestalt of the gesture and the meaning it conveys then extend over the entire two statements, resonating with the notion that every single person works exactly 100 percent of the time, that there is no 'slacking off'. The kinesthetic form of the gesture—the sensation it generates: pointed pressure exerted by index and thumb—appears to be critical here.

(5.38)
1   H   Every technician here they're working hard
2   I invest everybody time o•ne hundred percent

Thus, a corporeal schema and experience, as it is generated by picking up and holding something very small, and firmly, and the sensation that making the gesture evokes are made relevant to the situation.

Index up

Equally conventional as the precision grip is the gesture of raising the index finger (Streeck 2008c), which conventionally marks what is being said now, or about to be said, as salient. It is a gesture that announces heightened importance of a bit of speech. In (5.39), 'index up', coupled with an eyebrow raise, cues the subsequent 'plot' of Hussein's story of his Saudi Arabian workdays.

(5.39)
1   H   When •I go home
2   my voice cannot reach from room to room

In (5.40), index up is coupled with an accented negation marker, 'not', which initiates a salient proposition. Kallmeyer and Schmitt (1996) have called the pragmatic effect of markers such as these 'relevance up-step'.

(5.40)
1   H   I make sense when I talk with the people
2   n•ot because of language

Fig. 5.39 'My voice cannot reach from room to room'

Fig. 5.40 Index up: 'not because of language'

In (5.41), index up 'condenses' the sense of 'one' with that of salience.

(5.41)
1   H   For o•ne reason maybe
2   because

'Index up' is a *visually* salient act: the hand with its extended index finger rises in center space and attracts attention. But it also a distinct kinesthetic schema, not only because of the unique ('digital', Deleuze 2003) posture of the hand, but because the hand is brought in a position that it rarely reaches in conversation, and points in a direction that is equally rare in pointing. The gesture, more than other gestures, acts against the force of gravity and thereby provides the speaker with a kinesthetic experience of 'up'.

Counting

A gestural practice Hussein readily performs when an occasion for it arises is to count by hand (or, at least, to initiate a counting sequence). He has several ways of doing this: counting on one hand, first extending the thumb, then the index finger, and so forth; tapping the tip of the index finger of one hand either to the thumb or the pinky of the other hand and then proceeding outward or inward and grasping the fingers, one by one, in either order. These schemata are structured cultural practices, as is the coupling of counting gestures with list constructions of various kinds: of things to do, things needed, circumstances, or clauses. Counting, more than many other gestures, appears to be a deliberate and calculated affair, a rhetorical action. Communicatively, counting provides listeners with a preview of the structure of subsequent talk, suggesting that it will comprise multiple units. When these units are arguments, the gesture lends weight to them ahead of time, because it indicates that there is more than one. For this purpose, a single initial installment may suffice, because it implies that there will be other countable units and that the talk should be heard in this way.

   In the following conversation with the researcher, Hussein, who has just pointed out that he feels as if he is going crazy at times, talks about how much worse it was in his shop in Saudi Arabia. He lists the types of people he interacted with on an average day, and he begins to count by opening his left hand, looking at it, and tapping the little finger with the extended right index finger (Fig.5.42.1). Then he moves on to the ring finger. When he has exhausted the four fingers, he makes a fist (Fig.5.42.3).

Figs. 5.42.1–3 Counting: 'between your employees, between customer'

(5.42)
1   H   Afternoon you see about hundred hundred fifty p**eo**ple
2   between y•our employ**ee**s
3   betw•een customer came to pick up car
4   and people they give 'em ri:de
5   p•eople they come just-
6   they wanna introduce them to me:
7   or introduce me to them
8   to give me business

In (5.43), Hussein modifies this cultural routine on the spot. The second item on his list is a catch-all list completor: 'everything [else] I need'. Hussein first counts 'one' by tapping his index finger, but then he completes the list in one stroke, striking all four fingers, as he says 'everything'.

(5.43)
I'm gonna •buy the door
buy •everything I need

We can consider this a local adaptation of a gestural listing practice, invented as a new circumstance arises, the possibility or need to abandon list making

Figs. 5.43.1–2 Premature list completion

Fig. 5.44 Sustained counting posture

and do so with a 'catch-all' item. (But, of course, the practice could be a habit, even a cultural practice, rather than a local convention. At the present stage of gesture documentation, we cannot know.) This extract thus exemplifies a recurrent feature of gestures, that the relationship between cultural form or practice and local instantiation is often open-ended. Undoubtedly, the counting schema Hussein enacts is shared culture, but would we say the same thing about striking four fingers while saying 'everything'? The body that gestures and enacts shared practices is an individual body in unique circumstances. It fashions 'next actions' out of the available material, and these can come from the shared culture, or from the physical and semantic contingencies of the situation and their interaction with affordances of the hand.

In (5.44), Hussein's hands, once they are done counting, then hold each other—fairly bending each other out of shape—for another twelve units of talk, one index finger bending the little one of the other hand. The list is complete after three items (line 4), but the posture the gesture has now become is not dismantled until sixteen utterance units later (line 20).

(5.44)
```
1    H    ... part of my professional
2         the way I talk with my customer
3         the way I diagnosis their problem
4         the w•ay I treat him
5         I always make money
6         but I neve:r- ( - - - ) thought to make money one time
7         from any customer
          ( - - )
8         because I want him again
9         .hhh and most my customer I appreciate their business
10        but most of people
11        they thank me
12        before they leave
13        by service I did
14        because they feel they did good
15   J    Right.
16        And they come back
17   H    And they come back
18        and they said
19        We just came
20        because somebody told us about you
```

By maintaining his counting posture, Hussein maintains himself in a distinct corporeal state. Cognitive psychologists have studied why people, particularly young ones, use their hands when they count and perform other numerical operations. They explain the practice as a form of 'off-loading': when numbers (or mathematical concepts) are given material, kinesthetic form, they do not need to be retained in short-term memory. The body can function like other 'external' information storage devices (Goldin-Meadow, Alibali, & Church 1993; Hutchins 2005; Wilson 2002). Counting during talk in interaction may be a similar kinesthetic mnemonic, keeping the speaker 'on track' during a multi-unit telling. With each next count, the completion of a unit and the initiation is registered. Maintaining the posture, Hussein maintains and displays a particular mode of engagement for the duration of a larger thematic unit.

Rotation

A less distinct group or method of gesture involves rotations of a single index finger, or both index fingers, or both hands circling one another. These gestures must be distinguished from those that draw a circle in a depictive

Fig. 5.45 Rotation: money transaction

Fig. 5.46 Rotation: 'to give me business'

mode. Discussing gestures of precision grip, we have distinguished between the hand's shape and the kinetic-kinesthetic action the hand performs, arguing that the former (and perhaps the latter) may be coincidental and irrelevant to how the gesture communicates. Here, we are dealing with similar motion patterns—rotation—but usually it appears to be possible to make out whether the gesture is meant to show a form (in literal or metaphoric mode) or rather a circular or cyclical process. In (5.45), the gesture is combined with reference to a money transaction.

(5.45)
1   H   Any money you g•et here
2   just come

In (5.46), forward rotation of the two hands figures a transaction of giving.

(5.46)
1   H   or introduce me to them
2   to gi•ve me business

Figs. 5.47.1 – 2 Rotation: 'get the car out quick'

Fig. 5.48 Rotation: 'production'

In (5.47) it alludes to the 'rotation' of the car through the shop.

(5.47)
1   H   get the car out qu•ick

In (5.48) the gesture is coupled with 'production', showing it as ongoing operation.

(5.48)
1   H   The VIN number the-
2   the vin number,
3   the pro•duction date

When he talks about what it is like to be thinking about his business, Hussein first performs himself thinking by adopting a thinking posture (resting his head on his hand). Then, saying, 'I just start thinking', he makes two circles by rotating his hands at the wrist. The gesture figures an activity as cyclical motion, but it is not clear whether it refers to thinking, business, or running a business.

Figs. 5.49 Rotation: 'thinking about running business'

Fig. 5.50 Rotation: 'Sometimes I feel crazy'

(5.49)
       (- - - - - - - -)
1   H   .hhh and I just- (- -) start thi•::nking about
2   (- - - -) how I run my business

A moment later, his head propped up on the right hand again, Hussein reports that he sometimes feels that he is 'going crazy'. He moves to rotate the index finger three times near his head. Undoubtedly the gesture figures 'going crazy'.

(5.50)
1   H   I told her I feel sometime
2   I'm cra•:zy.

Alternation (left – right, back – forth)

The majority of the joints of human arms and hands are such that motions along one axis are afforded; limbs alternate between excursion and return, extension and flexion. These are basic patterns of the human life form. Furthermore, our bodies are bilateral, providing us with pairs of arms and hands. Both of these structural affordances and constraints can be in play during conceptual gestures of alternation. Hussein performs many back and forth, or left-right-left, movements with his fingers or hands (as he often builds large gestures that employ bilateralism in significant ways). Either kind of gesture, interestingly, seems to be made when the talk conveys or implies (logical) disjunction, an either–or relationship.

The disjunction of left and right has a literal application in a context where space is thematic:

(5.51)
1   H   Which •side of the engine?
2   Because they're going to ask,
3   which side.

In (5.52), Hussein's hands are raised and held with the palms opposing each other at a distance. His turn includes a disjunction of numbers. The first and second numbers are combined with a body shift, first in one, then the opposite direction, and the third with a smaller repeat of that back-forth-shift. The hands come to rest in the middle.

(5.52)
1   H   During the day I see at least- at least •twenty to •forty,
2   maybe thirty in average customer.

But other alternation schemata such as excursion+return can also signify conjunction. As he adds up the number of his technicians, Hussein makes an alternating movement with his index finger, which is pointing up. The gesture here conjoins 'both locations'.

Fig. 5.51 Alternation: 'which side?'

Fig. 5.52 Alternation: 'twenty to forty, maybe thirty average'

Fig. 5.53 Alternation: 'ten to fifteen/both locations'

(5.53)
77   H   And now here it's really big different
78   its-a slowed down already
79   because you have sixteen technicians
80   ten • to fifteen by both location

'Business going good'

Among the gestures of which only one or two instances occur in the corpus, we have already encountered the 'stepping up' gesture that accompanied reference to self-betterment by studying in school. Another, more idiosyncratic, perhaps unique, gesture accompanies 'business going good': the left hand is held palm up, and the right hand, palm down, moves over and across it, the two together seemingly depicting gliding along a smooth surface.

Fig. 5.54 'business going good'

Fig. 5.55 'finished'

(5.54)
1   H   I'm happy
2   because bu•siness going good

Another gesture that involves skin contact between the hands is the emblem of wiping hands, one of Hussein's 'finish' gestures.

(5.55)
1   H   maybe half an hour
2   we're fi•nished

This, without doubt, is a cultural convention, even if its distribution is unknown: wiping one's hand to signify 'finish' is a metonymy familiar to many.

5.10   The opacity of a gesture: slicing

The last gesture type we examine is a rapid downward, occasionally forward motion, made with the hand held in palm-vertical (palm-side) position. The motion evokes a slicing or cutting act (cf. Calbris 2003a). This gesture

Fig. 5.56 CUT: 'don't call'

appears to have an unequivocal, yet non-intuitive, significance in Hussein's conversations. Invariably, the gesture is coupled with an utterance that either asserts or implies that something is not the case, something that it is wrong, false, incorrect. The gesture seems to be implicated in separating true from false. This connection is seen when Hussein tells the researcher that he told his wife that she calls him at work too often.

(5.56)
```
1    H    Even my wife if she call me
2         some time two three time
3         if a day I tell her
4         You call too much
5         don't c•all please if
6         you're not emergency to call
7         you don't need to
8         And I just answer
9         the necessary answer
          ( - - - )
10        just it
11        I don't have time personal
```

In (5.57), the gesture is made when he says, 'You don't find technicians with experience.'

(5.57)
```
1    H    .hhh You do•n't find also technicians
2         with experience
```

A moment later, as Hussein is contemplating the need to keep some emotional distance from his business, he makes an 'index-up' gesture, a precision grip ('exactly'), and then, as he formulates negative clauses ('if I'm not worried', 'if I cannot be worry'), cutting gestures.

Fig. 5.57 CUT: 'you don't find'

Fig. 5.58 'I cannot be worried'

(5.58)
1 H and I know exactly
2   if I'm not worry about-
3   if- I cannot be wo•rry like this on my business

In (5.59) as well, the gesture is combined with a negative clause. Hussein is talking to a customer. The gesture is synchronized with 'don't'.

(5.59)
1 H You have sticker probably in windshield
2   if you d•on't maybe

In (5.60), the gesture is made when Hussein says to Art that Uncle Ahm 'doesn't know'.

(5.60)
1 H I want to just to make sure
2   the door back together
3   because he don't kn•ow how to put the wires

Fig. 5.59 CUT: 'if you don't'

Fig. 5.60 CUT: 'he don't know'

In (5.61), the cutting gesture is made when Hussein reports how sometimes what a customer tells him will turn out to be false.

(5.61)
1   H   First I put the year-model of the car
2   make sure
3   sometime the customer tell you something
4   and you go by what he told you
5   or what the customer said
6   you find wr•ong

In (5.62), the case is more complicated. The gesture is made several times during an utterance that constitutes a list of positive assertions. But their upshot is negative. While he makes the gesture, Hussein affirms that the three components of the charging system of Ms. Nancy's car are working, which means that the charging system *cannot* be the problem source.

Fig. 5.61 CUT: 'you find wrong'

Fig. 5.62 CUT: Excluding possible causes

(5.62)
1 H   Then the ba•ttery good
2   alternator perfect
3   starter okay
4   One thing left.

All instances of gestures of the CUT type I have found in this corpus, except one that accompanies the phrase 'another part to cut' and 'literally' enacts cutting, have been associated with a notion of negation. This does not mean that they are tokens of conventional 'negation' gestures (for counter-examples, see Streeck 2008c); they may betray an idiosyncrasy, a personal habit or method for displaying that a proposition or presupposition is negated. But what explains the gesture's form, why is the significance of negating 'picked out' by this form? It is difficult to establish a connection. It is possible that the cutting gesture marks a dividing or separating of what is and what is not the case, of true and false, instead of signifying negative polarity, as grammatical forms of negation do. The need to negate or reject makes the true–false dichotomy relevant, and it is this 'higher-level' structure, the dichotomy itself, that is articulated by the gestural act. Incidentally, 'dicho-tomy' means 'dividing in two', and the cutting or slicing gesture could be called the 'dichotomy gesture'.

5.11   The body's position in the world

Calbris (2011) posits, as do I, that gesture is grounded in the body's indigenous position in the world, its life form: its forward-looking attitude toward the world, its relatedness to objects, obstacles, and forces. For example, she writes about gestures that respond to interruptions that

> the Level Hand brusquely positioned in front of the speaker seems to physically want to stop something from coming up from the ground ... ; it symbolically suspends an ongoing process, and in doing so, it pragmatically requests that the process of producing the ongoing utterance is not interrupted. (Calbris 2011: 229)

In (5.63), Hussein's gesture appears to stop the customer's incipient action (speaking), to be holding back his talk. At this moment, a sequence has just been completed and it is open who will take the next turn. Hussein turns to his right and readies his arm, apparently to pick up a pen, but then, as the customer begins to tell more of his sad story ('what happened is'), he briefly shapes his hand, still holding the pen, so that its palm faces the customer as he initiates his own, competing turn. The customer falls silent.

Fig. 5.63 Holding an incoming turn at bay

(5.63)
1 V Okay
2 H [- - • - -]
3 V what happened is uh
                        [
4 H   Let's say now...

Let us call this gesture HOLD-AT-BAY. In (5.64), Hussein makes it when he is rejecting the sense his interlocutor has made of his prior utterance, as it is displayed in the answer. Hussein's gesture does not stop a turn, but *rejects* what the addressee's prior turn had conveyed.

(5.64)
1 H I'm n•ot saying this here
2   let's say different way.

When he launches his own proposal how he will take care of Victor, Hussein's gesture seems to be holding Victor's worries at bay.

Fig. 5.64 'I'm not saying this'

Fig. 5.65 Keeping worries at bay

Fig. 5.66 Closing an activity

(5.65)
42   No, l•et's fix necessary work
43   to get your car back.

The gesture can also stop an action in its tracks when the talk it accompanies does not manifestly include a rejection. In such a case, the gesture conveys that sense on its own. In (5.66), Hussein has inspected and then helped with a young mechanic's work on an Audi. He has concluded that Alex is not up to the task, makes a downward HOLD-AT-BAY gesture toward the car, and states that he himself and Victorio should take over the job. The gesture, through its location in space, appears to convey 'no more engagement [for Alex] with this engine'.

(5.66)
1   H   I wanna• get maybe Victorio, me

How can we account for the *doings* of these gestures, both conceptual and pragmatic; what and how do they contribute to the moment? Let us review what we have found.

5.12   Motor cognition

Our analysis of Hussein's gestures in this chapter has pointed out a number of important features; among these are:

- many conceptual and pragmatic gestures appear to be schematic versions of familiar real-world, object-focused acts;
- they emerge spontaneously; their temporality proves that they cannot be elements of some deliberate 'utterance plan';
- they are unattended by their makers; the speaker generally is not consciously aware of making them;

- nevertheless, like all motor actions, the speaker senses them; they produce kinesthetic sensations that *can* rise to consciousness after the fact;
- listeners rarely respond to these gestures overtly, and we therefore have no evidence to rely on when we want to find out what sense they make of them; nor do they show signs of non-understanding or confusion.

Note, again, that not all of these features are shared by other forms of gesturing: as we have seen in Chapters 3 and 4 (see also Streeck 2009a: ch.5), when humans point, explain an object at hand, or depict something not present in the here and now, their gestures are demonstrably part of a deliberate utterance plan: speakers attend to and monitor their own gestures. Thus, it would be a mistake to lump all modes of gestural meaning making together and assume that they are cognitive phenomena of the same kind. Here, we want to understand how spontaneous, simple, pragmatic, and conceptual gestures make sense, gestures, in other words, whose production the speaker is visibly unaware of. (In the following, I will generally only refer to conceptual gestures; pragmatic gestures are embodied concepts for communicative action and in this respect a subtype of the larger type 'conceptual gesture' or 'conceptual action'.) That even this mode of gesturing is trainable (and has been trained since antiquity), that public speakers and anyone else is *able* to become aware of their gestures and then to begin to gesture methodically and deliberately, must not distract us from the fact that in everyday social interaction this is rarely the case. Rather, the fact that these gestures are *not* made deliberately must be our point of departure for explaining how they make sense. These gestures are not made by the speaker *in order to* express an idea, structure the turn at talk, or hand it over; rather, these gestures—and the meanings they embody—*happen to* the speaker.

In the following I will offer the outlines of a novel answer to the question how conceptual gestures mean. As readers familiar with gesture research will notice, my account has much in common with recent work in cognitive linguistics on metaphorical gestures; but it radically departs from this work in that it regards physical action as a mode of thinking, and gesture as an abstracted, yet fully embodied mode of physical action, rather than taking gestures as expressive of independent cognitive processes. While my account shares this perspective with others, it is novel insofar as it takes the *kinesthetic* nature of gestures as its point of departure, that is, the fact that gestures generate *feelings of action* in the speaker, of actions whose motor patterns are familiar from material, public life. For an interactionist to turn to kinesthesia as a ground for meaning and understanding requires justification, because we usually are committed to studying communication as a *public* process: only what interlocutors can perceive can be the basis for their understanding of what someone means, and what that person *feels*—their kinesthetic sensation of their own motor-actions—is not perceptually accessible to the interlocutor and can therefore not be part of an emerging shared understanding. However, I hope to show that this line of reasoning is grounded in a misconception of how humans perceive the body motions of others, a 'visualist' misconception widely held until not too long ago, but recently called into question.

To lay out a neuroscience-informed account of the way in which conceptual gestures make sense for their makers and interlocutors, we can turn to Marc Jeannerod's book *Motor Cognition* (2006). Jeannerod is a neuroscientist who has studied motor action, especially of the hands (Jeannerod 1984, 1997; Jeannerod, Arbib, Rizzolatti, & Sakata 1995), and *Motor Cognition* provides an integrated view of the state of the art of neurological research on the neurocognitive features and implications of motor action. Jeannerod's model is remarkable, however, in the ways in which it avoids the twin pitfalls of Cartesian dualism and materialism (physicalism) that hobble so much of cognitive science: (1) Jeannerod holds that motor actions are cognitions, rather than the *results* or *expressions* of 'mental' cognitions; (2) his model implies a dialogical (interactive) view of the embodied self; and, (3) in an ingenuous interpretation of the findings about 'mirror neurons', he demonstrates that the resonances with the actions of others that mirror neurons explain are not at all the result of 'mirroring', but of participation in a shared life-world or culture: mirror neurons encode actions with which we are familiar and that we can recognize. Jeannerod presents motor action as a kind of tacit dialogue of the embodied self: the subtitle of his book is 'what actions tell the self'. This is precisely the question we must ask about conceptual gestures: what do they tell the speaker? Jeannerod emphasizes the *autonomic* character of the great majority of our motor actions, the fact that they are spontaneous and often inaccessible to conscious control, yet nevertheless 'cognitive'. So how is it possible that 'autonomic' gestures can tell anything to the speaker's inattentive self?

Key to Jeannerod's model are *motor images*. Motor images are the neural networks activated during the performance of skilled, routinized actions such as getting dressed, taking a bath, making breakfast, as well as playing soccer or piano. Motor images are the schemata involved, for example, when a hand, as soon as the arm begins to move, configures itself to successfully grasp a glass of a certain weight and stability in order to then bring it to the mouth (or, alternatively, move it to the side). 'Implicit motor imagery [is] widely used when preparing actions in everyday life' (28). A characteristic of these actions is that we perform them spontaneously, automatically, without focused attention or consciousness, and usually without even being aware of the component motor acts building up the activity. In fact, many features of these actions are not even accessible to consciousness. 'Consciousness of action is bound to *posterior* signals arising *from the completion of the action* itself' (58, emph. J. S.). 'Consciousness reads behavior rather than starting it, . . . [it] represents a background mechanism for the cognitive rearrangement after the action is completed, e.g. for justifying its results' or rearranging its conditions after failure (65), it belongs to the 'narrative' rather than the 'embodied self' (Gallagher 2005; Jeannerod 2006: 64).

Jeannerod also calls motor images 'action representations'. Both terms lend themselves to misinterpretation: what Jeannerod means by the term are simply the patterns of activation of neurons that correspond to the performance of types of motor actions. They have no imagistic quality, but they allow our bodies to rehearse future actions. Jeannerod explicitly contrasts 'action representations' with 'visuomotor representations': visuo-motor representations encode visual properties of objects' (Jeannerod 2006: 6). 'Generating a motor response to a stimulus and building a perceptual experience of that same stimulus [are] . . . distinct processes' (47). In other words, when we perceive an object or a situation, our body enacts an autonomic enactive response to it—a reach, a refusal, and so forth —which is distinct and different from our production of a visual image of the object or situation. Jeannerod uses the terms 'pragmatic' and 'semantic processing' to refer to this difference. Moreover, when we perceive objects, there is a difference between the encoding of visual properties and that of 'pragmatic properties' (or affordances) of objects (110): we can have a distant observer's or an agent's experience. However, the two systems are connected and inform one another.

Motor images, thus, involve anticipations. They are schemata that facilitate anticipation of the further development of the action and what its successful completion will feel like. In technical terms: the motor image is compared to a 'reafferent copy' of the executed act, and when the action has reached its anticipated completion, they match. Therefore, motor images have been described as 'forward models'.[6]

---

[6] 'A forward model . . . runs in parallel with the actually executed movement. . . . Using information about the movement properties of muscles and limbs, the forward model

The performance of skilled actions can thus be described as a feedback loop in which 'forward-looking' motor images are continuously compared with 'reafferent flow', with 'reafferent copies' that encode the end states of acts. We tune our actions, adapt them to their objects and circumstances, as when a hand adapts its prehensile posture when it takes hold of a cup. In this fashion, we learn. But reafferent flow does not depend on the presence of objects; 'empty' motor actions such as dancing and gesturing also, of course, produce and depend on 'reafferent copies'. To reiterate: When an action is performed, the motor image that is its neural component is retained ('afference copy') and then compared online with 'reafferent flow', information coming from the body's contact with the external world, as well as proprioceptive information (kinesthetic sensations of the action as it is going on: 'reafferent copies'). This constitutes a constant feedback loop by which we keep track of the success or failure of our actions, by which we tune our motor acts, and by which we learn and retain kinesthetic memories or 'tacit knowledge' (Polanyi 1966).

Because of their dialogical nature, motor acts are cognitive acts. Moreover, skilled motor acts are self-organizing: they are not controlled by a central executive organ, but emerge as autonomic responses to objects and situations, and they self-tune as they run their course. This is an important consideration when we seek to explain conceptual gesticulation. Moreover, motor actions are also, in all forms of life, cognitive acts in a broader sense. A body motion enacts the organism's recognition of a relevant feature of a situation and selects it as significant for the organism. It *makes sense* of its situation. Through its movement biography, an organism builds its *Umwelt* (von Uexküll 1957).

---

simulates the unfolding course of the movement, in parallel with the actual movement occurring in the external world. Any discrepancy between the forward model's simulated movement and the desired movement results in corrective commands being issued' (Wilson & Knoblich 2005: 466). Wachsmuth and Knoblich discuss in this context 'the parallels between the computations that occur in motor control and in action observation, imitation, and social interaction. In particular, they examined the extent to which motor commands acting on the body can be equated with communicative signals acting on other people and suggest that computational solutions evolved for motor control in natural organisms may have been extended to the domain of social interaction. They hypothesize that during action observation, by comparing the predictions of one's own motor system with the state of a system being observed, the motor system can be used to understand the actions of others. This could underlie our extraordinary ability to detect and identify biological motion. . . . The social interaction loop would then involve that an actor generating motor commands causes communicative signals which, when perceived by another person, can cause changes in their internal mental state that in turn can lead to actions which are perceived by the actor' (Wachsmuth & Knoblich 2004: 4).

> An autopoietic system always has to make sense of the world so as to remain viable. Sense-making changes the physicochemical world into an environment of significance and valence, creating an *Umwelt* for the system. (Thompson 2007: 146–147)

'The external world is constituted as such for the system by virtue of the system's self-organizing activity' (27). At any moment, movement is significant by selecting a 'subjective' feature of the situation (a 'value', Zlatev 2003), that is, an aspect of *Umwelt* that is relevant to the organism's self-sustenance and that is brought into being *by* the organism's act.

The dialogical nature of the production of motor acts is the key that enables us to unlock the secret of gestural conceptualization. It is only through the execution of the gestural motor act that our body produces 're-afferent copies' and thus makes their cognitive content available to the speaker. By 'cognitive content' I mean the significance and intentionality that the motor act of which the gesture is a schematic version enacts in the lived-in world. It is the (kinesthetic) feedback the body produces in the execution of the action that feeds back into the speaker's ongoing conceptual activity. It is not the case that the gestures express conceptual content that could also be left unexpressed, that they are deliberate visualizations of concepts that the speaker 'has on his mind'. The motor images that are the neural components of physical-cognitive actions encode *pragmatic* features; they are not, as Jeannerod emphasizes, 'visuo-motoric representations' (which they would be under a dualist account, which takes gestures as encodings of mental images). No attention is usually paid to conceptual gestures' visual features, unless these are made salient in the conversation. Conceptual and pragmatic gestures encode *pragmatic* features of stimuli at hand or 'in mind'.

Let us apply this account to gestures: what/how do gestures tell the self?

- Gestures are patterns of action;
- they 'make sense', that is, they go with the drift of the situation and 'take hold' of it, 'pick out a significance' such as the action being performed, an act by the listener to which it responds, the search for a word, or a stimulus arising from the conceptual activity of speaking.

Gestures activate meanings inherent in everyday motor actions, such as the 'point' of a grasping action (i.e., to take hold or possession of an object) or the fact that cutting means to divide into two When a motor action is completed a 'reafferent copy' of the motor image is fed back into the speaker's neural circuits: the speaker feels his gestures, and what he feels are familiar meaningful motor acts.

Thus, rather than assuming that the speaker makes these gestures *in order to express* certain meanings, we assume that the speaker-as-body produces autonomic bodily responses to stimuli, in analogy to the way an enculturated body responds to the appearance of a desired cup with an automatic grasping act. Gestures are cognitions, not the outer signs of 'inner' cognitions.

Gesturing is not only communication with another, but also a tacit, implicit dialogue of the embodied, speaking self. The dialogue usually remains covert and unrecognized, but occasionally it rises to consciousness, for example, when a speaker suddenly 'catches himself' having made a certain gesture and then interprets or corrects it (Streeck 2009a: ch.7).

In real-world action, this reafferent stream often includes sensory information about contact with objects. This is not the case in gestures. In gestures, the reafferent stream is purely kinesthetic. The stroke of a gesture, that is, the phase of the movement that is performed with accelerated effort and speed, might 'increase' or 'sharpen' reafferent flow, whatever this means in neurological terms: it produces a stronger sensation. It enhances the 'feeling of action'. It helps the gesture, as felt action, to 'register'. It brings the gesture closer to consciousness (which it sometimes reaches). It strengthens the speaker's experience of agency. This became apparent when I reviewed variations in the way Hussein closes his hands when he gestures: sometimes by relaxing his fingers after a gesture, sometimes rapidly and with effort. Especially when he searched for a word and then seized upon it with his hand did it become visible how a seizing gesture can be a meaningful act of bodily self-organization by the way it marks the moment as a distinct, meaningful and sensible experience.

5.13   Understanding the gestures of others

When, instead of performing an action, we observe, hear about, or imagine it, no reafferent copy is sent to our brains, but our motor cortex is nevertheless activated: it generates the same motor images that underlie the execution of these actions. From the perspective of research on embodied interaction and communication, the most important finding from cognitive neuroscience, repeated and demonstrated in a multitude of studies of various kinds, is that perceiving the motor actions of others is not a purely visual affair, but activates the motor control system of the perceiver. In fact, the same is true when we remember or imagine motor actions or are being told about them, even when we hear or read metaphors based on motion verbs. To put it in simple terms, while we do not literally *feel* the motor actions of others, our own motor control system resonates with them in a kind of unmediated body-to-body understanding. That we *see* the actions of others is almost incidental to the logic of this understanding; to the extent to which we can perceive them through other senses (e.g., by sensing the air waves in their wake), the mechanism of understanding should be much the same. Thus, surprisingly, a key to the understandings others achieve of someone's motor actions lies in the very feelings (sensations) of action the actor creates in him- or herself. If my account is valid, it is the kinesthetic patterns that provide the speaker with meaning and organize his or her speaking, and the listener makes sense of their overt manifestations by responding with analogous or complementary, yet tacit (covert) patterns of enaction.

Thus, 'motor cortex should be considered a cognitive area ... rather than simply an area devoted to motor execution' (Jeannerod 2006: 36). Motor cortex (and premotor cortex) is always active when motor action is at issue. The fact that we usually do not move when we imagine ourselves (or observe someone else) moving is not due to the absence of motor-related activity in our nervous systems, but rather to the inhibition of the *execution* phase of the motor patterns that are activated in us. Execution commands are given 'downstream' from the motor cortex, 'possibly at the spinal cord or brainstem level' (Jeannerod 2006: 40). In other words, actions are continuously prepared in the brain, but their execution is blocked before execution commands can reach the limbs.

A similar view, focused on gesture, has been formulated by Kinsbourne (2006): body motion and the perception of human motion are initially not separated; the newborn infant responds to body motions of others by imitating them.

> For an infant, to consider a movement is to perform it. To activate the movement pattern in the nervous system (for consideration) and yet not perform it requires inhibitory ability that has not yet emerged. As the nervous system matures, ... the individual becomes able to decompose the synergisms, and undertake any single component movement while holding the rest in check. Or, he can intend or consider an action, but hold its outward manifestation in abeyance by inhibition. (Kinsbourne 2006: 206)

Kinsbourne also asserts the identity of movement and cognition during infancy:

> In infancy . . . thinking and moving have not yet dissociated. Infants' bodily actions are the result of brain activations which themselves represent what the infant is thinking. The infant's thought processes are all embodied. Embodiment of mental activity is not a sporadic event. Rather, it is how thinking began, and the embodiments that are observed in adults are residua of their infant origins. (207)

When we observe the gestures of others, we obviously do not feel the feelings of action these gestures generate in them. Technically speaking, no afferent copy reaches our brain. And yet, our motor cortex generates the same neural patterns as if we executed the action. We do not feel, but recognize and understand it. An observer's motor images can be called representations without subject. In sum, while listeners usually perceive gestures visually, it is motor cortex that resonates with them and 'understands' them by recognizing familiar action patterns. This is *preconceptual* motor cognition, but it is the basis for any implicit or explicit conceptual understanding of gestures. The fact that listeners do not execute the implicit motor acts that constitute (part of) their understanding, as a conversation analyst would want them to, does not mean that the gestures are irrelevant to them.

However, only *known* motions trigger in the observer 'a motor plan to execute the perceived action' (Jeannerod 2006: 105). Currently, it is popular to explain our understanding of the bodily actions of others by reference to 'mirror neurons'. Mirror-neurons are neurons in the F5 area of the premotor cortex (and possibly also in other cortical structures) that encode not only actions that are executed, but also those observed in others. Mirror-neurons encode, in Jeannerod's words, 'goal-directed actions, but irrespective of the agent who performs' (2006: 110). Moreover, mirror neurons such as those corresponding to grasping also respond to the presentation of an object, even if it is not grasped (i.e., the motor system produces a 'coupled' or 'coupling' response, matching the object with the act of obtaining it). In other words, mirror neurons are in play whenever a known action comes into play. According to Rizzolatti & Craighero (2004), when a monkey perceives an action that is in its repertoire, the action is automatically retrieved (with all relevant kinetic and kinesthetic features.) But this means that mirror neurons rather represent a 'vocabulary of object-oriented actions' (Jeannerod 2006: 109) and 'cannot be considered as "perception" neurons' (111). The term '*mirror* neuron', in other words, is a misnomer. These neurons are not specialized for mirroring, but for recognition. They form a 'vocabulary' of actions that an individual knows how to perform and has practiced; they fire whenever an instance of such an action is being observed. Their operation depends on participation in a community in which these actions are shared.

The physical actions humans carry out in the world are almost always transparent; they are transparently meaningful to others. We would not need neuroscience to tell us that, but neuroscience helps us understand the biological mechanisms involved. And even neuroscience confirms what researchers in the interpretive tradition have always argued, that mutual understanding depends on participation in a shared life-world or culture. The conclusion to be drawn with respect to gestures is that they are transparent and recognized in the same fashion in which other motor actions are. This is how conceptual gestures contribute to the sense made in conversation: they express what the body has to say about a matter or the situation at hand, not what the speaker says *by means* of the body. They are bodily concepts, practical concepts, and their contribution would be somewhat diminished if we called them 'preconceptual'. They can be considered preconceptual only from the point of view of linguistic conceptualization, which they ground and anchor (Hutchins 2005), but which they do not need: every practiced act is a conceptualization of some intentional object or circumstance. Finally, a gesture can at any moment *become* conscious, be recognized by the person who has just made it or is still making it, and gesture can be fully enlisted by a playful communicator, for limited occasions. Human gesturers are capable of taking an 'eccentric position' in relation to their gestures, and thus to the significance or 'intent' expressed in them (Plessner 1975). In this fashion, gestures become a medium of self-reflection.

5.14 Autopoiesis by gesture

Movements can become habitualized, and habitualized movements incorporate an *Umwelt*. As Thompson writes, 'the lived body constitutes itself and its surrounding environment through the involuntary formation of habits, motor patterns, associations, dispositions, motivations, emotions, and memories' (2007: 30). To put it differently, iterable movement patterns (habits, a habitus) are the result of the communicating body's self-organization over biographical time. Hussein's repertoire of gestural sense-making habits, too, is the result of ongoing self-making. But by habitually gesturing in certain ways, Hussein is also continuously making and remaking the person that he is, and, given that making gestures is a kinesthetic experience, the man who *feels* a certain way.

I have used the term 'gesture ecologies' to distinguish the ways in which gestures 'functionally' participate in the communicative situation, what they are 'about', and how they are perceived in relation to the environment at hand. In Chapters 3 and 4, we saw how gestures adapt to settings while structuring them, and earlier in this chapter, how gestures' orientations are embedded in the intercorporeal context of the moment. But there appear other, more elusive ways in which a configuration of circumstances that we can call 'ecology' shapes Hussein's gesticulation. Comparing Hussein's gesturing in the conversation with the researcher about his work with those during the consultation with the customer in financial trouble, we see differences that are striking, even though he is seated in the same chair in the same office, behind his desk. There is much diversity in Hussein's gestures when he talks to me; their intentional arcs are shifting, they vary in size, and they are entirely unpredictable. When he talks to the distressed customer, Hussein's gestures are far less varied, larger in size than most in the other conversation, and after a while, they seem nearly predictable. Many of the gestures are open-handed, palm up, gestures of presenting, giving, and shrugs, most of them large and bilateral. It is striking how differently Hussein comes across, compared to the morning conversation. In Texas, where he resides, the disposition he displays through his gestures in the second scene would approvingly be called 'swagger'.

What explains these differences in gestural style between the two conversations? Is it the different role relationship between the parties, or the nature of the activity, or is it related to the fact that Hussein previously had only one, but now has two conversation partners and is oriented toward both of them, an intercorporeal setting that 'triggers' bilateral gestures? Is the repetitiveness of the gestures here a consequence of the repetitiveness with which he makes offers to

Fig. 5.67.1 I will o•rder the pa:rt

Figs. 5.67.2–3 put the ' (- •s -) ca•:r together as mechanical

Fig. 5.67.4 then you able to dr•ive your car.

Fig. 5.67.5 without o•pen the door now

Fig. 5.67.6 O•kay? .hh a::nd

Fig. 5.67.7 wu- • we will prepare

Fig. 5.67.8 I'm 'onna b•uy the door

Fig. 5.67.9 buy e•verything • I need

Fig. 5.67.10 k•eep it available

Figs. 5.67.11–12 if I fi- because we b•usy now on body work a•lso.

Victor, or frames statements as offers? Or does Hussein behave the
way he does because the occasion gives him an opportunity to perform his generosity and largesse for the camera? Humans do not
respond to their circumstances like effects do to causes, and answers

Figs. 5.67.13–16 Let the m•en work on our car for s•ale and c•ustomer c•a:r

Figs. 5.67.17–18 and do nec•essary wo•rk to give you your c•ar back.

to these questions will forever remain unverifiable attributions, as would be statements in this matter by Hussein himself. What we can say with certainty, however, is that his gesturing not only varies moment by moment in response to communicative needs or emerging significances of the moment, but also in a broader fashion between occasions. To gain a full picture of the person Hussein, as it presents itself at the 'surface' of his observable actions, we would therefore need to observe him in many more circumstances than in the work-place alone.

We have already examined several of Hussein's gestures in this con-versation, and we can illustrate Hussein's gesticulation *style* during this engagement with a single sequence. We notice at several points that Hussein's gestures are expansive where, in other contexts, they would not be.

Almost all of Hussein's gestures during the forty-one clauses of this discourse, and a great many among those he makes during the rest of his conversation with his financially distressed customer, are made with both arms and hands; they are large, the hands are open, and the movement opens up toward the customer. Today's average psychologist, if asked to research possible links between Hussein's gestures and his personality, would possibly include him in a large sample and then map frequency, size, and other aspects of his gestures onto independent measures of personality, or personality self-assessment. A different approach would ask if and how gesturing 'a lot', or in certain ways, or repeatedly of certain others or in certain situations, contributes to the *making* of a person that is perceived, by others and/or himself, as, say, an 'extrovert' or 'a generous person'. What kind of recurrent experience of the embodied self is generated by the repeated making of gestures of certain kinds: broad and large ones, angular ones, forceful ones, restrained ones, and so on? Undoubtedly, we feel ourselves gesturing, and our habitual gestures are part of our 'body schema', our specifically configured set of 'I can's'. How our habitual experiences of our speaking and gesturing selves contributes to our embodied sense of self is an open question. The conversation between Hussein, the customer, and, peripherally, the researcher, would be a place to start such an investigation on the scale of a single encounter.

5.15 Conclusion

Pointing and showing are deliberate and methodical communicative activities, taking place at the center of the parties' field of visual and cognitive attention. They are also coherent methods: once a showing procedure has been initiated, the type of subsequent strokes is some-what predictable, at least in Hussein's case, whose showing methods are sediments of innumerable hands-on instructions and explanations. In contrast, Hussein's gesticulation, like everyone's, is spontaneous, not planned, and characterized by incessant, unpredictable changes in form, imagery, and reference. We saw Hussein making slicing or cutting motions when polarities of right or wrong and true and false became thematic, and we saw him mark a point he was making, or the completion of a point, or the completion of an interaction, by forcefully closing his hand. But we also saw him close his hand in this fashion when he found a word he was searching for, when he asserted his professionalism, and when he claimed that he makes sense when talking to customers. I have called this type of gesture 'conceptual' because such a gesture enacts a schema—a 'wrestler's grip',[7] a 'take'— under which the referent, whatever it is, is subsumed. I have proposed that listeners and observers, although often incapable of formulating the sense of the gesture, more often than not agree as to what they make of it.[8]

That gesticulation is spontaneous means that it is self-organizing or *auto-poietic*, that it unfolds without the intercession of a controlling executive organ, a supervising mind. Spontaneous conceptual gestures are a world-knowing body's *autonomic*, 'haptic', cognitive responses to emerging significances in the situation at hand. They 'pick out' a single significance (or condense two) by enacting a schema that 'goes with' or 'fits' it, in much the way a metaphor 'fits' its target. As talk about drinking may elicit a HOLD response (an enactment of a bottle-holding schema), a 'tip of the tongue' moment can make the hand take on a prehensile posture, and when the word is found the hand seizes it and thereby reflexively makes sense of the word-searching moment. The gesture 'formulates' the moment that it gives sensible form.

If we are truly interested in understanding the nature and logic of spontaneous gesturing, we gain little by thinking of them as expressions of a speaker's thoughts. We would only be trying to explain, as ethno-methodologists have never tired to point out (Garfinkel 1967), something that is overt and accessible by something that is not, as the doing of a 'ghost in a [body] machine' (Ryle 1949). Moreover, we could not explain what moving the hands contributes to thinking, how gestures organize thought, what the specific material advantages are of 'acting out'. I believe that

---

[7] Thus the root meaning of 'schema'.

[8] Provided their ability to see gestures like ordinary speakers in ordinary interactions has not been obscured by the influence of folk and academic psychological theories that commonly and falsely attribute gestures to emotional states, dispositions, desires, and traits.

gesturing is a *mode of thinking*, not an expression of thoughts (although it is perfectly legitimate, of course, to say: 'From your gestures I can tell what you are thinking.') Western folk models of the mind as well as academic Western philosophy and psychology have for a long time been dualist, explaining overt intelligent and intelligible behavior as the result of 'internal' or immaterial processes (D'Andrade 1987). This is what makes it so difficult to find a nondualist language for the description of embodied thought (Reddy 1979).

The forms conceptual gestures take show that they are abstract versions of physical actions in the material world. This was especially evident when Hussein, talking on the phone, enacted schematic versions of the actions he was talking about, and later, when he described to me what the problem with Ms. Nancy's car was and how he fixed it. In that case, the abstraction was minimal and recent: the hands re-performed actions they had performed a few minutes earlier, although, as all depictive gestures, in a version enhanced for communication. The body still remembered these actions. But even conventional conceptual gestures have their origin in, and derive their meanings from, ordinary physical actions, though not this particular body's actions—anybody's actions. The meanings that inhere in them as everyday worldly actions, actions such as taking, holding, turning, giving, and so on, make these *genuine* contributions to conceptual activity, which, because it is public, benefits the listener as much as it does the speaker.

Conceptual gestures, like all gestures, are doubly interactive: they are elements of the interaction between speaker and listener (and sometimes other participants), but they are also products and elements of the speaking body's interaction with itself. Gestures have something to say to the self. Acting out a 'cept', completing a physical gesture, even subconsciously, registers a *feeling of action* in the speaker, the more clearly the more energetically it is done. By making gestures, the speaker's living body orients itself to the cognitive and social landscape at hand as an acting body, and it makes sense in the manners in which acting in the material world makes sense: a talked-about dashboard is something that can be fondled, a word can be taken in hand, incorrect statements can be separated from correct ones by making a cut. Even where it concerns virtual and abstract domains, the conceptual and social activity of speaking remains bodily action.

I have described gesticulation as a subjectless activity, uncontrolled by any entity other than the living body itself, which organizes itself through these autonomic acts in response to, or more commonly in anticipation of, emerging significances of the communicative moment. Gesticulation is auto-poietic activity on a number of scales: the emergence of the gesture is auto-poietic, and, although this chapter has focused on Hussein's habitual gestures, not all gestures that are made are habit enactments. Furthermore, gesture habits—or habitualized gestures—represent a living body's communicative self-organization on a biographical scale, much like the repertoire of speaking practices that we will examine in the next chapter. Because gesturing evokes kinesthetic sensations—feelings—repeatedly making gestures that evoke a particular kind of feelings can also make the speaker feel himself, consciously or not, a particular kind of person. Thus, by relaxing into an almost unbroken series of open, 'giving', 'offering', and 'letting go gestures' made by wide-open arms, Hussein may be creating and sustaining within himself the feeling of being a generous person (whereas his Texan compatriots might credit him with 'swagger'). Finally, Hussein is also just another cog in the reproduction of some (unspecified) culture's traditional gesture 'code' and bodily techniques (Mauss 1973).

The turn to neuroscience I have taken in this chapter must not be taken as a suggestion that the explaining of intersubjectivity and intercorporeality should be handed over to it. Rather, the fact that neuroscientists have demonstrated that socialized bodies resonate with other socialized bodies, that our motor cortices generate activation patterns that match those of the actions that we observe, provided we know how to perform them, relieves us of the task of explaining that resonance ourselves.[9] Socialized human bodies are transparent in an immediate way for bodies socialized in the same material culture. Socialized bodies intuitively understand what other socialized bodies are up to. There is no need for intervening conceptual thought, categorization, or inference drawing.

But neuroscience can only play a subsidiary role in interaction research and its investigations of coordination, cooperation, and shared understanding. Gestures, like other communicative acts, can only be understood in contexts; without a specifying context, a gesture cannot mean a thing. And this context is, in the first place, the social action sequence, and the 'place' within it at which it is made. Only the close contextual and sequential analysis of gestures can ever clarify how gestures mean in communication and what a single gesture means, or is understood to mean, in any real moment. Neuroscience tells us about the neural anatomy and processes that make the understanding of conceptual gestures possible, but cannot explain how the understanding of the situated meaning of a gesture is

---

[9] Coming from a linguistic and sociological research tradition, scholars in our field are usually not well prepared to deeply analyze resonance between moving human bodies.

achieved. Only the microscopic analysis of real-time, real-life, real-culture interaction can do this.

But this analysis, particularly that of gesture, will also benefit from a lesson that comes to us from another corner of the natural sciences, biology or 'life science', namely what it and its philosopher commentators (Sheets-Johnston 2012; Thompson 2007) tell us about movement:

- Movement is significant: it enacts a 'subjective feature' of the situation (a 'value', Zlatev 2003), an aspect of *Umwelt* that is relevant to the organism's self-sustenance and that is brought into existence by the organism's act.
- Every movement is cognitive: it embodies the organism's recognition of a feature of the situation that is relevant to its sustenance. An amoeba's motion away from certain molecules selects 'toxicity' as a relevant feature and couples cell and environment. Life scientists informed by Maturana and Varela's (1980) work on autopoiesis as a principle of life call this 'sense-making':

   > An autopoietic system always has to make sense of the world so as to remain viable. Sense-making changes the physicochemical world into an environment of significance and valence, creating an *Umwelt* for the system. (Thompson 2007: 146–147).

- Movements can become habitualized. Habitualized movement patterns incorporate a world (an *Umwelt*).

   > The lived body constitutes itself and its surrounding environment through the involuntary formation of habits, motor patterns, associations, dispositions, motivations, emotions, and memories (Thompson 2007: 30).

With a touch of the fingers, Hussein establishes 'coarseness' as a relevant (action-implicative) feature of the surface at hand (see Chapter 4); with a grip of the hand, he enacts 'having a firm grip' as a relevant property of his professional identity; making large forward-rotating gestures, he enacts 'intercorporeality' as a relevant feature of the talking that he is talking about. In other words, conceptual gestures make sense in the way in which the movements of all mobile life make sense, not in the way of manufactured signs or pictures. (That is the province of gestural depiction, where a different logic is in effect.)

6   Speaking

Mr. Chmeis' repertoire of linguistic practices reveals his self-making on the biographical scale: the day shows a transitory stage of an evolving system, his English. Following a brief assessment of the gaps in Mr. Chmeis' grammatical and lexical resources, this chapter focuses on three areas of language mastery: *action design*, how he designs his utterances as intelligible social acts, including directives, and which routines he has evolved for coping with recurrent communicative action tasks; *information design*, how he designs his utterances to convey information to, and obtain it from, others; and rhetorical and poetic practices and devices that he uses when he tells stories about his work life. Various forms of parallelism and other esthetic methods are not only imprints of an ancient rhetorical tradition, but also means to move the story forward, to facilitate the progression from one utterance to the next; these can be considered poetic methods of speaking.

6.1   An adaptive repertoire

Hussein could not do his work, much less his communication work, without speaking, without knowing and using a language. Every moment we have examined has been a moment of talk: information is gathered, 'situation awareness' (Norman 1993) is achieved and distributed, jobs are allocated through speech. Jobs and the practical actions and tools they involve are typified and sedimented in a common vocabulary. Car parts are identified by a shared technical vocabulary, which is almost all English. Hussein's communicative acts are in part made up of conventional constructions of English and Arabic, in part of personal habits and self-made English linguistic tools that deviate from standard grammar. Sentences may lack a copula, or tense or person-marking, or show interferences from Arabic syntax. One could regard Hussein's

English at the time as a 'petrified learner grammar', an interim, but frozen stage of second-language acquisition, doomed to imperfection. But one can also regard Hussein's documented speech on any given day as an interim product of an ever-evolving, self-organizing set of speaking resources, in which standard English grammar provides a normative model that intersects with self-made, habitualized (idiolectal) constructions. It is an ecological adaptation to communicative circumstances that falls short of native-like competence, but meets all recurrent speaking needs. For as Hussein correctly observes, he 'makes sense when he talks with his customers.'

To give a full account of Hussein's speaking practices in this book is impossible, because this would make for another book-length *practice grammar* of Hussein's English, covering the syntactic patterns he uses in designing linguistic actions, as well as a lexicon, including his work-related vocabulary. The primary aim of this book is to take stock of and account for the bodily practices in which linguistic actions enfold. Speaking, of course, is also a bodily activity and syntax is a set of patterns that organizes bodily behavior. But language is an organization *sui generis*, and reconstructing and describing it, even as a collection of practices, would require an extensive, methodologically innovative identification of (habitual) constructions and their mapping onto the multiple functions that speech serves, including informational and social ones. Thus, I will describe only a small subset of the constructions Hussein deploys in his speech, attempting to include what appear to be the most salient speaking activities he engages in on this day. I begin by listing the most striking and recurrent normative 'deficiencies' in his English. An enormously important question, rigorously pursued by conversation analysts, is how speakers deploy linguistic formats to design the *actions*, such as requests and informing, that they perform moment by moment; this is the theme of Section 6.3. Equally important is how Hussein uses linguistic resources to efficiently acquire and disseminate information, which will be the theme of Section 6.4. In examining Hussein's speech for its *information design*, I draw on the work of construction grammarians, notably Lambrecht (1994). Hussein's English-speaking skills, or rather the skills he brings to bear on speaking English, come into full view only in conversations, for example, when he reflects on his workdays by telling a story: he deploys poetic and rhetorical devices known since antiquity. I will devote the last section of this chapter to those.

Table 6.1 Nonstandard features in Hussein's English

no copula	The wire still good?
	Because the idle low I believe
no auxiliary	We going to fix it.
auxiliary mis-selected	The oil is damage all the rubber
no tense marking	The oil is damage all the rubber
no number marking	The one go up front?
no relative pronoun	The one go up front?
no possessive marking	They bring Corsica part
idiosyncratic causative: make	And now it make missing
adverb misplaced	Then you need too this
auxiliaries reanalyzed as sentence-adverbs	We may should . . .

6.2   Features of Hussein's 'learner grammar' of English

Some of the main characteristics that distinguish Hussein's English from standard grammar are shown in Table 6.1.

In normative terms, Hussein lacks the means to express syntactic and semantic relations, apart from grammatical categories such as tense and number. He seems unable to express identity of referents by using relative pronouns (cf. 'the one go up front'), or, occasionally, semantic roles such as agent and patient ('this the one done transmission?'). And he sometimes mis-positions adverbs ('then you need too this'). At times, Hussein becomes aware of his grammatical errors and corrects them. For example, this mis-positioning of the adverb, 'too', was corrected in the next turn: Hussein said, 'you may need this too.' In these cases it appears that Hussein masters the standard format or structure, but has not fully routinized it. The only time during the day when grammatical errors do make communication difficult occurs during a phone conversation when Hussein orders car parts and constructs a phrase in which the head and modifier are in the reverse order from English: he tries to order a *headlight door* ('light-door'), but calls it a 'door-light', which causes confusion because door-lights in fact exist, but not for the car model in question. Hussein visibly incorporates the corrected version of the part name to his memory: he grabs a pen, as if to write it down.

6.3   Action design: routines

Since Wittgenstein's *Philosophical Investigations* (1953), philosophers, sociologists, anthropologists, and, eventually, linguists in increasing numbers have realized that speaking is, in the first place, a form of social interaction and that each utterance is a social act. Conversation analysts have drawn radical consequences from the insight that spoken utterances are social actions, transforming Wittgenstein's (1953) critical philosophy of language games into a coherent and extremely productive empirical research agenda. They maintain that we design units of talk so that they are intelligible to *this* recipient at *this* moment in *this* conversation as actions of a particular type, transparently relevant to the context at hand (Drew 2013; Levinson 2013). Conversation analysts consequently rediscovered grammar as a resource for interaction (Ford, Fox, & Thompson 1998). They became interested in how grammar works as a resource for *action design*, including the ways in which utterances absorb grammatical material provided by preceding utterances and thereby achieve conversational coherence and progression. In linguistic terms, this interest focuses on the relations between grammatical forms and pragmatic functions of action types. However, the coupling between grammatical forms and action types is weak: grammatical forms are typically suited for many different types of actions. For example, a sentence type such as interrogative is not only used in questions, and questions are not only asked in interrogative form (Schegloff 1984).

A long-neglected dimension of language structure, intonation, came under a conversation-analytic lens in the 1980s (e.g., Selting 1988, 1992). While much of this work focused on the vocal design of turns in relation to turn-taking (e.g., how the completion of a turn is projected ahead by pitch movements; de Ruiter, Mitterer, & Enfield 2006 for an overview see Couper-Kuhlen & Selting 1996), an increasing number of studies has been devoted to prosodic cues that mark the type of action the turn is designed to accomplish. Intensively studied action types include questions (Selting 1992); responses to questions (Ford, Fox, & Hellermann 2004; Raymond 2010); and repair (Selting 1988, 1996), and there has been some work on the prosody of announcements and informings (Goodwin 1996), as well as complaints (Ogden 2010). Yet other researchers have investigated prosodic phenomena that operate, not within, but across, turns and are elements of sequence organization (Schegloff 2007), for example, 'pitch resets' that mark the initiation of a new sequence (Couper-Kuhlen 2004). In the following, purely descriptive section, I describe a sample of the most conspicuously routinized ('prefabricated') linguistic action resources that appeared in the course of the day. They span the range of 'levels' of language structure and include lexical routines, constructions, and what I call, with some discomfort, 'scripts', a term that has become associated with 'mental scripts', activity representations 'in the mind'. Here, the term simply refers to a sequence of speech acts that usually occur in fixed order. I describe conversation management routines; work-allocation routines (directives) and speech acts during immediate physical cooperation; and, very briefly, 'front-stage' routines. Then I turn to the information design of Hussein's utterances.

We can consider an utterance an instance of a linguistic routine when it (a) shares a distinct lexical or grammatical form with other instances and (b) does similar 'jobs' across contexts or within certain kinds of contexts. Theoretically, one can consider linguistic routines habitualized solutions to recurrent communication tasks. Predictably, the type of utterances that appear most readily as 'tokens of types', as 'enactments of sedimented practices', can readily be associated with Hussein's various managerial roles, which we will discuss in the next chapter: for example, he has routines for making inquiries and announcements, both of which enable him to cope with his tasks as manager of knowledge and information; he has routines for giving directives (task allocation) and for ordering parts (resource management). Other routines have more general applications, including methods for answering the phone and for greeting, and there are generic routines such as 'no problem', 'okay', and 'make sure', as well as methods for 'modulating' and 'recipient-designing' actions, for example, using politeness markers when making a request of a customer. Yet other practices are specific (or adaptive) to complex activities in which there may not be a clear segregation or complementarity of roles, as there often is when Hussein gives directives or makes inquiries. The following overview of Hussein's speaking practices is a sample that 'gives an impression of how he speaks', but it is neither a complete picture (because, with one exception, only relatively simple communication tasks are included), nor does it give a precise and full account of the linguistic forms and constructions involved. Nevertheless, we can see how certain overriding characteristics of Hussein's speech—notably syntactic constructions and intonation contours—are responsive to the multiple constraints and requirements under which he operates.

Conversation management

Every conversationalist needs to know how to initiate and end a conversation, and how to respond to an opening and join a termination. Conversationalists also need listeners' practices. Because these tasks are ubiquitous in conversational life, the routines involved are highly typified, short, efficient, and shared. Yet they are also adaptive to contingent, unanticipated circumstances, and thus even the routine case must be considered an 'achievement' over and against ever-lurking opportunities for derailment. A selection from this set can be considered Hussein's conversational *signature*. Foremost among these, as we will shortly see, is his very distinct way of saying 'Hi-Tech Automotive' when answering the phone. Table 6.2 shows a small sample of conversation-management routines.

Some of these routines have distinct intonation contours, for example, summonses. The noise in the shop often requires Hussein to call on a technician twice, and he uses a distinct tone pattern for the pair: the first summons has a rise and high-level tone, the second a rise-fall. That these contours are habitualized can be gleaned from the fact that they are highly predictable.

When he answers the telephone, Hussein self-identifies by what an American hears as 'uh-high tectuhmotive': the phrasing is peculiar. Not so the prosody, which sounds familiar to American ears. Beginning on a mid-tone, his pitch lowers until he ends—'tive'—with a rise to high and a fall to mid-high.

Table 6.2 Conversation-management routines

Summons	Art? Art
Self-identification	u-High techtomotive
Address terms	Sir, Ma'm
Discourse-markers/response tokens	Okay (several varieties)
	Now.
	No problem

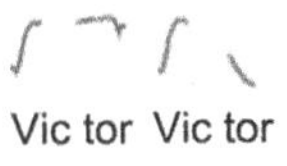

Vic tor Vic tor

Fig. 6.1 Summons

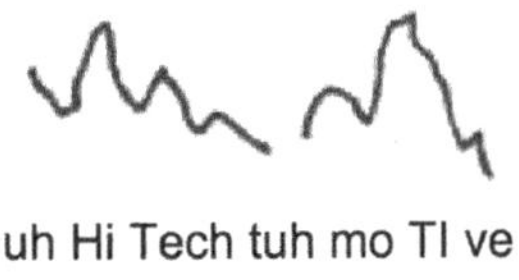

uh Hi Tech tuh mo TI ve

Fig. 6.2 Answering the phone: self-identification

These typified intonation contours are prosodic 'signatures' that enable Hussein's interlocutors, more than voice recognition alone, to recognize who they are talking to. Such typifications are commonplace, of course; everyone has their own way of saying 'hello' when they answer the phone, and Hussein's prosodic signatures are more conspicuous only because they combine with nonstandard phonological patterns.

Greeting routines are enacted when Hussein places a call or greets an arriving customer or delivery person, and, although their pitch level changes with the level of background noise and the distance between the parties, the intonation contours of his greetings appear quite the same across situations. Their 'formality' or 'politeness' is not only expressed by the address term, but also 'modulated' in unexplored ways by the tone with which they are uttered (a rising tone is heard as a friendly summons, a falling tone as an equally polite, but more 'matter of fact' form of addressing the other).

Like the beginnings of conversations, their closings are also occasions to 'do politeness': to use address terms, express gratitude, and say good-bye. These endings also appear typified to a great extent in Hussein's speech, and as with greetings, their prosodic contours appear similar in face-to-face interactions and on the phone.

Table 6.3 Selected scripts

Greeting
Greeting + Self-identification
Ordering parts
Ending a conversation

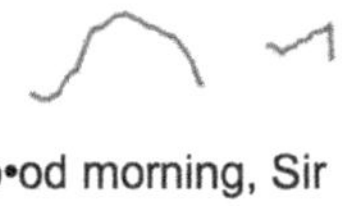

Go•od morning, Sir

Fig. 6.3 Greeting

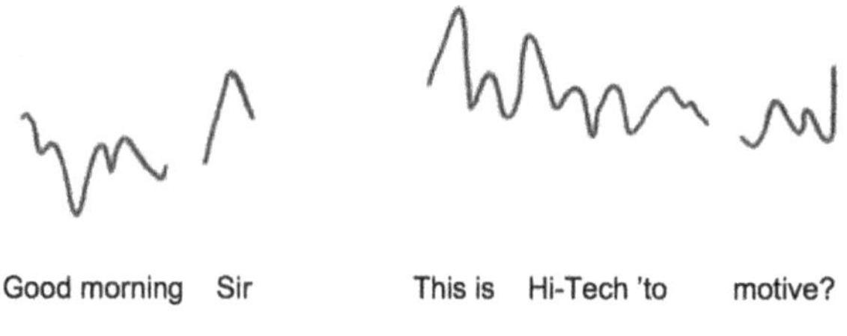

Good morning   Sir   This is   Hi-Tech 'to   motive?

Fig. 6.4 Greeting and self-identification

okay Sir thank you bye bye

Fig. 6.5 Ending a phone conversation

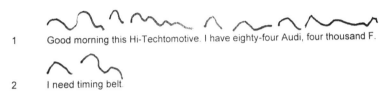

Fig. 6.6 Ordering parts

'Scripts' are multi-turn routines, including formulaic ways of opening, closing, and conducting types of conversations or conversational sequences that follow a protocol, such as greetings, but also larger, formulaic activities such as ordering a replacement part. Some of these are shaped by the constraints of other representation media involved, such as lists, forms, and part numbers. In these contexts, Hussein's prosody appears to be highly routinized, resulting in parallel tone sequences from situation to situation.

The following example of a part-ordering script opens with a greeting, with pitch falling stepwise from high to low and then rising to high, followed by a self-identification, which begins with a high tone on 'this' and then falls continually until it rises again on the final syllable, indicating that there is more to come. Next, the 'year model' of the car is identified in a continuously falling contour, which we hear as 'matter of fact'. Everything in these last two clauses ('I have – I need') is new information, and there is only one high accent on the subject ('I'), until the information has been conveyed in its entirety. However, secondary stress focuses attention on a detail, the series identifier 'F', which is spoken with rising intonation, indicating yet more to come. This is the statement of the need, an identification of the part requested. The label carries a strong rise-to-fall, terminal accent. The clauses are thus tied by intonation, and it is therefore appropriate to think of them, which each constituting a different speech act, as a 'prepackaged' script, a routinized, formulaic speech act series.

These scripted routines show Hussein's skills at using prosody as a means to give his chained utterances a predictable structure, to structure information, and at the same time to give his routine talk personal style.

Allocating work: directives

A critical part of Hussein's managerial work is to allocate jobs to his employees and to inform them about the details of the work to be done. Hussein typically motivates directives by formulating purposes or motives, or he combines them with an announcement of what he himself will do. In other words, directives are not only issued, but accounted for, providing Hussein's coworkers with rationales for his actions and the ones he demands of them. Once a job has been assigned and is being carried out by a technician, Hussein must find out what they need to complete the job. As this information often only emerges as 'the field is cleared'—the transmission taken apart, the dirt removed from the engine—technicians often also approach him with requests for parts or further instructions. Hussein is called upon as resource manager.

Directives—instructions to take specific actions—occur in two kinds of contexts that differ fundamentally in their ecology, although one can easily transform into the other. The first of these contexts are interactions in which Hussein allocates work that is to be done at some future point in time, that is, *after* the interaction is over. The other kind are situations in which Hussein and a technician are working on a job together and Hussein utters directives that are to be acted upon *now*. I call these contexts 'cooperation'. The timing, syntax, and prosody of directives are predictably quite different between the two contexts.

Hussein has a highly differentiated repertoire of request/directive formats. They can be distinguished by the type of causativity involved as well as by the politeness strategy deployed. Yet it is sometimes not possible to determine, on the basis of the form alone, for example, whether an 'impersonal', 'passive directive' ('this need to be fixed') is uttered because the agent of the requested action is deliberately left unspecified or to make the directive more polite. Context usually resolves this ambiguity.

'Straight', unmarked imperatives ('spray little bit') are far more common during cooperation, and when they occur during job assignments, they are usually not the first, but the second or third directive in a series, instructing for a complex action. A 'signature' directive of Hussein's is 'make sure + clause' ('make sure everything work'), which is a 'summary directive' issued, typically at the end of a set of instructions. 'Impersonal directives', which

Table 6.4 Types of directives: allocating work

straight imperative	Spray little bit.
	Make sure everything work.
impersonal, active, necessity	I need this car up.
impersonal, passive, necessity	Need to be tied.
impersonal, oblique, necessity	This man maybe need oil change.
'inclusive we', personal, active	And this we need to see also
'inclusive we', impersonal, active	We need somebody pull the engine.
'inclusive we', imperative, personal, active, self-reflexive	Let's take all the used tire across the street.
felicity condition addressed	Can you get the jeep outside?
	If you have any closer paint
announcement, self-allocation of work	I wanna go get you letter title

occur in both active and passive constructions, leave the actor unspecified: I 'need this done' (active) and 'this needs to be done/needs doing' (passive). Hussein very often uses the 'inclusive we' pronoun instead of referring to himself, appealing, as it were, to a common goal, interest, and perspective on the situation. This is, of course, a conventional way of making polite requests. But note that this collective 'we' can also be the 'causative subject', the procurer, not the agent, of the action, such as when he says, 'we need somebody [=else] pull the engine'. Hussein is prone to utter 'let's imperatives' ('let's + infinitive verb'), which literally is a request, addressed to speaker and hearer, for permission to do the act, but has long become a frozen politeness formula. Hussein also deploys 'negative politeness' strategies (Brown & Levinson 1987), such as asking whether 'felicity conditions' of the request are met, that is, whether the addressee is in a position to carry out the act: 'Can you get the Jeep outside?', or referring to a specific condition for the act, but leaving the act itself unspoken ('if you have closer paint').

Example (6.7) is a characteristic sequence of directive and account. The account shares information about the state of an engine and thereby links symptoms to actions to be taken. The intonation appears typified, an enactment of a prosodic routine in which the upward contour of the first clause, which gives a reason, projects a second reason to come.

Hussein deploys a range of alternative constructions and contours and makes variable and spontaneous choices among them, which gives his interactions an unscripted, lively quality. This is also true of his request intonations: they vary greatly with the level of background noise, the temporal constraints of the situation, and perhaps degrees of urgency or 'arousal'.

Table 6.5 Directives, feedback, and accounts during cooperation

'pre-directive'	Go ahead
directive	Let's see
• initial	Go ahead crank it
• continuing	Keep going
	More [more more]
	Up [up up]
specification	Just hand maybe tight
complex instruction	Push this all the way inside and put clamp here
feedback	Okay
	More more
'auto-directive', announcement	Let me crank.
goal statement, inclusive directive	We need to get the car start.
prognosis (hedged)	We may able to …

We need somebody pull the engine. There is knocking? and the oil-pressure low

Fig. 6.7 Directive + accounts

Cooperation

While 'allocating work', as used earlier, means 'delegating work', work is also allocated, but in different ways, when Hussein and a technician diagnose or repair a car together and 'all hands' are needed for the task. I call this context 'cooperation'. Cooperation naturally involves directives, instructions to the technician or apprentice how to participate *now*, as well as feedback once the action is under way, much of it in the form of further, truncated directives ('keep going', 'more', 'okay'). A 'pre-' or 'dummy' directive, for example, 'go ahead [crank it]', is uttered when the addressee is directed to perform a *new* action, different from the one he is currently in the process of performing. 'Auto-directives' have the form of reflexive 'let'-directives ('let me') and are announcements of an action Hussein is about to take. Finally, Hussein accounts for the requests he makes by formulating goals and giving prognoses, usually hedged by a modal adverb: 'we may able to'. In this fashion, he not only legitimizes

Table 6.6 Front-stage speech acts

informing	It's done
	It's ready
	About an hour
	First of all, visual inspection no charge
offer	Let me fix mechanical
recommendation	What we need maybe one day
prognosis, hedged promise	We may able to
directive	Turn the engine off please
negotiating, meta-communication	You have to go very fair

mh back back more more more   more more   more more more?   back   That's it.

Fig. 6.8 Directives during physical cooperation

the exercise of authority, but teaches: he makes his automotive reasoning transparent.

In contexts of cooperation, the prosody of directives is far more formulaic and standardized than when Hussein allocates jobs, but the directives are also 'minimized' in their syntactical structure and timed to cohere with the unfolding of the technical activity under way. The following is a characteristic sequence. Here, Hussein and his apprentice Alex are troubleshooting the engine of an Audi and adjusting the timing belt; Hussein fastens one wheel with a screwdriver while Alex tightens a bolt.

Front-stage speech acts and tactics

A last, heterogeneous group of speaking routines comprises various 'front-stage routines' by which Hussein transacts business with customers. These occur on the phone, when he responds to inquiries, or when he does the paperwork during an intake or checkout. The routines unsurprisingly contain many expressions of politeness, deference, and generosity. For informings on the phone, Hussein appears to also have a few formulas, such as 'it's done', 'it's ready'.

Hussein's interactions with customers of course involve a broad range of speech acts: responding to inquiries; making proposals, recommendations, and offers; informings; greetings; and apologies. But, as we have seen in particular in Hussein's interactions with Richie, the potential buyer of a white Jeep, Hussein also uses *tactics* (de Certeau 1984) to bypass uncomfortable or difficult possible paths the interaction could take. One such tactic is the 'abuse' of action formats and routines for uses for which they were not designed. Tactics are *practiced ad hoc solutions* to local circumstances, rather than implementations of prefabricated plans. Examples of tactics include flights into irony, teases, and also Hussein's use of (conversational) repair in his sales negotiation with Richie (see Chapter 1), in which he derails her demand to know the price at which he bought the Jeep by acting as if he does not know what car she is talking about, and requesting repair, and then launching a second repair initiation.

(6.1)
8   R   =Okay, (- -) I don't wanna buy the car.
9   What'd you pay for the car?
        (- -)
10 H   Which car?
11 R   This car.
12 H   What I pay?
13 R   Yeah.
14 H   I bought it from the auction. (-)
15   With- damage in the body and I have to fix it.

6.4   Creating situation awareness

The two aspects of Hussein's linguistic management, assigning work and managing knowledge, are not separated from one another; after all, a question is a request for action, and a command often provides knowledge of facts. Yet knowledge management brings another aspect of speaking practice—of utterance design—into play, information design. Managing the flow of information and knowledge across members of the team and ensuring that everyone concerned has adequate 'situation awareness' (Norman 1993) are of particular importance, because of Hussein's role as a relay in all information transmission. The most important action formats occurring in this context, inquiries (questions) and informings, have already been discussed.

An activity in which knowledge management takes on more complex and diversified forms because it is combined with the joint finding and

Table 6.7 Speech acts involved in the creation of situation awareness

inquiry	What year model
	What Mike he has now
	What about the van
	What you still have on that car
	What's wrong with this
	This truck the one done transmission?
'conditioned inquiry', request for clarification	Which one you mean
	The one go to the front?
informing	Mike he coming now
	This cross the street
	We have another car to cut
	We almost finish
prediction	We may use later on

Table 6.8 Speech acts during inspection of work

directive	Look
(focusing attention)	See what happen here
'pointing'	This here
	This here Uncle Ahm
noticing + directive	This here? Need to be all fixed
(topicalization + comment)	This here need to be
	This man maybe need oil-change
noticing	Antifreeze leaking
(all new information)	

'disclosing' of significances in the world, the shared gathering of information, are inspections, when Hussein 'checks up' on a technician's ongoing work. On the day I filmed Hussein, it mostly involved younger members of the team, who were tasked with getting refurbished cars ready for sale. This is a context in which what we could call 'pointing constructions' are particularly common, that is, utterance formats whose first parts are usually coupled with some pointing gesture, the part achieving indexical reference, and whose second part specifies an action to be taken on the object.

Another type of activity combines elements of inspection with elements of cooperation. Hussein calls this activity 'troubleshooting'; I call it 'diagnosis'. These are interactions in which Hussein, either with a customer or a technician, seeks to find out what causes the symptoms that have brought the car and its owner to the shop. As during inspections, Hussein may

Table 6.9 Speech acts during diagnosis

directive	Watch this
(focusing attention)	Listen to this compressor
	Listen to the clutch when it's kick
diagnosis	Clutch is kind of loose
	Charging system perfect
	I think timing belt jump
	Maybe battery low
	The idle low I believe
noticing, informing	Now no fuel
	Too much gas now
	Exhaust leak somewhere
directive (requesting action)	Go ahead start the car
proposing action	We may should put new timing belt

Table 6.10 Speech acts associated with resource management

inquiry	What you need, door?
	We got everything you need?
conditioned inquiry, repair initiation	Only one you need
	Ordering parts

notice something, a feature or event, and focus the listener's attention on it, and then formulate a hypothesis, often including an epistemic disclaimer or 'hedge', a modal adverb like 'maybe' or an epistemic verb like 'believe' or 'think'. Diagnosis can require physical cooperation with a technician or customer to produce the symptoms at issue, for example, start the car so he can hear the engine. Directives request cooperation and direct attention, while various kinds of informings reveal to the other what Hussein perceives and what diagnostic conclusion he draws from the perception.

A further set of managerial tasks associated with knowledge management concerns the management of resources: knowing what is needed, where it can be obtained, and what the costs of obtaining it will be. Hussein routinely checks on technicians to find out what replacement parts or tools they require, and then orders them, or discusses with an employee whether and where a part can be procured. With the exception of the part-ordering script we have already observed, the practices in this category overlap with those in the 'work allocation' and 'knowledge management' groups.

6.5 Information design

Let us examine more closely how Hussein manipulates the syntax (word order) and prosody, specifically stress placement, when he passes information on to others. For this, it is necessary to lay some groundwork and explicate a handful of basic concepts of *construction grammar* that concern utterances' information design. Lambrecht, along with Kay (1987), Fillmore (1991), Goldberg (1995), and other developers of construction grammar, introduced the term 'information structure' on the basis of the observation that construction alternatives in a given language ('allo-sentences') are motivated by constraints on how new information can be introduced into the discourse so that listeners can track it and relate it to previously shared ('old') information, as well as to the interactional context of the moment. In other words, different sentence formats handle the distribution of old and new information differently.

In information-structural terms, sentence-like utterances (utterances by which a speaker expresses a proposition) consist of a *topic-expression* and a *comment-expression*: an identification of the entity being talked about and a phrase that expresses what is being said (asserted) about it. This latter part of the utterance, which provides new information, is called 'focus'.[1] 'Focus' is that 'portion of a proposition which cannot be taken for granted at the time of utterance. It is the unpredictable element in an utterance' (Lambrecht 1994: 207). When the topic is known, utterances have a characteristic prosodic structure: there is minor stress on the topic expression, and the main stress falls on the comment or focus expression. Bolinger wrote that prosodic stress 'marks the "point" of a sentence' (1994: 152).

Unfortunately, there is an overlap in terminology that gives 'focus' two almost contradictory senses, and one may wonder if linguists would have labeled the new information 'focus' if they had studied language use in work settings. At Hi-Tech, focusing *attention* is an essential task, and it is usually done by pointing gestures that are coupled with deictic expressions. In Lambrecht's terminology, the expressions are topic-expressions, whereas the comment that the speaker makes—the predication—is called 'focus'. Thus, the focus-expression is *not* the part of the sentence that focuses attention, but the part that is usually uttered *after* attention has been focused by the topic-expression. To avoid confusion, I use the terms 'topic' (or 'topic constituent') and 'comment' (or predicate/predication),

---

[1] To be precise, 'topic' and 'focus' refer to pragmatic relations between constituents and the proposition that is being expressed. One constituent is the *topic* of a proposition, the other its *focus*.

rather than 'focus', and continue to use 'focus' and 'focusing' to refer to devices and practices designed for focusing *attention*. But I will retain Lambrecht's terminology when distinguishing different kinds of focus relations in a sentence or utterance ('focus types').

There are three focus types. In 'predicate-focus' constructions, the most basic one, new information is given in the comment, whereas the topic is presupposed to be known. In predicate-focus constructions, main stress falls on the predicate, minor stress on the topic-expression. Thus, the speaker may have said sentence (1) in response to the question 'what happened to your car?'

(6.2)   My car broke d**ow**n.

'Sentence-focus' constructions, on the other hand, are used when the entire sentence provides new information. In English, sentence-focus constructions have the same syntactic form as predicate focus, but they have different prosody: they only carry one accent, which falls on the subject.[2]

(6.3)   My c**a**r broke down.

As Lambrecht notes, this sentence is not about the car, but about the speaker, and it may be uttered in response to the question, 'What happened to you?' or 'Why are you late?' The speaker, indexed only by the possessive 'my', is what the utterance is about, that is, the topic. We can illustrate the difference with an example related to Hussein's telephone conversation with Ms. Nancy. After Hussein hangs up the phone and turns to me, he says:

(6.4)   She's outside New Braunfels
         and her car broken down.

The clause in line 1 is about Ms. Nancy, and Hussein presumes that I know (or that it is irrelevant for me to know) who 'she' is. Clearly, the clause is

She's outside New Brownsville

and her car broken down.

Fig. 6.9 Sentence-focus intonation

---

[2] In other languages, rather complex morphosyntactic constructions may be required to build 'sentence-focus' utterances, e.g., in French, 'J'ai ma voiture qui est en panne'.

The clutch kind of loo:se I think

Fig. 6.10 Predicate-focus intonation

about her; she is the topic of the sentence, and that 'she's outside New Braunfels' is the focus, 'new information', and this sentence, too, is about Ms. Nancy. This sentence has *predicate focus*. The clause in line 2 has 'sentence focus': both 'her car' and 'broken down' are newly introduced into the talk, they are 'new information'. Only 'car', the sentence subject, is marked by stress. The sentence accent is on 'car', not 'down'. In contrast, when Hussein and Art are listening to the rattling noise coming out of the air conditioner of a car 'when it's kicked', he produces two accents. With the phrase 'the clutch', he introduces the topic; the accent on 'loose' indicates that this feature of the clutch is the focus of the sentence.

Hussein appears to have a profound and subtle understanding of English intonation. English is a language that has rigid SVO word order. As a result, the basic English SVO construction is 'unmarked with respect to its information structure' (Lambrecht 1994: 131). The difference is mainly communicated by prosody: in 'predicate-focus' sentences, in which the new information is about an already known topic, only the subject is stressed.

'Argument-focus' sentences are those in which not the entire predicate, but only one of its arguments is 'new information' and focused. English can handle these, too, without altering the canonical SVO order, simply by stressing the focused argument. Thus, in the following sentence, everything but the prepositional (or oblique) argument 'head-gasket' is old information.

(6.6) This comes out of the **hea**d-gasket.

English, like other languages, has alternative constructions for drawing attention to the focus and topic of a proposition. For example, in the following SVO sentence, 'only one' is the focus.

(6.7) You need only **o**ne?

But the focus can also be moved to the left, that is, uttered first, in a sentence with inverted word order.

(6.8) Only **o**ne you need?

Lambrecht calls this construction type 'focus movement', 'left focus'; we might also call it 'focus first', in deference to the temporal nature of these positionings. 'Fronting' the focus in this way is a means to draw attention to and emphasize it. This, then constitutes another 'layer' of language form, and syntax (placement) and prosody can serve similar functions: in addition to marking old and new information, prosody can be modulated to emphasize non-focused items, to mark the unexpected (by contrastive stress), and to display stances such as disagreement, surprise, or calm. While we cannot investigate these modulations here, it very much appears as if Hussein masters these all.

In addition to focus 'movements', there are also topic 'dislocations', which allow speakers of languages to 'topicalize' a non-subject constituent (provided the language has 'subjects' and subjects are topics in canonical sentences). 'Left dislocations' (topic-first constructions) put the topic in initial position, and the topic is 'copied' or 'resumed' by a pronoun in the main clause; 'right-dislocation' means appending the topic after the clause, in which case it may be cataphorically indexed by a pronoun.

(6.9)   Some of the technicians they hate me.

('Topicalization' is also a term used more restrictively to topic-first constructions in which no additional pronoun refers to the topic.) A third construction type are 'clefts', in which the topic and the new information are distributed across two interlinked clauses.

(6.10) But uh about the oil leak
       if you have a chance to stop by one day?

Hussein makes abundant use of topicalization constructions; they are, to an extent, a distinctive component of his linguistic 'information management' machinery, and, given that they are less common in English, they appear to reflect an 'interference'—or should we say support?—from the syntax of spoken Arabic. These are some examples:

Table 6.11 Topic-first and topic-last constructions

Topic first: 'left dislocation', 'left topic'	Some of the technicians they hate me. And then the technician they get confused. Some people they ask for ideas.
Topic last: 'right dislocation', 'right topic'	It's cracked, both. Those going to salvage auction now, these car. What he has, Cedric.

As the topic can be 'fronted' and thereby made salient, so can the sentence 'focus', that is, the piece of new information provided in the sentence about the topical referent. Lambrecht calls this the 'focus movement construction' (1994: 225). In (6.11), it is understood that Victorio needs a fuel injector. Hussein answers:

(6.11) Only one you need?

Here, 'only one' is the sentence focus.[3]

To fully appreciate how Hussein's (or anyone's) utterance design—the constructions he instantiates—facilitates his communicative work, one must investigate them in the context of practical action. It is here that they show their adaptability. An example is how Hussein deploys topic-comment structures when he inspects the work of a technician and identifies spots that need his attention; where the topic constituent and the comment are sometimes separated by seconds, the first part formulates the moment of discovery and specification of an item, the second the action to be taken in relation to it. Often in such cases, topic 'left dislocation' can be found. The sentence is delivered in two intonation units, and the first is coupled with a pointing gesture.

(6.12) This
       cross the street.
(6.13) This here
       need to be all fixed
(6.14) This here need to be tied all
(6.15) The front right-side tire
       you need to switch with that tire

Here we find utterance design optimally adapted to the structure of basic communicative acts of 'inhabiting', namely inspecting and conceptualizing the world at hand for the benefit of another. The sentence format of these linguistic actions—deictic reference + predication—is of course very common in human languages, because it matches the structure of action.

Questions

As important to Hussein's work as disseminating information by 'indicative' sentences is his acquisition of information through questions. Hussein's question design shows some deviations from standard English.

---

[3] The terms 'topic' and 'focus' (in Lambrecht's sense) equally apply to interrogative and imperative sentences as they do to indicatives.

Table 6.12 Yes/no question formats

Yes/no question format: no inversion, no auxiliary	We got all the part you need? You got the part for the Corsica? You adjust mixture?

Table 6.13 Wh-question format

Wh-question format: no inversion, no auxiliary	From where you got this cap. What Mike he has now.

But this deviation is not so much a deviation in the forming of constructions as an inability to use them in the given context. What we find are 'work-around' solutions to the problems this deficiency causes. Some of these can be attributed to his difficulty in using pronouns to form relative clauses, others to the absence of auxiliaries. Moreover, Hussein never uses inverted word order to mark questions, as standard English does.

Hussein also maintains SVO order in wh-questions; again we can explain the structure by the absence of the copula or an absence of inversion. In wh-questions, the focus—the 'point' of the sentence—is by definition the question word, that is, the 'new information' it is designed to elicit.

Note that in the sentence 'What Mike he has now' (in Table 6.13) several construction practices discussed here converge: the preservation of SVO in wh-questions; the lack of question intonation; but also 'left dislocation' of the topic and cross-reference by a pronoun 'inside the clause' (cf. 'Mike he has').

6.6 Poetics and autopoiesis

The reader would get a terribly skewed and impoverished impression of Hussein's speaking abilities if I only showed how he talks on the job, during entirely functional and time-compressed activities, however skillful his communication may be. All of my friends and colleagues who met Hussein at his shop commented on his charisma, but his skills at designing talk and performance—his 'rhetorical range'—only reveal themselves fully in leisurely, story-prone situations. As a guest at Hussein's large and frequent parties, I have seen him 'at the top of his game', but because there he spoke Arabic unless he spoke to me, I could therefore not follow the game. But there were also some moments during this day when he took a few minutes to relax in his office or on the front bench and to explain to me what I was filming.

Crazy days

Around nine o'clock in the morning, I sit with the camera on my shoulder opposite Hussein in his small office and he begins describing to me what his workdays are like, giving me his perspective on things, and portraying his own self-reflections. He gives me context for what I am recording. He casts this in the form of a story and becomes animated as he animates himself and other characters. His pitch range rises to 315 kHz (in comparison to 110 kHz during many interactions with technicians), and the frequency of steep drops and rises in pitch increases. And Hussein builds his talk scaffolded by ancient rhetorical, poetic, and dramaturgical devices. I will identify and describe these now by roughly following the chronology of the telling, occasionally drawing comparisons to utterances from other story parts. I exclude Hussein's musings about how he makes sense when he speaks with his customers, because I have so closely analyzed it in Chapter 5 that it would be boring to the reader. I call Hussein's story *Crazy Days*, as this is, by and large, the image of his workdays that he is talking to convey: perhaps the present day seems quiet, but I should have seen him on other days, let alone in his shop in Riyadh! To Hussein, though, it appears that only a crazy man could keep up this pace, multitasking as he does. So, then, is he crazy? The distance between the enactive and the self-reflecting Hussein sitting at home with a glass of Bourbon is large.

Hussein launches his telling when I tell him that I am astonished by the sheer multitude of tasks he deals with moment after moment, how he often manages to juggle several roles at once. Hussein raises his index finger, flagging an important contribution to the topic, and says, 'Tell you one thing' and 'I don't know if I ever spoke about that with you.' This sentence addresses the need for relevance of what is to come, but it also already casts Hussein in a metacognitive, self-reflective state, a stance he takes during much of what is to come. What the 'that' is that Hussein may or may not have previously talked to me about is never quite specified. The story, however, is about Hussein thinking about his crazy days. In a standard story beginning, 'one time...' (once upon a time), he introduces the setting and main character: 'One time I was sitting by myself at home.' This could be a setting for an unexpected, intrusive event or for happenings that rather take place within the character: a story about thinking. Then, another character is introduced, his wife, a potential listener, so that the story about his thoughts can be told as a story about a conversation about his thoughts. Yet throughout, the perspective from which events are told, even what the story is about, shifts. In other words, the story frame serves to organize a multiplicity of themes and ways of seeing things.[4]

(6.16)

1	H	Tell you one thing
2		I don't know if I ever spoke about that with you
		(1.2)
3		One time I was sitting by myself (.) 't home
4		with my wife, weekend.
		(- -)
5		Drinking Chevis, my favorite drink, Chevis
11	H	ptt and it's- just start thinking about
12		hh how I run my business.

We notice a poetic device, alliteration, in line 4.

4   **with** my **wife**, **weekend**.

Alliteration and other forms of parallelism become rather frequent in Hussein's emerging telling.

Hussein now frames the story as a conversation with his wife. But as he begins, he sees me fiddling with the camera, which causes him to make sure he is still being filmed. He frames the story as a document.

15		.hhhh and I told my wi:fe
16		I don't kno:w
		(- -)
17		how hard I- (-)
18		you're still- we're still in it
19	J	No no no it's okay

He continues:

20	H	I tell her I don't belie:ve
		(- -)
21		because she don't know about my business
22		I tell her I don't believe how I can do: that every day
23		for twenty yea:rs

And then he switches focus and frame: he casts himself from the ambivalent perspective of his employees, as someone who has a social role to play, the

---

[4] A repair sequence establishing that 'Chevis Regal' signifies Chivas Regal (lines 6–10) is deleted from the transcript. Similarly, sections that contain material that may be relevant to the interaction, but not to the phenomena in question, will be omitted in other transcripts in this chapter. They are included in the full transcript in Appendix 2.

role of role model, but who is not appreciated in that role by all. In this segment, we detect numerous poetic devices.

Hussein continues:

24		and mo- some of the technicians they ha:te me
25		and some of the technicians they lo:ve me
26		more than they love their family
27		because they build themselves,
28		in my experience they do a lot better
29		.hhh when they: uh- (- - -) copy me.
30	J	M hm
31	H	Special people they wanna (- -) prove themse:lves
32		they wanna learn the business
33		and they go and open own business
34		those people they appreciate me because
35	J	Right
36	H	they successful.

We notice another case of parallelism or repetition:

24	and mo- **some of the technicians they** ha:te **me**
25	and **some of the technicians they** lo:ve **me**
26	more than they love their family

Here, Hussein copies almost the entire clause, including its prosody, and thereby frames and highlights the antithesis *hate – love*. We also find repetition across lines 25 and 26:

25	and some of the technicians **they lo:ve** me
26	more than **they love** their family

As well as alliteration[5]:

25	and some of **the t**echnicians **th**ey lo:ve me
26	more **th**an **th**ey love **th**eir family

We finally take note of the three-part structure of this statement, which instantiates another classic rhetorical form: an antithesis is set up and highlighted through parallel construction, and the third line 'takes it to another level': it compares, generalizes, concludes, or states the thematic relevance of what the antithesis signifies. This form is also instantiated in the following extract in which Hussein asserts the value of having accumulated experience ('I did this before.'):

---

[5] I have included /t/ in this series because of its phonetic proximity to /th/; this is not literally alliteration.

117   something wrong then **they cannot**- (- -) tr*i*ck **me**
118   **they cannot** (-) ch*ea*t **me**
119   because I did this befo:re

In a later segment, we find a three-part list, followed by a rhyming (cf. 'way') 'upshot':

147   H   this (.) part of my professional
148   **the way I** talk with my customer
149   **the way I** diagnosis their problem
150   **the way I** treat him
151   **I always make** money

Parallelism and other such utterance-design devices can be—and have been—analyzed from at least four perspectives: for their esthetic properties, which is the classic *poetic* perspective; as persuasive devices, that is, as devices to engage and persuade audiences, which is the *rhetorical* perspective; from a *text-linguistic* perspective, as means of anaphora that provide textual coherence; and as devices by which an improvising speaker scaffolds his progression from word to word, from utterance to utterance (from line to line); this is a perspective derived from the study of *oral poetry* (Finnegan 1977; Havelock 1963), a mode of speech production illustrated today by *freestyle* rap. Whereas in traditional forms of oral poetry, parallelism (or repetition) of all kinds has been shown to play decisive roles in organizing and sustaining memory, in the context of *freestyle*, the rapper's incessantly pressing task is to make it to the next line. The rapper's linguistic skills are already tuned to parallelism because of the need to rhyme,[6] and other forms of repetition not unlike the ones observed here enable the rapper to get from line to line: when the format of a beginning line is that of the previous one, thought can be focused on the line that will come next. Hussein, I believe, at times betrays a poet's tuning to the music of language, as he builds engaging lingua franca narratives and shows a public speaker's persuasion skills at the same time. He must have imported these from Lebanon with ease.

39   All day like this
40   J   Hm
41   H   all day like this.

Further occurrences of alliteration are:

59   .hh afternoon I **m**eet **m**aybe **m**any **m**any people.
62   That's **w**hy I use to **w**ear **o**ne like this

---

[6] Rhyme is the form of parallelism that fairly defines our traditional forms of poetry.

66   wireless microphone to sp<u>ea</u>k **w**ith the people
107   I leave him **a**lone **li**ttle bit

These alliterations may seem random and coincidental or 'not even there', existing only in the beholder's eye. However, in light of the many alternative ways available for saying the same things and the frequency of consonant repetitions, we can appreciate that this is not a by-product of semantic word-choices alone.

Further occurrences of alliteration are:

59   .hh afternoon I **m**eet **m**aybe **m**any **m**any people.
62   That's **w**hy I use to **w**ear **o**ne like this
66   **w**ireless microphone to sp<u>ea</u>k **w**ith the people
107   I leave him **a**lone **li**ttle bit

Alliteration in line 59 is blended with assonance, and together with equidistant stresses, these devices can give Hussein's speech rhythm:

59   .hh afternoon I meet **may**be **ma**ny **ma**ny people.

Repetition of sentence parts is a device that is used when a list is constructed:

50   afternoon you see about hundred hundred-fifty peo:ple
51   **between** your **employees**
52   **between customer** came to pick up car
53   and people they give them ri:de
54   people they come just-
55   they want to introduce them to me:
56   or introduce me to them

This segment contains other examples of parallelism:

53   and **people they give** them ri:de
54   **people they come** just-
55   **they wan**t to introduce them to me:
56   or introduce me to them

as well as a case of a kind of parallelism with reversal of elements:

55   they want to **introduce them to me**:
56   or **introduce me to them**

Full repetition is, of course, also a device to convey just that: repetition. It is common during dramaturgical enactments. In this example, the repetition is combined with depictive gestures:

39   **All day like this**
40 J   Hm
41 H   **all day like this**.

Text linguists regard repetition and other forms of parallelism as cohesive devices: what belongs together is constructed in like manner. From a 'freestyling' perspective, however, it can also serve as a device for the speaker to effortlessly move from one topic to another, or one perspective to another. Here, parallelism is used in the transition from a narrative statement in the second person to generic 'you', by which Hussein 'zooms out' to a bird's-eye view of his shop in Riyadh, after having depicted that shop in a way that had included the listener as would-be participant.

44   you can- **you can't** follow me in that shop
45   because **you talk** about forty-five person,

And, arguably, even a simple construction like the following, in which elements are simply reordered, can relieve the speaker of a certain amount of construction effort, if we want to see it in cognitive-psychological terms. A more general explanation would be that the speaker 'keeps an ear on his talk' and lets his esthetic sense, his *pattern recognition*, guide him in moving from utterance to utterance: he copies (some of) what he hears himself say.

62   That's why I use to wear one like this
66   wireless microphone to speak **with the people**
67   **not with people** face to face

Another formulaic device Hussein uses at one time as a 'progression device', along with an emphatic phrase ('at least at least'), can be called 'calculating' or 'arithmetic':

47   during the day I see at least at least **twenty to forty**
48   **maybe thirty in average** customer

The following segment collects a few of the devices we have identified.

104   Every technician here they working ha:rd
105   I invest everybody time one hundred percent
106   And sometime I feel tired,
107   I leave him alone little bit
108   to brea:the
109   I said he needs (- -) break
110   he needs to work easy now
111   he don't wanna (- - -)

112 they don't wanna work rushed
113 but some time (- -) I know this job has to be finished
114 by hour or two hour or less or more

We have already noted the muted alliterations in the first two lines. Then comes a three-part structure in which the first two parts are tied by repetition and assonance. Note also the near-rhyme 'leave- breathe':

106 And sometime **I feel** tired,
107 **I leave** him alone little bit
108 to brea:the

Then comes what is projected as a three-part list, but contains a shift in reference that breaks the parallelism of 'he [needs, does]'. The three-part structure has the logical form of assertion-assertion-negation; that is, the third contains an antithesis to the first two. And the third part, which seemingly begins with a statement about a particular technician, is cut off and replaced by a statement about (all) technicians; the third part contains a generalization.

109 I said **he needs** (- -) break
110 **he needs** to work easy now
111 **he don't wanna** (- - -)
112 **they don't wanna** work rushed

Hussein concludes with a prepositional phrase that is built as a disjunction of disjunctions, a pair of pairs: (hour or two hour) or (less or more).

113 but some time (- -) I know this job has to be finished
114 by **hour or two hour** or **less or more**

Dramatization

Hussein dramatizes events several times during his monologue. Two instances are very brief, but nevertheless alert us to possibilities of dramatizations, affordances provided not least by the many roles the speaker's body can take in them. In the first, Hussein shifts his narrative perspective to the second person, using what appears as 'generic you': 'and if you see that shop in Saudi Arabia'. But then, as he continues, that 'you' is fairly called upon the scene, as a singular observer physically affected by the goings-on. Hussein says, 'you can't follow me in that shop', and as he does, his gesture push back the observer who is following him. This is a micro-performance, fleeting and inconsequential, and yet, when a distant scene is being depicted, the large and forceful hand gestures and bodily stance of the speaker have an immediate felt effect on the listener, who vicariously and schematically experiences the goings-on in the shop in Saudi Arabia.

56   And if you s•ee that sh<u>o</u>p in Saudi Arabia
57   • that   it'•s- (- - - -)
58   you c•an- you can't follow me in that shop
59   because you • talk   about forty-five p•erson,

Personification is another possibility. The speaker's body can act out the human actions that the talk attributes to an entity that literally has no body. In this case, it is the voice, which, Hussein says, 'reaches', as his hand reaches far forward.

Fig. 6.11 And if you s•ee that sh<u>o</u>p in Saudi Arabia

Fig. 6.12 • that

Fig. 6.13 it'•s- (- - - -)

Fig. 6.14 you c•an- you can't follow me in that shop

Fig. 6.15 because you • talk

60	When I go ho:me
	(.)
61	my voice cannot r•each from room to room.
62	That's why I use to wear one like th•is
63	(-)

Fig. 6.16 about forty-five p•erson

Fig. 6.17 When I go ho:me my voice cannot r•each from room to room

64 J   Oh, microphone
65 H   micropho:ne
66   wireless microphone to sp<u>ea</u>k with the people
67   not with people f•ace to face
          [
68 J   Right
69 H   I just push the button here a•nd speak with my •tech<u>ni</u>cian

Hussein depicts a generic workday in Austin in two stages, by an abstract, dynamic sketch and by re-impersonation. The sketch are zigzag gestures, coupled with the 'viewing instruction' 'all day like this, all day like this'. The hands make rapid, jagged motions, and the voice draws attention to them: 'like this'. This production is a 'multimodal' formula depicting how Hussein runs from place to place all day. (Note that Hussein's hands

Figs. 6.18–19 That's why I use to wear one like th•is.Not with people f•ace to face

Fig. 6.20 I just push the button here

here do not represent his hands at work: their motions are impersonal depiction devices, 'gesture paintings'; Streeck 2008a.)

```
36   H   I told her I feel sometime
37       I'•m crazy.
         (1.0)
38       All • day   l•ike
39          th•is
40   J   Hm
41   H   all d•ay like this.
```

A bit later, Hussein's body transforms into an impersonation of itself: he enacts his own actions. The text is cut like a fast-paced action movie.

```
84   how I answer the phone
85   sometime I am handling two three line
     quick wo- altogether
```

86   and in meantime I'm checking invoices
87   and I'm going
88   sometime this way
89   the technician here

Fig. 6.21

Fig. 6.22 I told her I feel sometime I'•m cr<u>a</u>zy

Fig. 6.23 All • day

Fig. 6.24 l•ike

Figs. 6.25–26 th•is. All d•ay like this.

90 they expect me outside
91 suddenly they see me in front of them
92 then I done here
93 then I change my- (- - - -) way
94 then I go this way
95 to see something else going over there

Fig. 6.27 •how I answer the phone

Figs. 6.28–29 sometime I am handling two th•ree l•ine

Fig. 6.30 q•uick wo- altogether

But as vivid as the text is, it is also embodied through spatial-gestural actions.

83   .hh •how I answer the phone
84   sometime I am handl]ing two th•ree l•ine
85   q•uick wo- altogether

Fig. 6.31 and in m•eantime

Fig. 6.32 I'm ch•ecking invoices

Figs. 6.33–34 and •I'm going sometime th•is way

86	and in m•eantime I'm ch•ecking invoices
87	and •I'm going
88	sometime th•is way
89	the t•echnician here

Fig. 6.35 the t•echnician here

Fig. 6.36 they ex•pect

Figs. 6.37–38 me outs•ide. Su•ddenly they see me in front of them

90	they ex•pect me outs•ide
91	su•ddenly they see me in front of them
92	.hhh •then I done here
93	then •I change my- (- - - • -)

Fig. 6.39 then I change my- wa• y

Fig. 6.40 to see so•mething else

Fig. 6.41 going over th•ere

94		wa• y
95		then I go th•is way
96		to see so•mething else going over th•ere
97	J	Yeah

Figs. 6.42–43 a•nd then the techn•ician

Figs. 6.44–45 they g•et conf•used

Fig. 6.46 they don't kn•ow how to catch me

98   H   a•nd then the techn•ician
99   they g•et conf•used
100   they don't know how to c•atch me
101   they don't know how to r•un   aw<u>ay</u> from m•e.
102   .hh•h This the only way I make money

Figs. 6.47–48 they don't know how to r•un away from m•e

Fig. 6.49 hh•h This the only way I make money

Only the first few gestures in this section are true reenactments: his hand is holding the telephone receiver. After that, his hands overwhelmingly represent him, as he runs here and there, or they position other participants in space. At one point, Hussein depicts the confusion of his subordinates by gestures to his head.

Coda

At the end, Hussein once again summarizes how he runs his business, but this time he does it in moral terms: by formulating his business ethic, he states his business model, again deploying the same poetic-rhetorical devices.

151   I always make money
152   but I neve:r- (- - -) thought to make money
153   one time from any customer
        (- -)

154   because I want him again
155   .hhh and most my customer I appreciate their business
156   but most of people
157   they thank me
158   before they leave
159   by service I did
160   because they feel they did good
161   J   Right.
162   And they come back
163   H   And they come back
164   And they said
165   we just came
166   because somebody told us about you
167   and they mention some name.
168   That it's what make me feel more better
169   and do more better.

6.7   Conclusion

In this chapter, I have analyzed samples of Hussein's linguistic practices in the typical contexts that make up the better part of his day and show him in his main managerial roles: as manager of people, who directs their actions, and as manager of information, who must maintain and provide situation awareness. I have described Hussein's routine ways of making and answering phone calls, of greeting customers, of soliciting and distributing information, and the design of his directives when he assigns technicians their jobs and when he cooperates with them. We saw that Hussein skillfully manipulates the syntax and prosody of his utterances, almost entirely in line, it seems, with standard English syntax and prosody. Lacking certain relative pronouns and attributive constructions (relative clauses), Hussein finds syntactic 'work-arounds' to get his point across. In the last part of this chapter, I have exposed Hussein as an 'oral poet', someone who occasionally employs poetic and rhetorical devices, most of them versions of parallelism, familiar from rhetorical tradition, and requiring a musically tuned ear. Folklorists (Finnegan 1977) and classicists (Havelock 1963) studying oral poetry have described these methods as a kind of memory technology and methodology for speaking, for progressing from utterance to utterance, from line to line, while having some utterance-design tasks taken care of by quasi-automatically building parallel constructions. Hussein uses parallelism also when he dramatizes events; dramatizations include exuberant mimetic reenactments. It is during face-to-face conversations in which he talks about his life that Hussein has an opportunity to call on his entire rhetorical repertoire, and the charisma some customers attribute to him is partly informed by seeing him in this role.

While I have described only a smattering of speaking practices, I believe that these are representative of the most important communicative tasks Hussein faces and the main managerial roles he plays during the day— this day. More than his bodily communication practices, for which a normative standard is either not known or does not exist, his speaking practices show an evolving, adaptive repertoire, a system forever in transition. Some of Hussein's idiosyncrasies shown here have since given way to standard constructions. On one or two occasions during this day, we saw Hussein correcting himself, replacing a nonstandard by a standard form, reordering a compound to match English word order.

One dimension of Hussein's speaking that I have not yet properly addressed is the institutional or *transactional* nature of some of his speech acts, the forces they have within a web of entitlements and obligations, that is, in the communicative life of the *organization* called 'Hi-Tech Automotive'. I do so in the next chapter.

7   Getting Things Done

Finally, Mr. Chmeis is given his due as a *self-made man*, an entrepreneur, business owner, and principal of an organization. The chapter title alludes to his authority to delegate physical agency to others, his 'agency at a distance'. As a principal of an organization, Mr. Chmeis is authorized to perform directive speech acts, and he makes commitments and incurs sanctionable obligations when he performs certain other speech acts. These acts can be called *transactions*, acts that alter the webs of duties and rights within and beyond the organization. They will be analyzed by using a found meta-language and the typology of forms of *causativity* its grammar offers. As sole manager of Hi-Tech Automotive, Mr. Chmeis is also the hub of a *distributed cognitive system*. And when he participates in a car's repair (as he frequently does), he transforms a bit of the material world. To account for the flow of activity and Mr. Chmeis' main managerial roles in it, this chapter is structured from the vantage point of a single car, a Mercury Capri, and its movement through the *operating chain* of intake, diagnosis, part ordering, repair, and checkout. This is the first car to arrive in the morning and the last to leave. Its time at Hi-Tech is extended because of a judgment error on Mr. Chmeis' part, which prompts him to take remedial action himself.

7.1   The story of the red Capri

The first 'patient' to arrive at the 'clinic' in the morning is a red Mercury convertible, a '91 Capri, and, as things turn out, it will also be the last one to leave. The owner had called the day before and made arrangements to have the front brakes checked. When he brings the patient to the shop in the morning, the 'doctor' greets him (see Chapter 1). Altogether, the Capri will spend an entire hour in Hussein's personal care and additional hours in the care of staff. The analogy to a clinic is not entirely ironic: the activities performed in a repair shop are quite analogous to those in a clinic. Many cures involve 'surgery', and where restorative surgery does not suffice, replacement organs are available or can be ordered. In this chapter, we trade the perspective of the agent for that of the patient, the 'undergoer', the car, which we follow through the shop to understand the sequence of activities that forms one complete operational cycle. A helpful analytic tool is the praxeological concept of the 'operating chain' (*chaîne operatoire*, de France 1983), which refers to the sequence of actions through which a compound activity such as setting a table for dinner or preparing a meal is accomplished. At Hi-Tech Automotive, operating chains are the sequentially ordered steps taken to 'heal' a car, from intake interview through part ordering and delivery, the series of actions by which the problem is fixed, to the check-out procedures. While actions taken ultimately fall under the purview of laws, a number of speech acts that are part of the *chaîne operatoire* bring about legal or quasi-legal facts: obligations, supported by the possibility of sanctions. The operating chain is the core organizing frame that interconnects all activities and provides human actors with a techno-logical map for making sense of what is going on and for planning or designing their own actions while considering those of others.

Throughout this book, I have examined and made sense of Hussein's words and actions only within the context of the immediate situation. But neither Hussein's identity nor the meanings and expectable consequences of his acts are delimited to the situation at hand. What his doings amount to is *organizing*: he *enacts* and, in cooperation with others, *sustains* an organization. Hussein is an entrepreneur and manager. Many of his actions implicate him in a web of obligations and presuppose a web of entitlements due to his position as principal. An often neglected feature (but see Heath and Luff 2012; Heritage 1984) that many, but by no means all, human actions possess is that they bring about *institutional facts*. Thus, by promising to a customer that the car will be ready at a certain time, Hussein places himself under an obligation to make sure that it is; a promise is an institution. By pointing to a car and saying 'I need this car up' to an employee, Hussein places the employee under an obligation to 'make sure' that *someone* will put the car up; he delegates his 'institutional' or 'remote agency' to someone else. Taylor (2011) has called this type of interactions *transactions*, and we draw on his framework to delineate which of Hussein's actions have transactional qualities and how, in performing them, Hussein *enacts the organization*. To this end, we need to discuss what we mean by agency and to distinguish different types of organizationally relevant agency.

Tracing the operating chain through which a single car moves gives us an opportunity to collect the communicative actions Hussein performs at its different stages, what parts of his repertoire of practices are called upon, and what obligations he incurs and imposes, that is, how he performs as an *institutional* actor. We also see Hussein enacting what we may call his primary roles: as *doer*, someone who changes the world by physically 'doing things'; as *manager*, someone who gets others to 'do things', through communicative action; and as *performer*, someone who orients to his own actions as a *performance*, staged, for example, to entertain and play with customers. By far the most important role Hussein plays is that of manager. Managing Hi-Tech Automotive also involves the management of information: cognizance of the various operating chains currently in motion— situation awareness, his own and that of other members of the team. His job is not only to get others to do things, but also to enable them to do these things, and so he needs to know what his technicians, or the car, need to get the job done. Constantly during the execution of these tasks, Hussein relies on what he calls his 'experience', which he defines as 'having done this before'. When he participates in a job, his embodied experience as a former technician comes into play. As this book is about Hussein's communicative work, it must exclude Hussein's silent cognitive labor, what is going on 'in his mind' as he does other things (he rarely if ever sits by himself thinking). Mental activities are evidently indispensable components of Hussein's management; we have access to them only to the extent to which they take place in public interaction.

We can draw on three analytic frameworks to elucidate how Hussein's moment-by-moment words and actions weave themselves into the fabric of the shop's operation: Hutchins' 'cognitive ethnography' of 'distributed cognitive systems', as loosely or tightly coupled wholes (Weick 1976), which solve cognitive problems through the dynamic, improvisational, yet methodical coupling of its parts by means of media of communication. Taylor (2013) analyzes organizations as the ongoing product of *transactions*, that is, of communicative actions that bring about actionable and accountable social facts. Goodwin (forthcoming), finally, gives us a perspective on Hi-Tech Automotive as a *co-operative transformation zone* (or an ever-evolving set of such zones), zones in which the world is changed in characteristically human fashion: 'by flexibly combining different kinds of ... materials ... into local contextual configurations, ... where each component mutually elaborates the others' (Goodwin 2011a: 4). In the following, I will briefly lay out these frameworks and then, after a summary of the stations the red Capri travels through, analyze key moments in light of them.

7.2 Hi-Tech as a distributed cognitive system

The cognitive ecology (Hutchins 1995) of Hi-Tech Automotive includes a vast array of human actors, routine practices, bodies of knowledge, skills, and artifacts (tools, machines, representations) that are linked within an ever-evolving ecology of communication. Insofar as the operation of the shop is geared toward problem-solving, it can be characterized as a 'distributed cognitive system'. Hutchins writes about the notion of 'distributed cognitive system' that it

> permits one to move the boundary of the cognitive unit of analysis out beyond the skin of the individual to include the material and social environment as components of a larger cognitive system. This focuses attention on the processes by which people take advantage of both internal and external resources to organize their actions. ... This means that work materials are more than stimuli for disembodied cognitive systems. Work materials become elements of the cognitive system itself, and cognition becomes an emergent property of the interactions among people and work materials. (E. Hutchins, http://pages.ucsd.edu/~ehutchins/)

The concept of cognitive systems externalizes thought processes, and this is necessary because human cognition is enmeshed in culture: it makes use of cultural tools, including language. Cognitive activities are also embedded in material settings: we use information that is available to our senses, arrange objects in ways that facilitate cognitive tasks, and (today) make use of a broad array of inscriptions (writing, lists, diagrams, etc.). All of these actions are essential components of thought processes or *cognitive activities* (Lave 1988; Norman 1993). Finally, cognition often involves other people; it is a social, distributed process (Resnick 1991). And while this is fundamentally true of all basic cognitive activities (from which 'internal' cognitive activities are derived), it is particularly evident in places where people work together. A rapidly growing group of cognitive scientists, led by Lave (Rogoff & Lave 1984), Norman (1993), and Hutchins (1995), has therefore set out to study cognitive practices in the everyday lives of people, where they are usually scaffolded and mediated by an environment rich in heterogeneous, adaptive cognitive artifacts.

Describing teamwork in an airline cockpit, Hutchins observes that the distribution of a chunk of knowledge in such a system is a

propagation of a representational state [information] across representational media. In [a] cockpit, some of the representational media are located
within the individual pilots. Others, such as speech, are located between the
pilots, and still others are in the physical structure of the cockpit. Every
representational medium has physical properties that determine the availability of representations through space and time and constrain the sorts of
cognitive processes required to propagate the representational state into or
out of that medium. (Hutchins & Klausen, 1996: 32)

But knowledge is not only distributed via dedicated communication chan-
nels and practices; rather, the performance of practical actions is itself
communicative: socialized members of the practice community can read
much information from the visible physical conduct of others, and Hussein
certainly gains insights into the progress of a job from fleeting glances at the
technicians' positioning and motions. It is important not to lose sight of this
underpinning of skilled perception and bodily resonance, lest the cognitive
operation of the shop is misconstrued as traffic in symbols alone.

One can describe Hussein as the *hub* (or *lynchpin*) of a distributed
cognitive system. Knowledge (information) is distributed across
a heterogeneous multitude of loci: a particular technician may have
special skills; a bit of glue put on a brake pad shows a technician what
to do with it; a part number is hidden in a library of lists; a phone
number is known 'by heart'; an oil leak reveals itself. To become part of
an operating chain, a bit of information must travel through Hussein,
with few exceptions. Hussein 'propels' information through the system,
and he must maintain *situation awareness* (Norman 1993: 142), be aware
of what is going on. Where a car is in its operating chain can be read off
its location, the body posture of a technician, a replacement part still
waiting on a shelf, or an entry in the job sheet. Norman has investigated
a multitude of ways in which humans stack their environment so that it
embodies knowledge for them, to enable themselves to *off-load* memory
tasks: desk corners where things not to be forgotten are placed, post-it
notes, lists, piles, refrigerator doors, cabinets (Norman 1992, 1993; see
also Hutchins & Klausen 1996).

> Information in the world can be thought of as a kind of storehouse of
> data. ... The world remembers things for us, just by being there. When
> we need a particular piece of information we simply look around, and there
> it is. (Norman 1993: 147)

We have seen in Chapters 1 and 2 how Hussein, as he walks from place to
place, usually in pursuit of information or to deliver it, scans the world

around him, reading information off of it that is relevant to the operation. But of course the shop also employs a number of technologies specifically designed to store information. These included at the time of the recording a notebook, a ledger serving as a payment calendar, a rolodex, an electronic rolodex (never used), a cordless phone that stored ten telephone numbers, and numerous catalogs and lists of parts, as well as the Blue Book, which lists average sales prices for used cars. By far the most important information artifact, however, is the job sheet. Table 7.1 shows the most frequently used information technologies.

Most of these are vintage technologies now; only job sheets and notebooks are still in use at Hi-Tech. The way job sheets bring different genres of information together in one, moveable plane—customer contact information, technician tasked with the job, parts needed, part costs, labor and labor costs, taxes, signatures, and the official Hi-Tech Automotive logo plus contact information—appears to be enduringly adapted to ensuring situation awareness and meeting the administrative needs of the auto shop, as well as to the *chaîne operatoire* in whose context information is gathered and distributed: the job sheet is portable, enduring, and capable of accumulating a succession of layers of information, in ways similar to the flight strips used by air-traffic controllers (Sellen & Harper 2002). For Hussein's employees, there is a simple and universally used practice for retrieving all manner of information: going and asking Hussein. Situation awareness in most matters resides with him.

7.3 Hi-Tech as a cooperative transformation zone

Hi-Tech, despite the complexity of the cognitive work going on, is not primarily a 'knowledge organization', but a place where manual labor gets done and the tangible world gets changed (or repaired). Certainly, wherever humans communicate, the world is changed. Interaction is *cooperative transformation* (Goodwin forthcoming). However, while humans inhabit and transform the world by *doing* things, they have made it by *making* things. The making of things, however, is not the province of Hi-Tech Automotive. Karl Marx would not have considered the work that goes on at Hi-Tech Automotive productive labor: nothing really gets produced, only restored. Marx would chalk up car repair to the 'reproduction costs of capital', in this case of reproducing that capital that most of Hussein's customers possess, their labor force. They are in need of a car to get to their jobs, and Hussein's shop 'adds value' to their labor force. But no 'real value' is created when a car is kept running.

Table 7.1 External memory storage

Notebook: records of customer calls, misc. information; accessible to everyone

Payment calendar: records of payments by customers with outstanding loans

Electronic rolodex (not used), rolodex and phone with stored numbers

Job sheet: records parts used, part costs, customer information, license plate number, year model, mileage; labor and labor costs; sum total, taxes, signatures, date

Library of part-lists

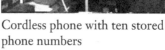

Cordless phone with ten stored phone numbers

However, Goodwin suggests that the logic is always the same whenever we are dealing with human activities. His anthropological theory of human action reveals and foregrounds the homologies between the production of a single, situated action and the production of material culture, whose building blocks—for example, tools—have the same combinatorial structure as moments of cooperation and communicative understanding. He casts light on human action as a never-ending 'ratcheting up' of cultural materials. Our focus here is far narrower, and Hussein's actions, which leave few tangible products, provide scant illustration for Goodwin's theory of cooperative action. But we would miss out a small, yet decisive part of Hussein's day and identity, which is grounded in cumulative, practical experience, in his knowing what it feels like to repair a car. Ultimately, the combinatorial structure of practical moment-by-moment cooperation constitutes the micro-links in the *châine operatoire*.

Goodwin writes that

> human action has an intrinsic combinatorial structure. It is built by flexibly combining different kinds of ... materials ... into local contextual configurations, ... where each component mutually elaborates the others to create a whole that is different from any of its parts. ... Action is constituted through both simultaneous and sequential co-operations. ... This public, combinatorial structure [contextual configuration, J. S.] makes distinct forms of cognition and social organization possible. For example, actors occupying alternative positions within the endogenous activities that an action is helping to pursue can both contribute to the organization of the current action, and build subsequent action, by performing different kinds of operations on the varied materials provided by the contextual configuration used to build that action. ... Such visible combinatorial structure leads to the unfolding of ongoing action through decomposition of the materials provided by a prior contextual configuration, and their reuse in different form in the organization of a subsequent action. Participants are thus engaged in continuous attention to, and monitoring of, the precise materials being used to build the events of the moment. ... The combinatorial structure of human tools creates networks that link widely dispersed groups into shared projects as different kinds of actors, including some widely dispersed in time and space, contribute alternative materials to common tool, project and course of action. ... The ability to build action in concert with others while performing systematic operations on a substrate accumulated through historical sedimentation within particular societies, makes possible unique forms of social learning and the proliferation of diverse cultures, settings and languages which provide the relevant infrastructure for the constitution of appropriate action within specific communities and professions. All of these phenomena manifest a common formal

organization that includes the construction of actions and tools through a process that brings together structurally different kinds of materials into webs of relationships where they mutually elaborate each other. (Goodwin 2011a: 4–7)

This describes precisely how work and communication are conducted at Hi-Tech Automotive and how the actors, actions, and materials that are brought together in a *chaîne operatoire* are also linked to a multitude of other actors, actions, and materials through vast networks of human activity and world-making.

7.4 Hi-Tech as an organization

Hussein participates in these networks not least through actions by which he incurs and imposes obligations: he makes commitments and is entitled to exert authority over the actions of his employees on the basis of a contractual commitment they have made to him. A part of the communicative acts Hussein performs during the course of the day are, though usually indistinguishable by their form, functionally different from other communicative acts insofar as they carry institutional force: they are sanctionable according to the rules of economic and legal networks. Stewart refers to these as *transactive* acts; they are parts of institutional transactions.

> Human communication … is *trans*active, and not merely *inter*active. The distinction is this. When you get married you have taken on a *transaction*-based set of mutual obligations, legitimated by society and enforceable in law. The more informal reception that follows is a scene of *interactions*, although even here the latter are framed by transactional understandings, such as the obligation of the groom's parents to host a reception for the guests. (Taylor 2011: 1277–1278)

Hussein's 'transactional' communicative acts are not different in appearance from purely 'interactional' acts; they are not specifically marked, and certainly Hussein does not utter 'explicit performatives' ('I hereby promise you that your car will be ready by four.') What distinguishes *transactions* is that they, in Taylor's words, 'establish a calendar of rights and obligations'.

> Hiring onto a firm is an example of a transaction, and again it establishes a calendar of rights and obligations. The interactions that follow must now be weighed against the background established by the initial transaction, and the web of relationships they have become thereby enfolded within. Interactions are always set against their transactional framework. Organization, it follows, is initiated and established by transactions; its day-

to-day commerce, however, is typically interactive. But both transaction and interaction, we should remember, are practical instances of communication. It is [this] reasoning, however, that we need to pay particular attention to: that of our grounding in materiality, when we engage in communication. The only way to connect with anyone communicatively is through the generation of what Mead termed 'gestures'. (Taylor 2011: 1277–1278)

The oral and embodied practices used for transactions are the same as those enacted in mere interactions, although their enactment 'counts as' something else, or rather counts in a different way. The matter is different with inscriptions, many of which have transactional force (bills, receipts, signatures, etc.) by design.

Hussein's linguistic and institutional agency can thus be explained with respect to speech acts: it is an entitlement to perform certain classes of them. Constellations of agency define power relations enfolded in an organization. One of the hallmarks of Hussein's agency is the entitlement to transfer physical agency, that is, to 'make someone' do something, rather than doing it himself; it is the power of directive.

Evidently, not all of Hussein's communicative actions are transactive: asking a technician a question ('what Mike he has to do now?'), advancing a diagnosis ('oil pressure low I believe'), or suggesting a line of action ('maybe come back in a week') are acts that cannot be sanctioned if Hussein errs or the act is otherwise defective. This is different when he tells the Mercury owner the price he will charge him, or signs the job sheet. In the former case, obligations for participants are those that are generally in force in conversation (truthfulness, relevance, etc.), and these obligations extend to everyone at Hi-Tech. But only Hussein can, for example, sign a form or utter a command.

There is also a more encompassing way to describe Hussein's agency in the shop. Bypassing recent debates about agency in sociology and other disciplines, we can instead turn to natural languages and how they conceptualize and distinguish types of human agency. Natural languages, in contrast to 'actor-network theory' (Latour 2005) and other 'post-humanist' frameworks (Kohn 2013), distinguish between beings by attributing to them different degrees of animacy and agency, and humans are universally assigned the highest rank on the animacy hierarchy (Comrie 1981), measured by the range of positions they can take in a clause and the degree of 'control' they have over other clause-constituents, as well as by the fact that, universally, human-actor events require the least amount of coding, that they are 'unmarked'.

Simple (unmediated) agency is expressed by *transitive* constructions, which present an agent acting on an object, which is typically lower in animacy or specificity. Many languages also have simple constructions to refer to actions the agent does to self, or that two or more agents do to one another (middle voice, reciprocals, etc.) Another important semantic 'prime' is *causativity*. 'Causative verbs' (e.g., 'to set') are verbs that refer to actions that bring about, or bring an object into, a state, which is described by a 'stative verb' ('to sit'). Often, 'stative' and 'causative' versions of a verb are paired, as in this example. A causative verb such as 'to kill' was thus 'decomposed' by linguists as 'CAUSE (state)' or 'cause-to-die'. Here, the actor is acting directly on the object, exerting 'immediate agency'.

A different kind of agency is 'agency at a distance', 'agency once removed', events in which one agent (the 'principal') gets, usually by means of communication, another actor to do a certain act. Some natural languages offer subtle distinctions between different types of agency at a distance. The Philippine Ilokano language distinguishes, by means of simple prefix choice (pa-, pag-, and pang-[1]), between 'making someone do something' (causing P to cause X), 'having it done by someone' (causing that it is done by someone, the immediate agent remaining unspecified), and 'making someone make someone do it ('causing P to cause Q to cause X'). Incidentally, this typology of causation at a distance almost corresponds to a set of organizationally relevant distinctions among Hussein's actions, and thus of the types of agency he exerts: he either *does something* (e.g., puts Ms. Nancy's 'inner carburetor bracket' in its place); or he makes someone else, an addressee, do something ('go park the car over there'); or he makes his addressee have it done by someone ('I need the car up', spoken to Kenneth, who does not put cars up himself). To complete the typology of Hussein's institutional agency and to properly typify the speech acts he performs, we would need to add constructions or verbs that cast Hussein as an institutional actor, that is, as someone entitled to incur sanctionable obligations, even on behalf of others, and who is authorized to bring about sanctionable institutional facts. Searle (1971) offers the terms *commissives* and *declarations* for the corresponding types of speech acts.

7.5   Operating chain: the car as patient

We now return to the events surrounding the red Mercury Capri. Once the owner has dropped it off to have the brakes padded and the engine checked

---

[1] Ilokano has an astonishingly rich causative derivational morphology, enabling such words as 'the one you have caused the X to be written with' (i.e., the instrument of writing that is beyond my own reach).

for an oil leak, Hussein checks for the information he needs to order the pads and, once they arrive soon after, unpacks and puts glue on them. Then he sends them to Cedric. In the meantime, someone has put up the car on a hydraulic bridge. Hussein does some of the brake work himself, until he leaves the job to Cedric. When the brakes are done and the car has been lowered, Hussein drives it out into the driveway, where he meets another customer, Richie (see Chapter 1). Some time later, he instructs Hakim where to steam-clean the engine, even though Hakim is worried that the steam might mess up the electricity. Later again, the owner of the Capri arrives, pays the bill, and receives Hussein's instructions concerning the oil leak. Hours have passed when the customer returns. He reports that the engine is stuttering. Hussein notes for the camera that this is the complaint I have been waiting for, since I had asked about complaints, yet none had so far occurred. Then he inspects the car, identifies the location of the oil leak, and, after assembling a team and the tools needed, blow-dries the carbure-tor of the Capri in cooperation with Victorio, again leaving the job for the technician to complete. In his final work-related speech act of the day, he asks Victorio whether the job has been done.

Table 7.2 gives an overview of the 'stations' in the Capri's operating chain.

7.6   Knowing

Hussein's information-processing activities in the course of the cure of a car can be grouped into four kinds: gathering, processing (including re-coding), disseminating, and recording information in an external medium (an optional stage).

Acquiring knowledge

There are many ways to distinguish forms of knowledge, and we narrowly focus in this chapter on 'information', knowledge that can be expressed in symbolic form (although it not always is). This type of knowledge or situation awareness that Hussein acquires and distributes is of three kinds: (1) factual ('propositional') knowledge about states of objects, acquired by way of sensory exploration and knowledge-based inference; (2) information about symptoms, linguistically 'coded', but often also ges-tured, obtained in conversations with customers; and (3) knowledge repre-sented in symbolic, often numerical, form, including phone and part numbers. In the course of the Capri's operating chain, a moment of *sensory*

Table 7.2 The Mercury's operating chain

Fig. 7.1.1 8:10 a.m.: First inspection

Fig. 7.1.2 Intake

Fig. 7.1.3 Hussein enters customer information in the worksheet.

Fig. 7.1.4 Hussein checks the Capril's mileage

Fig. 7.1.5 Hussein looks for the 'year model' of the Capri.

Fig. 7.1.6 Hussein checks the brake rotors.

Table 7.2 (cont.)

Fig. 7.1.7 Hussein looks up the supplier's phone number.

Fig. 7.1.8 Hussein orders brake pads.

Fig. 7.1.9 After the brake pads have been delivered, Hussein unpacks them and squeezes glue on them.

Fig. 7.1.10 Hussein gives the glued pads to Victor to give to Cedric.

Fig. 7.1.11 Hussein continues putting glue on the pads.

Fig. 7.1.12 Hussein unscrews one wheel.

not visible: Cedric completes the brake job, lowers the car, and drives it to the front.

Table 7.2 (cont.)

Fig. 7.1.13 9:50 a.m. After the brakes are done, Hussein drives the Capri to the driveway, where he meets another customer.

Fig. 7.1.14 Hussein explains to Hakim where to steam-clean the engine.

not visible: Hakim takes the car to the car-wash and steam-cleans the engine

Fig. 7.1.15 The owner picks up his Capri; 'checkout'.

Fig. 7.1.16 Two hours later, the customer returns and complains that the engine is now stuttering.

Fig. 7.1.17 Hussein discovers an oil leak.

Fig. 7.1.18 Hussein and Victor blow-dry the contacts of the Capri.

Table 7.2 (cont.)

Fig. 7.1.19 Hussein asks Victor whether
the Capri has been fixed.

knowledge acquisition occurs when Hussein checks the Mercury's brakes. He
has told the owner that the price of the brake job will depend on whether
the rotors have to be ground down. To determine whether they will, he
needs to find out whether the brakes are squealing. Like many symptomatic
noises cars make, the brakes only squeal when the wheel is turning; to
conduct a diagnosis, Hussein must therefore make the wheel turn. This is
a common constraint on car inspections: in order to obtain a symptom, for
example, a symptomatic sound, someone needs to operate the controls or
move some part of the car. The brake check, however, is a two-party
diagnostic action that Hussein can distribute within himself: his hands
turn the wheel and his ears listen to determine whether this action produces
a squealing sound. The test comes out negative. Because he carries out the
task by himself, there is no need to label his sensory experiences now.
In contrast, when Hussein and Art together elicit, notice, and diagnose
the 'rattling noise' coming from an air conditioner (see Chapter 2), sharing
and agreeing on sensory and diagnostic categories was key to the success of
their activity.

Another moment of sensory knowledge acquisition during this episode
is Hussein's quiet inspection of the oil that covers the Mercury's engine, as
Richie is waiting on him. The upshot is that he will send Dr. Marwan to
steam-clean the engine, because there is so much oil that he cannot locate
the leak. This is a preliminary inspection. But there is no evidence on the
tape that he checked the engine again after the cleaning.

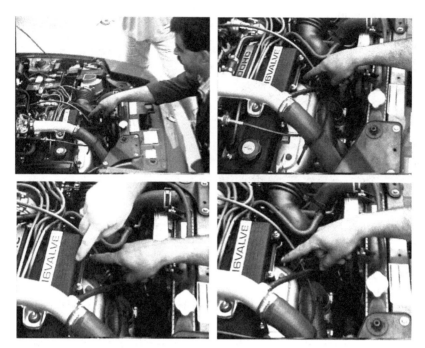

Figs. 7.2.1–4 Hussein discovers the oil leak

The third instance of sensory exploration is the inspection, after the customer has returned, of the damage that Hakim's steam-cleaning has done; it becomes a moment of discovery and disclosure.

```
(7.2)
17         All this- a::ll this (goo) up there
18         (               ) transmission and (      )
19         does this come out of the head-gasket or
20         cuz it looks- (          )
                    [
21    H                      Yeah, I will get the light on that
22         and it- Sure
23    C    see where it's coming from (but     )
24    H    We have • bad leak here
25         you see • here leak?
26    C    What is that • yeah
27    H    The valve • cover gasket
28         we should take care of it
```

Hussein's eyes discover the oil leak, and his index finger traces it. In one compound cognitive act, he finds and *discloses* the source of the problem the customer had asked him to find. As he gains insight, so do the bystanders. The owner then joins him in the pointing. This is one of the affordances of hand gestures: several can collaborate in the clearing of a perceptual field.

The acquisition and recording of symbolically coded information takes up a much bigger part of the time that Hussein devotes to the Capri. All of the information he gathers is recorded on the job sheet. The layering of information on the job sheet begins when the customer enters his personal information (name and phone number), which will be used when Hussein calls him to tell him his diagnosis of the brakes and later informs him that the car is ready. Hussein's active part in recording information begins when he reads the mileage off the odometer and the 'year model' number off the sticker on the door of the Capri and adds them to the memory store that is the job sheet. This information, preserved on moveable paper (Latour 2005), later enables him to call a supplier for brake pads (whose part number is 'one three nineteen'). But before he can make the call, he needs the supplier's number, which he finds, rather surprisingly, in the phonebook. He then transmits the information obtained from the car—year model, etc.—to the supplier, as he orders the brake pads. The information he, in turn, obtains from the supplier is whether the parts are available. Transactions with suppliers are highly routinized, as we have seen in Chapter 6.

However, in this case, the situation turns out not to be routine and to require additional knowledge management or information processing. Having determined that all four brakes need new pads, but having ordered only the fronts, presumably because he thought that they still had the rear pads in stock, Hussein goes to the storage room only to discover that they are out of them. He now spends minutes in the storage room to locate the part number for the rear pads in one of the many black binders on the shelf. When he has found it, he returns to the counter and calls the supplier again to order them. He gives him the part number ('three sixty-six', 7.3, lines 10, 15, 25) and authenticates this information by mentioning that he obtained it from 'the book'. Now he can remember the supplier's number, but it takes the supplier more than thirty seconds to find out whether they have the rear pads in stock. During this time, Hussein replaces the paper roll in the diagnostic computer in the shop. He eventually learns that rear pads—the 'three sixty-six'—are not available.

Figs. 7.3.1–4 Hussein checks part number and calls supplier

(7.3)

1	H	Pete this me again

          (1.0)

2   Send me also the rear pad.

          (0.9)

3   Yeah, three sixty-six, I think.

          (1.0)

4   Three sixty-six

5   I just check the book au-

6   I'm out of those also.

          (1.5)

7   Three sixty-six and that one three nineteen.

          (14.0)

8   Yah.

          (19.0)

9   You got it?

          (3.3)

10   You have the front ehh

11   okay then send me the front

12   and find me the other

13   and the other-

14   You want me call eh

          (0. 9)

15   somebody else or you may find him also.

          (0.9)

16   You don't stock the three sixty-six.

          (0.5)

17   Okay send the front then.

          (0.4)

18   Thank you.

When he is done putting the paper roll into the computer, Hussein calls another supplier. He knows that supplier's phone number by heart. As he is on the phone, he returns to the Mercury and checks the year model on the door again. He tells the person on the other end that it is '11 of 90 in 1991'. This order is successful.

(7.4)

1	H	Good morning, Joe
2		This Hussein.
3		I have nineteen-ninety one Mercury Capri XRT
4		I want rear brake pad if you have.

We observe components of the 'cognitive ecology' of Hi-Tech Automotive here, specifically a difference between embodied and entextualized information. We saw Hussein walk to the Capri to get the 'year model number' and relay it to the supplier at the other end of the line. The phone is in his office. (He makes the second and third calls from his cordless phone.) He physically bears the information, and information born this way by humans has a propensity to decay. However, Hussein also entextualizes and inscribes the information, committing it to durable, external form on the job sheet, where it will remain available as long as he and others know where the job sheet is; the place for it, while a car is in the shop, is on the counter. By gathering and transmitting this information and transmitting it to a supplier in the context of placing an order, he, the data, and the supplier also become entangled in a web of economic relations. All of these relations go through Hussein, as does all relevant information.

Automotive thinking

'Information processing' would not be a good label for what goes on 'in Hussein's head' after he has collected the relevant information he needs to make diagnostic and managerial decisions. The metaphor has been introduced in connection with a view of human cognition as a processing of abstractly (symbolically) coded 'data', but Hussein's automotive thinking (cf. Harper 1987; Sennett 2008) involves the whole person, what he, like everyone else, calls 'experience', especially his accumulated sensory experiences, professional feeling (kinesthetic intuition; see Goodwin [1994] on professional vision), and knowledge about cause-and-effect relationships in automotive technology, including dispositions of makes and 'year models'. Hussein's automotive thinking was on display, for example, when he diagnosed Ms. Nancy's car, and it is on display now in how he looks at the engine of the Mercury and sees the oil leak right away, in the evening, when the engine has been cleaned but is now stuttering. Hussein then articulates his hypothesis about the water damage in hypothetical-propositional terms:

(7.5)

18	Hussein	What I thi:nk
19		when Dr. Marwan he washed this area probably
20		the distributor cap could be cra:cked
23		maybe it got some moisture inside
24		from the water.
25		And now it make missing
26		what they'll call that, cross-fire.

This is a characteristic coupling of actions when Hussein diagnoses a car's trouble in the presence of a customer or technician, and for both, it can also constitute a moment of learning: the cause–effect relationship abstracted from the present context is applicable in other contexts as well. When a technician is involved the organization learns.

Disseminating knowledge

Hussein, thus, often conveys a finding or diagnosis on the spot, for example, when he reveals the oil leak by a gesture and the customer's hand joins him in tracing the leak. In this context, speech is indexical ('we have oil leak here'). At other times, for example, on the phone, disseminating knowledge may require extensive linguistic 'coding'. Here he is on the phone, explaining to the customer in the morning the condition of the brakes.

(7.6)

1	H	Uh(h) we can
		(0.2)
2		if you like we can try to save the rotor without umm him right now
3		if it has any problem in the future
4		then we have to(hh) pull the rotor
5		and turn him
6		because this expensive job to take the rotor
7		and turn him in the machine.
8		(Hhh) We can put i- just regular pad in the front
9		and regular pad in ba:ck
		(0.7)
10		(Hhh) >You're looking about< seventy dollar in the front
11		seventy dollar in the back.

Much of what is being conveyed here would be available as shared sensory experience were the customer by the car with Hussein. Tasks such as the verbalization of diagnostic judgments and articulating automotive thinking make considerable demands on Hussein's vocabulary and skills at information design, as it requires the encoding of causal, conditional, and counterfactual relations between clauses. There is no evidence that would suggest that he tends to fail at this task.

By definition, Hussein disseminates knowledge when he gives instructions to technicians. But usually he goes beyond asserting a desired state of affairs by motivating the directive. Thus, when, after the Mercury's intake, he demands of nobody in particular that 'he needs this car up and the tires off', he also tells the unspecified recipient why: 'I want to check brake.' He provides everyone within earshot with situation awareness. As it turns out, Cedric 'takes it from there', and he will later fix the brakes without Hussein ever explicitly instructing him to do so: he simply has Victorio bring him the brakes with a directive made of glue inscribed on them.

Hussein's instructions are indexical and yet explicit when he instructs Hakim how to steam-clean the engine: his hands specify the referents of his indexical expressions: 'This area needs washing.' When Hussein talks to his senior technicians Art and Victorio, his instructions often have a dialogical, negotiated character, because he solicits their perspective and insights. Here, however, Hussein dismisses Hakim's warning that water might get into the engine. A physician without automotive knowledge, Hakim anticipates the complications Hussein's prescribed cure might cause.

(7.7)
1 Hakim Shoo elak el maudoo?
         What's your situation?
2 Hussein Yam elak wen el mantahah le bedeh ekhoud sheil haydeh.
           I'm telling you the location where I need to take and remove this.

Figs. 7.7.1–2

Fig. 7.7.3

Fig. 7.7.4

3 H	•Shouf el zet hon hek?
	You see the oil here like this?
4 Hm	Eh.
	Yes.
5 H	Hal• mantahah bedah ghaseel.
	This area needs washing.
6	Hon mish darooreh tkib ekteer.
	Here it's not necessary to throw a lot.
7	Eh hon• aza ejah ma behim.
	Yes, it doesn't matter if it gets on here.

Fig. 7.7.5

Fig. 7.7.6

8 Hm   Ma behim•? Mab tihktaaya?
        It doesn't matter? It won't stall it?

9 H   Hon• kamen ghaselah bel maayh.
        Wash it here also with water.

10   Lak, el seeyarah ndeefeh, mah rah tihktah.
        No, the car is clean it won't stall it.

Hussein freely and generously shares his automotive knowledge with his customers and repeatedly during this day instructs someone how to maintain their car by monitoring it for various symptoms. He does this with the Mercury owner twice, during the first check-out, in response to a question (7.8), and when he shows him in the evening that the car needs new cables.

Fig. 7.7.7

(7.8)
1   C   You gotta grind it down in a couple of months, huh?
        (- - - -)
2   H   Hmm?
3   C   uh- grind down the rotors in a couple of months?
4   H   No! Check if you have any probly- find any problem by squealing
5   then we may need to taken 'em and grind 'em
6   Now I left them as is
7   still thick and in good shape I think

The hub of a cognitive system

The operation of Hi-Tech, notably the flow of information, is highly centralized: Hussein is the hub. He is not only in charge of all purchasing, pricing, and management decisions, but also conducts most transactions with customers, including preliminary diagnoses of what is wrong with the car. He is also the 'attending surgeon' who is responsible for determining 'what the patient needs' and how to fix him, and does minor surgery himself. Hussein's main 'extension' (McLuhan 1994) is a cordless phone, which enables him to make calls to suppliers or 'across the street' to get Hassan's advice while he is working on a job. To this day, it is almost always Hussein himself who answers the phone when one calls the shop.

Hussein's organizing has more dimensions—more 'systems' are involved—then we can analyze here. For example, he must manage his employees' time: know if and how they are engaged, how much longer their current jobs will take, how much the job to be allocated will take, who is competent to do it, whether someone else is available to assist, and so on.

This is the temporal dimension of his situation awareness. Ordering parts, judging whether buying a new replacement part for an old car is a wise investment, knowing where new and used replacement parts can be found, and making sure there are enough tools, constitute his 'resource management'. And then there are cycles of information, action, and decision making involving his landlord, his lawyer, his accountant, his bank, suppliers, and others, which embed High-Tech Automotive in extended economic and social networks. These are outside the scope of our analysis.

7.7 Doing

Hussein, having done some work by himself in the morning, joins the Capri's 'cooperative transformation' when he and Victorio together blow-dry its carburetor, contacts, and spark-plugs together. Unfortunately, the transformation zone proper, which is also their 'domain of scrutiny' (Goodwin 1994), is not within view of the camera. Therefore, we cannot see the phenomena to which they react, for example, the degree of moisture inside the spark-plug shafts. Nevertheless, we can observe the 'laminating' structure of the activity (Goodwin forthcoming), how an act by one party provides the material from which the other will fashion the next act. Goodwin illustrates this by the collaborative production of utterances as well as by the sequential and mutual enabling of practical acts within processes of material cooperation. It is mainly the latter form that we can observe in this *chaîne opératoire*.

This part of the cure of the red Capri shows us for the last time acts of 'clearing', 'showing', and 'disclosing' as we have seen them many times before, acts that transform an opaque field into an intelligible field for action.

Having had to attend to business with his accountant, Hussein returns to the Mercury and gets final confirmation that water got inside the electric system. Victorio is presently bending over the engine and beginning to screw off one of the caps, and Hussein asks, 'water inside also?' (line 10). 'Inside' refers to the shaft that holds the spark-plugs. Hussein's hand reaches next to Victorio's as if it wanted to participate in the action.

Hussein leaves and goes to the toolbox, does not find what he is looking for, and asks the men who work in the vicinity, 'You have air-blower here?' Thus, he initiates his part in the activity by assembling needed resources. He explains to Victorio, 'We need before we take the plug, put air blower' and 'We got one with Arturo.' He formulates the need for a tool and its purpose and thereby foreshadows the actions to be taken; he provides situation awareness. Victorio, taking this informing as a request for action,

Fig. 7.9.1 Hussein looking for blow-dryer

at once calls out, 'Arturo', and Hussein continues (to Arturo), 'Give me the air blower, the one skinny.' Hussein and Victorio co-construct the turn with which they get someone else to do something that will make continued activity possible. Agency is distributed.

(7.9–1)

1	H	At least it came here drive.
2		We need not tow to take it back.
3		He probably he got some wire maybe mixed up.
4		Maybe we got wire mixed?
5	V	No.
6	H	Where was [it?
7	V	[( )].
8	H	Where.
9	V	Water inside.
10	H	Water inside also?
11	V	Yeah.
12	H	You have air blower here.
		(1.5)
13	H	We need before we take the plug- put air blower to get-.
14	V	( ).
15	H	Well: we need to blow air first [before you get the plug.
16	V	[(
17	H:	We got one with uh:: Arturo.
18	V:	Arturo?
19	H:	Give me the air blower, the one skinny?
		(1.0)
20		The air blower you have. The skinny one.
		(21.0)

Fig. 7.9.2 Hakim assessing the damage he has done

It takes a while for the air-blower to turn up. In the meantime, Hakim inspects the damage he has done.

Having procured the air-blower, Hussein establishes two more *enabling conditions*: he attaches a tip to the air-blower and asks Hakim, in Arabic, to get fender covers. He completes one job himself and delegates the other one. Victorio brings a different tip and takes the one that Hussein had just attached off, while Hussein goes to get a blue fender cover. Kenneth comes with a red one, and they cover the two fenders of the car to protect them from the imminent 'shower'. How it comes about that Kenneth and Hussein bring the covers, rather than Hakim, who was tasked to do this, is not clear. Hussein begins to blow air around the valve cover. Then he instructs Victor to 'take that plug. Let's see how it look'. Hussein wipes it clean and looks at it, blows air on the contact one more time, and then begins to screw it back on. This is a repetitive *chaîne opératoire* at Hi-Tech: an action reaches a point where resources for cooperation are needed, these are solicited and given, and the action continues. 'Public, combinatorial structure . . . can both contribute to the organization of the current action, and build subsequent action, by performing different kinds of operations on the varied materials provided by the contextual configuration used to build that action' (Goodwin 2011a: 4–5).

(7.9–2)

          [[H blows air again]]

28   (9.0)

29   H   Take that plug. Lets see how its look.

          [[H blows air on the engine]]

          (14.0)

Figs. 7.9.3–4 Blow-drying the engine

Fig. 7.9.5 Hussein cleans spark-plug

Then, Hussein organizes a search for a missing spark-plugs, which he quickly locates himself:

(7.9–3)
34   H: One. Two. Three? Where's the fou[rth.
35   V: [(   ) no.
36   H: I don't see it. Four plugs- we need- oh here.
37   There is one more.

More blow-drying by Hussein follows, and more cooperation, facilitated by brief, 'minimized' directives.

(7.9–4)
50   V   (Hh Hh Hh)
51   H   Give me the last one please.
52   Let him do it.
53   H   Victor.
            (2.0)
54   H   Give me this one also.
55   Get this also.

Fig. 7.9.6 Cooperation with bystanders

Hussein screws the plugs back in. Finally, as he receives an oral report from Victorio that Ashraf has found a sub-frame for Uncle Ahm across the street, Victorio takes over. When Hussein returns his attention to the Capri, he observes Victorio engaged in a line of action he does not approve of. He interrupts him and, obscured from the camera, appears to reconfigure the setting so that Victorio can see it in a way that will make him understand the alternative solution Hussein is about to propose.

(7.9–5)
```
57   H:   Uh- Hold on.
58        I ha- I have solution.
59        Hold on. Hold on.=
60   V:   =(    ).
61   H:   We don't want to take.
62        No no. We don't wanna take it.
63        Look.
64        Here.
65        I'll get [it. We do]n't need to
66   V:           [(        )]
          (2.0)
```

Hussein takes over and demonstrates the solution himself, and again he enlists Victorio's cooperation. The ensuing dialogue shows more clearly than most scenes that we have observed how closely physical and linguistic action become intertwined and entrained during physical activities and how these activities impose their logic of action on the formatting and sequencing of talk.

Fig. 7.9.7 Cooperation

Fig. 7.9.8 'Watch now, I got shower.'

(7.9–6)
67   H: I got it. Here.
          (2.0)
68   H: You pull it now.
          (6.0)
69   V: Oo::h! [[whistles]]
          ((H blows air on part))
          (6.0)

Finally, Hussein gives a public show of the success of his procedure: he produces a cloud of steam, a 'shower' (water is being blown out of the shaft).

(7.9–7)
67   H: Watch now.
          (4.0)

Fig. 7.9.9 Hussein goes across the street

68 H: I got shower.
        ((H blows air on engine))
        (11.0)
69 H: Okay.
        (10.0)

Having shown that the method is working, Hussein signs off. He announces that he will go across the street to check up on Uncle Ahm. He ends his engagement with a prognosis and a commitment: if the Capri will not get dried today (as it likely will), it will be tomorrow.

(7.9–8)
72 H: I think that like this we ca- wo- we will be done.
73 V: Yeah: but (   ).
74 H: Okay you answer the phone
75   I'm going to go see across the street Uncle Ahm.
76   I think we'll get it fixed like this.
77   If not we will work on it tomorrow.

Goodwin writes:

Participants build action by performing co-operations, both simultaneously and through time, on the materials provided by others. . … Action with such a formal structure constitutes cognition as a form of social practice as participants both perform operations on the utterances and materials provided by others, and are faced with the task of understanding in detail what others are doing so that they will be able to participate appropriately in the courses of common action that constitute the endogenous activities that sustain and modify the settings they inhabit. (Goodwin forthcoming: 7)

7.8   Getting things done: managing

Social systems and organizations can in part be described as webs of
entitlements to, and constraints upon, immediate agency and agency at
a distance. 'Causation at a distance', mediated by another person, is
always a privilege, an entitlement, entangled in institutional relations.
For a directive to achieve its purpose, certain social conditions must be
met. The types of directives Hussein issues suggest that there is
a three-tier positional hierarchy at Hi-Tech, with him at the top,
senior employees, who are entitled to issue directives, in the middle,
and junior apprentices at the bottom, who do not have anyone to
delegate immediate agency to, or the authority to reject or question
directives.

I have described the design of Hussein's directives in Chapter 6 All
of the directives Hussein uttered concerning the red Capri are listed in
Table 7.3. Most of these are short, 'unmitigated' directives, and they
occur in contexts of visible, cooperative practical action where their
motivation is transparent: 'give me this one also', 'get this also', 'you
pull it now', 'hold on'. Where the situation does not transparently
motivate them, directives are usually given an explicit motivation:
'let's get screwdriver *to clean the cap*', 'take that plug, *let's see how it
look*', 'hold on, *I have a solution*', 'you answer the phone, *I'm going to see
Uncle Ahm*'. Motivating directives is part of Hussein's 'leadership style'.
We cannot tell the social status of the addressee from the form of his
directives: 'open the hood' is addressed to a customer, 'give me the last
one, please' to an employee. The same is true about gestures: pointing
gestures, beckoning, and so on, are equally suited, in this setting for
addressees of all stripes. (And yet, occasionally, as we have seen in
Chapter 3, a gesture can exhibit Hussein's institutional agency, if only
by its timing.)

The other type of institutional, transactional communicative acts
that Hussein performs are *commissives*, acts by which he incurs obligations. There are too many in this episode to list. Among them are the
examples in Table 7.4.

Commitments are implicitly made when Hussein orders parts ('okay
send the front then'), because orders imply a commitment to pay for the
goods. We see Hussein act on his commitments when he steam-cleans the
engine without charge.

Table 7.3 Hussein's directives during the Capri episode

I need this car up
and I need tires off I want to check brake
This area needs washing.
Wash it here also with water.
You need to follow me
Open the hood.
Let's get Philips screw driver WD-40 to clean the cap.
Give me the air blower the one skinny?
Let me see.
Watch your face.
Take that plug.
Let's see how its look.
Okay we don't want to pull the plug out then.
Just let's= Just the water?
And then- try to start.
Give me the last one please.
Let him do it him do it.
Give me this one also.
Get this also.
Uh- Hold on. I ha' I have solution. Hold on. Hold on.=
No. We don't want to take. No no. We don't want to take it.
Look. Here.
You pull it now.
Watch.
Watch now.
Okay, you answer the phone.

7.9 Performing

We turn to a final, minor, dimension of Hussein's communicative work, that of being a performer, someone who 'stages a show' for an audience. One might argue that his entire day is a performance, as he acts in the presence of a camera and once demands, 'Put this in your tape,' and at another time asks, 'Are we still on?' But there is no evidence that Hussein adopts this self-reflexive stance toward his own communication and action throughout the day. Occasionally during the day we have indeed seen Hussein 'put on a performance' and modulate the interaction into an entertaining, jocular key. By 'performance', then, I refer with Goffman to communicative actions primarily designed to entertain, not to inform (1974).

Table 7.4 Transactive speech acts during the Capri episode

	Promise:
	Yeah, I will get the light on that. Sure.
	I'm gonna give you a call.
	Commitment (to a price):
	If- uh pad and rotor need to be turned
	it's just to be about hundred dollars
	if it's just pa:d without turning rotor
	it will be less.
	Yeah, if the rotor good
	the:n (.) just (- -) about maybe sixty-nine ninety-fi:ve.
	If the rotor bad
	then we need to knock the rotor
	and grind it.
	If the rotor were ou:t
	then more hundred
	more than hundred
	Commitment (to time of delivery):
C	But y- got it- you have that (wrapped) at four o'clock,
	ain't you ( )
	[
H	Oh yeah
	Committing a work-order to paper:
	Let's put the brake check
	(4.8)
	an:d the-
	(- - - - - - - -)
	oil lea- **oi**l leak check.

A plethora of verbs in different languages that are used as terms of analysis muddle the conceptual landscape. The English verb *to act* refers both to 'ordinary' actions and to *acting*, the actor's craft. Some theorists have claimed that all social action is acting and that in our social lives we are performers projecting a character on a stage. Confusion is created when different usages of the verb 'to perform' are conflated as if they all meant the same thing: performing an act, performing a task, performing a role, and performing a character. That the verb can occur with these categories of objects has led some to conclude that, since all (social) acts are performed, all social action is performance.

But empirical observation clearly reveals that not all social and communicative behavior is 'performed' or constitutes a 'performance' in the theatrical sense, that is, displayed with an eye to how it appears to the audience. Dramatized performances obviously abound in social life, and frequently their audience is the co-interactant. But performance includes a layer of self-reflexivity that much of our participation in interaction lacks.

We have seen Hussein perform surprise and terror when he described how he almost hit a delivery woman's car (Chapter 5), and we have seen Richie perform Hussein in pain (Chapter 1). These are dramatizations. Performances in Goffman's sense—stylized presentations of self—occur twice during this episode. In them, we see Hussein 'front-stage'. Thus, when he first greets the Capri owner in the morning, he straightens his bearing and faces and directs his gaze toward him, entirely unlike during his interactions with his technicians; and a while later, when he unpacks the brake pads and hands them to Victorio without ever looking up, but, when a pair of customers arrives, he turns, straightens, and fully faces them before he performs a greeting routine.

The modulation or 're-keying' (Goffman 1974) of interaction that we call 'play' is different from theatrical and 'front-stage' performance: it does not cast the other as audience, but as co-player. Play shares with theatrical performance an element of fictionalization: things are not what they seem (Bateson 1972). Social play allows players to put otherwise 'hidden' selves on display. As a mechanism for drawing pleasure from contradictions (Bateson 1949; Freud 1960), humor and play are apt at transforming and resolving conflict in social interaction (as Hussein did when he joked to Richie, 'If you don't wanna buy it, I'll sell it to Russia'). In this episode, play occurs when Hussein says to the customer, laughing:

H: I tell you you're not losing nothing
    because we wash it.
    If you wash it
    you're going to spend maybe hundred dollars
    to do this (hh) j(hh)ob (hh hh hh hh hh).

Dialogues such as these, which contain an element of teasing, are part of the fabric of Hussein's relationships with some of his customers. These will likely see in him less the performed Hussein, the 'front' he presents to them in his polite and sometimes exuberant greetings, but rather the playful Hussein he reveals when he 'breaks frame' and teases or banters with them.

Fig. 7.10 The day ends

7.10   The last act

Hussein's last job—the last act as owner and principal of Hi-Tech Automotive—is to ask Victor whether the red Mercury Capri has been fixed. Victor says yes, and Hussein, turning to the camera and grinning, says 'make him happy'. He leans back, stretches his arms, and says, 'now I go home and drink two Chevis Regal'. Then he divests himself of his coat, the microphone, and his workday self.

7.11   Conclusion

Accompanying a single car on its all-day journey through the shop has provided us with a synopsis of the main managerial capacities in which Hussein conducts his communicative labor: as manager of information—the hub of a distributed cognitive system; as principal of an organization, entitled to issue directives and incurring sanctionable obligations when doing business with customers and suppliers; and as coworker or 'foreman' when he participates in the manual work that is the material foundation of Hi-Tech Automotive. Hussein's *transactive* speech acts (Taylor 2011—those that have sanctionable, agreed-upon, institutionalized social, economic, or legal consequences—are not marked as such by their form. They are indistinguishable from 'ordinary' speech acts such as informings and (indirect) promises, as Heritage and Clayman (2010) have pointed out; their institutional forces surface only when something violates commitments and remedial action is required. We saw Hussein honoring his commitments when he began the process of blow-drying the red Capri. As owner of the business he was the principal of the act of steam-cleaning it before, even though someone else did it. This is implied in his contractual relationships with both the owner of the car and his employee, Hakim. He had also directed Hakim to do so over Hakim's objections, who saw the damage coming; in that regard Hussein lives to a commitment that is institutional only to the degree to which institutional meanings ('constitutive rules'; Searle 1969) and commitments are institutionalized in everyday speech acts ('you cannot blame someone for the consequences of an act that you requested of him, if it was properly executed').

I have distinguished between different types of agency in Hussein's managerial actions, different acts of deferring or delegating 'immediate' (physical) agency to others: Hussein can cause something to happen (perform the action himself); he can direct the addressee to do it; he can request that the action be done by someone (unspecific); and he can direct someone specific to have the action done, either by someone specific or unspecific. As I have pointed out, there are natural languages that treat these distinctions as basic, as fundamental hierarchical forms of social relatedness in action, in making things happen, getting things done. I have also used terms such as 'personal' and 'impersonal' and 'active' and 'passive' to distinguish types of directive by which agency is transferred. Delegating agency is of course what managing is all about: getting things done by productively getting others to do it.

Hussein's final managerial act of the day, and his last work-related speech act, is to check with Victorio whether the Mercury Capri is done. When Victorio says yes, Hussein takes off his coat and the microphone. And so his workday ends, and with it our journey with him through eleven hours of one human life, a life spent and made in the main by communicating with others. In the final chapter, I will take stock of the 'cultural composite' we have encountered in Hussein and look back at him as an exemplar, a specimen of the self-made, self-making lived body, cultural actor, and social persona that every one of us is. In the postscript, I will reflect on the autopoietic process that this investigation itself has been, and how 'theory' and generalization 'autonomically' emerged from disciplined observation.

8　Self-Making

8.1　The anthropology of making

This book is a pointillist portrait of a person and, hopefully, works somewhat like a Chuck Klose painting:[1] as a mosaic of pieces, each of which is a picture in its own right, but shows only a slice of its subject, yet in its home context—a genre painting. Those who know him should yet be able to recognize Hussein Chmeis as they know him, with his distinct habits, charisma, and leadership and communication styles. We, however, will now take a step back to where only his silhouette can be seen, where he appears as a *model of the human actor*, displaying features that everyone of us possesses. What distinguishes Hussein in this book from other models of the actor is that he is in part fleshed out, an empirical model, rather than a generic, abstract, and hypothetical one.

I have used a simple heuristics of body parts—or rather of modalities of communication—to structure the analysis and order the scenes that make up the whole Hussein in his life-world on an average workday. At one level, this is a troublesome way to proceed: after all, never is only one body part involved in communication; it is always the whole body that communicates. However, the different communication modalities that we distinguish in everyday life and our research—gaze, gesture, posture, speech, and so on—are each to a greater or lesser extent and in their own way subject to social regulation, and a case can be made that human multimodal communication is indeed a *composite* of component systems of

---

[1] For example: http://vertufineart.com/wpcontent/uploads/2013/03/Chuck_Close_Lyle_ 2010.jpg

practices, that each has its own evolutionary history (Streeck 2008b). Levinson and Holler propose that

> language normally occurs embedded within an interactional exchange of multi-modal signals. If this larger perspective takes central focus, then it becomes apparent that human communication has a layered structure, where the layers may be plausibly assigned different phylogenetic and evolutionary origins. ... This perspective helps us to appreciate the different roles that the different modalities play in human communication, as well as how they function as one integrated system despite their different roles and origins. (Levinson & Holler 2014: 1)

The picture that emerged in this book is compatible with this perspective. There is a difference in the framework of analysis, however. I do not abstract communication as a signaling system, or as a system of signaling systems, from the communicators' bodily *inhabiting* of the world, from the daily practical labor of world-making in which communicative abilities have evolved and in which they are embedded. Humans are 'always already' *transparent* to each other as they go about their business of inhabiting the same world. The modalities of embodied communication, most certainly gesture, have arisen from and within the context of practical action, not as signaling systems *sui generis*, even though some have evolved into such systems (and are continuing to evolve into such systems, for example, when a gesture is abstracted from situated action and then becomes a common symbol in a group; LeBaron & Streeck 2000), or where 'home sign' systems develop (Haviland 2013). This perspective—a *dwelling* perspective—is informed by Ingold's anthropology (Ingold 2000, 2011). Ingold emphasizes the continuity of world-making (niche-building) and meaning-making across all forms of organic life, notwithstanding the distinct human ability to 'ratchet up', refine, and reanalyze shared skills, forms, stories, and practices—culture—from generation to generation (see Streeck 2015). Humans do not so much impose orders of symbolic meaning onto the world, but they gather and enact meanings in the world and thereby create *Umwelten* (Uexküll 1957) in ways that are continuous across life-forms.

We have closely observed how Hussein makes gestures, but the making of gestures also speaks to a more profound human ability, namely to make things (Streeck 2007b). Making things out of things by two hands under a watchful eye is the most characteristic 'pose' of the human life-form. The importance of world-making to the human life-form has previously been emphasized by philosophical anthropologists, a school of thought originating in the 1920s, informed both by phenomenology and the theory of evolution, and by Mead's (1934) evolutionary theory (Gehlen 1988; Plessner 1923, 1975, 1980; see also Berger & Luckmann 1967; Honneth & Joas 1988). In an essay on art, philosopher Alva Noë has recently formulated this view of the human life-form as *homo faber*, an *anthropology of making*, in straightforward terms:

> Making stuff is special for us. Making activities ... constitute us as a species. Artists make stuff because in doing so they reveal something deep and important about our nature, indeed, ... our biological nature. ... Human beings ... are designers by nature. We are makers and consumers of technologies. Knives, clothing, dwellings, but also language, pictures, email, commercial air travel and social media. Tools and technologies organize us ... insofar as they are embedded in our lives. ... Take a doorknob, for example.... Doorknobs exist in the context of a whole form of life, a whole biology—the existence of doors, and buildings, and passages, the human body, the hand. (Noë 2015)

8.2 Embodiment and the modalities of communication

In the first chapter, we learned that the simple activity of locomotion, of getting from one place to another, subtly encodes social meaning: walking—modulating gait and bearing—is an opportunity to project purpose, destination, availability. Today, we view gait in strictly functional terms—even urban traffic is treated as if it were only a navigational problem (Goffman 1971; Mondada 2009); this contrasts with older interpretive frameworks for scrutinizing the way people walked with respect to what it revealed about moral character, social standing, and aspiration; typically, these frameworks were designed to naturalize one's own cultural movement style as the most effective, least pretentious, the only legitimate one. Locomotion—walking together—can also be used as an opportunity to 'dance together', to 'step a relationship into being'. Dance, like pedestrian navigation in densely populated environments and many sports, calls upon the body's ability to anticipate the movements of other bodies. Without anticipation, synchronous motion could not be achieved. This deeply embodied and ancient species-unspecific ability is a reliable, autonomic mechanism deployable even in sophisticated, self-reflexive, even ironic—in other words, distinctly human—negotiations.

Hussein's eyes, like anyone's, are preoccupied for much of the day with the corporeal, 'technical' necessities of material action: monitoring the hands as they take, handle, probe, use, and make things, as well as seeing ('reading') the environment. For modern humans, this includes frequent reading of inscriptions. When other humans are present and cooperation is to be organized, the need to coordinate the movement of the eyes, to achieve 'joint attention', arises as a task for which pointing methods have been habitualized everywhere. When the activities of others matter to one's own project, situation awareness becomes a concern. Situation awareness often has a social structure; it is unequally distributed (Hutchins 1991). For Hussein, being exclusively responsible for maintaining situation awareness creates the need for frequent scanning, monitoring, and supervision.

During much of the day at Hi-Tech, people are free to do what they want with their eyes at any moment and are accountable for where they have directed their attention only, as it were, at the end of the day. During cooperation, they must maintain joint attention. However, when people enter into a state of face-to-face *conversation* where other activities are attended only peripherally, if at all, gaze becomes entangled in a system of constraints. During face-to-face conversation, the allotment of gaze appears to be subject to a fairly rigid social control grid, which reduces possible gaze directions and movements to a small set of distinct states: looking at or away from the other; being or not being in the process of turning one's gaze to the other; turning away. Hussein's conversations were almost all 'functional'—not flirts—and thus they did not give us an idea of the relational possibilities that this system nevertheless opens for us, for example, through the negotiation of extended mutual gaze. Within Hussein's mundane conversations and business transactions, mutual gaze seems to have the characteristics of a minimal social contract. Mutual gaze 'registers' new action projects as well as consequential, 'transactive' speech acts.

Pointing, and what I have called 'showing', is foundational 'equipment for living', one set of methods for inhabiting and making the world. Enacting them, we disclose meanings that inhere in the world for us, make a visible, yet opaque, world seeable and intelligible. Beyond directing attention, pointing gestures can frame the way we see things. Pointing and bodily showing involve highly differentiated, context-adaptive techniques—a toolkit. Pointing methods can be landscape-specific and shaped by cultural systems of spatial orientation and wayfinding (Haviland 1993, 2003; Levinson 2003). Methods of corporeal showing can embody the way of life of a practice community (dancers, car mechanics, rock climbers). Whenever the hands show the world at hand, they have an opportunity to reveal something that they know about it. Imagine showing a child how a thumbnail cinema works: we have no program for the instruction, but our hands will figure one out. They will find a way to make intelligible and replicable by

other hands what they already know how to do. In such moments, in the most
mundane actions, we confront the creativity of life in the form of creativity of
adaptive motion.

This creativity is even more on display during gesticulation, one of the
least regimented human communication activities: nobody is forced to
gesticulate (no matter that not gesticulating may look odd); the words
spoken are intelligible on their own merit and gesticulation seems
superfluous and was often condemned (Schmitt 1990), even though in
modern societies, it is subject to only few, loose restrictions. The result is
considerable, perhaps immeasurable, individual variation—*individuation*.
In gesticulation, we can therefore forever witness the evolution or self-
replenishment of a communicative resource, the reproduction of a social
medium, through individuated spontaneous action. Gesticulation is creative communication that always, at least potentially, transcends received
strictures, as if new words came out of people's mouths every time they
speak. Some developmental neuroscientists (Kinsbourne & Jordan 2009)
have suggested that the non-performance of overt, bodily actions in
response to the actions of others—*not* to mimic a facial expression, *not* to
reach out with one's hands for an object—is an achievement, an inhibition
that requires a certain maturity of the central nervous system. One can
speculate that the idiosyncrasies of gesticulation are due not so much to
individual differences in inventiveness, but to differences in inhibition, in
acquired habits of suppressing the body's autonomic activity in communication with other bodies.

I do not pretend to have provided any new insights into language and
speaking. Within the context of this study, however, and its ambition to
understand as much as possible about the self-making of a communicating
person, the inherently transitional character of Hussein's repertoire of
speaking practices and linguistic constructions has been important to
note. 'On-the-job learning', or learning by cooperative speaking, especially
in the case of a second language learner, amplifies the ubiquitous inter-
twining of individual language making (the making of a repertoire of
constructions by imitating those used by others and understanding how
they work in context), the making of a life-world, and the making of a social
self.

Furthermore, we saw how, during one of the few occasions on this day
when Hussein produced extended, multi-turn talk—stories about his days
at work—his speaking—the 'line-by-line' progression of his talk—exhibited patterns familiar to us from poetics, rhetoric, and text linguistics and
usually conceived as aesthetic, persuasive, or coherence devices. All of them

involved some form of parallelism.[2] From the perspective of the study of oral poetry, these practices appear as methods of 'oral composition' (Finnegan 1977), as methods by which the ever-present problem of getting from one line to the next line is solved. The methods are musical in nature and, in the case of ordinary speakers such as Hussein, to a great extent unconsciously practiced. Yet they require a musical tuning to the sounds of one's own speaking: the next line is built by recognition of a sonic pattern in the last. Oral poets learn to trust the autonomy of this process so that they can concentrate on remembering content or finding a new pattern for a future line (Streeck & Henderson 2010). Hussein appears to rely on this poetic automatism from time to time. Here we find autopoiesis in both the life science and the poetic sense: it is an autonomic process like gesticulation, and its mechanism is replication of form.

Last, we have taken note of the institutional or transactive character of some of Hussein's speech acts. By speaking, he enacts, reproduces, and presupposes social institutions, which are themselves of different origin and scale: contracts, laws, debts, entitlements, and so on. Speech acts themselves are human institutions (D'Andrade 1984), involving commitments, presupposing statuses, establishing realities that are binding for everyone. Ever since Ryle (1949) discussed the social accountability of the ascription of emotions, Hart (1955) analyzed the ascription of responsibilities and rights, and Austin (1962, 1970) conducted his performative analysis of vows, statements, and excuses, ordinary language philosophers and, subsequently, sociologists (see especially Heritage 1984, 2008; Heritage & Clayman 2010; Heritage & Greatbach 1989) and anthropologists (Rosaldo 1990), have worked out parts of this web of institutions that is incessantly enacted in quotidian interaction. It is likely that some of these institutions such as questions and informings are as old as humanity itself, while others are institutions of particular societies and embedded in culture-specific webs of norms, entitlements, language ideologies, and systems of belief. While such transactive speech acts are typically not distinguished by their linguistic form, small bodily acts such as shifts in gaze can mark—and show a person's orientation to—the exalted, transactive nature of the talk under way. This reflexive orientation to one's own communication, as well as the poetic ways of speaking that are possible because one can hear oneself speak, illustrate the *ex-centric positionality*

---

[2] Jefferson (1996) has described poetic forms such as rhymes, antinomies, and inversions in the context of speech errors, as well as rhetorical devices such as lists (Jefferson 1990).

(Plessner 1923) of the human life-form, its ability to take a stand on itself in light of its own objectivations.

The living human body in communication is an institutional actor, someone who enacts cultural meanings and communal institutions. It is useless—implausible anthropology—to abstract away from these entanglements and try and study the human organism in a culture-, institution-, history-, and power-free zone. It is also implausible to study embodied communication without acknowledging the individuation and spontaneous intelligence of bodily action and the fact that, as movement, it is also in an important way life.

8.3 Autopoiesis in the auto shop

This book has focused on the self-organization of an individual actor in moments of praxis. This perspective brings into relief the always open-ended relationship between practice/habit/routine and contingent situation, between 'sediment' and 'spontaneity' (Merleau-Ponty 1962), between repetition and change. Intelligent body motion, including gesture, is fluid and adaptive, and whether a given gesture instantiates a convention (a socially shared form), is a personal habit, or a situated 'invention', is, at least initially, up for grabs. Occasionally, we see Hussein 'groping' (Noland 2009), striving for 'maximal grip' (Dreyfus 2002). Because I could not be certain which gestures were tokens of types, my focus had to be on the *process* or *acts of typification*, on how Hussein subsumed features of diverse situations under similar gestural forms. In its temporality—its demonstrable spontaneity, emanating without Hussein's awareness—his gesticulation revealed its nature as an autonomic, self-organizing (autopoietic) process that shares structural features with all other forms of living motion, in particular in the ways in which living movements make sense in a situation. I have thus reconceptualized gesture as a language-independent, action-based form of bodily intelligence, grounded in human 'dwelling' (Ingold 2000). Gesticulation is transparent to others within a shared life-world, in ways analogous to those in which practical bodily actions are transparent (Andrén 2010).

While we have observed self-organization during gesticulation, we have also found it in Hussein's linguistic habits. Studying them, we recognize self-organization on a different time-scale, not situation but life-time: Hussein's English linguistic repertoire at the time consisted, of course, to a very large extent of words, constructions, and prosodic routines shared with the speech community at large; yet the 'idiolectal' features of his language use—the constructions that, while not standard, have nevertheless become habits—can *only* meaningfully be regarded as products of self-organization and individuation because they are not shared with others and cannot have been acquired from them.[3]

Hussein's self-making—his ongoing enacting, reproducing, and modifying of a repertoire of habits, of skilled dispositions to respond to evolving situations—takes place under specific economic and institutional conditions: control of capital and means of production (tools, machines, etc.), wage labor, sole ownership of the shop, and so forth. His becoming a self-made man—an entrepreneur—is not any more representative of 'the human condition' than that of other humans in privileged positions. Their self-making depends on the limitations it imposes on the self-making of others. This dimension of Hussein's autopoiesis has remained in the background of this study, and it would require a decentered perspective, focused on how Hussein appears to others and how others, through their actions, bring about 'their Hussein'.

Nevertheless, we have seen, especially in Chapter 7, that Hussein's actions are frequently implicated in and sustain economic, institutional, and power relations. His agency extends beyond the current moment because he can order others to do things, in which case their actions become attributable to him as 'principal' (Goffman 1983); he, not the technician, will be held liable. In turn, Hussein's 'causative' agency is the result of preexisting entitlements, defined by labor laws and locally by contracts. Some of Hussein's communicative actions—those that define his status within the organization—are transactive (Taylor 2011): they alter the state of the web of commitments and entitlements that Hussein is entangled in. The living being that is the center of Hussein's communicative activity, as everyone's, is thus always and irreducibly also an institutional agent. This dimension of communicative action cannot be 'naturalized away'. It is central to Hussein's ways of acting, visible in the care he often exerts in performing certain acts, and it is generally constitutive of human sociality.

8.4 Serious embodiment: reviving life

If we really desire to understand how the human body participates in cognition, communication, and social life, we have no choice but to accept two premises: first, that 'the body' is in each case an individual body, a *lived*,

[3] I do not mean to suggest that only 'idiolectal' features are products of self-organization. The acquisition of standard forms is also a process of self-organization, and the repertoire as a whole constitutes a mixture of forms/practices acquired by emulation and imitation.

not an anatomical or semiotic one, the product of a lifetime of living and individuation, of sustaining itself by inhabiting the world with particular, concrete others. Any abstraction away from the singularity of each human body risks missing the very essence of what being a living body means. Second, then, to understand the body and give it its proper place in our social theories, we must understand it as *life* and recognize in its communicative movements the logic that is characteristic of the self-organization of all life and movement. In the seemingly least important and consequential form of communication in which Hussein engages, his gesticulation, the process was on display: ongoing, unpredictable, autonomic creative action, targeted movements by which the speaking and thinking body organizes itself in, and thus makes sense of, an emerging situation. To understand gesture, we must understand it as an evolutionary elaboration of 'worldly' bodily action, not as a store of expressive forms by which mental content is encoded and what is being said is made evident, 'visualized'. Gesticulation cannot be described and explained within the traditional categories of subject, agent, and communicative intent, for the one who makes the gestures is an autonomous, unsupervised living body, making sense of the oncoming world by moving toward it, grasping it, taking hold of it, and moving ahead on its 'path of observation' (Gibson 1986).

A gaping hole in my portrait of Hussein remains, however, and it is where his face ought to be. I have hardly looked at it at all, and then only to see where he directed his eyes. I have justified this with the insufficient quality of the data: one often cannot see Hussein's face, or what his interaction partners can see in it, and one rarely sees it closely enough to recognize the play of expressions and micro-expressions (Ekman & Friesen 1975). I have also not made any attempt to describe and understand Hussein as an emotional man, to analyze *affect* in his communication. Empirical research on affect in interaction is at a very early stage. There is little clarity as to which phenomena are relevant (but see Peräkylä & Sorjonen 2012), nor is there a broadly agreed upon conceptual and theoretical framework (but see Fuchs 2017).

Finally, I have given short shrift to Hussein, the moral actor, the reflexive, responsive person who evaluates and decides his courses of action in light of values, norms, standards, and the interests and rights of others (as weighed against his own). The ways in which he motivates directives is perhaps indicative of Hussein's lived 'management ethos'. We have also heard Hussein sum up his ethics or business philosophy in the coda of his description of a generically crazy day in his life:

> I always make money
> but I never thought to make money
> one time from any customer
> because I want him again.

But to do justice to this aspect of Hussein's being, to portray him in light of his own self-understanding, I would have had to talk to him at length, and that would have disrupted the reality of the workday I wanted to document. It would also require a different methodology, not micro-ethnography. Hopefully the reader has nevertheless been able to recognize a coherent, distinct, and moral person in these small scenes from a day in Hussein's life.

Autopoietic research: a note on methodology

Gregory Bateson, who compared himself to an 'explorer who cannot know what he is exploring until it has been explored' (Brockman 1977: 4), wrote in his 'Experiments of thinking on ethnological material':

> Whenever we pride ourselves upon finding a newer, stricter way of thought or exposition; whenever we start insisting too hard on 'operationalism' or symbolic logic or any other of these very essential tramlines, we lose something of the ability to think new thoughts. And equally, of course, whenever we rebel against the sterile rigidity of formal thought and exposition and let our ideas run wild, we likewise lose. As I see it, the advances in scientific thought come from a combination of loose and strict thinking, and this combination is the most precious tool of science. (Bateson 1972: 75)

We need 'looseness of thought', but we also need that looseness to 'be measured up against a rigid concreteness' (ibid.).

The conduct of this study has been such an oscillation between 'rigid concreteness' of strict analytic procedure and sudden 'hunches' that a phenomenon that had turned up during this arduous exercise might be indicative of 'something bigger', something 'generic', something that might tell me something more profound about human communication. In my prior research, my 'discovery' that people sometimes look at their hands when they gesture had precipitated 'hunches' about differences between modes of gesturing and about the human ability to take a reflexive—or 'ex-centric' (Plessner 1923)—stance on their own bodily objectivations (Streeck 1993), that gesture is also a dialogue within the self. When I studied Hussein, the way he touched a newly painted fender and thereby disclosed its texture to Omar yielded ideas about transmodal capacities of hand gestures, their ability to translate tactile and haptic sensations into another sensory modality, to make something feelable visible. And rigorous scrutiny of the temporality of his gesticulation made me think of these acts as 'subjectless actions', to begin to see the autonomy of the communicating body, not the mind-tool, signalizer, and embodiment of larger social forces that figures prominently in contemporary lay and academic discourse. My turn to the living organism as the self-making core of a self-made man is turn with unknown consequences: what model of the actor and speaker would one end up with once one really lets go of the 'subject' or 'homunculus' that controls bodily action in our explanatory models? What is evident is that any empirical reconstruction of the accountable actor as a product of a self-making body will be an arduous ascent. Methodological rigor does not guarantee insights, but neither is it dispensable, as Bateson pointed out: it is required for the laying down of the path toward the hunches.

Research of the kind conducted here has been characterized as *abductive*. This term, introduced by C. S. Peirce (1901), refers to logical inferences that derive a hypothesis from an observation—a hypothesis that would explain the occurrence of the event that has been observed. In other words, a phenomenon is analyzed as a single case, with the aim of finding a general pattern that accounts for its emergence in its context. The explanation is then tested by examining what appear to be parallel phenomena in other contexts, with the aim of establishing whether the same hypothesis would explain their emergence in them. If it does not, the hypothesis or 'pattern' must be revised.[1] Timmermans and Tavory write that Peirce considered abduction the 'only logical mechanism that introduced new ideas into a body of scientific knowledge' (Timmerman & Tavory 2012: 170).

> Abduction is the form of reasoning through which we perceive the phenomenon as related to other observations either in the sense that there is a cause and effect hidden from view, in the sense that the phenomenon is seen as similar to other phenomena already experienced and explained in other situations, or in the sense of creating new general descriptions.
> (Timmerman & Tavory 2012: 171)

Researchers of everyday life treat every phenomenon as surprising unless it is familiar from prior research, often research done by others.

Abduction is a slow procedure, characterized by continuous shifts between a purely descriptive and a theoretical orientation to the data. But

---

[1] A classic example of the revision of a hypothesis or account to accommodate a 'deviant' case is Schegloff's (1968) revision of his account of the sequential pattern of telephone openings to accommodate a single case that did not fit the hypothesis that 499 others had.

the slow pace of abduction has the advantage of allowing generalization and theory to grow at their own unpredictable pace.

But does 'abduction' mean abducting or being abducted? It appears that the 'hunches' that Bateson referred to are what Peirce regarded as 'the only logical mechanism that introduced new ideas', the finding of a pattern that can explain the phenomenon. Abduction, in other words, necessitates 'loose thinking' (and room for loose thinking): the ability and opportunity to let oneself be abducted by autonomically evolving lines of thinking and inquiry, before returning to the 'rigid concreteness' of case-by-case analysis, applying the same *inductive* procedures again and again.

An interesting fact about our field is that many practitioners, although they are often involved in collaborations and regularly participate in collective 'data sessions', never delegate the analysis of their data to assistants in the way common in other disciplines. They much rather do 'the work' themselves, often by themselves, like woodcarvers or writers. This may be so because the combination of the meditative practice of data analysis with the freedom and fatalism to let hunches happen as they wish, without the need to answer to hypotheses that the very research that follows the hunches could make obsolete, is conducive to an evolving observational science that repeatedly reconceives the phenomena it studies. It is a context in which the researcher is allowed not to know what he is exploring and living cognition can remain unpredictable.

Appendix: Activity log

Friday, March 24, 1995
  begins 7:30 a.m.
  ends 7:50 p.m.

Tape 1

00-00	puts on coat
	paper work
3-50	empty office
5-45	Hakim
6-04	Omar arrives
7-05	Art, tow truck
7-17	greets Victor
8-11	checks car in shop
8-28	Cedric, instructions
9-00	checks car in shop
9-31	Victor, planning, diagnosis
10-00	checks car 1
10-47	Art, consultation, interpretation of noise, collaborative diagnosis
	gestures
14-54	Hakim
15-04	first customer
	office, work order
18-08	incoming call: Kenneth
18-30	customer 1
18-50	checks red Mercury

Tape 1 (cont.)

20-00	drives Mercury into garage
20-54	Victor, Audi, collaborative diagnosis
22-00	front desk, talks to me: offers more time
23-20	mobile paperwork
23-30	Victor, Audi, collaborative diagnosis, spark
27-04	paperwork at white car
28-50	brake check red Mercury, DW 40
30-10	computer, diagnosis
30-34	office
31-05	front desk, checks phone number
31-22	incoming call: customer, taking order, figuring problem
32-40	call: Pete, Hi-Lo
33-00	front desk, switches phones, order for brakes, availability check
	'send them to me'
34-20	talks to me
	'don't like to waste a moment'
34-57	Hakim
35-05	to shop, red Mercury
35-36	storage room, checks part numbers
35-55	call, Hi-Lo
	rear pads also, part numbers
30-35	back to shop, phone, computer
38-00	call ends
39-50	call: Joe, rear brake pads
40-16	front desk, call: Mercury owner, diagnosis, price
41-00	delivery of front pad
42-15	switch to incoming call: customer
	checks ticket
43-02	I ask questions
	'how do you know about each car'
	'I know. I always inside.'
	'Most of my time because inside the shop, not in the office.'
	'and then I'm going inside my head who goin' to do this a job, who the other one.'
44-20	'what do you write'
	importance of year model
45-56	incoming call: Chuck Howley, property, business, employees
47-29	Victor
	'give this to Cedric'

Tape 1 (cont.)

47-53	customers on trip to Houston arrive
	air condition lever problem
	prognosis: half an hour
49-50	Hakim, instruction
50-15	Victor, Audi
	collaborative diagnosis
	Chito
	Alex, work assignment
	tells him to leave tools at car
51-58	Hakim
53-10	incoming call: John
	wants appointment
	'bring it by; I'll do my best'
56-39	worker outside
57-09	shop
	red Mercury, brake work
58-56	work on little red car, dashboard
	gets tools, flashlight, screwdriver
1-05-19	front desk, call: Hassan, for help
	checks mobile phone; it works
1-07-07	Hassan arrives, at red car
1-07-56	incoming call, Lebanese
1-08-40	Hassan, red car
	explains work to me
1-09-40	Cedric, puts wheel on Mercury
	work on wheel, Mercury
	explains what he does in shop
	'I not only give order, do same thing'
	Cedric
	gets tool
	screws on wheels
	'hand tight'
1-12-30	puts away tool
1-12-45	incoming call: customer, axle problem, diagnosis
1-13-56	phone, inspects car
	inside car
1-14-47	customer, diagnosis, 'idle low'
	keys
1-15-53	Hassan, red car
	I talk about what I learn

Tape 1 (cont.)

	'you use only your brain'
	'we never fix anything'
	'without teach how do life can continue'
1-18-06	Victor, leaves note
	'what year model'
	'in Spanish'
	explains conversation to me
	about call for parts
	batteries
1-20-42	Hassan, red car
1-20-54	Arturo, transmission
	diagnosis
	'wanna check with customer about this'
	background music
	'let me get okay on this'
1-22-15	front desk, Hakim, Hassan
1-22-35	goes outside
	Hassan, red car
1-23-10	front desk, Hakim
	call, Lebanese
1-23-50	call: Albert Martinez
	unavailable, leave message
	background music
1-24-20	front desk, paperwork
	Hakim, chat
1-25-42	calculator
1-26-00	call: towing of GMC
	incoming call
1-26-20	red car
1-26-20	second incoming call: send somebody
	customers waiting
1-27-21	back to first incoming call: transmission, diagnosis
1-28-12	Arturo, banter
1-28-12	Lebanese interlude
	customers waiting
	'half an hour'
	'done, already done, five more minutes'
1-29-15	Hassan, red car
	Hakim
1-30-00	H finishes work on red car

Tape 1 (cont.)

1-32-20	shop, gets tool
1-32-55	inside red car
1-33-11	close up: hands, face
1-35-11	call: Hassan
	explains problem to me
1-35-38	calls on Hakim, work order
1-36-13	goes inside, Lebanese (off)
	Hassan, red car
	both in red car
1-38-10	Hakim
1-38-35	inside red car
1-39-10	Hakim
1-39-39	front desk: customers waiting, background music
1-40-10	call: Lebanese
1-40-30	front desk, call: Steve
1-11-05	Hakim
	call continues
1-42-10	blue car
	call continues
1-42-53	inside red car, call continues
1-43-30	front desk, call continues
	Paperwork
1-44-05	red car
	call: conversation
1-44-30	gets tools
1-44-57	inside red car
1-45-40	puts away tools
1-45-59	red car done
	drives red car
1-46-25	front desk, red car customers, paperwork
1-47-08	call: credit card
1-47-29	delivery man: Snap On
	I talk
1-48-15	customers, good-bye
1-48-30	delivery man
	'Arturo said you need'
	payment
1-49-15	office, delivery man, insurance problem
	safe, money for Arturo
	needs record from Snap-On for insurance claim

Tape 1 (cont.)

1-51-01	office, alone
	drinks OJ
1-51-50	'start again now'
1-52-05	drives red Mercury outside
1-52-40	white convertible
	R, potential buyer
1-52-20	incoming call, Lebanese
	red Mercury
	R waiting
1-54-10	second incoming call
	'just come back'
1-54-28	R, negotiation
1-55-55	'Okay how much did you pay'
2-00-48	incoming call

Tape 2

00-00	about R
	'she likes me; she hugs me'
00-57	moves white car for oil change
01-22	Victor, instructions
01-55	I ask about locking up of tools
02-07	checks blue car
03-02	shop, tool box
03-30	Hakim
03-39	red Mercury
03-51	office, eats banana
04-40	Hakim
	at red Mercury
05-22	gives credit
05-30	little break
	'they don't wanna see me around'
	I talk, 'this is so interesting'
07-20	'I tell you one thing,' story
08-45	'all day like this'
09-35	'that's why I used microphone'
14-00	about meditation

Tape 2 (cont.)

14-21	'I don't have time for personal'
	'all my life work'
16-19	incoming call
	'when I go home, go to sleep'
17-15	'first time I come to United States'
17-35	incoming call, price of diagnosis
18-28	delivery man
19-20	TV, calculator
19-43	'start back again inside'
20-00	instructions, fender
20-40	second red car
	Hakim brings parts
21-20	Kenneth
21-29	office
23-07	money
	Kenneth
	banter about camera
23-58	bananas
24-20	'you like UT' (to Kenneth)
25-00	'good place to make money'
25-21	'for example long time', story
	Kenneth, banter
	story continues
26-33	incoming call overseas, Lebanese
27-24	'Insha'Allah'
29-07	call ends
	to Kenneth, 'how much you sold the Hyundai'
29-37	office, empty
32-17	front desk, Hakim, Hassan, Kenneth
	gestures
33-51	shop
	'see that technician'
34-06	explains transmission
	Chito
37-22	close up, Chito explains
38-26	about birthdays
38-42	Victor, Audi, consultation
39-40	explains about Audi and Victor
	close up
	Victor

Tape 2 (cont.)

41-20	customer arrives, wants old part (splint) from junk yard
43-16	'professor teach in UT'
43-53	'Victorio give him screwdriver'
44-08	Mike, inspection, instructions
45-26	incoming call
	'is ready, Sir'
46-15	incoming call, Lebanese, sits on car
47-30	explains phone calls
	relationships with other Lebanese
50-00	shop
50-25	Victor, Audi
	close up
52-49	Kenneth, needs a ride
	'are you gonna make me some money today'
53-32	incoming call
54-11	front desk, sorts mail
54-45	Kenneth
55-18	Victor, Audi
	gets phone
55-58	office, Kenneth, paperwork
56-36	call, timing belt for Audi
57-16	about credit
57-59	Victor, close up
1-00-49	gets tools
	compression check
	diagnosis
1-03-24	distributor broken
	explains to me
1-04-55	customer needs help at junkyard
1-06-15	customer advertises Hi-Tech
1-06-49	Hakim
	goes to junkyard, close up, wreck
	gets bolt out
	dialogue with customer
1-09-30	unscrews door
	Victor comes
	close up
1-12-49	gets tool
1-13-55	back at car
1-14-37	done

Tape 2 (cont.)

	talks with customer
	examines object
1-15-25	puts door back in
1-16-10	incoming call
1-16-30	second incoming call, 'which Pontiac'
	walks back
1-17-10	calls for Victor
	at tool box
1-17-59	Cedric comes, instructions
1-18-38	shop, cleans up
1-19-23	Victor, distributor
1-19-38	front desk, Kenneth
	quiet, background music
	electronic rolodex
1-20-00	call, about used distributor for Audi
	paperwork
1-22-01	calls for Hakim
	TV
1-22-47	office, paperwork
1-23-34	calls out to Kenneth, ad in paper
	paperwork
1-26-25	incoming call, 'Kenneth, line 2'
1-27-16	incoming call, customer, complains, H. forgot, 'stop by'
1-28-21	Kenneth, financing
	paperwork
	rolodex
	I talk
1-29-15	call: Martinez
	unavailable, ask for call back
1-30-07	call, unavailable
1-30-30	calls out to Kenneth
	paperwork
1-31-40	incoming call, Lebanese
1-33-01	I ask permission for phone call
1-33-21	incoming call, Lebanese
1-34-08	call to Sam
	credit card
1-34-45	incoming call, Lebanese
1-36-36	calls out to Kenneth
	paperwork

Tape 2 (cont.)

1-44-29	leaves office
	shop, cleans up
1-45-07	Victor, Audi
	about distributor
1-45-45	talks to me, about available time
1-47-18	incoming call
1-47-47	(incoming) call, Kenneth: transmits phone number between them
1-48-35	Art
	shop, Alex, van
1-49-13	Mike, instructions
1-50-30	inside large car
	reads papers
1-52-07	incoming call, for Kenneth
1-53-12	'we must go across street'
1-54-28	Hakim
	H made mistake: year model wrong
	'my mistake'
1-55-35	explains to me
1-55-47	Ashraf
1-56-10	Audi
1-56-31	banter, Ashraf and I
	'what do you call this research'
1-57-27	about Ashraf
	'he get teach in my business in Saudi Arabia'

Tape 3

00-00	Uncle Am
	'you got everything you need'
	'everything over there' (other side)
01-24	hood, inspection
02-03	Hassan, Omar, instructions
	inspection
03-30	Uncle Am
	Corsica part
03-59	Hassan, Omar, Corsica
04-30	Omar, lamp fitting
05-21	open hood, instructions
	lamp fitting, close up
07-42	other car, engine, inspection
	explains to me 'this car done', 'ready for paint'
	planning of spray booth
08-24	about Uncle Am
06-47	Art, 'they call him grandpa'
09-02	about Hakim
09-29	dogs, 'what's wrong, baby'
	Ashraf, Omar, Uncle Am
10-53	incoming call: Audi customer, prognosis
12-31	Omar
12-57	about call from Audi customer
	'who can just picture him picking up the phone as if she is sitting across the street'
13-23	Omar
13-40	under bridge, Ashraf
	I talk about white sneakers
14-48	at van, Ashraf
15-00	inspection of head gasket
	Ashraf
16-06	waiting for Art
	about Art, 'the troubleshooter'
	'he take time, read the book, read computer'
17-00	inspection of car
17-54	Alex has questions, at car
18-37	Art
18-53	phone rings
20-03	moves fender
20-31	announces return to Hi-Tech 1

Tape 3 (cont.)

20-40	calls Uncle Am
	inspection
	'customer come to get estimate'
22-16	inspection
22-44	Art, Uncle Am, inspection
24-11	Corsica
	light, light fitting
25-24	Victor
	call: Hakim, 'we need one injector'
26-17	call, unsuccessful
	Uncle Am, light
	work on light, close up
24-17	leaves
28-00	back at office
28-20	call: door light for Corsica—head light door, language problem
	paperwork
30-20	call continues, 'I don't have book to check part'
	paperwork
31-19	calls out to Kenneth, copy, file
32-10	file for Nissan
32-40	leaves office
	shop, inspection
33-25	Mike, instruction
34-10	dries hands
35-00	Victor, 'what year model this Buick'
35-29	discovers leak
	Housem (cab driver) arrives
35-41	Housem, Lebanese
	Victor, inspection
36-44	office
	incoming call, 'what car', 'come any time you like'
37-30	Housem
	eats apple
38-45	'double check'
39-42	Lebanese, 'professor at UT, research'
41-37	incoming call: line one
43-06	call, unsuccessful
43-70	leaves
43-50	Kenneth

Tape 3 (cont.)

45-36	front desk, Kenneth only
48-10	Chito, uses phone
	(off:) 'without insurance, they go after my business'
50-00	'cars have to look better'; 'cars need to be in excellent shape'
54-00	lunch
	Ashraf, Hakim
	Ashraf, about himself
56-50	office, Kenneth
57-15	'can I go eat now'
57-25	lunch, Hakim, Ashraf
	conversation with Hakim
	gestures
	'nasty things'
59-39	outside
	(off)
1-00-00	'we're not equipped for this'
	(bad sound)
1-00-00	customer, radiator
1-01-34	explains to me, 'correct distributor'
1-02-00	lunch
	'coffee too much'
1-04-40	'introduce him to nice student'
	Senior Fellows Class
1-05-27	shop, lunch, incoming call
	car won't start
	phone instruction, phone start
	Kenneth
1-08-00	'can I talk with some man over there'
	near New Braunfels
	gestures
1-09-27	explains to me
	'don't too much money'
	Kenneth
1-10-33	outside
	instructions to Hakim, directions
	radiator
1-10-56	Victor
	leak in radiator
1-11-16	Kenneth
	'go check what they're doing'

Tape 3 (cont.)

1-11-20	incoming call, Lebanese
1-11-49	Hakim
	radiator
	directions
1-12-43	Housem
	about video
1-13-11	incoming call: potential buyer
	'I'll call you when we get anything'
1-13-45	Victor, short block
	Kenneth
1-14-26	Hakim, starter
1-15-09	Housem
	Kenneth
	Arturo
1-15-59	drives white car
1-16-12	shop
	outside, white car
1-16-37	Housem
1-16-57	carry engine to truck
	Victor
1-17-14	tool box
1-17-34	gets Cedric tool
	Housem
1-18-07	tool box
	'put air'
1-18-42	Kenneth
	'check what old man needs'
1-19-10	fixes tire
1-19-50	fixes tire, close up
1-20-36	Art
1-21-30	gets tire kit
	tool box
1-22-00	gestures to Cedric
1-23-01	close up
1-24-37	calls Arturo
	Cedric
1-25-00	rolls out tire
1-25-09	old man
1-25-40	incoming call, phone start
1-26-37	old man
	starter
	'68 Plymouth

Tape 3 (cont.)

1-27-20	call: '68 Plymouth starter
1-28-05	Hakim
1-28-21	Victor, instructions, shop
1-29-25	old man, starter, price
	'you looking about $110'
1-30-50	front desk
1-31-15	old man, work order
1-32-17	calls out 'go ahead'
	drives cab
	cab radio
1-33-05	old man
	inside '68 Plymouth
1-34-13	Victor, 'get Cedric to change oil'
	starter
	'you and me we have something else'
1-34-40	shapely woman (Susan)
1-35-11	call: customer
1-35-23	'bring car here now'
	shop
1-35-45	'what you want'
	incoming call, Lebanese
1-36-26	front desk, incoming call
	'take break couple of minutes'
	paperwork
1-37-03	Cadillac
	diagnosis, computer,
	background music ("Desperado")
	Victor, 'fender cover'
	Mike
1-38-37	ride for old man
1-38-50	Art, asks for money
1-39-24	female customer
1-39-31	incoming call, Lebanese
	paperwork
1-40-10	call
	'what year model'
	Lebanese
	paperwork
1-41-22	Art, towtruck
	paperwork
	car to salvage auction
1-43-00	office, paperwork

Tape 3 (cont.)

1-43-27	woman asks for Kenneth
1-43-51	Audi
	explains to me
	timing belt, jump
	close up
1-44-59	'you don't need car'
	Victor
	computer
1-45-27	'double check'
	diagnosis, plugs
	'free testing', Cadillac customer
1-46-06	puts plugs away
	inspection of plugs
	Victor, 'run another test'
	Mike, 'go to Hi-Lo'
	'what year model'
1-49-40	no output
	'missing one wire for connection'
	Victor
	incoming call, Lebanese
	no output
1-51-05	incoming call, John (supplier)
	starter for '68 Plymouth
	two-motor mound
1-52-27	Cadillac, Victor
	metric conversion
1-53-20	Housem, gets tire
1-53-40	letter for John
	office, insurance
1-54-26	delivery man, signature, about camera
1-55-02	about ballgame
	John
	'one time we made fault because we do not file right',
	insurance
1-56-07	Cadillac, diagnosis
1-57-03	about insurance agent
1-57-20	Arturo, language
	'I need one man'
1-58-02	'get Cedric for you', 'Mike can help you'

Tape 4

00-00	Mike, instructions
01-20	red car
02-20	Cadillac
02-37	Arturo
02-50	office, Kenneth
04-12	woman customer
	other woman customer
	paperwork
06-25	'we'll back to you'
06-41	with first woman
	outside, at car
	oil check
07-22	incoming call
	'wanna be in movie'
	'let's get a nice car'
07-49	'I joke with you movie'
	oil check
08-19	diagnosis
	rubber band
09-07	Yvonne, symptom, overdrive
09-54	Kenneth
	call, Lebanese
10-04	Kenneth, front desk
	'going to test drive with Yvonne'
	explains to me
10-41	test drive
11-12	Yvonne 'sent many friends'
	hears exhaust leak
12-07	'you make research'
12-57	my house
15-20	about Manuel and Mario
10-44	gestures at wheel, open hand
16-54	'all divorced', gestures
18-09	overdrive
18-40	close up: RPM
19-30	'it may happen': gesture
20-24	about Jeep
20-40	Yvonne gestures
21-25	about Sergio
27-50	back at Hi-Tech

Tape 4 (cont.)

28-25	inside car
	micro check
29-34	Victor
	Hakim
30-00	office
	Hakim
	checks delivery
30-13	incoming call: 'What you wanna know', starter
31-13	Hakim, money
	credit card
	chat
33-15	Ansar
33-31	'Hello, you made it'
	to me: 'you were taping me'
	phone start customers have made it to the shop
	'congratulations'
33-59	'let's go to the car now'
	'Hi, Ms. Nancy'
	gets tool
35-27	diagnosis
	gets tool, test instrument
	explains diagnosis
37-16	'I wanna make something here wrong'
38-35	car starts
	smoke in the back
	choke problem
39-05	incoming call
	'Maxima need another week'
40-00	'put this in your tape'
39-57	choke, close up
41-34	try smoke
	tool box
42-11	no more smoke
	works on choke
42-30	close up
44-21	gets part
	Art
	Omar
45-25	ties choke
	no charge

Tape 4 (cont.)

46-35	to me: 'if you check market for only money'
47-25	explains problem
	gestures
47-55	'she misdescribed to me'
	'they expect crooked business'
49-18	shop, Kenneth, banter
5-07	office, title, debt
51-10	Kenneth, about job
51-17	customer with financial problems (Victor?)
	explains accident
	prognosis
	'make it as cheap as possible'
	gestures
	financing
53-07	incoming call
	customer talks to me
53-50	customer explains accident
	problem with police
	'I still owe him 120 bucks'
	'lost my apartment'
	'Mona found herself another man'
	cleans up desk
	credit
	paperwork
	insurance
57-51	insurance
	financing
59-05	incoming call, Lebanese
	title
59-58	'you still owe $8,000'
	what year model
	gestures
1-02-37	credit cards
1-03-40	'you're good person'
	gestures
1-05-20	customer Victor makes payment offer
1-06-20	'what we're going to do now, Victor'
	gestures
1-08-24	'I'll work with you'
	I talk about liability insurance

Tape 4 (cont.)

	loaner car totaled
	'why I should sign work order'
	gestures
1-11-45	incoming call: Audi customer
	good news
	'car never seen like that'
	175 compression
1-13-06	Omar
1-13-30	break
1-13-50	guy with not enough boost
1-14-06	incoming call, opening hours
1-15-00	'where's Victor'
	calls on Kenneth
	Ashraf
1-16-40	calls on Victor, Hakim
	April 84
	Capital Chevrolet
	Corsica
1-17-44	Mike, instructions
	Hakim
	Kenneth
1-18-30	incoming call: old man
	'Yes, Sir; it's ready'
1-19-07	calls on Mike, pick up old man
	explains to me
	cars for sale
1-20-45	front desk, customer for pick up
	Victor
	keys
	leaves
1-22-27	office, drinks water
	about Kenneth
1-13-07	signature
	outside
	Victor
	gets reading on RPM
	truck
	better power, boost
1-24-17	RPM reading
	close up

Tape 4 (cont.)

1-24-40	incoming call
	inspects car
	'what's in the car'
	trunk
1-25-23	banter with Lebanese man who comes to borrow tools
	'ask him ask him'
1-26-13	office
1-26-44	Victor
	checks leak, gives tools
1-27-23	Victor, timing belt
	'Maxima ready'
1-27-52	front desk, Kenneth, old man
1-28-59	two teenage boys come for Probe
	Yvonne is back for Maxima
1-28-49	inside Maxima
1-29-27	Yvonne, Maxima
	gets Ali for work on Maxima door
1-30-47	explains Ali's job
1-30-57	Arturo
1-31-11	office
	Yvonne
1-31-24	Kenneth, Longhorn disposal
1-32-28	about Kenneth
1-32-31	incoming call, Lebanese
	calls on Ali
	paperwork
1-38-40	Ali, Lebanese
1-33-27	drives white Jeep
1-40-00	bench, break
1-40-17	bench, break
	'all day you move'
	'like yesterday twenty years, always busy'
	calls
1-41-50	list of call types
	Kenneth
	reports new car problem
	'when I go home'
	'my father farmer', bakery, butcher shop
	small convenience store
	'I write for him'

Tape 4 (cont.)

	'I get respect like businessman when I was eight'
	health problems
	'pain when I started take it easy'
1-46-40	Ali, signature
1-47-13	customer gets Dr. Pepper
	about buying and selling cars
	'I grow up on the service'
	'respect for service'
1-48-30	'but service that, you talk about experience'
	customers with complicated problems
	places that should be closed down
	certificates
	stealing
	customers who cry
	how others make several times as much
1-52-31	'I hope someday somebody will get on top of that'
	experience
1-53-33	the laws should support everybody
	'I can't scare the lady'
1-54-40	Mike, reducer
1-55-06	office, Mike, money
1-55-55	'you work hard all day following me'
	bench, break
1-56-50	potential buyer with kid
1-57-09	bench, break
1-57-17	Cedric, radiator hose
1-57-40	truck
	ask Victor
	Victor
1-58-17	incoming call for Kenneth, on the line
	front desk, Kenneth

Tape 5

00-00	front desk, Kenneth, Hakim
01-06	Alex
02-21	junkyard
02-48	closing ticket
	job done
03-32	part for Uncle Am
	Hakim
	leak
07-39	shop, Arturo
	'I will go write them down'
	Cedric
	clean up shop for today
05-24	Victor, GMC
05-56	AC off
	front desk
	Kenneth
	ticket
06-22	Victor
	'fix that Subaru'
06-28	incoming call: Nadia
06-34	Subaru ready?
	brake light switch
	could not get it
	Magnolia Café customer
	Art
07-27	customer
	'owe money on ticket'
	'when you gonna pay the rest'
	credit
08-18	office, ticket, calendar
09-10	calls out to Kenneth
	take break now
09-27	potential buyers, family
10-00	bench, break
	soda for kids
	Kenneth
11-31	'Grand Am sold'
11-49	instructions
	to me: 'what can I help you, nothing', 'no movement, nothing'
13-27	Rodney King trial, video

Tape 5 (cont.)

15-12	about Ali and Ansar
	respect
	stealing
16-45	mean people
17-04	Housem
	money
	banter, Kenneth
18-34	Housem, conversation
	banter
	Victor
20-55	'everybody asks about camera'
21-20	Mike, money
	what car Mike gets to drive
22-50	Kenneth, reports deal
23-15	about Kenneth
	'he is smarter than me'
24-29	Omar, brings car for inspection
	wax
28-20	close up
27-48	red cover
	goes to shop
28-20	calls on Victor, others for black spray paint
29-00	spray paint
31-49	Omar sprays
	compliments 'excellent'
33-30	'you wanna buy now'
	about sale
34-11	close up
34-59	shop, to Arturo
	'are you sleeping'
35-15	Mike
35-58	'sleeping'
	inspection
	'no way, José'
36-30	call
36-50	Victor
	Audi
37-05	front desk
	call, Lebanese
37-51	talks to Ali and Asran, in front of TV

Tape 5 (cont.)

	ribs
	gestures
39-05	transmission customer
	'readying your ticket'
	Kenneth
	paperwork
	explains camera
42-33	Kenneth, ad in paper
43-12	call, Hassan: ad in paper
	'he will talk with you'
44-06	customer complaint red Mercury
	'put this on camera'
44-44	lawyer with obnoxious child
45-20	check red Mercury
45-30	'let's get screwdriver'
	inspection
	close up
	explains problem to me
46-37	Victor returns
	diagnosis: cross fire
	engine drew water during steam wash
47-27	Hakim
47-36	customer
	gestures
48-35	office, lawyer
48-00	incoming call, Lebanese
	money
51-09	'hi, Mom!'
	copier
	boy 'can I break the camera'
52-58	lawyer leaves
53-00	about lawyer
53-14	men asks for Cedric
53-30	about taxes
	about loyalty to customer
	Clinton advisor customer
54-58	electronic rolodex
55-29	prospect of invitation to his house
56-13	office
	Hassan, Ali, Asran

Tape 5 (cont.)

	paperwork
	advances to employees
59-44	about Hassan's name
	checks
	credit card slips
	paperwork
1-04-17	about complaint: crossfire
	Ali
	Ali at desk
1-05-00	red Mercury
	language
	'maybe we got wire mixed'
1-05-22	gets tool
1-06-20	air blower
	close up
	water
	Hakim
1-09-13	Ashraf
	about subframe
1-10-25	incoming call
	to Kenneth: 'here, you answer the phone'
1-10-50	across the street
1-11-00	Uncle Am, inspection
	frame
	Corsica
	light
	language
1-12-15	about Uncle Am
	'can weld wood to wood'
1-13-00	about tomorrow
1-13-14	Cedric
	asks for advance
	'everybody need money'
	about advances
	I: 'how do you find mechanics'
1-14-27	Arturo
	asks for advance
1-15-53	Ashraf, Hassan, Omar, customer
	chat, Lebanese
	gestures

Tape 5 (cont.)

1-17-13	identical cars
1-18-03	Ashraf
	discussion
	cash
	in back lot
	Hassan
1-19-45	inspection
1-120-22	calls on Uncle Am
1-20-35	Uncle Am comes
	subframes
1-21-15	light
	language
1-21-49	light
	language, understanding problem
	Omar
1-22-31	inspection
1-23-09	light, instructions
1-23-41	Omar
1-23-55	asks for my name
	'you need more'
	go back
1-24-43	back at Hi-Tech 1
	Jeep
	Hakim
	Ali
1-25-10	incoming call, Lebanese
1-23-25	Victor
	asks for advance
	'Mercury fixed?'
1-25-30	office
	'now relax and drink a couple of Chivas'
	gives me microphone
	takes off coat
1-27-15	turns off credit card phone
	lights out

Bibliography

Alkemeyer, T., Brümmer, K., Kodalle, R., & Pille, T. (2009). *Ordnung in Bewegung: Choreographien des Sozialen: Körper in Sport, Tanz, Arbeit und Bildung* (1. Aufl. ed.). Bielefeld: Transcript.

Alkemeyer, T., Budde, G., & Freist, D. (Eds.). (2013). *Selbst-Bildungen. Soziale und kulturelle Praktiken der Subjektivierung*. Bielefeld: Transcript.

Andrén, M. (2010). *Children's Gestures from 18 to 30 Months* (Travaux de l'Institut de Linguistique de Lund ed. Vol. 50). Lund: Lund University.

Andrén, M. (2014). On the lower limit of gesture. In M. Seyfeddinipur and M. Gullberg (Eds.), *From Gesture in Conversation to Visible Action as Utterance* (pp. 153–167). Amsterdam: Benjamins.

Austin, J. (1962). *How to Do Things with Words*. Oxford: Oxford University Press.

Austin, J. L. (1970). *A Plea for Excuses. Philosophical Papers* (2nd edition) (pp. 175–204). Oxford: Clarendon Press.

Austin, J. L. (1971). Performative – constative. In J. R. Searle (Ed.), *Philosophy of Language* (pp. 13–22). Oxford: Oxford University Press.

Balzac, H. d. (1968 (1833)). Théorie de la démarche. *La Comédie Humaine* (Vol. XII) (pp. 259–302). Paris: Les Editions du Delta.

Baron-Cohen, S. (1995). *Mindblindness: An Essay on Autism and Theory of Mind*. Cambridge, MA: MIT Press.

Barresi, J., & Moore, C. (1996). Intentional relations and social understanding. *Behavioral and Brain Sciences*, 19, 107–154.

Bateson, G. (1953). The position of humor in human communication systems. In H. von Foerster (Ed.), *Cybernetics: Circular Causal and Feedback Mechanisms in Biological and Social Sciences; Transactions of the Ninth Conference*. New York: Josiah Macy Jr. Foundation.

Bateson, G. (1972). *Steps to an Ecology of Mind*. New York: Ballantine.

Bateson, G. (1979). *Mind and Nature: A Necessary Unity*. London: Wildwood House.

Bavelas, J., Chovil, N., Lawrie, D. A., & Wade, A. (1992). Interactive gestures. *Discourse Processes*, 15, 469–489.

Bavelas, J. B., Coates, L., & Johnson, T. (2002). Listener responses as a collaborative process: The role of gaze. *Journal of Communication*, 52(3), 566–580.

Bergen, B., Narayan, S., & Feldman, J. (2003). Embodied verbal semantics: Evidence from an image-verb matching task. Proceedings of the Twenty-Fifth Annual Conference of the Cognitive Science Society.

Berger, C., & Schmidt, S. (2009). Körperwissen und Bewegungslogik. Zu Status und Spezifik körperlicher Kompetenzen. In T. Alkemeyer, K. Brümmer, R. Kodalle, & T. Pille (Eds.), *Ordnung in Bewegung: Choreographien des Sozialen: Körper in Sport, Tanz, Arbeit und Bildung* (1. Aufl. ed., pp. 65–90). Bielefeld: Transcript.

Berger, P. L., & Luckmann, T. (1967). *The Social Construction of Reality*. Garden City, NJ: Doubleday.

Bourdieu, P. (1990). *The Logic of Practice*. Stanford, CA: Stanford University Press.

Brandstetter, G. (2007). Tanz als Wissenskultur. Körpergedächtnis und wissenstheoretische Herausforderung. In S. Gehm, P. Huseman, & K. von Wilke (Eds.), *Wissen in Bewegung. Perspektiven der wissenschaftlichen und künstlerischen Forschung im Tanz* (pp. 25–36). Bielefeld: Transcript.

Bressem, J., & Mueller, C. (2014a). The family of away gestures: Negation, refusal, and negative assessment. In C. Müller, A. Cienki, E. Fricke, S. H. Ladewig, D. McNeill, & J. Bressem (Eds.), *Body Language Communication. An International Handbook on Multimodality in Human Interaction* (Vol. 2, pp. 1592–1604). Berlin: Mouton de Gruyter.

Bressem, J., & Mueller, C. (2014b). A repertoire of German recurrent gestures with pragmatic functions. In C. Müller, A. Cienki, E. Fricke, S. H. Ladewig, D. McNeill, & J. Bressem (Eds.), *Body Language Communication. An International Handbook on Multimodality in Human Interaction* (Vol. 2, pp. 1575–1591). Berlin: Mouton de Gruyter.

Brockman, J. (1977). Introduction. In J. Brockman (Ed.), *About Bateson* (pp. 3–20). New York: E. P. Dutton.

Brown, P., & Levinson, S. C. (1987 (1978)). *Politeness. Some Universals in Language Usage*. Cambridge: Cambridge University Press.

Bühler, K. (1985). *Sprachtheorie. Die Darstellungsfunktion der Sprache*. Berlin: Ullstein.

Butterworth, G. (1995). Origins of mind in perception and action. In C. Moore & P. J. Dunham (Eds.), *Joint Attention: Its Origins and Role in Development* (pp. 29–40). Hillsdale, NJ: Lawrence Erlbaum Associates.

Calbris, G. (1990). *The Semiotics of French Gestures*. Bloomington: Indiana University Press.

Calbris, G. (2003a). From cutting an object to a clear cut analysis: Gesture as the representation of a preconceptual schema linking concrete actions to abstract notions. *Gesture*, 3(1), 19–46.

Calbris, G. (2003b). *L'Expression Gestuelle de la Pensee d'un Homme Politique*. Paris.

Calbris, G. (2011). *Elements of Meaning in Gesture*. Amsterdam: Benjamins B. V.

Call, J., & Tomasello, M. (2005). What chimpanzees know about seeing revisited: An explanation of the third kind. In N. Eilan, C. Hoerl, T. McCormack, & J. Roessler (Eds.), *Joint Attention* (pp. 45–64). Oxford: Oxford University Press.

Certeau, M. d. (1984). *The Practice of Everyday Life*. Berkeley: University of California Press.

Chance, M. R. A., & Larsen, R. R. (Eds.). (1976). *The Social Structure of Attention*. New York: Wiley.

Cicero, M. T. (1942). *De Oratore*. Cambridge, MA: Harvard University Press.

Cienki, A., & Müller, C. (Eds.). (2009). *Metaphor and Gesture*. Amsterdam: Benjamins.

Clark, H. (2003). Pointing and placing. In S. Kita (Ed.), *Pointing: Where Language, Culture, and Cognition Meet* (pp. 243–268). Mahwah, NJ: Lawrence Erlbaum Associates.

Comrie, B. (1981). *Language Universals and Linguistic Typology*. Chicago: University of Chicago Press.

Condillac, E. (1746). *An essay on the origin of human knowledge, being a supplement to Mr. Locke's essay on the human understanding*. London: J. Noursse.

Cook-Gumperz, J., Corsaro, W., & Streeck, J. (Eds.). (1986). *Children's World and Children's Language*. Berlin: Mouton de Gruyter.

Cooperrider, K., & Nuñez, R. (2009). Across time, across the body: Transversal temporal gestures. *Gesture*, *9*(2), 181–206.

Corbeill, A. (2004). *Nature Embodied: Gesture in Ancient Rome*. Princeton: Princeton University Press.

Corsaro, W., & Streeck, J. (1986). Studying children's worlds: Methodological issues. In J. Cook-Gumperz, W. Corsaro, & J. Streeck (Eds.), *Children's World and Children's Language*. Berlin: Mouton de Gruyter.

Coulter, J., & Parsons, E. D. (1990). The praxiology of perception: Visual orientations and practical action. *Inquiry*, 33(3), 251–272.

Couper-Kuhlen, E. (2004). Prosody and sequence organization in English conversation: The case of new beginnings. In E. Couper-Kuhlen & C. E. Ford (Eds.), *Sound Patterns in Interaction* (pp. 335–376). Amsterdam: Benjamins.

Couper-Kuhlen, E., & Selting, M. (Eds.) (1996). *Prosody in Conversation. Interactional Studies*. Cambridge: Cambridge University Press.

Croft, W. (1990). *Typology and Universals* (Vol. 1). Cambridge: Cambridge University Press.

Croft, W., & Cruse, D. A. (2004). *Cognitive Linguistics*. Cambridge: Cambridge University Press.

Cuffari, E. (2012). Gestural sense-making: Hand gestures as intersubjective linguistic enactments. *Phenomenology and the Cognitive Sciences*, 11, 599–622.

Cuffari, E., & Streeck, J. (2017). Taking the world by hand: How (some) hand gestures mean. In C. Meyer, J. Streeck, & J. S. Jordan (Eds.), *Intercorporeality: Emerging Socialities in Interaction*. Oxford: Oxford University Press.

D'Andrade, R. G. (1984). Cultural meaning systems. In R. A. Shweder & R. A. LeVine (Eds.), *Culture Theory. Essays on Mind, Self, and Emotion* (pp. 88–121). Cambridge: Cambridge University Press.

D'Andrade, R. (1987). A folk model of the mind. In D. Holland & N. Quinn (Eds.), *Cultural Models in Language and Thought* (pp. 112–150). Cambridge: Cambridge University Press.

de France, C. (1983). *L'analyse praxéologique. Composition, ordre et articulation d'un proces*. Paris: Editions de la Maison des Sciences de l'Homme.

de Ruiter, J. P., Mitterer, H., & Enfield, N. J. (2006). Projecting the end of a speaker's turn: A cognitive cornerstone of conversation. *Language*, 515–535.

Deleuze, G. (2003). *Francis Bacon: The Logic of Sensation*. Minneapolis: University of Minnesota Press.

Deppermann, A., & Günthner, S. (Eds.). (2015). *Temporality in Interaction*. Amsterdam: Benjamins B. V.

Donald, M. (1991). *Origins of the Modern Mind*. Cambridge, MA: Harvard University Press.

Drew, P. (2013). Turn design. In J. Sidnell & T. Stivers (Eds.), *Handbook of Conversation Analysis* (pp. 131–149). Chichester: Blackwell.

Dreyfus, H. L. (1991). *Being-in-the-World. A Commentary on Heidegger's 'Being and Time'*. Cambridge, MA: MIT Press.

Dreyfus, H. L. (2002). Intelligence without representation – Merleau-Ponty's critique of mental representation. *Phenomenology and the Cognitive Sciences*, 1, 367–383.

Dunbar, R. (1998). Theory of mind and the evolution of language. In J. R. Hurford, M. Studdert-Kennedy & C. Knight (Eds.), *Approaches to the Evolution of Language* (pp. 92–110). Cambridge: Cambridge University Press.

Durkheim, E. (1982 (1895)). *The Rules of Sociological Method*. London: Macmillan.

Efron, D. (1972 (1941)). *Gesture, Race and Culture*. The Hague: Mouton.

Ekman, P., & Friesen, W. V. (1969). The repertoire of nonverbal behavior: categories, origins, usage, and coding. *Semiotica*, 1, 49–98.

Ekman, P., & Friesen, W. V. (1975). *Unmasking the Face: A Guide to Recognizing Emotions from Facial Clues*. Englewood Cliffs, NJ: Prentice-Hall.

Elsner, M. (2000). *Das vierbeinige Tier. Bewegungsdialog und Diskurs des Tango Argentino*. Frankfurt/M.: Lang.

Emirbayer, M., & Mische. (1998). What is agency? *American Journal of Sociology*, 103(4), 962–1023.

Enfield, N. J. (2009). *The Anatomy of Meaning*. Cambridge: Cambridge University Press.

Engestroem, Y. (1987). *Learning by Expanding: An Activity-Theoretical Approach to Developmental Research*. Helsinki: Orienta-Konsultit Oy.

Fillmore, C. (1971). *Santa Cruz Lectures on Deixis*. Bloomington: Indiana University Linguistics Club.

Fillmore, C. (1982). Towards a descriptive framework for spatial deixis. In R. J. Jarvella & W. Klein (Eds.), *Speech, Place, and Action* (pp. 31–60). Chichester: Wiley.

Fillmore, C. (1991). On Grammatical Constructions. Ms. Berkeley: University of California.

Finnegan, R. (1977). *Oral Poetry*. Bloomington: Indiana University Press.

Flusser, V. (2014). *Gestures*. Minneapolis: University of Minnesota Press.

Ford, C., Fox, B., & Hellermann, J. (2004). 'Getting past no': Sequence, action, and sound production. In E. Couper-Kuhlen & C. E. Ford (Eds.), *Sound Patterns in Interaction* (pp. 233–271). Amsterdam: Benjamins.

Ford, C. E., Fox, B. A., & Thompson, S. A. (1998). Social interaction and grammar. In M. Tomasello (Ed.), *The New Psychology of Language* (Vol. 2, pp. 119–144). Mahwah, NJ: Lawrence Erlbaum Associates.

Foucault, M. (2010). *The Government of Self and Others*. New York: St. Martin's Press.

Freud, S. (1913). *The Interpretation of Dreams*. New York: Macmillan.

Freud, S. (1960). *Jokes and Their Relation to the Unconscious*. New York: Norton.

Fuchs, T. (2017). Intercorporeality and interaffectivity. In C. Meyer, J. Streeck, & J. S. Jordan (Eds.), *Intercorporeality. Emerging Socialities in Interaction*. Oxford: Oxford University Press.

Gallagher, S. (2005). *How the Body Shapes the Mind*. Oxford: Oxford University Press.

Garfinkel, H. (1967). *Studies in Ethnomethodology*. Englewood Cliffs, NJ: Prentice-Hall.

Gehlen, A. (1988 (1958)). *Man: His Nature and Place in the World*. New York: Columbia University Press.

Gelhard, A., Alkemeyer, T., & Ricken, N. (Eds.). (2013). *Techniken der Subjektivierung*. München: Wilhelm Fink.

Gibson, J. J. (1962). Observations on active touch. *Psychological Review*, 69, 477–491.

Gibson, J. J. (1977). The theory of affordances. In R. Shaw & J. Bransford (Eds.), *Perceiving, Acting, and Knowing: Toward an Ecological Psychology*. Hillsdale, NJ: Lawrence Erlbaum Associates.

Gibson, J. J. (1986). *The Ecological Approach to Visual Perception*. Hillsdale, NJ: Lawrence Erlbaum Associates.

Giddens, A. (1984). *The Constitution of Society: Outline of the Theory of Structuration*. Berkeley and Los Angeles: University of California Press.

Gilbert, M. (1990). Walking together: A paradigmatic social phenomenon. *Midwest Studies in Philosophy*, 15(1), 1–14.

Goffman, E. (1959). *The Presentation of Self in Everyday Life*.

Goffman, E. (1963). *Interaction Ritual*. New York: Anchor Books.

Goffman, E. (1964). The neglected situation. *American Anthropologist*, 66(6, part 2), 133–136.

Goffman, E. (1969). *Strategic Interaction*. Oxford: Blackwell.

Goffman, E. (1971). *Relations in Public: Microstudies of the Public Order*. New York: Basic Books.

Goffman, E. (1974). *Frame Analysis*. New York: Harper & Row.

Goffman, E. (1981). *Forms of talk*. Oxford: Blackwell.

Goffman, E. (1983). The interaction order. *American Sociological Review*, 48, 1–17.

Goldberg, A. (1995). *Constructions*. Chicago: University of Chicago Press.

Goldin-Meadow, S., Alibali, M. W., & Church, R. B. (1993). Transitions in concept acquisition: Using the hand to read the mind. *Psychological Review*, 100, 279–297.

Goodman, N. (1976 (1968)). *Languages of Art* (2nd ed.). Indianapolis, IN: Hackett.

Goodwin, C. (1980). Restarts, pauses, and the achievement of a state of mutual gaze at turn-beginning. *Sociological Inquiry*, 50, 272–302.

Goodwin, C. (1981). *Conversational Organization: Interaction between Speakers and Hearers*. New York: Academic Press.

Goodwin, C. (1994). Professional vision. *American Anthropologist*, 96(3), 606–633.

Goodwin, C. (2000). Action and embodiment within situated human interaction. *Journal of Pragmatics*, 32, 1489–1522.

Goodwin, C. (2003). Pointing as situated practice. In S. Kita (Ed.), *Pointing: Where Language and Cognition Meet* (pp. 217–242). Mahwah, NJ: Lawrence Erlbaum Associates.

Goodwin, C. (2007). Environmentally coupled gestures. In S. D. Duncan, J. Cassell, & E. T. Levy (Eds.), *Gesture and the Dynamic Dimension of Language: Essays in Honor of David McNeill* (pp. 195–212). Philadelphia: Benjamins B. V.

Goodwin, C. (2011a). Contextures of action. In J. Streeck, C. Goodwin, & C. LeBaron (Eds.), *Embodied Interaction: Language and Body in the Material World* (pp. 182–193). New York: Cambridge University Press.

Goodwin, C. (2011b). The Formal Organization of Human Action. UCLA: unpublished ms.

Goodwin, C. (2012). The co-operative, transformative organization of human action and knowledge. *Journal of Pragmatics*.

Goodwin, C., & Goodwin, M. (1996). Seeing as situated activity: Formulating planes. In Y. Engeström & D. Middleton (Eds.), *Cognition and Communication at Work* (pp. 61–95). Cambridge: Cambridge University Press.

Goodwin, M. H. (1996). Informings and announcements in their environment. In E. Couper-Kuhlen & M. Selting (Eds.), *Prosody in Conversation: Interactional Studies* (pp. 436–460). Cambridge: Cambridge University Press.

Gullberg, M. (2003). Eye movements and gestures in human face-to-face interaction. In J. Hyönä, R. Radach & D. H. (Eds.), *The Mind's Eye: Cognitive and Applied Aspects of Eye Movement Research*. London: North-Holland/Elsevier.

Gullberg, M., & Holmqvist, K. (1999). Keeping an eye on gestures: Visual perception of gestures in face-to-face communication. *Pragmatics and Cognition*, 7(1), 35–63.

Güney, S. (1997). Managing Multiple Frames in Everyday Interaction: Shifting Personas of a Car Mechanic. Master's Thesis: The University of Texas at Austin.

Habermas, J. (1981). *Theorien des kommunikativen Handelns*. Frankfurt/M.: Suhrkamp.

Haddington, P., & Keisanen, T. (2009). Location, mobility and the body as resources in selecting a route. *Journal of Pragmatics*, 41, 1938–1961.

Haddington, P., Mondada, L., & Nevile, M. (Eds.). (2013). *Interaction and Mobility: Language and the Body in Motion*. Berlin: de Gruyter.

Haller, M. (2009). Bewegte Ordnungen: Kontingenz und Intersubjektivität im Tango Argentino. In T. Alkemeyer, K. Brümmer, R. Kodalle & T. Pille (Eds.), *Ordnung in Bewegung: Choreographien des Sozialen: Körper in Sport, Tanz, Arbeit und Bildung* (1. Aufl. ed., pp. 91–106). Bielefeld: Transcript.

Hanks, W. F. (1990). *Referential Practice: Language and Lived Space among the Maya*. Chicago: University of Chicago Press.

Hanks, W. F. (1996). *Language and Communicative Practices*. Boulder, CO: Westview Press.

Hanks, W. F. (2005). Pierre Bourdieu and the practices of language. *Annual Review of Anthropology*, 34, 67–83.

Harper, D. A. (1987). *Working Knowledge: Skill and Community in a Small Shop*. Chicago: University of Chicago Press.

Harrison, S. (2010). Evidence for node and scope of negation in coverbal gestures. *Gesture*, 10(1).

Hart, H. L. A. (1955). *The ascription of responsibility and rights*. In A. N. Flew (Ed.), *Logic and Language*. First Series. Oxford: Blackwell.

Hausendorf, H. (2003). Deixis and speech situation revisited. In F. Lenz (Ed.), *Deictic Conceptualization of Space, Time, and Person* (pp. 249–269). Amsterdam: Benjamins.

Hausendorf, H., & Schmitt, R. (2010). Opening up openings. Zur multimodalen Konstitution der Eröffnungsphase eines Gottesdienstes. In L. Mondada & R. Schmitt (Eds.), *Situationseröffnungen. Zur multimodalen Herstellung fokussierter Interaktion* (pp. 53–101). Tübingen: Narr.

Havelock, E. A. (1963). *Preface to Plato*. Cambridge, MA: Harvard University Press.

Haviland, J. B. (1993). Anchoring, iconicity, and orientation in Guugu Yimidhirr pointing gestures. *Journal of Linguistic Anthropology*, 3, 3–45.

Haviland, J. B. (2003). How to point in Zinancantan. In S. Kita (Ed.), *Pointing: Where Language, Culture, and Cognition Meet* (pp. 39–70). Mahwah, NJ: Lawrence Erlbaum Associates.

Haviland, J. B. (2013). The emerging grammar of nouns in a first generation sign language: Specification, *iconicity, and syntax*. *Gesture*, 13(3), 309–353.

Heath, C. (1986). *Body Movement and Speech in Medical Interaction*. Cambridge: Cambridge University Press.

Heath, C., & Luff, P. (2012). Embodied action and organizational activity. In J. Sidnell & T. Stivers (Eds.), *The Handbook of Conversation Analysis* (pp. 283–307). Chichester: Blackwell.

Heidegger, M. (1962 (1926)). *Being and Time*. New York: Harper and Row.

Heine, B., Claudi, U., & Hünnemeyer, F. (1991). *Grammaticalization: A Conceptual Framework*. Chicago: University of Chicago Press.

Heller, A. (1984). *Everyday Life*. London: Routledge & Kegan Paul.

Heritage, J. (1984). *Garfinkel and Ethnomethodology*. Cambridge: Polity Press.

Heritage, J. (2008). Conversation analysis as social theory. In B. Turner (Ed.), *The New Blackwell Companion to Social Theory* (pp. 300–320). Oxford: Blackwell.

Heritage, J., & Clayman, S. E. (2010). *Talk in Action. Interactions, Identities, and Institutions*. Chichester: Wiley-Blackwell.

Heritage, J., & Greatbatch, D. (1989). *On the institutional character of institutional talk: the case of news interviews*. In??? (Ed.), *Discourse in Professional and Everyday Culture. Linkoping Studies in Communication* (pp. 47–98). Linkoping: University of Linkoping.

Hewitt, A. (2005). *Social Choreography: Ideology as Performance in Dance and Everyday Movement*. Durham, NC: Duke University Press.

Hickok, G. (2009). Eight problems for the mirror neuron theory of action understanding in monkeys and humans. *Journal of Cognitive Neuroscience*, 21(7), 1229–1243.

Hirschauer, S. (2013). *Verhalten, Handeln, Interagieren. Zu den mikrosoziologischen Grundlagen der Praxistheorie*.

Hockey, J., & Allen-Collinson, J. (2013). Distance running as play/work: Training-together as a joint accomplishment. In P. Tolmie & M. Rouncefield (Eds.), *Ethnomethodology at Play* (pp. 211–224). Farnham: Ashgate.

Honneth, A., & Joas, H. (1988). *Social Action and Human Nature*. Cambridge: Cambridge University Press.

Hopper, P. J., & Traugott, E. C. (1993). *Grammaticalization*. Cambridge: Cambridge University Press.

Horowitz, A. (2013). *On Looking: Eleven Walks with Expert Eyes*. New York: Scribner.

Humboldt, W. v. (1988 (1836)). *On Language*. Cambridge: Cambridge University Press.

Husserl, E. (2012 (1912)). *Ideas: General Introduction to Pure Phenomenology*. Hoboken: Taylor & Francis.

Hutchins, E. (1991). The social organization of distributed cognition. In L. B. Resnick, J. M. Levine, & S. D. Teasley (Eds.), *Perspectives on Socially Shared Cognition* (pp. 283–307). Washington, DC: American Psychological Association.

Hutchins, E. (1995). *Cognition in the Wild*. Cambridge, MA: MIT Press.

Hutchins, E. (2005). Material anchors for conceptual blends. *Journal of Pragmatics*, 37, 1555–1577.

Hutchins, E. (2006). The distributed cognition perspective on human interaction. In N. J. Enfield & S. C. Levinson (Eds.), *Roots of Human Sociality* (pp. 375–398). London: Berg.

Hutchins, E., & Johnson, C. M. (2009). Modeling the emergence of language as an embodied collective cognitive activity. *Topics in Cognitive Science*, 1, 523–546.

Hutchins, E., & Klausen, T. (1996). Distributed cognition in an airline cockpit. In Y. Engeström & D. Middleton (Eds.), *Cognition and Communication at Work* (pp. 15–34). Cambridge: Cambridge University Press.

Ingold, T. (2000). *The Perception of the Environment: Essays on Livelihood, Dwelling and Skill*. London; New York: Routledge.

Ingold, T. (2004). Culture on the ground – the world perceived through the feet. *Journal of Material Culture*, 9, 315–340.

Ingold, T. (2011). *Being Alive. Essays on Movement, Knowledge, and Description*. London: Routledge.

Ingold, T., & Vergunst, J. L. (2008). Introduction. In T. Ingold & J. L. Vergunst (Eds.), *Ways of Walking. Ethnography and Practice on Foot* (pp. 1–20). Aldershot: Ashgate.

Jackson, M. (1989). *Paths Toward a Clearing: Radical Empiricism and Ethnographic Inquiry*. Bloomington: Indiana University Press.

Jeannerod, M. (1984). The timing of natural prehension movements. *Journal of Motor Behavior*, 16(3), 235–254.

Jeannerod, M. (1997). *The Cognitive Neuroscience of Action*. Oxford: Blackwell.

Jeannerod, M. (2006). *Motor Cognition. What Actions Tell the Self*. Oxford: Oxford University Press.

Jeannerod, M., Arbib, M. A., Rizzolatti, G., & Sakata, H. (1995). Grasping objects: The cortical mechanisms of visuomotor transformation. *Trends in Neuroscience* 18(7), 314–320.

Jefferson, G. (1990). List-construction as a task and resource. In G. Psathas (Ed.), *Interaction Competence* (pp. 63–92). Washington, DC: International Institute for Ethnomethodology and Conversation Analysis & University Press of America.

Jefferson, G. (1996). On the poetics of ordinary talk. *Text and Performance Quarterly*, 16(1), 1–61.

Joas, H. (1996). *The Creativity of Action*. Cambridge: Polity Press.

Johnson, M., & Rohrer, T. (2007). We are live creatures: Embodiment, American pragmatism and the cognitive organism. In T. Ziemke, J. Zlatev, & M. F. Roslyn

(Eds.), *Body, Language and Mind* (Vol. 1: Embodiment, pp. 17–54). Berlin: Mouton de Gruyter.

Jonas, H. (1966). *The Phenomenon of Life: Toward a Philosophical Biology*. Chicago: Chicago University Press.

Kallmeyer, W., & Schmitt, R. (1996). Forcieren oder: Die verschärfte Gangart. In W. Kallmeyer (Ed.), *Gesprächsrhetorik* (pp. 19–118). Tübingen: Narr.

Kay, P. (1987). Linguistic competence and folk theories of language: Two English hedges. In D. Holland & N. Quinn (Eds.), *Cultural Models in Language and Thought*. Cambridge: Cambridge University Press.

Keevalik, L. (2015). Coordinating the temporalities of talk and dance. In A. Deppermann & S. Günthner (Eds.), *Temporalities in Interaction* (pp. 309–335). Amsterdam: Benjamins B. V.

Keller, R. (1994). *On Language Change: The Invisible Hand in Language*. London: Routledge.

Kendon, A. (1967). Some functions of gaze direction in two-person conversation. *Acta Psychologica*, 26, 22–63.

Kendon, A. (1980). Gesticulation and speech: Two aspects of the process of utterance. In M. R. Kay (Ed.), *The Relationship between Verbal and Nonverbal Behavior*. The Hague: Mouton.

Kendon, A. (1990). *Conducting Interaction*. Cambridge: Cambridge University Press.

Kendon, A. (1995). Gestures as illocutionary and discourse structure markers in Southern Italian conversation. *Journal of Pragmatics*, 23(3), 247–279.

Kendon, A. (2004). *Gesture: Visible Action as Utterance*. Cambridge: Cambridge University Press.

Kendon, A. (2009). Manual actions, speech and the nature of language. In D. Gambarara & A. Givigliano (Eds.), *Origine e sviluppo del linguaggio, fra teoria e storia*. Società di Filosofia del Linguaggio, atti del XV congresso nazionale. Arcavata di Rende (CS), 15–17 settembre 2008 (pp. 19–33). Rome: Aracne editrice s.r.l.

Kendon, A. (2012). Language and kinesic complexity: Reflections on 'Dedicated gesture and the emergence of sign language'. *Gesture*, 12(3), 308–326.

Kendon, A., & Versante, L. (2003). Pointing by hand in 'Neapolitan'. In S. Kita (Ed.), *Pointing: Where Language, Culture, and Cognition Meet* (pp. 109–138). Mahwah, NJ: Lawrence Erlbaum Associates.

Kesselheim, Wolfgang (2010). Wissenskommunikation multimodal. Wie Museumsbesucher sich über den Inhalt einer Museumsvitrine verständigen. In *Fachsprache: Internationale Zeitschrift für Fachsprachenforschung, didaktik und Terminologie* 32(3–4), S.122–144.

Kinsbourne, M. (2006). Gesture as embodied cognition: A neurodevelopmental interpretation. *Gesture*, 6(2), 203–212.

Kinsbourne, M., & Jordan, J. S. (2009). Embodied anticipation: A neuro-developmental interpretation. *Discourse Processes*, 46(2–3), 103–226.

Kita, S. (2003a). *Pointing: Where Language, Culture, and Cognition Meet*. Mahwah, NJ: Lawrence Erlbaum Associates.

Kita, S. (2003b). Pointing: A foundational building block of human communication. In S. Kita (Ed.), *Pointing: Where Language, Culture and Cognition Meet* (pp. 1–8). Mahwah, NJ: Lawrence Erlbaum Associates.

Klatzky, R. L., & Lederman, S. J. (1990). Intelligent exploration by the human hand. In S. T. Venkataraman & T. Iberall (Eds.), *Dexterous Robot Hands* (pp. 66–81). Berlin: Springer.

Kohn, E. (2013). *How Forests Think*. Berkeley & Los Angeles: University of California Press.

Lambrecht, K. (1994). *Information Structure and Sentence Form*. Cambridge: Cambridge University Press.

Lane, H. (1976). *The Wild Boy of Aveyron*. Cambridge, MA: Harvard University Press.

Latour, B. (2005). *Reassembling the Social: An Introduction to Actor-Network Theory*. Oxford: Oxford University Press.

Laurier, E. (2001). Why people say where they are during mobile phone calls. *Environment and Planning D: Society & Space*, 19(4), 485–504.

Lave, J. (1988). *Cognition in Practice*. Cambridge: Cambridge University Press.

LeBaron, C., & Streeck, J. (1997). Built space and the interactional framing of experience during a murder interrogation. *Human Studies*, 20, 1–25.

LeBaron, C. D., & Streeck, J. (2000). Gestures, knowledge, and the world. In D. McNeill (Ed.), *Language and Gesture* (pp. 118–138). Cambridge: Cambridge University Press.

Lederman, S. J., & Klatzky, R. L. (1987). Hand movements: A window into haptic object recognition. *Cognitive Psychology*, 19, 342–368.

Lempert, M. (2011). Barack Obama, being sharp: Indexical order in the pragmatics of precision-grip gesture. *Gesture*, 11(3), 241–270.

Leroi-Gourhan, A. (1993 (1964)). *Gesture and Speech*. Cambridge, MA: MIT Press.

Levinson, S. C. (2003). *Space in Language and Cognition: Explorations in Cognitive Diversity*. Cambridge; New York: Cambridge University Press.

Levinson, S. C. (2013). Action formation and ascription. In J. Sidnell & T. Stivers (Eds.), *Handbook of Conversation Analysis* (pp. 103–130). Chichester: Blackwell.

Levinson, S. C., & Holler, J. (2014). The origin of human multi-modal communication. *Philosophical Transactions of the Royal Society B*, 369(20130302).

Lllinas, R. R. (2001). *I of the Vortex. From Neurons to Self*. Cambridge, MA: MIT Press.

Mahon, B. Z., & Caramazza, A. (2008). A critical look at the embodied cognition hypothesis and a new proposal for grounding conceptual content. *Journal of Physiology*, 102(1–3), 59–70.

Malinowski, B. (1922). *Argonauts of the Western Pacific*. London: Routledge.

Mallery, G. (1978). A collection of gesture-signs and signals of the North American Indians with some comparisons. In D. J. Umiker-Sebeok & T. A. Sebeok (Eds.), *Aboriginal Sign Languages of the Americas and Australia* (pp. 77–406). New York: Plenum Press.

Marx, K. (1852). *The Eighteenth Brumaire of Louis Bonaparte*. Moscow: Progress Publishers.

Marx, K. (1973). *Grundrisse*. Harmondsworth: Penguin.

Marx, K., & Engels, F. (1960). *The German Ideology*, parts I & III. New York: International Publishers.

Maturana, H. R., & Varela, F. J. (1980). *Autopoiesis and Cognition. The Realization of the Living*. Dordrecht: Reidel.

Mauss, M. (1973 (1935)). The techniques of the body. *Economy and Society*, 2(1), 70–88.

Mayer, A. (2013). *Wissenschaft vom Gehen. Die Erforschung der Bewegung im 19. Jahrhundert*. Frankfurt/M.: S. Fischer.

McCullough, M. (1996). *Abstracting Craft: The Practiced Digital Hand*. Cambridge, MA: MIT Press.

McDermott, R., Gospodinoff, K., & Aron, J. (1978). Criteria for an ethnographical adequate description of concerted activities and their contexts. *Semiotica*, *24*(3/4), 245–276.

McDermott, R. P., & Roth, D. (1978). Social organization of behavior: Interactional approaches. *Annual Review of Anthropology*, 7, 321–345.

McLuhan, M. (1994 (1964)). *Understanding Media: The Extensions of Man*. Cambridge, MA: MIT Press.

McNeill, D. (1992). *Hand and Mind. What Gestures Reveal about Thought*. Chicago: University of Chicago Press.

McNeill, D. (2005). *Gesture and Thought*. Chicago: University of Chicago Press.

Mead, G. H. (1934). *Mind, Self and Society*. Chicago: University of Chicago Press.

Merleau-Ponty, M. (1962). *Phenomenology of Perception*. London: Routledge.

Merleau-Ponty, M. (1964). *The Philosopher and His Shadow*. In M. Merleau-Ponty (Ed.), *Signs*. Evanston, IL: Northwestern University Press.

Merleau-Ponty, M. (1968). *The Visible and the Invisible*. Evanston, IL: Northwestern University Press.

Meyer, C., Streeck, J., & Jordan, J. S. (Eds.). (2017a). *Intercorporeality: Emerging Socialities in Interaction*. Oxford: Oxford University Press.

Meyer, C., Streeck, J., & Jordan, J. S. (Eds.). (2017b). *Intercorporeality. Emerging Socialities in Interaction*. Oxford: Oxford University Press.

Meyer, C., & Von Wedelstaedt, U. (to appear). Enactive Intercorporeality in Sports: An Introduction. In C. Meyer & U. von Wedelstaedt (Eds.), *Enactive Intercorporeality. The Coordination, Concertation and Collectivization of Moving Bodies in Sports*. Oxford: Oxford University Press.

Mondada, L. (2009). Emergent focused interactions in public places: A systematic analysis of the multimodal achievement of a common interactional space. *Journal of Pragmatics*, 41, 1977–1997.

Mondada, L. (2012). Talking and driving: Multiactivity in the car. *Semiotica*, (191), 233–256.

Moore, C., & Dunham, P. J. (Eds.). (1995). *Joint Attention: Its Origins and Role in Development*. Hillsdale, NJ: Lawrence Erlbaum Associates.

Müller, C. (2003). Forms and uses of the palm up open hand. In C. Müller & R. Posner (Eds.), *The Semantics and Pragmatics of Everyday Gestures*. The Berlin Conference (pp. 234–256). Berlin: Weidler.

Müller, C. (2014). Ring-gestures across cultures and times: Dimensions of variation. In C. Müller, A. Cienki, E. Fricke, S. H. Ladewig, D. McNeill, & J. Bressem (Eds.), *Body Language Communication. An International Handbook on Multimodality in Human Interaction* (Vol. 2, pp. 1511–1522). Berlin: Mouton de Gruyter.

Müller, C., & Bohle, U. (2007). Das Fundament fokussierter Interaktion. Zur Vorbereitung und Herstellung von Interaktionsräumen durch körperliche

Koordination. In R. Schmitt (Ed.), *Koordination*. Studien zur multimodalen Interaktion (pp. 129–166). Tübingen: Gunter Narr Verlag.

Murphy, K. M. (2012). Transmodality and temporality in design interactions. *Journal of Pragmatics*, 44, 1966–1981.

Napier, J. (1980). *Hands*. New York: Pantheon.

Nishizaka, A. (2000). Seeing what one sees: perception, emotion, and activity. *Mind, Culture, and Activity*, 7(1–2), 105–123.

Noë, A. (2015). What art unveils. *The New York Times* (Oct. 5, 2015), Opinion Pages.

Noland, C. (2009). *Agency and Embodiment. Performing Gestures/Producing Culture*. Cambridge MA: Harvard University Press.

Norman, D. (1992). *Turn Signals Are the Facial Expressions of Automobiles*. Reading, MA: Addison Wesley.

Norman, D. A. (1993). *Things That Make Us Smart*. Reading, MA: Addison Wesley.

Nuñez, R., & Sweetser, E. (2006). With the future behind them: Convergent evidence from language and gesture in the crosslinguistic comparison of spatial construals of time. *Cognitive Science*, 30, 401–450.

Odling-Smee, F. J., Laland, K. N., & Feldman, M. W. (2003). *Niche Construction. The Neglected Process in Evolution*. Princeton, NJ: Princeton University Press.

Ogden, R. (2010). Prosodic constructions in making complaints. In D. Barth-Weingarten, E. Reber & M. Selting (Eds.), *Prosody in Interaction* (pp. 81–104). Amsterdam: John Benjamins.

Olson, D. (1994). *The World on Paper*. Cambridge: Cambridge University Press.

Peirce, C. S. (1901). *On the Logic of Drawing from Ancient Documents, Especially from Testimonies: Collected Papers* (Vol. 7, p. 219). Chicago: University of Chicago Press.

Peirce, C. S. (1995 (1940)). *Philosophical Writings*. New York: Dover.

Peräkylä, A., & Sorjonen, M.-L. (Eds.). (2012). *Emotion in Interaction*. Oxford: Oxford University Press.

Plessner, H. (1923). *Die Einheit der Sinne*. Bonn.

Plessner, H. (1975). *Die Stufen des Organischen und der Mensch*. Berlin: de Gruyter.

Plessner, H. (1980). *Anthropologie der Sinne*. Frankfurt/M.: Suhrkamp.

Polanyi, M. (1966). *The Tacit Dimension*. Garden City, NY: Doubleday.

Prinz, W. (1997). Perception and action planning. *European Journal of Cognitive Psychology*, 9, 129–154.

Prinz, W., Foersterling, F., & Hauf, P. (2005). Of minds and mirrors. An introduction to the social making of minds. *Interaction Studies*, 6(3), 1–19.

Quine, W. V. O. (1960). *Word and Object*. Cambridge, MA: MIT Press.

Quintilianus, M. F. (1922 (100)). *The Institutio Oratoria of Quintilian* (H. E. Butler, Trans. Vol. IV). London: Heinemann.

Radcliffe-Brown, A. R. (1965). *Structure and Function in Primitive Society*. New York: Free Press.

Raymond, G. (2010). Prosodic variation in responses: The case of type-conforming responses to yes/no interrogatives. In D. Barth-Weingarten, E. Reber & M. Selting (Eds.), *Prosody in Interaction* (pp. 109–130). Amsterdam: John Benjamins.

Reddy, M. (1979). The conduit metaphor: A case of frame conflict in our language about language. In A. Ortony (Ed.), *Metaphor and Thought* (pp. 284–324). Cambridge: Cambridge University Press.

Relieu, M. (1999). Parler en marchant: Pour une écologie dynamique des échanges de paroles. *Langage & Société*(89), 37–67.

Resnick, L. B. (1991). Shared cognition: Thinking as social practice. In L. B. Resnick, J. M. Levine, & S. D. Teasley (Eds.), *Perspectives on Socially Shared Cognition* (pp. 1–22). Washington, DC: American Psychological Association.

Resnick, L. B., Levine, J. M., & Teasley, S. D. (Eds.). (1991) *Perspectives on Socially Shared Cognition* (pp. 1–22). Washington, DC: American Psychological Association.

Rizzolatti, G., & Craighero, L. (2004). The mirror-neuron system. *Annual Review of Neuroscience*, 27, 169–192.

Rogoff, B., & Lave, J. (1984). *Everyday Cognition: Its Development in Social Context*. Cambridge, MA: Harvard University Press.

Rosaldo, M. (1990). The things we do with words: Ilongot speech acts and speech act theory in philosophy. In D. Carbaugh (Ed.), *Cultural Communication and Intercultural Contact* (pp. 373–408). Hillsdale, NJ: Lawrence Erlbaum Associates.

Rossano, F. (2012). Gaze Behavior in Face-to-Face Interaction. PhD Dissertation, Max-Planck Institut for Psycholinguistics, Nijmegen.

Ryle, G. (1949). *The Concept of Mind*. London.

Sacks, H., & Schegloff, E. A. (2002). Home position. *Gesture*, 2(2), 133–146.

Sandler, W. (2012). Dedicated gestures and the emergence of sign language. *Gesture*, 12(3), 265–307.

Schatzki, T. R. (2002). *The Site of the Social: A Philosophical Account of the Constitution of Social Life and Change*. University Park: Pennsylvania State University Press.

Schatzki, T. R., Knorr Cetina, K., & Von Savigny, E. (Eds.). (2001). *The Practice Turn in Contemporary Theory*. London: Routledge.

Scheflen, A. (1972). *Body Language and Social Order*. Englewood Cliffs, NJ: Prentice Hall.

Scheflen, A. E. (1974). *How Behavior Means*. Garden City: Anchor Press.

Schegloff, E. A. (1968). Sequencing in conversational openings. *American Anthropologist*, 70(6), 1075–1095.

Schegloff, E. A. (1981). Discourse as in interactional achievement: some uses of 'uh huh' and other things that come between sentences. Paper presented at the Georgetown University Roundtable on Languages and Linguistics 1981; Analyzing Discourse: Text and Talk, Washington, DC.

Schegloff, E. A. (1984). On some questions and ambiguities in conversation. In M. Atkinson & J. Heritage (Eds.), *Structures of Social Action*. Cambridge: Cambridge University Press.

Schegloff, E. A. (2007). *Sequence Organization in Interaction. A Primer in Conversation Analysis*. Cambridge: Cambridge University Press.

Schiffrin, D. (1987). *Discourse Markers*. Cambridge [Cambridgeshire]; New York: Cambridge University Press.

Schmidt, R. (2012). *Soziologie der Praktiken*. Berlin: Suhrkamp.

Schmitt, J.-C. (1990). *La raison des gestes dans l'Occident médiéval*. Paris: Gallimard.

Schmitt, R. (2012). Gehen als situierte Praktik: 'Gemeinsam gehen' und 'hinter jemandem herlaufen'. *Gesprächsforschung – Online-Zeitschrift zur verbalen Interaktion*, 13, 1–44.

Schmitt, R. (Ed.). (2007). *Koordination. Studien zur multimodalen Interaktion*. Tübingen: Gunter Narr Verlag.

Schutz, A. (1982). *Collected Papers* (Vol. 1–3). The Hague: Martinus Nijhof.

Searle, J. R. (1969). *Speech Acts*. Cambridge: Cambridge University Press.

Sellen, A. J., & Harper, R. (2002). *The Myth of the Paperless Office*. Cambridge, MA: MIT Press.

Selting, M. (1988). The role of intonation in the organization of repair and problem handling sequences in conversation. *Journal of Pragmatics*, 12, 293–322.

Selting, M. (1992). Prosody in conversational questions. *Journal of Pragmatics*, 17, 315–345.

Selting, M. (1996). Prosody as an activity-type distinctive cue in conversation: The case of s-called 'astonished' questions in repair initiation. In E. Couper-Kuhlen & M. Selting (Eds.), *Prosody in Conversation*. Interactional Studies (pp. 231–270). Cambridge: Cambridge University Press.

Sennett, R. (2008). *The Craftsman*. New Haven, CT: Yale University Press.

Sharrock, W., & Coulter, J. (1998). On what we can see. *Theory and Psychology*, 8(2), 147–164.

Sennett, R. (1977). *The Fall of Public Man*. New York: Knopf.

Simmel, G. (2009). *Sociology. Inquiries into the Construction of Social Forms* (A. J. Blasi, A. K. Jacobs, & M. Kanjirathinkal; Trans. A. J. Blasi, A. K. Jacobs, & M. Kanjirathinkal Eds.). Leiden and Boston: Brill.

Sinclair, N., & de Freitas, E. (to appear). The haptic nature of gesture: Rethinking gesture with new multitouch digital technologies. *Gesture*.

Sowa, T. (2006). *Understanding Coverbal Iconic Gestures in Shape Descriptions*. Berlin: Akademische Verlagsgesellschaft.

Stewart, J., Gapenne, O., & Di Paolo, E. (Eds.). (2010). *Enaction: Toward a New Paradigm for Cognitive Science*. Cambridge MA: Harvard University Press.

Streeck, J. (1983). *Social Order in Child Communication. A Study in Microethnography*. Amsterdam: Benjamins.

Streeck, J. (1993). Gesture as communication I: Its coordination with gaze and speech. *Communication Monographs*, 60(December 1993), 275–299.

Streeck, J. (1996). How to do things with things: Objets trouvés and symbolization. *Human Studies*, 19, 365–384.

Streeck, J. (2002). A body and its gestures. *Gesture*, 2(1), 19–44.

Streeck, J. (2007a). Geste und verstreichende Zeit: Stillstand und Bedeutungswandel. In H. Hausendorf (Ed.), *Gespräch als Prozess* (pp. 155–177). Tubingen: Gunter Narr.

Streeck, J. (2007b). *Homo faber*'s gestures. Review article on A. Kendon, *Gesture: Visible Action as Utterance*. *Journal of Linguistic Anthropology*, 130–140.

Streeck, J. (2008a). Depicting by gestures. *Gesture*, 8(3), 285–301.

Streeck, J. (2008b). Laborious intersubjectivity: Attentional struggle and embodied communication in an auto-shop. In I. Wachsmuth, M. Lenzen, & G. Knoblich (Eds.), *Embodied Communication in Humans and Machines*. Oxford: Oxford University Press.

Streeck, J. (2008c). Gesture in political communication: A case study of the Democratic presidential candidates during the 2004 primary campaign. *Research on Language & Social Interaction*, 41(2), 154–186.

Streeck, J. (2009a). *Gesturecraft. The Manufacture of Meaning*. Amsterdam: Benjamins.

Streeck, J. (2009b). Forward-gesturing. *Discourse Processes*, 45(3/4), 161–179.

Streeck, J. (2013a). Praxeology of gesture. In C. Müller, A. Cienki, E. Fricke, S. Ladewig, D. McNeill, & S. Tessendorf (Eds.), *Handbook Body Language Communication. An International Handbook on Multimodality in Human Interaction* (Vol. 1, pp. 674–685). Berlin: de Gruyter.

Streeck, J. (2013b). Interaction and the living body. *Journal of Pragmatics*, 46, 69–90.

Streeck, J. (2014). Mutual gaze and recognition. Revisiting gaze direction in two-person interaction. In M. Gullberg & M. Seyfeddinipur (Eds.), *From Gesture in Conversation to Visible Action as Utterance. Festschrift for Adam Kendon* (pp. 35–55). Amsterdam: Benjamins.

Streeck, J. (2015). Embodiment in human communication. *Annual Review of Anthropology*, 44, 419–438.

Streeck, J., Goodwin, C., & LeBaron, C. (2011a). Embodied interaction in the material world: An introduction. In J. Streeck, C. Goodwin, & C. LeBaron (Eds.), *Embodied Interaction: Language and Body in the Material World*. New York: Cambridge University Press.

Streeck, J., Goodwin, C., & LeBaron, C. (Eds.). (2011b). *Embodied Interaction. Language and Body in the Material World*. New York: Cambridge University Press.

Streeck, J., & Hartge, U. (1992). Previews: Gestures at the transition place. In P. Auer & A. di Luzio (Eds.), *The Contextualization of Language* (pp. 138–158). Amsterdam: Benjamins.

Streeck, J., & Henderson, D. (2010). Das Handwerk des Hip-Hop. Freestyle als körperliche Praxis. In C. Wulf & E. Fischer-Lichte (Eds.), *Gesten: Inszenierung, Aufführung und Praxis* (pp. 180–206). München: Wilhelm Fink.

Streeck, J., & Jordan, J. S. (2009a). Communication as a dynamical self-sustaining system: The importance of time-scales and nested contexts. *Communication Theory*, 19, 448–467.

Streeck, J., & Mehus, S. (2004). Microethnography: The study of practices. In K. L. Fitch & R. E. Sanders (Eds.), *Handbook of Language and Social Interaction* (pp. 381–405). Mahwah, NJ: Lawrence Erlbaum Associates.

Stukenbrock, A. (2009). Referenz durch Zeigen: Zur Theorie der Deixis. *Deutsche Sprache*, 37, 289–315.

Stukenbrock, A. (2015). *Deixis in der Face-to-Face Interaktion*. Berlin: de Gruyter.

Taylor, J. R. (2011). Organization as an (imbricated) configuring of transactions. *Organization Studies*, 32(9), 1273–1294.

Thompson, E. (2007). *Mind in Life*. Cambridge, MA: The Belknap Press of Harvard University Press.

Timmermans, S., & Tavory, I. (2012). Theory construction in qualitative research: From grounded theory to abductive analysis. *Sociological Theory*, 30(3), 167–196.

Tomasello, M. (1995). Joint attention as social cognition. In C. Moore & P. J. Dunham (Eds.), *Joint Attention. Its Origins and Role in Development* (pp. 103–130). Hillsdale, NJ: Lawrence Erlbaum Associates.

Tomasello, M. (2006). Why don't apes point? In N. J. Enfield & S. C. Levinson (Eds.), *Roots of Human Sociality: Culture, Cognition and Interaction* (pp. 506–524). Oxford: Berg.

Uexküll, J. v. (1957). A stroll through the worlds of animals an men: A picture book of invisible worlds. In C. H. Schiller (Ed.), *Instinctive Behavior: The Development of a Modern Concept*. New York: International Universities Press.

Wachsmuth, I., & Knoblich, G. (2004). Embodied Communication in Humans and Machines. Unpublished grant proposal. Bielefeld: Center for Interdisciplinary Research (ZiF).

Weick, K., & Sutcliffe, K. M. (2011). *Managing the Unexpected: Resilient Performance in an Age of Uncertainty* (2nd ed.). New York: John Wiley & Sons.

Weick, K. E. (1976). Organizations as loosely coupled systems. *Administrative Science Quarterly*, 21, 1–16.

Wilkins, D. (2003). Why pointing with the index finger is not a universal (in sociocultural and semiotic terms). In S. Kita (Ed.), *Pointing: Where Language, Culture, and Cognition Meet* (pp. 171–216). Mahwah, NJ: Lawrence Erlbaum Associates.

Wilson, M. (2002). Six views of embodied cognition. *Psychonomic Bulletin and Review*, 9, 625–636.

Wilson, M. (2006). Covert imitation: How the body schema acts as a prediction device. In G. Knoblich, I. M. Thompson, M. Gorsjean, & M. Shiffrar (Eds.), *Human Body Perception from the Inside Out* (pp. 211–228). Oxford: Oxford University Press.

Wilson, M., & Knoblich, G. (2005). The case for motor involvement in perceiving conspecifics. *Psychological Bulletin*, 131(3), 460–473.

Wittgenstein, L. (1922). *Tractatus Logico-Philosophicus*. London: Routledge & Kegan Paul.

Wittgenstein, L. (1953). *Philosophical Investigations*. Chichester: Blackwell.

Wolpert, D. M., & Miall, C. (1996). Forward models for physiological motor control. *Neural Networks*, 9(8), 1265–1279.

Zlatev, J. (2003). Meaning = life (+ culture). An outline of a unified biocultural theory of meaning. *Evolution of Communication*, 4(2), 253–296.

Author Index

Subject Index

440

The Learning in Doing series was founded in 1987 by Roy Pea and John Seely Brown.